The Price Index and its Extension

A theft amounting to £1 was a capital offence in 1260, and a judge in 1610 affirmed the law could not then be applied since £1 was no longer what it was. Such association of money with a date is well recognized for its importance in very many different connections. Thus arises the need to know how to convert an amount at one date into an equivalent amount at another date. In other words, a price index.

The ordinary consumer price index or CPI represents a practical response to the need. A sense for the equivalence that should give it some legitimacy, and the faithfulness, or truth, of a price index to that sense, becomes an issue giving rise to extensive thought and theory about price indices, to which over the decades a remarkable number of economists have each contributed a word, or volume. However, there have been hold-ups at a most basic level, cleared in this book. Beside the classical part of the subject that should command most attention, this volume ventures into further topics.

Afriat is rightly famous for his work in the field of the price index, and this latest book will interest economists of an academic and professional nature the world over.

S. N. Afriat, currently associated with the University of Siena, Italy, has a long and distinguished record of publishing at the interface of mathematics and economics. His most recent book *The Market: Equilibrium, Stability, Mythology* is also published by Routledge (2003).

Routledge Frontiers of Political Economy

The Price Index
and its Extension
A chapter in economic measurement

S. N. Afriat

Routledge
Taylor & Francis Group

LONDON AND NEW YORK

First published 2005
by Routledge
2 Park Square, Milton Square, Abingdon, Oxon OX14 4RN

Simultaneously published in the USA and Canada
by Routledge
270 Madison Ave, New York, NY 10016

Routledge is an imprint of the Taylor & Francis Group

© 2005 S. N. Afriat

Typeset in Times New Roman by
Newgen Imaging Systems (P) Ltd, Chennai, India
Printed and bound in Great Britain by
MPG Books Ltd, Bodmin

British Library Cataloguing in Publication Data
A catalogue record for this book is available from the British Library

Library of Congress Cataloging in Publication Data
A catalog record for this book has been requested

ISBN 0–415–32337–1

For P-L

Contents

TABLES

INFLATION RATES, INCREMENTAL RATES
AND INFLATION BIAS

Tables for the entire expenditure range
for the following income stratifications

Foreword

Sydney Afriat is the guru of the price index. As a young mathematician, he arrived at Richard Stone's Department of Applied Economics in Cambridge in the early 1950s, then the great center of research on theoretical and applied consumer behavior. He soon realized that neither he nor anyone else knew very much about what was meant by "the price index", in spite of being part of the everyday discourse of economics. In the half century since then, he has been exploring the foundations of the topic. Over the years, he has produced beautiful theorems on the topic, many of them completely unexpected even by the *cognoscenti* of the topic. And where he has led, the profession has followed, often many years later. Along the way, his work has fathered important incidental areas in economics, perhaps most notably the non-parametric analysis of demand.

Afriat is one of those rare and rarely gifted individuals who think differently from everyone else. What is obvious to him can sometimes seem bizarre to others, especially at first, and his vision of "the price index" often differs sharply from those that dominate the profession. Yet his work is a classic illustration of how much we learn from new ways of thinking, and how the bizarre and unfamiliar conceptions and results of an idiosyncratic leader can become the orthodoxy of the next generation.

This book presents a coherent discussion of fifty years of astonishingly creative work on the price index. Some of the analysis has appeared before, but much has not. Afriat's many friends will welcome this definitive account, as will those who have not previously had the opportunity to understand and enjoy the work.

Angus Deaton
Dwight D. Eisenhower Professor of International Affairs
Professor of Economics
Princeton University, USA

Preface

I received the interest in economic index-numbers from Richard Stone when I joined the Department of Applied Economics, Cambridge, in 1953. This book, which therefore marks the half-century since the work began, assimilates materials from my main published work in the area, together with additional items.

Among resources are two out-of-print books, *The Price Index* (Cambridge University Press, 1977), and *Logic of Choice and Economic Theory* (Clarendon Press, Oxford, 1987), Part III on "The Cost of Living", 185–256.[1] Newest parts beside this Preface include the book Introduction together with preambles to chapters. Additional resources include journal articles, chapters in volumes, unpublished reports, and other items; a partial list is supplied. The old books mostly support Parts I and II respectively of the new, while other items are included as appendices.

The introductory parts gives historical preliminaries and an overview of the subject area and of the book contents. This is followed by the main part having the form of a treatise drawing from the earlier books. After this is the collection of independent pieces, on special topics, or new unpublished material, or reproducing key published papers, represented as appendices.

The new book includes comment on how the subject stood at that time when the work began, and how the material set forth in it emerged, or reached objectives. My paper "On the constructability of consistent price indices between several periods simultaneously", in the volume *Essays in Theory and Measurement of Demand: in honour of Sir Richard Stone* edited by Angus Deaton (Cambridge University Press, 1981, pp. 133–61), is a singular item and contributes to a question that interested Stone.

The book is not an unrestricted survey tangling with a vast repetitive literature, more it is a treatise within clear boundaries dealing with a line in mathematical economics that represents an expansion—perhaps one should say inflation—around

---

1 About this book OUP have informed me that "We are in fact considering putting this on our 'Print on Demand' programme in the near future, which would make it available on demand", and it is to be included in the new OXFORD scholarship online (OSO) programme, see www.oup.com/uk/osodemo.

the commonplace price-index idea, the 'consumer price index', or 'CPI'. It is largely a document of my own work; in a way, therefore, it is more or less a typical 'collected papers', or 'selected papers' since there is confinement to a special topic. However, though a mass of material is offered in its unchanged original form going back some decades, there are also completely fresh statements, like this Preface, or the main book Introduction, or Introduction to Part I, or preambles coming before chapters. Overlap between parts of different vintage may accidentally contribute advantages for exposition.

Price index discussions that have reference to demand data have invariably dealt with data associated with two time periods, the base and current reference periods themselves, for instance the one or two hundred formulae dealt with in Irving Fisher's *The Making of Index Numbers*, in particular the Paasche, Laspeyres and Fisher formulae. A departure in my work has been the ability to deal with data for any number of periods. After a lecture I gave at Rice University, Houston, in 1962, exhibiting this ability, it was proposed to me by Edgar O. Edwards that I should give account of the work also with the traditional two-period data restriction because then it would be more easily understandable by the majority. My 1977 book *The Price Index* was a response to that suggestion. This had been reflected in the subtitle "Paasche, Laspeyres and Fisher" adopted initially but then abandoned, and now making the heading for Part I of this book which largely follows the original suggestion. Material in my 1987 book, from Part III on "The Cost of Living", is without that restriction and contributes to the material, and to the title, for the present Part II.

An early motive of the work had been to elaborate a concept of what really is a price index. Despite some notion of 'price-level' having a presence everywhere in economics, in both theory and practice, a deliberate concept had been hard to find, unless it be more or less the ordinary price index. I submitted to Joan Robinson, giving a lecture that gave prominence to the price-level, "There are many prices and so many levels, so what could be the significance of a single level?", and got an angry answer.

A theft amounting to £1 was a capital offence in 1260, and a judge in 1610 affirmed the law could not then be applied since £1 was no longer what it was. The association of any money with a date is well recognized, for its importance in very many different connections. There arises the need to know how to convert an amount at one date into an *equivalent* amount at another date.

What is a price index? To a mass of persons with any awareness about a price index, it is just a number issued to the public from the government Statistical Office that should serve for 'indexation' purposes, such as may affect wages, salaries, mortgages, loans and other contracts made in any period, to keep amounts at an acceptable level subsequently.

The ordinary *consumer price index* or *CPI* represents a practical response to the need. A sense for the equivalence that should give it some legitimacy, and the faithfulness, or *truth*, of a price index to that sense, becomes an issue giving rise to extensive thought and theory about price indices, to which a remarkable number of economists have each contributed a word, or volume.

However, for now evident reasons, including a misguided notion about index formulae and the escape of essential theorems, there had been hold-ups at a basic level, cleared in this book. Beside the classical part of the subject that should gain most attention there is entry into further topics.

With the usual diagram—tea on one axis and coffee on the other—Alan Brown explained the cost-of-living adjustment of an income in response to a price change, my first day at the Department of Applied Economics in 1953. I could not see what this had to do with a price index and how it could possibly be resolved by the use of one, as it usually is. He was submitting how a given utility can determine the *purchasing power correspondence* for money at different prices, connecting amounts that purchase the same level of utility at the different prices. The most than can be said generally about such a relation is that it is monotonic. But use of a price index as an indexation tool imposes that this relation should be a homogeneous linear relation, the price index being the slope. If it should be faithful to an underlying utility, *this has impact on the utility*. Neither he nor anyone else said that in those days.

For practice one book is important and without alternative: *Consumer Price Indices—An ILO manual*, by Ralph Turvey *et al.*, ILO, Geneva, 1989. It is the basis for a worldwide standardization of practice. There is no idea of competing with this book in its territory; however, it hardly touches theoretical issues. Another book *Index Numbers in Theory and Practice* by R. G. D. Allen (Macmillan, 1975) deals with both theory and practice to some extent, and in any case has its own distinct value. However, as concerns the price index, it gives no recognition of the 'homogeneity' that is quite essential to the concept—here he appears to have been in a large company.

Beside bearings on statistical method and strange mathematics, the material offered creates a substantial topic in mathematical economics with an interest of its own. It has fallout into a wider area, for instance giving rise to the so-called 'non-parametric or finite approach' to demand analysis, well known for the "Afriat's Theorem" of Microeconomics textbooks, that has had a range of applications, and served for invention of the frontier and stochastic frontier production functions at the start of the now much used 'data envelope analysis'.

H. Houthakker had been visiting the DAE a year earlier and his 'revealed preference' paper was circulating, spreading that influence. Robin Marris introduced the Laspeyres and Paasche indices and the question of their 'spread', and told me of Byushgens' remark that *Fisher's index is exact if it can be assumed that demand is governed by a homogeneous quadratic utility*—or something like that.

I still have never seen that paper but made a surmise immediately about contents and the communication has been the genesis for material in this book. At that time it prompted a non-homogeneous extension of Fisher's formula involving four periods simultaneously. This is my "Four-Point Formula" reported here in Part II which, from a remark of Houthakker a few years later, that $2 \times 2 = 4$, turned out also to be an extension of Wald's "New Formula", itself an extension of Fisher's formula. When submitted to a journal, the strangeness of computing with data for four periods instead of the usual two was too much to bear and it was not accepted.

A widely familiar story is that *the Laspeyres and Paasche indices are upper and lower bounds for the True index*,

$$P \leq T \leq L.$$

Hence if there exists a 'true' index, whatever that should signify, then necessarily

$$P \leq L.$$

This relation between the Laspeyres and Paasche indices, to be termed the *PL-inequality*, has been called *The Index Number Theorem* (Hicks' *Revision* of 1956, p. 181).

That certainly is no theorem, in the ordinary sense.[2] But the offer is provocative and my paper "On an identity concerning the relation between the Laspeyres and Paasche indices" was a response.

An observation that stands out immediately for very close attention is that *the PL-inequality implies Samuelson's revealed preference axiom*, as applied to the demand data available for the pair of reference periods. In other words, it is a strengthening of revealed preference consistency test which assures the data to fit some utility.[3] For fit with not any utility but a utility restricted to be homogeneous, as required for dealing with a price index, a stricter test would be needed—in fact, the PL-inequality![4]

It is possible to violate the PL-inequality while keeping revealed preference consistency. This goes somewhat beyond simply disproving "The Index Number Theorem".

We have lost a "Theorem" but the LP-inequality has gained another significance instead, where it is identified as the homogeneous counterpart of Samuelson's revealed preference condition, for the data to fit a homogeneous utility, as required for dealing with a price index.

How then is that condition extended to deal with more than two demand observations and provide a homogeneous counterpart for Houthakker's extension of Samuelson? That is a good question—with a perfect answer, as will be seen.

There are perhaps two versions of 'true index'. One, nebulous but with currency, is present in the argument that since L and P are upper and lower bounds their geometric mean, the Fisher index F, which lies between them should be a better approximation to the true index than either. Others allow it may be no nearer to the true index than either of the bounds L and P (R. G. D. Allen, 1975, p. 62).

---

2 There was a fleeting moment round that time when anything could be a "theorem" (maybe for poets).

3 Instead of going back the half-century to the start, or to *Discussion Paper* No. 177 (October 1964), now instead there are "Two new proofs of Afriat's Theorem" by A. Fostel, H. E. Scarf, and M. J. Todd, *Cowles Foundation Discussion Paper* No. 1415 (May 2003), Yale University. However, it is easier to prove the special case for two demand observations needed now, where Houthakker's test coincides with Samuelson's.

4 Here there is appeal to a 'homogeneous' counterpart of so-called 'Afriat's Theorem', with a test that strengthens Houthakker's, or rather, to the special case with two demand observations, where that stronger test reduces to the LP-inequality.

The other version, more matter-of-fact and making the approach of this book, treats the index, or whatever, as *computed* in respect to some utility that fits the data. Also against this clear approach, and again more in league with the nebulous, is the approach by means of algebraical formulae that has a culmination with Irving Fisher in *The Making of Index Numbers* (1922) with its one or two hundred formulae and famous "Tests". In that connection I am most happy to quote R. G. D. Allen where he quotes myself, with an extra comment on my "peculiar, indeed eccentric style with flashes ..." &c.:

> "It was as if an answer was proposed without first having a question ... many answers to no question in particular were proposed—the names of their proposers are attached to some of them" (p. 102)

Review of *The Price Index*
J. Roy. Stat. Soc. A 141, 3 (1978), p. 418

Just about all the formulae in that book, and everywhere else, are rational algebraic in demand data for the pair of reference periods. Here instead the Laspeyres formula stands out singularly, and if there is another formula to consider it would be more like what you may get by raising a matrix to powers in an alternative arithmetic where PROD means SUM and SUM means MIN, and from a sharing of mathematics with the Minimum Path problem of Ford and Fulkerson.

Let us call *the LP-interval* the closed interval with *L* and *P* as upper and lower limits, so the LP-inequality is the condition for this to be non-empty. While every true index is recognized to belong to this interval, it can still be asked *what points in this interval are true?* The answer is *all of them*, all equally true, no one more true than another. When I submitted this *theorem* to someone notorious in this subject area it was received with complete disbelief.

Here is a formula to add to Fisher's collection, a bit different from the others.

Index Formula: Any point in the LP-interval, if any.

Here ends an outline sketch of the most classical part of our subject matter, which will have a more fully explicit account in the main book Introduction, and in the text to follow. These introductory sketches may bring out the potential of this basic material for purposes of teaching where, despite its interest and importance, quite often there has been neglect. Beside such more essential matters, other phases in the book could be taken up for some interest they may offer in the way of mathematics, and mathematical economics.

This book touches on the price index in theory and practice, and on the essential limitation of the idea, and on lines of retreat from it which make an interesting inflation around the price index idea. One retreat is to go one rung up the ladder of generality and accept linearity, for purchasing power correspondence or expansion paths in the commodity space, without the homogeneity. All the same, it is very hard to envisage an actual abandonment of that single number and much respected social institution, the price index, to represent an official view for the community of how prices have changed. Knowing it is a quite crude compromised concept needed as a social institution, there may be not much point in refining it in some way without good reason.

There could be some reservations about work which is without dependence on empiricism as a contribution to any kind of economic knowledge. In fact, there is occurrence of complaints along such lines. But price indices are everywhere in economic thinking and statistics; and economic thinking is a great part of economic reality. The meaning of 'price level', as in the reported event when Joan Robinson was questioned, may give no concern in well known spheres of theory where by their nature form itself is an essential substance and a main support and is maintained with almost blameless fidelity; but outside those there is less easy submission.

The dependence on the price index in theory and practice makes desirable a crystallization of what is involved. With all the attention the subject has received it still has obscurities, the teaching of it, when not completely neglected, puzzles anyone confused by arguments that take place without proper definitions.

The result sought now is to give an explicit sense to familiar terms and statements, not actually to repudiate them. Especially there is the recognition, often absent, that the price index is an entirely 'homogeneous' idea. Against that is the knowledge that things in economic reality are thoroughly inhomogeneous—but that is another matter.

The index problem, taken up with interest at times and dropped at others, is always present, and it has usually been taken up during times of inflation. There can then be a questioning about the adequacy of the price index for its practical purposes. Inflation brings attention to price indices but on its own does not necessarily damage their reputation. An additional influence can be present, which has been described by Ralf Dahrendorf. This has bearing because a price index, in the theoretical notion a ratio of 'price-levels', is constructed statistically as some kind of average of price-ratios. He says: "... the end of expansion is also the end of the average.... At a time of general expansion, average figures gave some indication of a trend felt by most ... such averages are now [1974] losing much of their meaning.... The end of the average means that much more attention will have to be given to differences ...".

Obviously the impact of a price change on anyone depends entirely on what they want to buy. Purchasing habits vary widely, especially when there are widely different incomes. It is imaginable that prices may rise for basic necessities and fall for luxuries so cost of living may rise for the poor and fall for the rich while the 'price level' remains unchanged. Thus in spite of the implication of a price index that the impact—understood as proportional adjustment of income to offset the effect on purchasing power of the price change—is the same everywhere, it is in principle, and in reality, different where income and equally anything else is different. No one would care so much about this variation when most incomes are rising in purchasing power. But in contrary circumstances "... much more attention will have to be given to differences ...". It should no longer be plausible, even to convinced 'price level' believers, that the whole situation can be effectively summarized by a single number. It never has been plausible even though prodigious theories have depended on the idea; it has been tolerable only because it did not matter.

A case where it did matter, involving a pronounced bias of the price index specifically as between high and low incomes, and a fairly successful response made to this problem, with assistance of John Kuyper, is reported at the end of Part I.

However, to quote a reviewer of the proposal for this book, concerning problems of bias in price indexes not covered, particularly those arising from new goods and quality change:

> This is now a highly topical issue as a result of the Boskin report, and its dramatic claims regarding the impact of bias in the consumer price index on the US federal budget.

I follow advice to give this matter a passing reference. To quote the reviewer again:

> ... the price index is an important topic that has been neglected by the economics profession over the last few decades. The time may be right for the pendulum to swing the other way.

Unburdened of the 'Index Number Theorem' of Sir John Hicks and the one or two hundred formulae collected by Irving Fisher and the chronically unsatisfiable 'Tests', there could perhaps be a better mobility for the pendulum.

Also gathered from the reviewer: "... the international organizations collectively are soon going to publish a new consumer price index manual".

Acknowledgements

For a true index of debts accumulated over half a century I should make a start at the beginning, with several persons I have pleasure to blame for the initiation that has led to this volume.

At the very start is J. R. Bellerby, at the Agricultural Economics Research Institute, Oxford, during 1950–53, when I had been awarded the Rutherford Studentship to be his research assistant in work related to the Agriculture and Industry Enquiry. I had been a student in mathematics and this was my first encounter with the economics profession.

A next encounter was with Bob Clower, who came to see me in the corner of Wellington Square the sun never reached with some problem about a matrix. My thesis was on Matrix Theory and economists were beginning to have problems with matrices. He said then he hoped he was not disturbing me and when he turned up again recently, in Siena more than half a century later, I told him he had. After that I got to know other students in economics. About to leave Oxford, I went to say goodbye to Dr Burckhardt at the Institute of Statistics and, expecting to take a job in mathematics, mentioned I would be sorry to give up economics, whereupon he drew my attention to advertisement of a position at the Department of Applied Economics (DAE), Cambridge, three days before closing date.

So the scene changed again to Cambridge where I had been an undergraduate, and work with Richard Stone, Alan Brown, and Robin Marris at DAE put me on a path going towards this book, as also have associations with Angus Deaton, Terence Gorman and Amartya Sen which began about that time.

I should also mention Sir Roy Allen for a contact which though limited had been many sided, including reviewing each other's books. I am indebted to him for getting together with Nuri Jazairi, constant friend and collaborator in an encyclopaedia article, who had been his student at LSE and was brought up on my early index number papers.

Despite that any data I may actually use is more like form taken out of the air than bedrock historical or other statistics, J. S. G. Simmonds, Codrington Librarian at All Souls, beside kindness and conviviality during 1981–82 for which I thank him, also provided me with William Fleetwood's *Chronicon Preciosum Or, An Account of English Money, the Price of Corn, and Other Commodities for the Last 600 Years*.

I acknowledge with enduring gratitude friendship with Oskar Morgenstern begun in 1956 and marked by a productivity of Research Memoranda of the Econometric Research Program in Princeton 1958–62, in evidence in this book and all its material.

I have to express my appreciation and thanks to John Kuyper for his collaboration in the project with Statistics Canada data for investigating the bias of the CPI between high and low incomes, reported here in Part I, Appendix. The mastery he brought to the undertaking left me with a credibility I have been quite unable to support on my own in a different environment.

Axel Leijonhufvud, with friendly optimism for which I thank him, abandoned me to an interesting project from the World Bank with focus on Turkey in which I was able to make that discovery. It was during a period at the European University Institute, San Domenico di Fiesole/Firenze, as a Jean Monnet Fellow, and at Bilkent University, Ankara, prior to connection with the University of Siena. I express my thanks for hospitality at these institutions and their part in the thread of continuity necessary for this work.

Finally I am pleased to thank again Robert Langham and Terry Clague of Routledge very much for their collaboration that has made—as it did with another effort quite recently—a most welcome conclusion for this project.

Permissions

For materials reproduced, my thanks are due to:

Cambridge University Press
Blackwell Publishing Ltd, publisher of *International Economic Review*
Elsevier, publisher of *Journal of Econometrics*
National Bureau of Economic Research
Palgrave Macmillan

Their permissions extend to the following:

The system of inequalities $a_{rs} > x_s - x_r$. *Research Memorandum* No. 18 (October 1960), Econometric Research Program, Princeton University. *Proc. Cambridge Phil. Soc.* 59 (1963), 125–33.

The Price Index. Cambridge University Press, 1977. © CUP 1977.

On the constructibility of consistent price indices between several periods simultaneously. In *Essays in Theory and Measurement of Demand: in honour of Sir Richard Stone*, edited by Angus Deaton. Cambridge University Press, 1981. 133–61.

The construction of utility functions from expenditure data. *Cowles Foundation Discussion Paper* No. 144 (October 1964), Yale University. First World Congress of the Econometric Society, Rome, September 1965. *International Economic Review* 8, 1 (1967), 67–77.

Measurement of the purchasing power of incomes with linear expansion data. *Journal of Econometrics* 2, 3 (1974), 343–64.

The Theory of International Comparisons of Real Income and Prices. In *International Comparisons of Prices and Output, Proceedings of the Conference at York University, Toronto, 1970*, edited by D. J. Daly. National Bureau of Economic Research, Studies in Income and Wealth Volume 37, New York, 1972 (Ch. I, 13–84). © 1972 NBER.

The True Index. In A. Ingham and A. M. Ulph (eds), *Demand, Equilibrium and Trade: Essays in honour of Ivor F. Pearce*. Macmillan, 1984.

Introduction[1]

1 Laspeyres

2 Paasche

3 Revealed preference

4 Utility

1 The Preface ought to be read first, especially the part that deals with the PL-inequality. Reference should also be made to the appendix about Notation.

1 Laspeyres

A *price index* has reference to two periods, distinguished as the *base period* 0 and *current period* 1, so it can be denoted P_{10}. The sense of it is that different money amounts M_0, M_1 in the two periods that have the same *purchasing power* at prevailing prices p_0, p_1 should have the relation

$$M_1 = P_{10}M_0. \hspace{3cm} 1.1$$

To many with any awareness about it, a price index is just a number issued to the public from the government Statistical Office that should serve for 'indexation' purposes, such as may affect wages, salaries, mortgages, loans and other contracts, by use of the homogeneous linear *purchasing power correspondence* 1.1 with the given number P_{10} as slope.

The number with this use is not an arbitrary imposition, but a statistical construction by an accepted method, from which it should derive a legitimacy.[2] A most familiar theoretical approach to such legitimacy involves reference to a utility, which is restricted to fit given demand data by representing demand as providing maximum utility, for the cost. From such a utility, a purchasing power correspondence with the form 1.1 needs to be obtained, making P_{10} a *true index*, based on that data, or on a utility that fits the data. With the utility understood, the *purchasing power* of any money at given prices is just the utility level attainable with it.

Here it should be remarked that, with arbitrary utility, the most that can be said about the purchasing power correspondence derived from it is that it should be monotonic. Imposition of the special homogeneous linear form 1.1 would have impact on the presumed utility, by requirement of a special *homogeneity* property for it. A further issue is the existence of such a utility that fits given demand data.

---

2 *Consumer Price Indices—An ILO manual*, by Ralph Turvey *et al.* ILO, Geneva, 1989, has been the basis for a worldwide standardization of practice.

Suppose, in the way of available data, it is given that x_0 is demanded at prices p_0, so with a cost

$$M_0 = p_0 x_0. \tag{1.2}$$

For a utility that fits this data by representing it as having the attribute of efficiency, this cost M_0 is also the cost of attaining the utility of x_0 at the prices p_0. Then the cost M_1 of attaining that utility at the different prices p_1 is understood to be given by 1.1.

But the actual cost $p_1 x_0$ of x_0 itself cannot be less than this minimum cost of attaining just the utility of x_0, so

$$M_1 \leq p_1 x_0. \tag{1.3}$$

Now by 1.1, 1.2 and 1.3,

$$P_{10} \leq p_1 x_0 / p_0 x_0,$$

that is

$$P_{10} \leq \widehat{P}_{10}, \tag{1.4}$$

where

$$\widehat{P}_{10} = p_1 x_0 / p_0 x_0 \tag{1.5}$$

is the *Laspeyres price index* formula.

It has appeared that, with demand given for the base period, *any true index has the Laspeyres index as an upper bound.*

It is common for an official price index to have status as a Laspeyres index. The formula can be developed to show it in its practical form, as an average of price ratios

$$p_{1i}/p_{0i} \quad (i = 1, \ldots, n) \tag{1.6}$$

comparing current with base prices for the n goods, with *weights*

$$\sigma_{0i} = p_{0i} x_{0i} / p_0 x_0 \quad (i = 1, \ldots, n),$$

such that

$$\sigma_{0i} \geq 0, \quad \sum_i \sigma_{0i} = 1.$$

Thus,

$$\hat{P}_{10} = p_1 x_0 / p_0 x_0$$

$$= \sum_i p_{1i} x_{0i} / p_0 x_0$$

$$= \sum_i (p_{1i}/p_{0i}) p_{0i} x_{0i} / p_0 x_0$$

$$= \sum_i (p_{1i}/p_{0i}) \sigma_{0i}$$

showing that

$$\hat{P}_{10} = \sum_i (p_{1i}/p_{0i}) \sigma_{0i}. \qquad 1.7$$

From here apparently, as affecting practical procedure where there is a break-down into parts of the work involved, the goods can be partitioned into groups with price indices determined for the groups separately, which can then be recombined to form their average with weights belonging to the groups, to give the final result.

A one-time survey in the base period 0 to determine the weights σ_{0i}, beside prices which are to be recorded in this as in any other period, enables the price index to be maintained subsequently for any period where just prices are recorded. This is part of the *practical economy* of the Laspeyres index that has no doubt been influential for its adoption, beside the distinguished location in relation to the 'true index' that has been found for it, where it has the status of an upper bound. Beside this attribution, there is also no negative dogma to tell of any actual separation from the 'true index'—it may even be 'true' itself !

Two variations on the Laspeyres index can be described using the statement 1.7. The weights there are dated, with the base period 0 as their date, but they could be given another date different from the base and current periods 0, 1. Then we have a formula

$$\tilde{P}_{10} = \sum_i (p_{1i}/p_{0i}) \sigma_i. \qquad 1.8$$

where the σ_i are now not necessarily dated in the base period 0. Such a compromised Laspeyres formula is in some cases more like what is in actual use.

For the other variant, the arithmetic mean in the formula 1.7 is replaced by the corresponding geometric mean, to produce the formula

$$\ddot{P}_{10} = \prod_i (p_{1i}/p_{0i})^{\sigma_{0i}}. \qquad 1.9$$

Now by the General Theorem of the Mean, that a geometric mean does not exceed the corresponding arithmetic mean, we have

$$\overset{\leftrightarrow}{P}_{10} \leq \hat{P}_{10}, \tag{1.10}$$

with equality if and only if the price ratios 1.6 are all equal, so price inflation is strictly uniform over all the goods, in which case the two indices share this common value.

This *geometric Laspeyres* index could have a particular interest in high inflation conditions to offset the possible exaggeration of the inflation rate provided by the conventional arithmetic formula, since such exaggeration could be a force to increase the actual rate. However, it needs to be recognized that such compensation obtained from using the geometric formula could be overdone.

A notable feature of the geometric formula is that it exhibits the ideal model for a 'true' index, where it has the form of a ratio of 'price levels', though that by itself does not make it any truer than it might be. Let

$$P_t = \prod_i p_{ti}^{\sigma_{0i}} \quad (t = 0, 1), \tag{1.11}$$

so that, from 1.9,

$$\overset{\leftrightarrow}{P}_{10} = P_1/P_0, \tag{1.12}$$

showing the price index as a ratio of *price levels* P_0, P_1 given by 1.11. From this form it satisfies Fisher tests like time-reversal, and others, but not the chain test. But if the weights, dated in the base period and so variable, are given as fixed σ_i, as in the compromised Laspeyres formula 1.6, so the price levels are instead

$$P_t = \prod_i p_{ti}^{\sigma_i} \quad (t = 0, 1), \tag{1.13}$$

then the chain test, provided weights remain fixed, also is satisfied, and in fact every Fisher 'Test' one could wish. How is it then that this well-qualified index is not conspicuous among the one- or two-hundred formulae found in Fisher's *The Making of Index Numbers*?

2   Paasche

Unlike the Laspeyres index which involves the demand x_0 in the base period 0, the Paasche index instead involves the demand x_1 in the current period 1, as in the formula

$$\overset{\smile}{P}_{10} = p_1 x_1/p_0 x_1. \tag{2.1}$$

According to this the Paasche index is obtained by exchanging the base and current periods in the Laspeyres formula and taking the inverse,

$$\breve{P}_{10} = \hat{P}_{01}^{-1}. \qquad 2.2$$

Consider a true index P_{10} for a utility that fits the given data of demands

$$(p_t, x_t) \quad (t = 0, 1). \qquad 2.3$$

Then for the reverse index

$$P_{01} = P_{10}^{-1}, \qquad 2.4$$

also true with the same utility, by the relation of true index to Laspeyres, applicable in this case because of the fit with demand x_1, we have

$$P_{10} \leq \hat{P}_{10}$$

from which, by taking reciprocals and using 2.2 and 2.4,

$$\breve{P}_{10} \leq P_{10},$$

so now

$$\breve{P}_{10} \leq P_{10} \leq \hat{P}_{10}, \qquad 2.5$$

in other words, *the Laspeyres and Paasche indices are upper and lower bounds of the true index.* Hence, *if there exists a true index*, with the demand data 2.3, it follows that

$$\breve{P}_{10} \leq \hat{P}_{10}.$$

This relation of the Laspeyres and Paasche indices, termed the *LP-inequality* (see Preface), or LP-test, has been called *The Index Number Theorem.*[3]
    For a restatement,

$$p_1 x_1 / p_0 x_1 \leq p_1 x_0 / p_0 x_0,$$

equivalently, and more symmetrically,

$$p_0 x_0 p_1 x_1 \leq p_1 x_0 p_0 x_1,$$

---

3 By J. R. Hicks in his *Revision of Demand Theory*, 1956, p. 181. That certainly is no theorem in an ordinary sense, as remarked in the Preface with additional comment.

or

$$\hat{P}_{01}\hat{P}_{10} \geq 1.$$

or with

$$u_t = (p_t x_t)^{-1} p_t$$

this being the *budget vector* associated with the demand (p_t, x_t), it becomes

(LP) $u_0 x_1 u_1 x_0 \geq 1.$ 2.6

Concerning budget vectors it needs to be noticed that

$$
\begin{aligned}
u_i x_i &= ((p_i x_i)^{-1} p_i) x_i \\
&= (p_i x_i)^{-1} (p_i x_i) \\
&= 1
\end{aligned}
$$

and also

$$
\begin{aligned}
u_i x_j &= ((p_i x_i)^{-1} p_i) x_j \\
&= (p_i x_i)^{-1} (p_i x_j) \\
&= (p_i x_j / p_j x_j)(p_j x_j / p_i x_i) \\
&= L_{ij}(p_j x_j / p_i x_i),
\end{aligned}
$$

where

$$L_{ij} = p_i x_j / p_j x_j$$

is the Laspeyres index. Hence

$$u_0 x_1 u_1 x_0 = L_{01} L_{10},$$

and moreover

$$u_r x_i u_i x_j \cdots u_k x_s = L_{ri} L_{ij} \cdots L_{ks}(p_s x_s / p_r x_r),$$

so that

$$u_r x_i u_i x_j \cdots u_k x_r = L_{ri} L_{ij} \cdots L_{kr}. \qquad 2.7$$

From this it appears that the conditions

(K) $u_r x_i u_i x_j \cdots u_k x_r \geq 1,$ 2.8

and

(L) $L_{ri} L_{ij} \cdots L_{kr} \geq 1,$ 2.9

are equivalent.

3 Revealed preference

This condition (LP) in 2.6 has to be viewed in relation to Samuelson's Revealed Preference Axiom, or Test, which, suitably put, originally applied to a demand function and now just to a pair of demand elements, denies the possibility of the simultaneous inequalities

$$p_0 x_1 \leq p_0 x_0, \qquad p_1 x_0 \leq p_1 x_1$$

unless both be equalities, or equivalently

$$\text{(S)} \quad u_0 x_1 \leq 1, \quad u_1 x_0 \leq 1 \;\Rightarrow\; u_0 x_1 = 1, \quad u_1 x_0 = 1.^4 \qquad\qquad 3.1$$

This *Samuelson test applied to a pair of demands is necessary and sufficient for the existence of a utility that fits them.* The familiar theory for a demand function has no application to this proposition for a pair, which on its own is completely elementary, and is in any case a special case of a theorem for any finite collection.[5] Note that for a single demand (p_0, x_0) there is always a utility that fits, for instance

$$\varphi(x) = p_0 x,$$

but for more than one there is a positive restriction.

Obviously *the LP-test implies Samuelson's test*. For if the S-inequalities in 3.1 hold and one or other holds strictly, so the S-test is denied, then, multiplying the left sides and right sides, there is a violation of the LP-inequality, so

Not S $\Rightarrow$ Not LP,

equivalently

LP $\Rightarrow$ S. $\qquad\qquad 3.2$

This observation that *the PL-inequality implies Samuelson's revealed preference axiom*, as applied to the demand data available for the pair of reference periods, immediately *stands out* for the closest attention. The inequality is a strengthening of revealed preference consistency test which assures the data to fit some utility. For fit with not any utility but a utility restricted to be homogeneous, or conical, as required for dealing with a price index, a stricter test would be needed—in fact, the

---

4 Strictly, this is a minor relaxation of Samuelson's original condition, good for a demand function instead of a general demand correspondence, stated

$$u_0 x_1 \leq 1, \quad u_1 x_0 \leq 1 \;\Rightarrow\; x_0 = x_1.$$

5 Early proofs are followed by "Two new proofs of Afriat's Theorem" by A. Fostel, H. E. Scarf, and M. J. Todd, *Cowles Foundation Discussion Paper* No. 1415 (May 2003), Yale University. However, it is easier to prove the special case for two demand observations needed now, where Houthakker's test, appropriate for any number, coincides with Samuelson's.

PL-inequality![6] For want of this simple proposition, there had been *a real hold-up* in the proper treatment of the price index.

The LP-inequality has gained significance, where it is identified as the homogeneous counterpart of Samuelson's revealed preference condition, for the data to fit a homogeneous utility, as required for dealing with a price index.

How then is that condition extended to deal with more than two demand observations and provide a homogeneous counterpart for Houthakker's extension of Samuelson? That is a good question, with a good answer.

Consider any finite collection of demand elements

$$(p_t, x_t) \in B \times C \quad (t = 1, \ldots, m), \tag{3.3}$$

making the elements of a finite demand correspondence

$$D \subset B \times C$$

and the Houthakker condition

(H) $u_r x_i \leq 1, \quad u_i x_j \leq 1, \ldots, u_k x_r \leq 1$

$$\Rightarrow \quad u_r x_i = 1, u_i x_j = 1, \ldots, u_k x_r = 1.^7 \tag{3.4}$$

which is necessary and sufficient for the existence of a utility that fits the given demand elements. Also consider the condition, already encountered in 2.8 earlier,

(K) $u_r x_i u_i x_j \cdots u_k x_r \geq 1. \tag{3.5}$

which obviously is a strengthening of H,

$$K \Rightarrow H. \tag{3.6}$$

For any $\theta_t > 0$, let D^θ be the demand correspondence D where x_t is replaced by $x_t \theta_t$ on the ray through x_t. Let K(D) assert the condition K as applied to D. Because

$$u_r^\theta x_s^\theta = p_r x_s \theta_s / p_r x_r \theta_r = u_r x_s \theta_s / \theta_r$$

it appears that

$$K(D^\theta) \Leftrightarrow K(D).$$

---

6 Here there is appeal to a 'homogeneous' counterpart of so-called Afriat's Theorem, with a test that strengthens Houthakker's, or rather, to the special case with two demand observations, where that stronger test reduces to the LP-inequality.

7 The way we dealt with Samuelson, this is a minor relaxation of Houthakker's original condition, which was good for a demand function instead of a general demand correspondence, stated

$$u_r x_i \leq 1, u_i x_j \leq 1, \ldots, u_k x_r \leq 1 \Rightarrow x_r = x_i = \cdots = x_k.$$

There is the same result, though more directly, if prices are replaced by any points on the rays they determine in the budget space. For

$$u_t^\theta = (p_t^\theta x_t)^{-1} p_t^\theta = (\theta_t p_t x_t)^{-1} \theta_t p_t = (p_t x_t)^{-1} p_t = u_t.$$

It appears therefore that the condition K deals with the demand correspondence D not so much as a correspondence between points in the budget and commodity spaces B and C, as might be obtained from some utility, but rather as a *correspondence between rays* in those spaces, determined by such points, as would be obtained if it were a homogeneous utility. This is in harmony with K being established, as it will be, as the condition for the existence of not any utility that fits the demand data, like with H, but a homogeneous utility.

For a first step, it is seen that 3.5 is equivalent to the condition

$$u_s x_t \geq X_t / X_s \quad \text{for some } X_t > 0,$$

as comes from a result at first dealt with for a system in the form $a_{rs} > x_s - x_r$.[8] A restatement of this condition is that

$$(X) \quad p_s x_t / p_s x_s \geq X_t / X_s \quad \text{for some } X_i > 0, \tag{3.7}$$

or, with P_t for which

$$P_t X_t = p_t x_t, \tag{3.8}$$

that

$$p_s x_t / p_t x_t \geq P_s / P_t \quad \text{for some } P_i > 0,$$

that is

$$(P) \quad L_{st} \geq P_s / P_t \quad \text{for some } P_i > 0, \tag{3.9}$$

where

$$L_{st} = p_s x_t / p_t x_t$$

is the Laspeyres index.

As with condition (X), a necessary and sufficient condition for (P) is that

$$(L) \quad L_{ri} L_{ij} \cdots L_{kr} \geq 1, \tag{3.10}$$

or with

$$L_{rij\cdots ks} = L_{ri} L_{ij} \cdots L_{ks},$$

this can be stated

$$L_{r\cdots r} \geq 1.$$

8 See: Appendix 1, "The system of inequalities $a_{rs} > x_s - x_r$", *Research Memorandum* No. 18 (October 1960), Econometric Research Program, Princeton University. *Proc. Cambridge Phil. Soc.* 59 (1963), 125–33; and Appendix 8, "On the constructibility of consistent price indices between several periods simultaneously", in *Essays in Theory and Measurement of Demand: in honour of Sir Richard Stone*, edited by Angus Deaton. Cambridge University Press, 1981, 133–61.

This is the condition (L) encountered in 2.9 earlier, there seen directly to be equivalent to 2.8, which is (K), encountered again in 3.5.

With reference to condition (K), evidently

$$K \iff L,$$

and so, with 3.6, we have

$$L \implies H,$$

so it appears that *condition* L *is a strengthening of the Houthakker revealed preference consistency test* H.

4   Utility

Now to be seen is how, given any solution P_i of the system (P), be regarded as a system of *price levels*, a utility can be constructed that fits[9] the given demand data and is linearly homogeneous, or conical, and the *price index* P_{ij} that is *true* with this utility is given by the *price level ratios*

$$P_{ij} = P_i/P_j. \tag{4.1}$$

With the X_i determined by means of relation 3.8 from the solution P_i of system (P), so these are a solution of system (X), let

$$\begin{aligned}
\widehat{\varphi}_i(x) &= X_i u_i x \\
&= X_i (p_i x_i)^{-1} p_i x \\
&= P_i^{-1} p_i x,
\end{aligned}$$

and

$$\widehat{\varphi}(x) = \min_i \widehat{\varphi}_i(x), \tag{4.2}$$

so this is a concave conical polyhedral function. Now

$$\begin{aligned}
\widehat{\varphi}_i(x_i) &= X_i \\
\widehat{\varphi}_j(x_i) &\geq X_i
\end{aligned}$$

showing that

$$\begin{aligned}
\widehat{\varphi}(x_i) &= \min_j \widehat{\varphi}_j(x_j) \\
&= \widehat{\varphi}_i(x_i) \\
&= X_i,
\end{aligned}$$

---

9 A utility *fits*, or *is compatible with*, a demand means it represents the demand as efficient, as providing maximum utility for the cost, or minimum cost for the utility.

so we have

$$\hat{\varphi}(x_i) = X_i. \tag{4.3}$$

Hence from

$$u_i x \leq 1 \quad \Rightarrow \quad \hat{\varphi}_i(x) \leq X_i = \hat{\varphi}(x_i)$$

follows the minimum cost for the utility, or maximum utility for the cost, efficiency condition

$$p_i x \leq p_i x_i \quad \Rightarrow \quad \hat{\varphi}(x) \leq \hat{\varphi}(x_i)$$

which establishes that the utility φ fits the given demands

$$(p_i, x_i) \in B \times C \quad (i = 1, \ldots, m). \tag{4.4}$$

Now for any point $x_i \theta_i$ $(\theta_i > 0)$ on the ray through x_i the utility, by linear homogeneity, is $X_i \theta_i$ and the cost at prices p_i is

$$M_i = p_i x_i \theta_i.$$

Hence, in view of 3.8, any cost M_i will buy utility

$$X_i M_i / p_i x_i = M_i / P_i.$$

Therefore, to determine the purchasing power correspondence based on the utility, we have that the condition for money amounts M_i, M_j at prices p_i, p_j to buy the same level of utility is

$$M_i / P_i = M_j / P_j,$$

that is

$$M_i = P_{ij} M_j,$$

where

$$P_{ij} = P_i / P_j,$$

this now being established as the true price index belonging to this utility.

Another concave conical function $\check{\varphi}$ which fits the demand data and is such that

$$\check{\varphi}(x_i) = X_i. \tag{4.5}$$

and has the same associated price index as $\hat{\varphi}$, is the polytope type function given by

$$\breve{\varphi}(x) = \max \left\{ \sum_i X_i t_i : \sum x_i t_i \leq x, t_i \geq 0 \right\}, {}^{10}$$

4.6

and if φ is any other concave conical utility that fits the demands and takes the values X_i at the points x_i, then

$$\breve{\varphi}(x) \leq \varphi(x) \leq \widehat{\varphi}(x)$$

4.7

for all x.

It should be seen what light these conclusions have to shed on questions for the classical case where there are just two periods 0, 1 with demand data

$$(p_t, x_t) \quad (t = 0, 1),$$

4.8

just for the two price index reference periods themselves.

The system (P) in this case consists of the inequalities

$$(P) \quad L_{01} \geq P_1/P_0, \quad L_{10} \geq P_0/P_1 \qquad \text{for some } P_0, P_1 > 0,$$

4.9

where

$$L_{ij} = p_i x_j / p_j x_j$$

is the Laspeyres index. Equivalently

$$(P) \quad P_{10}^{-1} \leq P_1/P_0 \leq L_{01},$$

4.10

where

$$P_{10}^{-1} = p_0 x_0 / p_1 x_0$$

is the Paasche index. It is concluded, despite manifest disbelief (see Preface!), that any point in the Laspeyres–Paasche interval is a true index, for some utility that fits the data. Of course if more data is brought in, there are more constraints and the interval where the true index is indeterminate, will narrow.

---

10 The function of this form introduced by Afriat (1972) is the constant-returns 'frontier production function' that gives a function representation of the production efficiency measurement method of Farrell (1957) that marks the beginning of 'data envelope analysis' (DEA).

The above provides the following:

Theorem *For any given finite collection of demand elements*

$$(p_i, x_i) \in B \times C$$

with Laspeyres indices

$$L_{ij} = p_i x_j / p_j x_j$$

with chain products

$$L_{rij\cdots ks} = L_{ri} L_{ij} \cdots L_{ks}$$

and cycle products

$$L_{rij\cdots kr} = L_{ri} L_{ij} \cdots L_{kr}$$

the condition

(L) $L_{r\cdots r} \geq 1$

for Laspeyres cycle products all at least 1 is necessary and sufficient for the existence of a solution to the system of inequalities

(P) $L_{ij} \geq P_i / P_j$,

to determine price levels P_i, and for the existence of a homogeneous utility that fits all the demands, and given any solution, if

$$\varphi_i(x) = P_i^{-1} p_i x$$

and

$$\varphi(x) = \min_i \varphi_i(x),$$

then φ is one such utility, with

$$P_{ij} = P_i / P_j$$

as the price indices it determines.

Considering the disposition of the original "Index Number Theorem" leaving a vacancy, this theorem could perhaps take its place, or even—or better since nothing like this was dreamt of in the original—just the special case involving two demand elements.

The homogeneous utility construction part of this theorem is a homogeneous utility, parallel to the general utility construction theorem, familiarity with which has been enhanced lately by the addition of two new proofs.[11]

11 "Two new proofs of Afriat's Theorem" by A. Fostel, H. E. Scarf, and M. J. Todd, *Cowles Foundation Discussion Paper* No. 1415 (May 2003), Yale University.

Introducing budget vectors

$$u_i = (p_i x_i)^{-1} p_i$$

and coefficients

$$D_{ij} = u_i x_j - 1$$

with chains

$$D_{rij\cdots ks} = (D_{ri}, D_{ij}, \ldots, D_{ks}),$$

the condition

(H) $D_{ri\cdots r} \leq o \implies D_{ri\cdots r} = o,$

for the denial of semi-negative cycles, is necessary and sufficient for the existence of λ_i, φ_i such that

(U) $\lambda_i > 0, \qquad \lambda_i D_{ij} \geq \varphi_j - \varphi_i,$

which determine polyhedral and polytope monotone concave utility functions

$$\hat{\varphi}(x) = \min_i \varphi_i + \lambda_i u_i (x - x_i)$$

and

$$\check{\varphi}(x) = \max \left\{ \sum_i \varphi_i t_i : \sum x_i t_i \leq x, \sum_i t_i = 1, t_i \geq 0 \right\}^{12}$$

which fit the given demand data and have value φ_i at $x = x_i$, and if φ is any other monotone concave utility with value φ_i at $x = x_i$, it fits the data if and only if

$$\check{\varphi}(x) \leq \varphi(x) \leq \hat{\varphi}(x)$$

for all x.

According to 3.6 above, the condition L in the Theorem proposed earlier is a strengthening of the Houthakker condition H dealt with just now. With this comparison between K and L there should be a related comparison between the conclusions drawn from them.

---

12 This formula is used to introduce the so-called 'frontier production function' of 'data envelope analysis' in my "Efficiency Estimation of Production Functions", Boulder Meetings of the Econometric Society, September 1971, *International Economic Review* 13, 3 (October 1972), 568–98. A note about origin of 'data envelope analysis' is in my book *The Market: equilibrium, stability, mythology*, Routledge, 2003, Note 4, 118–9.

For a utility φ with gradient g to be concave, it should have the property

$$\varphi(x) \le \varphi(\bar{x}) + g(\bar{x})(x - \bar{x}),$$

which shows that

$$\varphi(x) = \min_{\bar{x}} \varphi(\bar{x}) + g(\bar{x})(x - \bar{x})$$

In case it is linearly homogeneous, that is $\varphi(xt) = \varphi(x)t$, also

$$g(x)x = \varphi(x),$$

by Euler's theorem. Hence

$$\varphi(x) \le g(\bar{x})x,$$

so now

$$\varphi(x) = \min_{\bar{x}} g(\bar{x})x.$$

Given that $\varphi(x_i) = \varphi_i$, and with $g_i = g(x_i)$, the Lagrangian conditions for φ to be a maximum at $x = x_i$ subject to the constraint $u_i x = 1$ are

$$g_i = \lambda_i u_i, \qquad u_i x_i = 1,$$

λ_i being the Lagrangian multiplier. But, with homogeneity, also

$$g_i x_i = \varphi_i,$$

so now

$$\lambda_i = \lambda_i u_i x_i$$
$$= g_i x_i$$
$$= \varphi_i$$

$$\therefore$$

$$\lambda_i = \varphi_i.$$

Substitution in the conditions (U) then gives

$$u_i x_j \ge \varphi_j / \varphi_i,$$

or, what is the same, with φ_i now denoted X_i,

$$p_i x_j / p_i x_i \ge X_j / X_i,$$

which is just what we have for system (X) in 3.7.

This outcome provides a further view of the relation between the general construction of utility and the homogeneous case seen here to be derived from it by the imposition $\lambda_i = \varphi_i$ required by homogeneity.

Is the price level P_i the price of anything? It's the price of utility when commodity prices are given by the p_i of period i, so utility X_i of the original x_i costs

$$P_t X_t = p_t x_t,$$

exactly the cost of x_i. Of course this utility was not delivered so to speak as an inscrutible entity as it were on a plate, but as an ordinary basket of goods x_i, which has that utility, and cost.

But this role of price level as price of utility level goes further. The costs in the periods i, j of maintaining utility at a constant level X are

$$M_i = P_i X, \qquad M_j = P_j X$$

so

$$M_j / M_i = P_j / P_i$$

that is

$$M_i = P_{ij} M_j,$$

where

$$P_{ij} = P_i / P_j,$$

which again shows what we had before, but with the index now quite explicitly a 'constant utility' index. This 'constant utility' terminology used to be used as if it had reference to a distinguishing characteristic of an index, but in fact it does not since it touches a completely basic idea for the concept.

At this point after the Theorem enunciated earlier, a comment can be made about the Fisher 'Ideal' index, which is the geometric mean of the Paasche and Laspeyres indices. With the provisor $P \leq L$, for the existence of a true index, belonging to some utility that fits the data, we have $P \leq F \leq L$, so F is such a true index, and hence it is associated with a utility of the polyhedral form $\widehat{\varphi}$ given by 4.2, or the polytope form $\widecheck{\varphi}$ given by 4.6. Both these utility functions are on the 'non-parametric' model that, as production functions, have done service in production efficiency analysis and popular 'data envelope analysis' (DEA). What then should be made of Byushgens Theorem that associates Fisher's 'Ideal' index with a homogeneous quadratic utility? It could hardly make Fisher better on such grounds that an ordinary quadratic is more reassuring than a freak non-parametric type.

Part I

Laspeyres, Paasche and Fisher

Introduction
—theory and practice

1   Comparisons

There is a dilemma in the comparison of two periods of time: they must have comparable features to bring them into a relation with each other at all, but also there is an essential separation so it is difficult to know what finally to make of the comparison. In tenth century Spain, a simple view was offered: the world is created afresh at every moment . . . This is certainly one way to abolish problems of comparison and connection. However, others, historians, economists, statisticians, or anybody else, believe things are not always so new: they dwell on connections, debts. In the other extreme, the only authority for the present is the past. In early economics, the correct price or wage is simply the price or wage that has been settled by custom and has the value which, so far as anybody can remember, it has always had. No doubt this is not as senseless as it might immediately seem from the standpoint of neoclassical economics. But it presupposes moral order, obedience to norms. There can be no price-cutting, and no charging of unexpectedly high prices. This makes sense in a steady way of life where supply and demand have created each other and settled down together. Whatever the limitations of this way of thinking, it is at least rational. Walras pursues the opposite in a logical way, but at the same time he helps foster a myth, which we have also from Adam Smith. However, with Smith it is not a deliberate and indispensable truth to be pursued with trappings of science. From him it can appear as a fantasy inadvertently inherited from predecessors. In the alternative system, which is more familiar to us at least intellectually, price-cutting and boosting is permitted freely, there is no law but competition, but out of this competition emerges the *optimal result*.

Here is not really a proposition that something—it is not said or known what—is at a maximum. It is an exhortation which connects, better than with anything in the differential calculus, with the tenth century philosopher: the Walrasian economy is always newly at its best at any moment. There can be no argument that it should be any different. Therefore it is pointless to do accounts which compare one moment with another. But standing out in practice is the opposite, familiarly old attitude, which is that the past has authority for the present. Price indices express respect for that authority. They offer a kind of exchange rate between £s in different periods; accounts in one period can be converted to show them as if they were accounts in another period, and then they can be compared with corresponding accounts in that other period. In particular, wages can be compared. A force acting on what a wage should be this year is what it was in some former year converted into this year's £s. Sums today are measured by a yardstick which has reference to the past. The 'index number problem' can be understood as the problem of fashioning such a yardstick. There is a dilemma, because the present has to be placed in the past, but the present has a separation from the past which erases reference marks which could assist in the positioning. There are calibration difficulties. Different approaches to the problem are distinguished by the choice of calibrating instruments.

A price index signifies a special form of instrument whereby prices, though they are many, have a 'level' in any period. Exchange rates between periods are then ratios of price levels, these being determined by 'price indices'. But this only gives a form and does not tell how it is to be realized, or why such a simple form should be suitable.

A change through time can be recognized only by means of some element which persists unchanged. If a material body is undergoing deformation in time, this can be known only by means of a measuring rod which is transported through time without deformation. With a price index which measures change in the 'level' of prices, there is dependence on a hypothetically unchanged construction, a special type of utility function. This function could be a very simple one determined from a single bundle of goods. This would be the case with a practical price index like the Consumer Price Index (CPI) used in North America. But no purpose is served by bringing in utility functions at all in this case. Utility functions give service in theoretical discussions, where they contribute structure which is part of the matter. But the data used in practice cannot bear that structure.

Practice can stand without theory; or, it constitutes its own theory. All that is accomplished by expressing anything in practice in terms of utility theory is to show it does not conflict with that theory. Practice is consistent with a poor specialization of that theory, so poor that nothing is added by bringing it in.

When prices change from one period to another, purchases made in one period at a certain cost have a different cost in the other. Should prices all rise so will that cost. If a wage does not increase enough to meet the extra cost, sacrifices have to be made and living-style suffers. The work done in a job might remain the same but the return received from it in terms of ability to purchase required goods becomes less. The unsettling effects are familiar. Agitation takes place everywhere for incomes and all payments to increase. It becomes important to have a general basis for deciding the amount of any such increase. The experience of rising prices therefore creates the social need to have an accepted yardstick for judging the modifications due to incomes and other payments which would compensate them for the effects of price increases.

In common practice it is a 'price index' which has use for such judgements. This is a number issued regularly from a government office which has official standing in the community as a description of how prices have changed in a given period. In many countries the CPI has this role, and practices in any other countries are similar. But there is a need served, reflected in the variety of uses, and then there are questions which feature in public discussions about whether this is fulfilled 'adequately'. The sense of such adequacy and how any question about it can be answered is not an altogether simple matter but has separate aspects. Two broad aspects, which encompass others, are about the character of the original statistical data, and then what is done with that data for whatever purpose. Interest here is in the latter of these aspects, especially in the question whether the extraction of a single number, the 'price index', from the available data is all that should be done with it.

It is likely that the procedures with price indices such as the CPI have been satisfactory enough over many years, so much so that perhaps any important modification would have been unwarranted—beside unwisely opening a pandoras box! But this finding is related to factors of historical experience which are capable of unfavourable fluctuations. There is demonstration of this in some recent years. Abrupt events give abrupt characteristics to inflation which destroy the possibility of an effective summary by any single number. Out of regard to this, there is reason to have more ample statistical reports which would communicate knowledge of inflation structure. Such structural information is essential for approaching matters to do with income distribution, changes in the relative position of different groups, taxation and inflation accounts in general. Questions to do with purchasing power measurement are not at all new; rather, they are among the oldest in economics. But there is a different emphasis in the way they are imposed nowadays.

Ralf Dahrendorf, in the remarks quoted in the Preface, points out a general phenomenon, illustrated by the interest given to differences of the effects of inflation on different consumer groups. Thinking in terms of price indices is not the natural way to recognize such differences. It should be established, what is the actual extent of these differences, and what is the effective and intelligible way of stating them in detail and in a summary fashion by means of suitable statistics. An example from early history shows plainly what is involved.

2   Fleetwood's student

> Since money is of no other use, than as it is the thing with which we purchase the necessities and conveniences of life, 'tis evident . . .

—this was a fleeting moment of practical concreteness before the rise of index number theory and doctrines of the 'price-level'. William Fleetwood, in 1707, calculated how much it would cost to live in a certain way in his day and four hundred years earlier. Since he was addressing the matter to a university student, he took as his example the life of a student, and its necessities (4 Hogsheads of Beer, 6 Yards of Cloth, 5 Quarters of Wheat, etc.). He found that "£5 in H.VI Days" would make a student "full as rich a man as he who has now £20." He might have taken any other representative type and instead of the figures (£5, £20) obtained some others, say (25, 50) for a Civil Servant. In fact, he could have sampled the population finding 16,000 examples of the way people live. Then the single point (5, 20) would appear as one in a cloud of 16,000. Taking the average point, the centre of gravity of the cloud, which in the rather sparse cloud formed by just these two points would be (15, 35), and the slope of the ray through that point, he would obtain

$$CPI = 35/15 = 2.3.$$

This is good luck for the Civil Servant and bad luck for the student. For, on issue of this number from H. M. Statistical Office in 1707, one would receive an adjusted income of £58.3, that is an amount more than the £50 needed, and the other would be given not £20 but only £11.7 on which he could not live as accustomed.

Of course, the bias could have been the other way round and in favour of the student. But there is no way of even taking notice of such bias, one way or the other, if it is a rule that just the CPI is to be used.

With reference to Figure 1, the CPI is used to specify a homogeneous linear relation between equivalent incomes, represented by the ray through the point A. If the inflation adjustments determined from it are applied to all incomes, the total adjustment for the total of all incomes is correct, but the allocation of the total to the individual incomes is not. One broad aspect of this misallocation is that one half of the population, the upper or lower half (in the figure, it is the upper half) receives an excess, and the other half has a defect of equal amount. Any line through A will have the same merit as the CPI-ray as giving a relation between equivalent incomes which provides the correct total adjustment. But there is just one such line which moreover can make no dispute between the upper and lower halves since it divides the total between them correctly. This is the line which passes through U and L, whose slope defines the marginal price index (MPI). Though this line gives the correct allocation between the halves, it need not give the correct allocation between strata within the halves, except when the population consists just two individuals, as in the chosen illustration which elaborates Fleetwood's calculation with one individual. This illustration can be taken further, by the method shown in Appendix I.

The average income £15 in H.VI days has been correctly adjusted to £35 in 1707. But the uniform proportion in which the adjustment is distributed to incomes is not correct. It would be better to use the average price index or API ($=$CPI) 2.3 to determine the average income

$$35 = 2.3 \times 15$$

for 1707 from that in H.VI days. Thus, in Figure 1, 2.3 is the slope of the ray through the overall average point A. Then instead of using the usual proportionate, or homogeneous linear relation

$$M_1 = 2.3 M_0$$

for adjusting individual incomes, calculate the MPI, 1.5, for adjusting deviations from the average, so as to form the general linear relation

$$M_1 - 35 = 1.5(M_0 - 15).$$

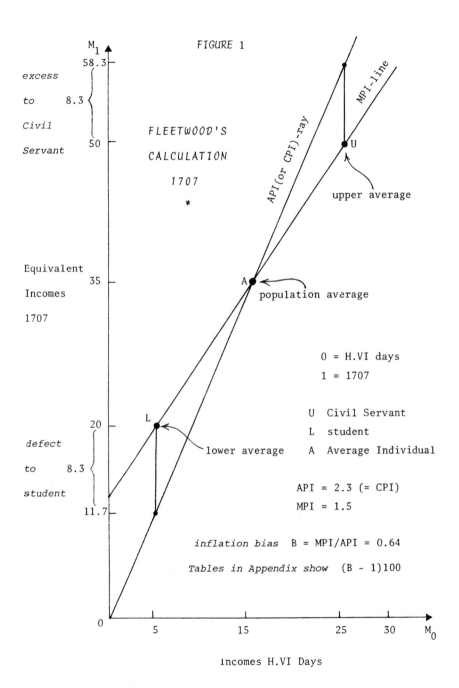

FIGURE 1

M_1

58.3

excess

to   8.3

Civil

Servant   50

FLEETWOOD'S

CALCULATION

1707

*

Equivalent

Incomes   35

1707

API(or CPI)-ray

MPI-line

U

upper average

A

population average

0 = H.VI days

1 = 1707

U   Civil Servant

L   student

A   Average Individual

L

20

defect

to   8.3

student

lower average

11.7

API = 2.3 (= CPI)

MPI = 1.5

inflation bias B = MPI/API = 0.64

Tables in Appendix show (B - 1)100

0

5   15   25   30 M_0

Incomes H.VI Days

In Figure 1, 1.5 is the slope of the line joining the points U and L which represent averages in the population where incomes are above and below the median. For the student with $M_0 = 5$, this relation gives

$$M_1 = 35 + 1.5(5 - 15) = 20,$$

and for the Civil Servant with $M_0 = 25$, the result is $M_1 = 50$, as required.

The API and MPI ideas, which in an alternative terminology are the inflation rate and incremental rate, for a group in the population and a range of expenditure items, are discussed in the Appendix together with illustration by calculations with Statistics Canada data. The student and the Civil Servant here should be understood as average representatives of two halves of the population, the division being by income level. The shift from the API (or CPI)-ray to the MPI-line shown in Figure 1 corrects the bias which gives an excess of inflation adjustment to high incomes, and a corresponding defect to low incomes. The bias could well be opposite. The report Prices and the Poor, which is discussed in the following section argues a bias unfavourable to low incomes in 1973. Our arithmetic with Statistics Canada data will confirm this, and quantify it. However, it will also be seen that in other years, for instance 1967, the sense of the bias is reversed, though the degree is less (see, for instance, Table II).

The CPI (=API) is often understood to have use as an inflation adjustor of all money amounts, regardless of whether these be actual incomes or any other type of amount. In this, it has the role of an *index of general purchasing power* of money. But just in the distinction between the API and MPI there is a refutation of the general possibility of having such an index which can meet criteria of fidelity in such a role. A much better candidate for a 'general purchasing power' role is the MPI. But then the role has to be restricted. While the MPI alone does not specify adjustments to incomes it can, in an intelligible way which can be developed, specify adjustments of all money amounts which modify incomes and which, to allow for inflation, are to be adjusted to represent the same modification 'in real terms'.

A simple but most important step, taken already in the way Fleetwood's calculation has been reported and elaborated, and which occurs throughout this work, is the change from thinking in terms of simply a 'price index' to thinking of *relations* between incomes with the same 'purchasing power' or of points in the space where such a relation is represented. Then a price index is seen as just a homogeneous linear relation on this space, and, when there is need, it can be abandoned for a relation which is more suitable.

A document which is an eloquent representative of a particular dissatisfaction in having the CPI as the single arbiter in all matters to do with inflation is:

Prices and the Poor—A Report by the National Council of Welfare on the Low-Income Consumer in the Canadian Market-place, 1974.

The phenomenon pointed out by Ralf Dahrendorf is on the surface of this report.

A key statement in it has immediate correspondence with the idea of Fleetwood:

> The adequacy of an income depends upon the expenses that it must be adequate to meet. A greater number of dollars is no gain at all if it buys no more than the lesser number formerly did (p. 1).

More of what?—there is an ambiguity here, found also in Fleetwood. It should be removed or there could be hazard of unprofitable talk about 'utility' such as followed Fleetwood. Instead it could be said: a greater number of pounds is no gain if it cannot buy exactly what the lesser number formerly did—that is the same bundle of goods. This is really what is meant, or at least this is the meaning which shows in the arithmetic of Fleetwood and of the CPI. Needless to say, if the greater number of pounds can buy exactly what the lesser did formerly, together with any saving, then it is a gain.

While Fleetwood's calculation dealt with the incomes of an individual, taking into account "the expenses that it must be adequate to meet", the CPI considers an entire community in the same fashion, as if it were an individual. Fleetwood calculates incomes M_0, M_1 which, in two periods, can purchase the same individual consumption. The 'CPI' for the individual is then M_1/M_0. But obviously, it is important to know both M_0 and M_1, and not just their ratio. With the CPI, in effect, there is calculation of total community incomes T_0, T_1 which in two periods can purchase the total community consumption as observed in some representative period (with the calculations to be done here is 1969). The CPI is then T_1/T_0. (Or introducing averages $\bar{M}_0 = T_0/N, \bar{M}_1 = T_1/N$ it is, more familiarly, $\bar{M}_1/\bar{M}_0$, though the total community has more reality than the 'average individual'.) But the community consists in many individuals. For anyone individual an M_0, M_1 might have been calculated separately, depending on the 'expenses' of that particular individual. There is no reason for M_1/M_0 for one individual to be the same as that for another, or for the community. With

$$T_0 = \sum M_0, \qquad T_1 = \sum M_1$$

and the M_1/M_0 varying, none needs coincide with T_1/T_0. Of course, should the M_1/M_0 all coincide with each other then they would coincide also with T_1/T_0. The validity of the CPI as a faithful representative of the inflation impact on all incomes depends on this special circumstance. The report *Prices and the Poor* compels attention to the unreality of such an assumption.

It is remarked

> ... a family with income of $5,000 will not (be able to) buy one-third of the goods and services (that can be) bought by the family with a $15,000 income.

(Without losing the sense, and to isolate a part of it, we can omit the words in parentheses.) In other words, when income is tripled, or multiplied by any factor, purchases are not then all scaled correspondingly. On the contrary, the pattern of consumption, the proportions of things bought, changes even drastically. Some of the things enjoyed by the rich, the poor cannot afford to buy at all. They have to concentrate their purchasing power on first necessities. Also the rich do not want to buy just so many times of everything the poor buy. On the contrary, they would rather have none of some things the poor must buy just in order to survive.

There are a number of other observations in *Prices and the Poor* which argue for the inadequacy of any uniform treatment of incomes such as that demonstrated in the uniform use of the CPI. Here the concern will be mainly with the aspect of the report going around this obvious but neglected variability of consumption patterns.

Certainly, the uniformity issue about the CPI affects all incomes, favourably or unfavourably. But there is an understandable emphasis on its importance for low incomes. The point is made with the story of the man who drowned, trying to wade across a river whose average depth, he had been assured, was a mere 18 inches. The crossing could, no doubt, have been made very routinely by a tall man, and no doubt this was a man of lesser height.

The argument is developed by pointing out that, according to 1969 data, families with less than $3,000 spend 27.9 per cent of their income on food, while those with over $15,000 spend only 13.4 per cent. Thus

> Any change in the price of food will have more than double the impact on those at the bottom of the income scale as it will have on those at the top.

Or again, the "average" family, or the entire community, spends about 15 per cent of income on housing, and about the same on transportation and travel. This is all that is taken notice of in constructing the CPI. However, the lowest-income fifth of the population spends three times as much on housing as on transportation and travel. But returning to food, in 1972 food prices began to rise more rapidly than other prices. The process continued through 1972 and then speeded up rapidly in 1973.

> By December 1973 the food price index was 15.7 points ahead of the general index.

Since the poor spend about 28 per cent of their incomes on food while the population spends overall about 18 per cent, the impact of inflation on the poor must be definitely greater than the average impact as given by the CPI.

Of course, the 'food price index', which is the CPI, computed for the population as if food was the only consumption, has the same defect already pointed out for the general CPI: it gives no recognition to the quite different diets enjoyed, or suffered, by rich and poor. Also, food prices do not all change together, but rather the variations, even for closely related foods, and for different grades of the same type of food, can be quite different. No simple and satisfactory correction of the CPI can be obtained for particular population groups merely by readjusting the weights on aggregate indices, like the 'food price index', to correspond to their particular budgets. It is necessary to go back to the original detailed, disaggregated data and start again. In practice some form of aggregation is rather necessary. But in principle, unless by chance this is organized on lines which maintain the distinctions which are to be revealed, if indeed this is possible, these distinctions will become masked to some degree in the results: they will become blurred in a shift towards the average. Nevertheless the higher the disaggregation, the better.

The year of *Prices and the Poor* is 1973; reference to Table IV(b) shows an overall population inflation rate of 7.0 in that year. But Table I(b) shows an inflation rate of 7.8 for the lowest octile, where incomes are under $2,500, and 6.7 for the highest octile where incomes are above $13,500. This strikingly confirms the qualitative conclusion obtained for that year by the argument from the more rapid rise of food prices and the greater share of income spent on food by the poor. However, let it not be assumed that the bias of inflation is always unfavourable to the poor. Table IV(d) shows an overall 'inflation bias index' of −0.5 in 1973, or a bias against low incomes of 0.5, which is the highest absolute amount of bias for all the years considered. However, the bias in 1971 is 0.4, against high incomes and in 1967, it is 0.3. Of course, in those years the inflation rate is lower than in 1973, and so the importance of any degree of bias is less.

It seems that inflation bias is increased when there are abrupt changes in the inflation rate. When the inflation rate has persisted around some particular level for a time, price changes could fall into harmony with it and this produces a uniformity, at least in medium term comparisons, if not in the short term. But a sudden change in the general or overall rate seems to be accompanied by non-uniformity. Abrupt economic events in the future could have this effect. We are reminded of the river of which only the average depth was known, and it would seem sensible to have a more detailed knowledge.

3 What is a price index?

Rather than search economic theory for the meaning of 'price index'—this leads into a labyrinth where meanings have become lost—it is simpler just to look at what a price index is in practice. All that is important for practice can then be gathered. But since the 'index' language of economics has a long history and complex associations, gathering strands of logic together with myth, it calls for a comment. The main point is the straightforwardness of the practical matter; it really lacks any of the mystery present with 'index numbers'.

One does not usually speak of 'temperature index'; it is enough to say 'temperature'. When it is known what is being referred to the reference is simply to that thing. Even with 'chill factor' there is a definition and we still know what we are talking about: the temperature which on a still day would produce the same rate of cooling on a standard body as the wind and temperature of the current day. Similarly, with the price of a commodity we do not have an 'index' of the price but just the price, that is, how much has to be paid—this is straightforward. The 'index' language comes in economics from compulsion to give numbers even when the meaning is not and perhaps cannot be known. When an unambiguous meaning for a number is not known it is an 'index'. The habit can inadvertently be carried into situations where there really is no occasion for it. This is the case with the CPI in its designation as a 'price index'. From the way the CPI is calculated its meaning is clear; just from its construction there is no compulsion to associate it with the 'price index' idea and another name could tell more plainly what it is. From an important point of view, it becomes a price index especially from the way it is used.

The 'price index' idea has one conspicuous meaning in the practical convention that any incomes M_0, M_1 in two periods which are to be determined as having the same purchasing power should correspond in a homogeneous linear relation

$$M_1 = P_{10}M_0.$$

Such a relation is specified by a single number P_{10}, its slope, and this slope is the 'price index'. There could be disagreement with this proposal as gathering essence of the idea. But there can be no controversy about meaning in the absence of a further distinction of meanings. Here there is settlement of a particular meaning, and a commitment to it. It might be objected that the choice is improperly narrow. Evidence for the judgement that it is not so, but, that it is everywhere at least implicit even if not always fully explicit in basic contexts and usages, is now offered.

The ideas of 'price index' and 'price level' are certainly linked, and it can only be supposed that numbers offered in the role of the former are quantifications of the latter. It seems impossible to argue about this since no one knows the meaning of 'price level' unless it is 'price index'. But there are many formulae for price indices. No matter, they are approximations to the 'true' index—true no doubt because it truly represents the 'price level'. This closes a circle of meanings. To escape, a price index in practice is simply understood to be a number which has a certain use, and it is this use which qualifies the CPI as a price index. There can be question then about the extent to which this use is justified in the social context and how that extent should be described statistically. A suggestion about this is in the Appendix to Part I. But the main propositions in this book are about the price index as a term which belongs to theory rather than to practice. It is important to see these two appearances of the term as separate. The connection between them, which is simply a dedication to the homogeneous linear relationship, is a matter of form and not of substance.

Two cardinal aspects of the typical price index of practice, the CPI, are its construction and use which are essentially as follows:

(a) *Construction.*   The CPI has reference to the total consumption of a community for a range of commodities, as recorded by a sample survey in a representative period, and compares estimates of the total cost of that consumption at the prices in a base period and in any current period. The percentage increase of that total cost from one period to another is the community *inflation rate* from one period to the other.

(b) *Use.*   From one period to the other any income must increase by the percentage given by the inflation rate if it is to maintain the same 'purchasing power'.

There are other uses, but this is a main one that has to be considered and to which the others should be related.

The price index of practice is by most accounts identified as a Laspeyres index. It is then put alongside another index which could just as well be calculated were there the data for it, the Paasche index. Then follows the 'limits' proposition, which makes these indices theoretical upper and lower units of the 'true' index. Attributes of the Laspeyres index in that theoretical context become transferred to the practical index, and become part of the doctrine about its meaning. But about this there can be complaints. To develop these, some ideas must be sorted out; certainly if there is to be objection to the identification of the practical index as a Laspeyres index, there has to be an understanding about what these are.

As a matter of definition, $p_1 x / p_0 x$ is the *inflation factor* for any bundle x, between periods where the prices are p_0, p_1. It should be asked if this automatically becomes a Laspeyres index merely by setting $x = x_0$, where x_0 is any bundle of goods which, somehow, has the date of the 0-period attached to it. Surely it does not, if the date of the bundle, or the bundle itself, is an accident. Some stringencies ought to be maintained in order to have a Laspeyres index, and not something which merely has the same form.

A typical practical index like the CPI can have this form in its original calculation. Thus it has a base year 0; but then there is a series of current years $0, 1, 2, \ldots$, not just *one* other, as there is in the theoretical context where it is brought together with the Paasche index (Chapter III). The CPI value for any current year i is

$$P_{i0} = p_i x_0 / p_0 x_0,$$

where x_0 is total community consumption in the base year. In other words, it is the inflation factor between the base and current year for community consumption in the base year. It is an inflation factor determined in respect to the total community (or the 'target' group) and, incidentally, used as if it were the inflation factor for every individual in the group, which of course it is not, but that is a separate matter. (See Appendix. Also note there has been confusion everywhere in using the terms inflation factor and inflation rate.) It becomes thought of as *the* inflation factor, from the base to any current year; this then leads to thought of the inflation factor between any two years i, j as being given by

$$P_{ij} = P_{j0} / P_{i0}$$
$$= p_j x_0 / p_0 x_0 / p_i x_0 / p_0 x_0$$
$$= p_j x_0 / p_i x_0.$$

In particular, the inflation rate across any one year is the inflation factor between it and the previous year. Thus

$$p_1 x_0 / p_0 x_0, \, p_2 x_0 / p_1 x_0, \ldots$$

are the inflation rates for the first, second, ... years. But only the first of these has the Laspeyres form. Generally, while the inflation factors P_{i0} qualify at least in form as Laspeyres indices, none of the *equally well considered* factors $P_{ij}(j \neq 0)$ do. Then, so to speak, though any P_{i0} might seem to be born as a proper Laspeyres index, it has sold its birthright as such when it is used to determine the other P_{ij} and is put on the same footing as them.

What has been pointed out is that community consumption in one particular year has been arbitrarily taken as the *standard* of community consumption, and this has been made the basis for determining inflation factors between any two years, in particular the inflation rates across each year. Thus year 0 is, by arbitrary adoption, the *year of the standard*, and then, consumption x_0 in that year determines the inflation factor

$$P_{ij} = p_j x_0 / p_i x_0$$

between any years i, j. While, with the particular case $j = 0$, P_{i0} does have the Laspeyres form, this is not significant. The year of the standard is arbitrary, so there is only an accidental coincidence of the year j with that year. With a Laspeyres index, the coincidence must be no accident.

Here is one manner of complaint about identification of a typical practical index as a Laspeyres index, going mainly around accidents about dates. Another manner involves the nature of the bundle x_0 as an aggregate. But first clear away all features on which the first complaint depended: suppose there are only two periods 0, 1 in view, and allow the coincidences of dates in the formula

$$P_{10} = p_1 x_0 / p_0 x_0$$

are essential, so it has the form of a Laspeyres index in an essential way. Is this then a Laspeyres index? Historically, it could well be; this could be the arithmetic formula originally exploited by Laspeyres. From its form, it is one of the 126 (or by another count, 145, see Introduction, Chapter III) formulae to be found in Irving Fisher's book. To make a distinction—though it is without any precise regard for history—let this be called the *original* Laspeyres index.

It has been argued that there is no good purpose, but a misleading intrusion, to even bring this formula in, when giving account of methodology of the CPI and the inflation rates. An enlargement of that methodology is in the Appendix. The question now is whether, with any advantage, the original index can be identified with what will be called the *theoretical* Laspeyres index, that is the index which enters with the role of upper limit in the 'limits' proposition (dealt with here in Chapter III). Doubts can be developed, on two independent scores: the nature of x_0 as an aggregate in the original index, and the presence of the Paasche index which is required with the theoretical index. The first of these by a mutual assistance of artifices can be put aside, though it still deserves pursuit. The second is more resistant.

It should be appreciated that an important value of this discussion—beside simply that it is compelled now—is to put restraint on a ready reflex which brings all things which have a look of Laspeyres indiscriminately together. Especially wanted, is to break the celebrated but spurious association between the practical index and the theoretical index. This has already been done: the significant practical index is

$$P_{ij} = p_j x_0 / p_i x_0$$

and, except when accidentally $i = 0$, it does not even have Laspeyres form. This brings about dissociation from both the original index and the theoretical index, since the form is essential in both. Especially in view here is North American practice; practice in the UK is somewhat different and a remark will be made about this difference later.

But still, it is interesting to pursue any possible link between the original and the theoretical indices. After all, the original (single and not serial like the CPI) index could have standing as a practical index; and in any case this is where the practical–theoretical association probably began, and then became maintained by the illusion that the modern North American year-to-year index is still a Laspeyres index of any sort.

The first ground for reservation about the practical–theoretical association is that x_0 is an aggregate. The price index of the theory shown in Chapter III involves the hypothesis that demand is governed by a utility order. That is, not only are wants, as expressed by the hypothetical utility or preference order, fully deliberate, but also there is perfectly precise programming with them. At least from the standpoint of theory, this is a bearable picture if the consumer is a single individual—in fact, economists are accustomed to it. But when the consumer is an entire community it is an absurd one—even though theoreticians have made strong efforts to come to terms with one definitely like it. How and on what basis is it possible for a community to arrive at a preference order in their aggregate consumption space? After all, each individual would consume only a bit of the aggregate, and it may not even be clear what bit; and in the classical picture the individuals are blind as 'windowless monads' (Leibnitz), they take no notice of each other, and so to each, the community does not even exist, let alone community preferences. Economic theory gives training in such questions; but rather than face difficulties, suppose they do not exist and that collective preferences for aggregate consumption already make sense. Then there still remains a difficulty: it is hard to entertain that precise aggregate consumption programming with the collective preferences should be accomplished as a result of every individual acting alone—free of any guidance from each other or from a Great Conductor. Certainly it is extravagant to treat any collection of individuals automatically as a single Gross Individual having deliberate preferences for aggregate consumption and acting on them very precisely. But at this point it should be noticed that something very much present has been left out: the homogeneity of utility, which is an indispensable part of any price-index thinking. Possibly, this inescapable imposition also permits entry of a different point of view which bypasses these obstacles.

Since

$$P_{10} = p_1 x_0 / p_0 x_0$$

is unchanged when x_0 is replaced by any point on the ray through x_0, it is a function not so much of the point as of the ray. With any collection of consumptions, the aggregate and average lie on the same ray. Therefore, it makes no difference to P_{10} whether x_0 is the aggregate or the average. Suppose all individuals were to be regarded as having the same utility, so their consumptions are different only because their incomes are different. With homogeneous utility, when prices are fixed the locus of consumption for all levels of income, or the expansion locus, is a ray. Then the consumption of all individuals in any period should lie on the same ray; and in reality they do not. The departure they have from being in the same ray can be regarded as due to 'error'. A statistical 'estimate' can be made of the ray from which they have erred. This ray, which should be a kind of 'average' of the rays through the individual consumptions, can be determined as the ray through the average consumption. In this way P_{10} with x_0 as average, which is the same with x_0 as aggregate, and as any point in the same ray, becomes regarded as determined for the ray which is the estimated locus of consumption for all individual consumers in period 0, and no longer as being simply for the aggregate. This dissolves the difficulty about the Laspeyres index being determined practically for an aggregate, while the theory applies to an individual. For now, the aggregate index becomes identified statistically with the Laspeyres index for an individual, in fact every individual. Here also is a rationalization of the way the practical index, determined for the aggregate, is used indiscriminately for every individual.

The characteristic property of a ray is that if any points lie on it, then so does their sum, and so also does their average. It gives basis for the 'homogenization' of a group of consumers by taking the ray through their average consumption as estimate of the locus on which their consumptions should, in principle, all lie. From this flows again the usual homogeneous treatment they receive from use of a price index in practice. Also with this homogenization of individuals, comes the possibility of treating the group as just another individual, governed by the same utility as they, whose income is the sum of their incomes and who with it purchases the sum of their consumptions. In other words, within the framework resulting from the homogenization, the picture of the group behaving like an individual, having definite wants and budgeting for them with precision, which has been claimed to be unsuitable, comes with an appearance of validity.

A device has been found for connecting the index for an aggregate with that for an individual, seeming to open a way for propositions from theory to have some bearing on practice; but this is what now has to be examined. Already it has been argued that the familiar current practice is divorced from any significant theory outside itself: it consists simply in determining inflation rates for a standard bundle of goods. Fleetwood did that in 1707. There is nothing further to add in that connection. The concern now must be with the simpler situation embodied in what has been called the original index, not serial but involving just two periods 0, 1. It should be seen what price index the theory shown in Chapter III has to offer there. As can be appreciated, that theory in earlier irresolute manifestations has been without a complete control for its interpretations, but with loose ends tied up it has become sterilized so as to be transparently without any immediate practical bearing.

The theory arbitrarily, from a tradition which could be regarded as an accident, concerns itself with just a pair of demands

$$(p_0, x_0), (p_1, x_1).$$

It then asks, or at least it should ask, if there exists a price index P_{10} compatible with these, and if there does then what are all its possible values. The answer is a formula for an interval, and this involves a pair of formulae for the endpoints which incidentally are the Paasche and Laspeyres formulae $\check{P}_{10}$, $\hat{P}_{10}$. If the interval is empty, which is when Paasche exceeds Laspeyres, which indeed could be the case,[1] then there is no compatible price index at all. Then Laspeyres is not even admissible as a price index, and nor is any other number. This situation leaves a practical–theoretical dilemma: there is an absolute practical determination to construct a price index—after all, the Government, and the People, are waiting to hear what it is—while there is the absolute theoretical conclusion that one does not exist which is compatible with the data. No doubt the practical–theoretical economic statistician would be dismissed and replaced by one who has an undivided appreciation of his duties. In effect this has already been done: no one in normal practice troubles with theory, and quite rightly. Practical need has dispersed the clouds of theory, even hosts of formulae, to settle on the one simple and sensible thing to do, which is closer to what Fleetwood did in 1707 than to anything else.

This argument could be prolonged: what if Paasche does not exceed Laspeyres, or what if Paasche is, as usual, not even known? But the point is already amply put. The interests dictated by social-economic needs and statistical practicalities are different from those which arise in the theoretical amplification.

From the standpoint of standard, or at least of North American practice, Paasche and Laspeyres are not Paasche and Laspeyres; they are inflation factors between two periods for two different standard bundles of goods. Of course, there would be interest to know what difference the change of standard makes to the inflation factor. But there is no general reason why the change should produce an increase or a decrease—there is no general inequality constraint between Paasche and Laspeyres, despite the "Index Number Theorem" (or non-theorem) of Sir John Hicks.

The standard bundle of goods should correspond to a prevailing pattern of living. It is determined by survey in a particular year; but pattern changes with time, so as years pass it loses present relevance (as did Fleetwood's bundle after 400, or was it 600 years). While in North America the standard bundle is based on a large survey sample and is renewed every few years, for instance in Canada it is based on a sample of about 16,000 households and was renewed in 1961 and 1969, in the UK it is

1 Examples are given by Irving Fisher in *The Making of Index Numbers* (1923), p. 503.

based on a small sample of about 7,000, and is renewed every year. The inflation factor across any span of years is then determined by compounding the inflation rates obtained in each of the years. This is still more remote from the Laspeyres index than anything in North America. It is more comparable with the Divisia index—but no more than the North American is comparable with Laspeyres. There is a strong merit in the UK practice. It is a practical merit, not accountable within the usual theory, where comparisons between times depend on hypothesis of a utility order which is independent of time, though there can be some appreciation of it by reference to that theory. A common complaint which applies to the North American index is that, because the standard bundle is fixed, when relative prices change it is not sensitive to 'substitution'. It is the familiar argument: if tea has a price rise relative to coffee, rather than buying still the original bundle, the same utility would be obtained at less cost by sacrificing some tea and buying more coffee, in other words the same standard of living would become represented by a different bundle of goods, one cheaper at current prices than the original. In *Prices and the Poor* (p. 29) it is pointed out that someone already buying only the cheapest food would have no substitute to go to, when food prices rise. Indeed, it is easy to talk about 'substitution' and to recognize its reality, but not easy to give it explicit description and allowance. However, with UK practice there is an implicit allowance, since the standard bundle is undergoing continual revision from current statistical observations.

Substitution can be illustrated from utility theory, as is familiar to every student. Demand analysts might then want to account it econometrically on the basis of utility—taking the means for a simple illustration as also the means for giving an actual account. But changing as rapidly as relative prices, is everything else in history affecting living patterns. Utility analysis would be a manner of attempting to identify a fixed structure underlying a surface of change. However, there is no general reason, and no statistical experience even suggesting its effectiveness for that. Rather, as soon as utility is thought about as fixed, it has to be thought about as changing, and if it is changing it cannot be observed—this is its *reductio ad absurdum*. However, UK practice is sensitive to substitution without venturing into absurdity.

A price index is directed to the relation between incomes in two periods which are to be regarded as being equivalent in purchasing power. It postulates a homogeneous linear relation, for which it gives the slope. Thus it involves a very special restriction on the relation. It is important to see this restriction, which from habit has become largely taken for granted, against the general background on which it is imposed. A recapitulation which is built on and illustrated by calculations in the Appendices for Part I, is as follows.

Any two different years where the prices of commodities are different can be indicated by 0 and 1. Where a comparison is to be given which distinguishes one period as the base period for the comparison and the other as the current period, these will be 0 and 1 respectively. It is recognized that an income of £M_0 held by some person in year 0 should have become an income of some £M_1 in year 1 if that person's way of life is not to have been disturbed by the price change. An understanding which prevails for general purposes is that the income M_1 is to be related just to the income M_0. Next to this is the broader recognition which gives relevance also to the type of the consumer, besides just the income level. But putting this broader view aside, there is the standard view that the income adjustment, over a period to offset the effect of a price change, should depend just on the income. Then the agreed social 'yardstick' for income adjustments will be a table showing various incomes in the first period and corresponding to them the equivalent incomes in the second period. This has the scheme

M_0	M_1	
⋮	⋮	
£4,000	£5,048	for example, $0 = 1969, 1 = 1974$
£5,000	£6,480	
⋮	⋮	

The same information could be given in the form

M_0	M_1/M_0
⋮	⋮
£4,000	1.262
£5,000	1.296
⋮	⋮

There is the general possibility here of having a different ratio M_1/M_0 corresponding to each income M_0. A distinctive feature of standard practice is that M_1/M_0 is a fixed number, constructed in respect to the two years 0 and 1, which applies uniformly to all incomes M_0. In other words, there is a simpler scheme,

M_0	M_1/M_0
⋮	⋮
£4,000	1.270
£5,000	1.270
⋮	⋮

the numbers in the second column being all the same. Another way of presenting this scheme is to specify the fixed number P_{10} used to form the homogeneous linear relation

$$M_1 = P_{10}M_0$$

between equivalent incomes in the two periods. This number is the price index.

This could seem a laboured account of a matter which is simple and familiar from everyday experience with price indices and in particular with the CPI. But the explicitness gives detachment from a simplicity and familiarity which has been so thorough as to obliterate perception of alternatives. It shows the price index as not an especially natural approach to the matter and allows the view of others which are more flexible.

The *unthinkability* of a true price index, as a practical matter rather than a formal concept, and with that the reality of the issues raised in *Prices and the Poor*, is obvious and has long had appreciation. Enquiry then could be about the burial of this appreciation, under a surface of simplistics in theory and rituals in practice which support each other in denying it. The appreciation is very simple, but the denial is vast and this has interest. There could be a not fully accounted, but compelling reason for it. The phenomenon seems important for features of it which appear in other contexts in economics. However, with the price index, a compulsion comes from the broad social reference it has together with the social requirement of simplicity. It is part of a social ritual, the agreeability of which is a historical variable.

Robert T. Michael (1975) gives this quotation:

A perfectly exact measure of purchasing power is not only unattainable, but even unthinkable. The same change of prices affects the purchasing power of money to different persons in different ways. For to him who can seldom afford to have meat, a fall of one-fourth in the price of meat accompanied by a rise of one-fourth in that of bread means a fall in the purchasing power of money; his wages will not go so far as before. While to his richer neighbour, who spends twice as much on meat as on bread, the change acts the other way.

A. Marshall
(1886)

I   Three problems

This work deals with three problems each more special than its predecessor. One purpose is just their formulation, but also they are solved and discussions go around the way this is done.

It might seem from simple logic that a problem could stand alone, in empty space, but this is not the usual way with problems. They belong to currents from which they cannot be separated, so if the current dries up perhaps they would disappear. These three problems are in a particularly well-known voluminous, sickly current: economic index numbers. In this there is a widespread practice, and then there are theories that go around but which, it has been argued, have little to do with the practice, and there are myths. Corners of the problems have broken the surface but they never would float into full view, and to make them do that could be an objective. There should be some appreciation also of the current which carries them since otherwise they would have not much sense.

Three well-known characters also are in that current, like those three men in a boat. These are the price index formulae of Lapeyres, Paasche and Fisher. With them is, if not a dog, an amount of baggage, including a True Index, an Ideal Index, a pair of "limits", a faulty Index Number Theorem, various utility functions, including quadratics, a device called Revealed Preference, related devices and so forth. The problems at first show no mention whatsoever of these characters, but when they are solved they take on the appearance of a boat which carries all three together with the baggage.

The familiar Laspeyres, Paasche and Fisher therefore are chief characters. But others claim attention. In fact they also are familiar and in other settings have appeared as chief characters themselves. It is interesting how they act together to make complication out of simple questions which in the end have simple answers. The answers could seem to have been known all along, had the questions been known.

To boil the subject down to three problems and their solution would do injustice to its pathology. The problems and the methods used for dealing with them make a structure with some interest in itself to any with the inclination; for them it could stand as a small monolith in rather empty space, in fact a chip from a larger one which might have subsequent attention. This would leave out the broth from which the crystallization took place but what remains is at least straightforward. The original traditional subject, however, does not have such a regular character. A microanalysis of it is not possible within the limited space and intentions here, nor perhaps would it do service. On that side as in economics, a cryptic macroanalysis can be more brief and also cut better.

The main work here can be regarded as a repair done on a limited part of what is understood as the Theory of Index Numbers, the part where Laspeyres and Paasche enter, and then Fisher. It is not a minimal repair: there has been interest in the methods exceeding the need of the application. By these methods everything is capable of being put more generally, but then more machinery must be brought in and connection with the ancient lore becomes buried in the weight of it.

The work therefore has different aspects. It is an exercise in making definitions and formulating questions and propositions in terms of them, within a framework made by ideas which are standard but are capable of non-standard variations which show them better for what they are. As such it is exercise in basic grammar of a part of economic theory.

Another aspect is mathematical. The reference everywhere here is to just a pair of demands, but statements have counterparts for any finite number, so this is an introduction to a more general mathematics. Here, the proofs of propositions are simple and immediate, while in the further theory, without adding to basic ideas, they are comparatively long and elaborate. This theory for a finite collection of demands, instead of for a demand function which is a particular kind of infinite collection, makes a development in demand analysis called Combinatorial Theory of Demand (Afriat, 1976). The book shows some main features of that subject in a simple form. A striking product is the equivalence of counterparts of the so-called Axioms of Revealed Preference of Samuelson and Houthakker to the consistency of a system of homogeneous linear inequalities, any solution of which permits the construction of a finitely computable utility function which fits the demand data. The integrability question which has a central place in corresponding theory for demand functions evaporates in this finite context and is replaced by a quite different pattern.

These are aspects of the work which, though not accidental by-products, are secondary to the declared purpose, which is to give a certain account of 'the price index'. Possibly there should be three main phases in a study of that idea: (i) every-day practices with price indices, the statistical arithmetic and conventional uses, (ii) theory about the price index, which should give account of it as a theoretical concept, and is often supposed to have a bearing on (i), and (iii) the appearances in many economic theories of the term 'price level', no doubt quantified by 'price index'. Here the main concern will be with (ii) for its own sake and also for impacts on (i). There will be no attention to (iii), though crystallization of the price index as a highly restrictive concept has a bearing there.

One type of discussion which is recognized as theory of index numbers is a branch of utility theory, and that will be a subject here. In the approach to be followed, questions are asked of the data and formulae come afterwards in the answers. Next to that is an approach to index numbers associated especially with

Irving Fisher, which can be distinguished from the utility theory though in many accounts they are separated. In that approach, formulae are considered involving price quantity data for two periods, in fact a very great variety of formulae and there is no limit to their proliferation. In this maze of index formulae, which Fisher compared and classified in various ways, it is a puzzle to know which one is the 'true index'. It is believed that prices, though they be many, have a 'level', and the 'true index' is a ratio which compares levels in two periods. Thus

$$P_{rs} = P_s/P_r$$

is the price index with r, s as base and current periods, where P_r, P_s are the price-levels. In that case, for any three periods r, s, t necessarily

$$P_{rs} P_{st} P_{tr} = 1.$$

This is Fisher's Circularity Test. Consequences of it are

$$P_{rr} = 1$$
$$P_{rs} P_{sr} = 1$$
$$P_{rs} P_{st} = P_{rt}.$$

These also are "Tests", the first being the Identity Test, the second being Fisher's Reversal Test, and the third his Chain Test. If there is a formula for the 'true index' it must satisfy these. The search made was disappointing, but Fisher had one which satisfies the Reversal Test and this is his 'Ideal Index'.

Since the Circularity Test, or the Chain Test which is its equivalent, is necessary and sufficient for any numbers P_{rs} to be the ratios of some numbers P_r, in particular of $P_r = P_{kr}$, for any fixed k, all that is involved here is what could be called the *Ratio Test*. Other conditions are claimed as "Tests" because they are consequences of this and they have no claim or meaning apart from it.

With $p_r \in \Omega_n$ as the prices in period r and $a \in \Omega^n$ some fixed bundle of goods,

$$P_{rs} = p_s a/p_r a,$$

following Fleetwood in 1707, is the *inflation rate* from period r to period s, for the bundle of goods a. These numbers satisfy the Ratio Test just from the way they are constructed. It could be wondered why this formula was not 'ideal' for Fisher. Possibly it was too dull but, if he was looking for a more interesting one which meets the proper qualifications, it does not exist, as Eichhorn (1976) has shown. Unaccountably he arrived at a compromise which is neither proper nor dull.

1 The 'Index Number Problem'

The so-called 'Index Number Problem' is an area of perplexity which comes from the use of terms whose meaning is not altogether known. From the insecure position that prices should have a 'level', that level, whatever it should be, can be denoted P. Then P, thus called into existence, joins the furniture of economic discussion. It is available to become a part in some edifice, and even in many since there is no habit to distinguish whether each appearance of P is really the same P or something entirely different. A problem arises because there could be a pause to examine how P should be determined, granted that it exists.

At the centre of the 'Problem' is the 'true index'. This has reference to two periods, and is to be determined from prices and quantity data in just those periods. There is no criterion to single out an index as the 'true' one, and no proper definition of 'index' except as a number which has a certain ritual in its production and use. An outstanding proposition is that the Laspeyres and Paasche indices are limits, above and below. Then the Index Number Theorem, so-called by J. R. Hicks (1956), is that one limit does not exceed the other. The affirmation is made regardless of the absence of any such necessity.[1] The geometric mean, which is the Fisher 'ideal' index, is a superior 'approximation' to either limit since it lies between them, and it is 'ideal' because it satisfied Fisher's Reversal Test. S. S. Byushgens (1925) remarked Fisher's index is 'exact' if utility should be representable by a homogeneous quadratic. The observation is still true though vacuous if no such representation be possible, but it raises question about such possibility. Samuelson pointed out, quite rightly, that the index problem involves an indeterminacy, liberating it from a pursuit of the 'true index' which, even if it existed and was by chance encountered, could never be recognized.

This well-known lore makes the subject for study and interpretation. A conceptual definition of a price index and of the relevance of the data to its determination gives a position for calculating the range of this recognized indeterminacy. The range could be empty—thus denying the existence of an object with such indeterminacy—and a question then is how to know by some test that it is not empty. Hicks' 'Index Number Theorem' bears on this test. It is not a theorem, but it could be a trace of a theorem which emerged at some moment but part of it, hypothesis or conclusion, got lost. Then a task is to reconstruct the missing fragment. The Reconstructed Theorem shows the usually considered inequality between the Laspeyres and Paasche indices as just the wanted test.

The entire matter has reference simply to a pair of demands, giving prices and quantities of the goods. Various familiar formulae apply to these and others can be added. For reference, various such features will be described in advance. But the genesis is to be entirely in certain questions asked of the data, and anything which is not in the surface of these must arise just out of their investigation. The immediate question (Problem I), which comes from the basic concern with purchasing power decision to which the index is directed, fails altogether to lead to the kind of statement wanted. Rather it contradicts the legitimacy of having a price index. This brings into relief that a special restriction is implicitly present in all thinking in terms of 'price indices'. This restriction will be stated in several different ways, one of which directly shows the use of a price index. It leads to a revised question (Problem II), and the theorems which are an answer to it give counterparts and

---

1 And the presence of counter examples, see Fisher (1923), p. 503.

enlargements of usual statements about the Laspeyres and Paasche indices. A further more restricted question (Problem III) elaborates Byushgens' remark about Fisher's index.

Though logically one could insist on a difference, the position at the end seems much the same as at the start. As in a very often quoted passage, "Everything is just as it was", and against "You'd generally get to somewhere else" is "Now, here, you see, it takes all the running you can do to keep in the same place. If you want to get somewhere else, you must run at least twice as fast as that." It is so also with the practice of index numbers since it still is at the point where it started with the calculation of William Fleetwood in 1707. The discussions since make a sustained current in economic literature, but still "Everything is just as it was."

Price indices are measurements without an ordinary object to measure. More, the object involved is a ritual with an embrace dictated from outside and unaffected by all the running you can do in the theory of index numbers. Only from change outside can come the needed extra speed to get somewhere else. Such change is much present and recognized though, as already proposed, it is of no concern here where attention is simply to the 'price index' of the 'Index Number Problem'. Even then the scope will be confined by a narrow understanding of the problem, where for data always just two periods are involved. But every aspect has a direct generalization involving any number of periods simultaneously. The questions to be dealt with are capable of alternative treatment, but there is influence from the particular methods used, which lead immediately to generalizations and are part of an approach which has other outcomes. To the suggestion that this is like "using an atom bomb to boil a kettle" (words of an editor delivering a rejection twenty years ago) an answer is that in any case here is (or was) an interesting way to boil a kettle, and especially so if otherwise the long-simmering kettle seems never quite to come to a final boil.

2   Formulae and tests

There are two periods of consumption, the *base* and *current periods*, 0 and 1, and in these quantities $x_0, x_1 \in \Omega^n$ of goods are demanded at prices $p_0, p_1 \in \Omega_n$. Then the incomes are

$$M_0 = p_0 x_0, \qquad M_1 = p_1 x_1$$

and, provided $M_0, M_1 > 0$, budget vectors

$$u_0 = M_0^{-1} p_0, \qquad u_1 = M_1^{-1} p_1$$

are determined, for which

$$u_0 x_0 = 1, \qquad u_1 x_1 = 1.$$

The Laspeyres and Paasche "price indices" are given by

$$\hat{P}_{10} = p_1 x_0 / p_0 x_0 = u_1 x_0 M_1 / M_0$$

$$\check{P}_{10} = p_1 x_1 / p_0 x_1 = (1/u_0 x_1) M_1 / M_0$$

and the Fisher index is

$$\bar{P}_{10} = (p_1 x_0 p_1 x_1 / p_0 x_0 p_1 x_1)^{\frac{1}{2}}$$

$$= (u_1 x_0 / u_0 x_1)^{\frac{1}{2}} M_1 / M_0.$$

Though it is not known what it is, the "True Index" is denoted P_{10}, and the "method of limits" of Keynes (*A Treatise on Money*, Vol. I) gives the proposition

$$\check{P}_{10} \leqq P_{10} \leqq \hat{P}_{10},$$

and the "Index Number Theorem" is that

$$\check{P}_{10} \leqq \hat{P}_{10},$$

which is equivalent to the condition

$$p_0 x_1 p_1 x_0 \geqq p_0 x_0 p_1 x_1,$$

that is

$$(\dot{H})\quad u_0 x_1 u_1 x_0 \geqq 1.$$

Samuelson's revealed preference argument applied to the demands (p_0, x_0), (p_1, x_1) gives

$$p_0 x_1 \leqq p_0 x_0, \quad x_1 \neq x_0 \; \Rightarrow \; p_1 x_0 > p_1 x_1$$

or the same condition with 0, 1 interchanged. Another statement which is symmetrical between 0 and 1 is

$$p_0 x_1 \leqq p_0 x_0, \quad p_1 x_0 \leqq p_1 x_1 \; \Rightarrow \; x_0 = x_1,$$

that is,

$$(H^*)\quad u_0 x_1 \leqq 1, \quad u_1 x_0 \leqq 1 \; \Rightarrow \; x_0 = x_1.$$

If $x_0 = x_1$ then $u_0 x_1 = 1, u_1 x_0 = 1$, so H^* implies

$$(H)\quad u_0 x_1 \leqq 1, \quad u_1 x_0 \leqq 1 \; \Rightarrow \; u_0 x_1 = 1, \quad u_1 x_0 = 1$$

and this is implied also by $\dot{H}$. With the further condition

$$(\dot{H}^*)\quad u_0 x_1 u_1 x_0 > 1 \quad \text{unless } \vec{x}_0 = \vec{x}_1,$$

$\vec{x}$ denoting the ray through $\vec{x}$, there is the scheme

$$\dot{H}^* \; \Rightarrow \; H^*$$
$$\Downarrow \qquad \Downarrow$$
$$\dot{H} \; \Rightarrow \; H$$

none of the converses being valid. This puts the "Index Number Theorem" condition $\dot{H}$ and the more restricted modification of it $\dot{H}^*$ in relation with the Samuelson condition H^* and its relaxed modification H.

3 Utility–cost

A point of *satiation* of a utility order R is any x for which $x < y$ and xRy for some y, that is any bundle which is as good as a larger one. Then $x < y \Rightarrow x\bar{R}y$ asserts the absence of such points.

A utility order is complete if for any x, y either xRy or yRx, that is $x\bar{R}y \Rightarrow yRx$, which can be stated $\bar{R}' \subset R$.

For a general order R there is need to consider *critical cost functions*

$$\hat{\rho}(p, x) = \inf[py : yRx]$$

$$\check{\rho}(p, x) = \inf[py : x\bar{R}y].$$

These, as will be seen, coincide when R is complete and without satiation, but otherwise they have to be distinguished.

Since xRx, by reflexivity, it follows that

$$\hat{\rho}(p, x) \leqq px.$$

If R is without satiation, so $x\bar{R}y$ for $y > x$, then

$$\check{\rho}(p,x) \leqq \inf[py : y > x] = px,$$

so also

$$\check{\rho}(p,x) \leqq px.$$

The significance of these functions for their application is shown in the following.

Theorem *For any utility order R and any p, x*

(i) if $M > \hat{\rho}$ then yRx for some y such that $py < M$.

(ii) if $M < \check{\rho}$ then $y\bar{R}x$ for all y such that $py \leqq M$,

provided R is without satiation.

Since (i) is immediate from the definition of $\hat{\rho}$, it remains to consider (ii).

Let $py \leqq M < \check{\rho}$, so xRy by definition of $\check{\rho}$. Then there exists $z > y$ such that $px \leqq \check{\rho}$, so xRz. But now if also xRx then, by transitivity, also yRz. But since $z > y$ this is impossible, by absence of satiation. Thus $y\bar{R}x$, and this proves (ii).

Corollary (i) *For any utility order R and any p, x*

$$\hat{\rho} \leqq \check{\rho} \text{ if } R \text{ is complete}$$

$$\check{\rho} \leqq \hat{\rho} \text{ if } R \text{ is without satiation.}$$

The first part is immediate from the definitions. For the second, if $M < \check{\rho}$ then $py \leqq M$ implies $y\bar{R}x$ for all y, by the Theorem. But this shows $M \leqq \hat{\rho}$, by definition of $\hat{\rho}$. Thus for all M

$$M < \check{\rho} \Rightarrow M \leqq \hat{\rho},$$

and from this follows $\check{\rho} \leqq \hat{\rho}$.

FIGURE 2

Utility-Cost

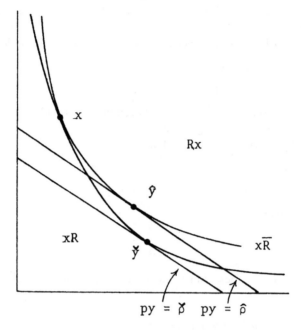

$$py = \check{\rho} \quad py = \hat{\rho}$$

R is without satiation, so $\check{\rho} \leqq \hat{\rho}$

and incomplete, allowing $\check{\rho} < \hat{\rho}$

$\hat{y}$, $\bar{y}$ are in the closures of Rx, x$\bar{R}$ where

py attains lower limits $\hat{\rho}$, $\check{\rho}$

R is typical of a revealed preference relation

with xR orthoconcave and

the consistency property xR ∩ Rx = {x}

and additionally Rx is orthoconvex

Corollary (ii)   *If R is a complete utility order without satiation then $\check{p} = \hat{p}$.*

The Theorem shows, under the stated qualification, that for any x and p the cost at prices p of purchasing a bundle as good as x is at least $\check{p}$ and at most $\hat{p}$. The application the functions will have in determining cost bounds depends on this property, together with the following, which is immediate from the definitions. Let R_0, R_1 be any two utility orders, and let $\hat{p}_0$, $\hat{p}_1$ and $\check{p}_0$, $\check{p}_1$ be the corresponding critical cost functions. Then

$$R_0 \subset R_1 \;\Rightarrow\; \check{p}_0 \leq \check{p}_1, \quad \hat{p}_1 \leq \hat{p}_0.$$

Consequently:

Corollary (iii)   *For any utility orders R_0, R_1 without satiation*

$$R_0 \subset R_1 \;\Rightarrow\; \check{p}_0 \leq \check{p}_1 \leq \hat{p}_1 \leq \hat{p}_0.$$

and $\check{p}_1 = \hat{p}_1$ if R_1 is complete.

A *utility function* is any $\phi : \Omega^n \to \Omega$. It *represents* the utility order R given by

$$x R y \equiv \phi(x) \geq \phi(y).$$

A *classical utility function* is semi-increasing, that is

$$x < y \;\Rightarrow\; \phi(x) < \phi(y)$$

and concave. These properties alone require the function to have a linear support at every interior point of Ω^n, but a classical function is required to have one also at any point on the boundary. For g to be the gradient of a linear support, or a *support gradient*, at a point x, the condition is

$$\phi(y) - \phi(x) \leq g(y - x) \quad \text{for all } y.$$

Then, with ϕ semi-increasing, necessarily $g \geq 0$. A *classical utility relation* is one which is representable by a classical function.

A *polyhedral* classical function is the especially simple type of function determined by a finite set of supports. It has the form

$$\phi(x) = \min_t \phi_t(x)$$

where the ϕ_t are linear, with gradients $g_t \geq 0$. While for any utility $\phi(x)$, the indirect utility function

$$\psi(u) = \max[\phi(y) : uy \leq 1]$$

is quasi-convex, and ϕ is recovered from ψ as

$$\phi(x) = \min[\psi(v) : vx \leq 1]$$

provided ϕ is quasi-concave, if ϕ is concave then ψ has the additional property that $\psi(\rho^{-1}u)$ is a concave function of ρ, and so has a support gradient $\lambda > 0$ at

$\rho = 1$, for which

$$\psi(\rho^{-1}u) - \psi(u) \leqq \lambda(\rho - 1),$$

giving

$$\left. \frac{d\psi(\rho^{-1}u)}{d\rho} \right|_{\rho=1} = \lambda$$

in case $\psi(\rho^{-1}u)$ is differentiable at $\rho = 1$. This λ, which here appears directly as the marginal utility of income, also appears as the Lagrangian multiplier in the condition

$$g \leqq \lambda u, \qquad gx = \lambda$$

for ϕ with support gradient g to be a maximum at x subject to the budget constraint $ux \leqq 1$, that is for x to be such that

$$\phi(x) = \psi(u), \qquad ux \leqq 1.$$

4   Cost-efficiency and efficacy

If a utility order R is given which is complete and without satiation so $\hat{\rho}$ and $\check{\rho}$ coincide in a single function ρ, then

$$M = \rho(p, x),$$

obtained from R, define the cost at prices p of maintaining a standard of living represented by a bundle x. Any income more than M is more than is necessary for the purpose, and any income less than M is less than sufficient (Section 3). This gives a concept of cost of living depending on a given utility relation R. The problem of the cost of living arises because usually the utility relation, by which it is intelligible as a concept and which is necessary for its determination, is not given. All that usually is given is a fragmentary scheme of data which has to be brought to bear in some way. An element of such data is a demand (x_t, p_t), of quantities x_t at prices p_t, observed in some period of consumption t. The utility order R is to be constrained by having a relation to (x_t, p_t). With several such demands being given at various time t, it is further constrained by being required to have that relation to each of them simultaneously. Then when R is constrained so is the value of $\rho(p, x)$ which depends on R. This shows a method by which the available demand data can be used if not to give a final determination of $\rho(p, x)$ then just to reduce its indeterminacy. But whatever might be proposed, it is sure that one way to maintain a standard of living represented by x, when the prices are p, is to have the income $M = px$ adequate to purchase x itself. Practical procedure of cost of living assessment relies on just this. But the concern now is with theory in terms of utility, which, though it is consistent with everything in usual practice, adds nothing essential to it.

The needed relation between a utility order R and a demand (x, p) can have several versions. Most familiar is that given by the condition

(H^*) $py \leq px,$ $y \neq x \Rightarrow xRy, y\bar{R}x.$

If R is represented by a utility function ϕ, so

$$xRy \Leftrightarrow \phi(x) \geq \phi(y)$$

this becomes

$$py \leq px, \quad y \neq x \Rightarrow \phi(x) > \phi(y).$$

But R can be understood to be any order, just reflexive and transitive and not subject to any additional restrictions. The condition asserts that, according to R, x is the unique maximum among all bundles which, at the prices p, cost no more than x. Another way of stating this condition is

$$py \leq px \Rightarrow xRy, \qquad yRx \Rightarrow py > px \quad \text{or} \quad y \neq x.$$

Then an apparent weakening of this condition, denoted H^*, is H given by the conjuction of

(H') $py \leq px \Rightarrow xRy,$ (H'') $yRx \Rightarrow py \geq px.$

The first part (H') here asserts that x is as good as any bundle which costs no more at the prices p. This is the principle of *cost-efficacy*, that the money spent on x has been spent effectively, since no better result is attainable with it at the same prices. Then (H'') is that any bundle which is as good as x costs at least as much, showing *cost-efficiency*, that it is impossible to reduce the cost and still obtain as good a result. These two conditions are generally independent. They represent the two equally basic criteria familiar in cost–benefit analysis. However, they become dependent if restrictions are imposed on R. Thus if $yRx, y < x$ is impossible then $H' \Rightarrow H''$, and if R is complete, so $y\bar{R}x \Rightarrow xRy$, and the sets xR are closed, the $H'' \Rightarrow H'$. For instance if R is represented by a continuous increasing utility function the $H' \Leftrightarrow H''$, and the same if the function is just lower semi-continuous and semi-increasing.

The condition $H = H(R; x, p)$ between a utility relation R and demand (x, p) define their *compatibility*, and the more strict H^* defines *strict compatibility*. They apply also to a utility function, through the relation it represents.

There is always some utility compatible with a single demand (x, p), $\phi(x) = px$ always being on example. But there does not always exist a utility which is simultaneously compatible with two or more given demands. To be able always to associate a utility with several demands simultaneously, H must be relaxed in some way. This can be done by introducing a further parameter e where $0 \leq e \leq 1$, representing a degree of cost-efficiency, and replacing H by $H(e)$ given by

$$H'(e) : py \leq pxe \Rightarrow xRy, \quad H''(e) : yRx \Rightarrow py \geq pxe.$$

This condition, defining *compatibility at a level of cost-efficiency e*, or *e-compatibility*, is valid unconditionally if $e = 0$, and it coincides with H if

FIGURE 3

Demand-Utility Compatibility

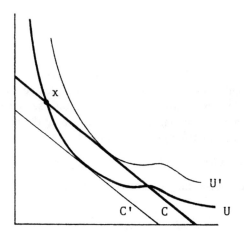

U   utility of x
U' utility of cost of x
C   cost of x
C' cost of utility of x
in any case

$$U' \geq U, \qquad C' \leq C$$

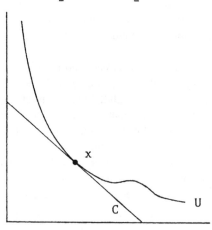

for compatibility between demand and utility

$$U' = U, \qquad C' = C$$

FIGURE 4

Partial Compatibility

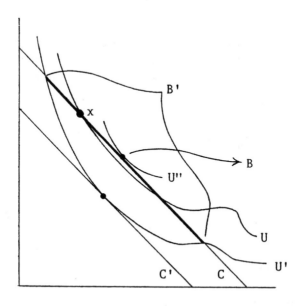

C   cost of x

C' part-cost of x

$$C' = eC, \qquad 0 \leq e \leq 1$$

U' utility of part-cost of x

U utility of x, U" utility of cost of x

partial compatibility: U ≥ U'

e-compatibility, or compatibility at

a level of cost-efficiency e

compatibility ≡ 1-compatibility

B' partial compatibility region, x ∈ B'

B compatibility point

$e = 1$, that is $H(1) \equiv H$. Then with any given demands, even if $e = 1$ is impossible there will be the position to give e, a small enough value to assure the existence of a simultaneously e-compatible utility, because $e = 0$ is always one such value and such values have a readily determined upper limit. This more flexible method based on $H(e)$ instead of H is suitable to the present subject. But for simplicity and to maintain a direct relationship with considered standard propositions, H will be adopted.

For R which is complete and non-satiated, so $\hat{\rho}, \check{\rho}$ coincide and can be denoted ρ, if also the sets xR are closed, so $H'' \Rightarrow H'$, making $H \Leftrightarrow H'$, then a statement of compatibility H between R and a demand (x, p) is simply

$$\rho(p, x) = px.$$

But since generally $\rho(p, x) \leqq px$, so $\rho(p, x) = epx$ where $0 \leqq e \leqq 1$, and the condition for e-compatibility $H(e)$ is

$$\rho(p, x) \geqq epx,$$

there is always compatibility at the level $e = e\,(R; x, p)$ thus determined. With $u = px$ and $u = M^{-1}p$ this level is

$$e = \rho(u, x),$$

and the condition H requires $\rho(u, x) = 1$.

5   The price index

A price index is, on the surface, a number which is calculated by some formula and put to a certain use. Since the formulae for a price index are numerous—Fisher considered 126 of them, at least—and there is no conclusive way of choosing one from the other—Fisher showed it hardly mattered—it is impossible to discover a theoretical concept just from these formulae. Evidence for the theoretical concept involved, therefore, must come from the use.

A price index P_{10} is calculated with reference to two periods 0, 1 in which the prices are different, and its use is to determine a relation

$$M_1 = P_{10}M_0$$

between any incomes M_0, M_1 in those periods which are to be accepted as having the same purchasing power. Inseparable from a price index is the presumption that the relation between equivalent incomes at different prices should be homogeneous linear. The entire meaning of a price index is that it should determine just such a relation by giving its slope. But the determination of equivalence between incomes has theoretical intelligibility with reference to utility. Thus, with a utility relation R and incomes M_0, M_1 at prices p_0, p_1, let x_0, x_1 be such that the demands (x_0, p_0), (x_1, p_1) are compatible with R and $p_0 x_0 = M_0$, $p_1 x_1 = M_1$, so these are bundles of goods, the incomes might purchase at those prices. Then the condition for the purchasing power equivalence of the incomes M_0, M_1 at prices p_0, p_1 is that the

FIGURE 5

Income Purchasing Power

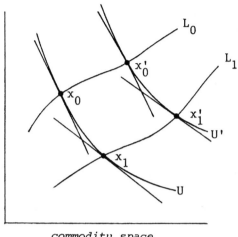

commodity space

p_0, p_1 any prices; L_0, L_1 corresponding expansion loci
U a utility level; x_0, x_1 bundles where U cuts L_0, L_1

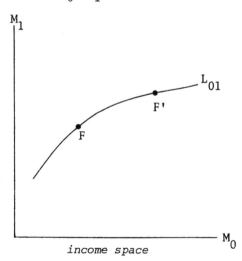

income space

L_{01} purchasing power relation, holding between incomes
M_0, M_1 having the same purchasing power at prices p_0, p_1;
it is described by points $F = (M_0, M_1)$ whose coordinates
$M_0 = p_0x_0$, $M_1 = p_1x_1$ are incomes purchasing the same utility U

bundles x_0, x_1 be indifferent in respect to R, that is $x_0 R x_1$, $x_1 R x_0$. This relation between M_0, M_1 obtained from any R and p_0, p_1 is a general monotonic increasing relation. That it be a homogeneous linear relation represents a special condition, which has various equivalent statements, as follows:

(i) In terms of preferences: $x R y$ *implies* $x_t R y_t$ *for all* $t \geq 0$.
That is, the utility order is conical.

(ii) In terms of expansion loci: *compatibility with R for any* (x_0, p_0) *is equivalent to that for* $(x_0 t, p_0)$ *for all* $t \geq 0$.
That is, the expansion loci are conical.

(iii) In terms of utility–cost: $\rho(p, x) = \theta(p)\phi(x)$ *where* θ, ϕ *are functions of* p, x *alone.*

(iv) In terms of purchasing power: *any* p_0, p_1 *determine* P_{10} *such that for all* (x_0, p_0), (x_1, p_1) *compatible with R the indifference of* x_0, x_1 *with respect to R is equivalent to the relation* $M_1/M_0 = P_{10}$ *where* $M_0 = p_0 x_0$, $M_1 = p_1 x_1$.

There is still another form of statement in terms of a utility function $\phi(x)$. Any budget constraint is described by $ux \leq 1$ for some $u \in \Omega_n$. Then the budget constraint has a utility value, determined as the maximum of utility attainable under it,

$$\psi(u) = \max[\phi(x) : ux \leqq 1].$$

The utility of any budget constraint $px \leq M$ where $M > 0$ is the utility of the constraint $ux \leqq 1$ where $u = M^{-1}p$, that is $\psi(M^{-1}p)$. The condition that any income M_0, M_1 have the same purchasing power at prices p_0, p_1 is now

$$\psi(M_0^{-1} p_0) = \psi(M_1^{-1} p_1).$$

This determines a correspondence between M_0, M_1 and the use of a price index requires this correspondence to have the form $M_1/M_0 = P_{10}$, where P_{10} is independent of M_0, M_1.

When there is a price index P_{10} it must have the form

$$P_{10} = \theta(p_1)/\theta(p_0).$$

So to speak, it is a ratio P_1/P_0 of "price-levels"

$$P_0 = \theta(p_0), \qquad P_1 = \theta(p_1).$$

The function θ is necessarily conical. So is the order R. Then if θ is a function given to represent R which is not itself conical it can be replaced by a function

FIGURE 6

Purchasing Power and the Price Index

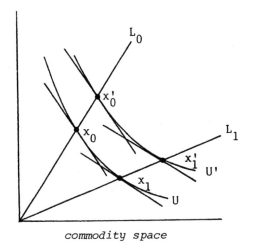

commodity space

p_0, p_1 any prices; L_0, L_1 corresponding expansion rays

U a utility level; x_0, x_1 bundles where U cuts L_0, L_1

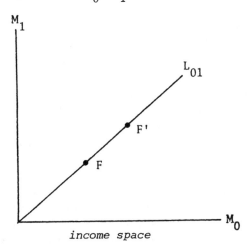

income space

L_{01} purchasing power relation, proportion $M_0 : M_1$ fixed

$M_1 = P_{10}M_0$ where P_{10} is the price-index

determined from one price position to the other

which is conical, and is equivalent in that it represents the same relation, and

$$X_0 = \theta(x_0), \qquad X_1 = \theta(x_1)$$

are "quantity-levels"

$$P_0 X_0 = M_0, \qquad P_1 X_1 = M_1.$$

Then $X_0 = X_1$ is equivalent to

$$M_0^{-1} P_0 = M_1^{-1} P_1.$$

That is

$$M_1 / M_0 = P_{10}, \quad \text{where } P_{10} = P_1 / P_0.$$

This brings forward the link with the aspect of price-index thinking, where prices have a "level", and a price index is a ratio of price levels. Then follows the notion that the price index is to be grasped statistically as some kind of average of individual price ratios—almost any kind of average was Fisher's conclusion after stydying together a great variety of series based on different formulae. It also reveals the sense of Fisher's Tests as tests that the set of price indices determined between pairs of periods should have consistency with their being a set of ratios. When there are just two periods 0, 1 these tests reduce simply to

$$P_{01} = P_{10}^{-1}.$$

6   Problems

The definitions which have been made, permit the following formulations.

Problem I.   *To establish a test for the existence of a utility order R with which the given demands (x_0, p_0), (x_1, p_1) are simultaneously compatible and then to determine the possible values of the cost $\rho(p_1, x_0)$ at the prices p_1 of maintaining the standard of living represented by the bundle of goods x_0, determined in respect to all such orders.*

Instead of $\rho(p_1, x_0)$ in this problem there is no reason not to consider $\rho(p_s, x_t)$ where s, t are periods different from the periods 0, 1 of the demand observations, or $\rho(p, x)$ for quite arbitrary p, x and for demand observations taken from a collection of any number of periods. But the usual custom is to consider indices between two periods based on the data from just those periods.

The method with this problem will be to find bounds on $\rho(p_1, x_0)$ without any additional restriction on R, and then, as a subsidiary problem, to show that any point in the interval determined by these bounds is attained for some classical polyhedral R. This shows that the bounds are in fact limits, and also that the values exhaust the interval between them.

It also shows that the subsidiary problem gives no different result from the main problem. The significance of this is that the special properties for a utility function which are usually assumed, and on which familiarly so much emphasis is made, are without necessity or importance. For at first here no special properties at all are required for *R*, and then all properties usually considered and more are imposed, *but they make no difference*, neither to the consistency test nor to the range of values determined.

This basic first problem leads to an unfamiliar result without intelligibility in terms of a price index. It is the problem actually presented by Alan Brown in the lecture of 1953 mentioned in the Preface. Recognition of the price index as entirely a homogeneous concept leads to a reformulation.

Problem II. *To establish a test for the exercise of homogeneous utility order which is compatible with the given demands. In respect to any such order R, the cost M_1 at prices p_1 of attaining the standard of living obtained by any income M_0 at prices p_0 has a fixed ratio P_{10} to M_0 , defining the price index with p_0, p_1 as base and current prices, and all possible values of this index are to be determined.*

The test obtained, which is, as it should be, more restrictive than that obtained for Problem I (see Chapter I, Section 2), is the often considered "theorem" that the Paasche index should not exceed that of Laspeyres. Then the required set of values is the closed interval, lying within the formerly obtained interval, with these indices as limits.

Fisher's "ideal" index lies between these limits, and Byushgens' remark about its connection with quadratics brings into view the following still more restricted problem.

Problem III. *To establish a test for the existence of homogeneous quadratic utility with which the given demands are simultaneously compatible and then to determine all possible values of the price index in respect to such utilities.*

Investigation of this problem, which could be a first response to Byushgens' remark, leads to the conclusion that the problem should be modified. Instead of asking for a compatible homogeneous quadratic utility, the existence of which is awkward, it is better to ask for a compatible homogeneous utility which has quadratic representation near x_0, x_1. Then the test is simple and, surprisingly, it is identical with that found for Problem II.

The automatic existence of compatible homogeneous locally quadratic utility whenever there exists a compatible homogeneous utility suggests a tolerance which will leave a general indeterminacy as found in Problems I and II, except just that the indeterminacy would be diminished still further by the additional quadratic restriction. This surmise could seem to be reinforced by there being an infinite variety of locally compatible quadratics, if there are any, assuming $n > 2$. In spite of all this, the indeterminacy is removed totally, without defect or excess, leaving a point determination which moreover is identical with the point provided by Fisher's index.

If homogeneity is abandoned, while retaining the quadratic requirement, simultaneous compatibility is possible in positive measure just with two further demands, but nevertheless indeterminacy is restored (Afriat 1956 and 1961, in Shubik 1967).

II   The general problem of limits

The distinction made between exchange-value and use-value for goods produces the idea that money, or—what is more specific and understandable—any income, has a purchasing power which is variable depending on prices. The distinction is recognized, but at the same time there is need to avoid the awkwardness of maintaining it fully. The need must be understood, because otherwise there can be bewilderment at consequences of it. One of these is the jump to the nebulous notion of the 'general purchasing power' of money, or its reciprocal which, no doubt, is the price level. Keynes, who made much of the price level, found it unsuitable and offered retreat to a more accommodating idea which allowed a "plurality" of purchasing powers (*A Treatise on Money*, Vol. I); but also this is nebulous, it being simply a relaxation of an already nebulous idea. A different and also familiar perplexity with the distinction is in general equilibrium and welfare theory. There the distinction is between the exchange-value of output of the economy at equilibrium prices and the use-value in the sense of collective welfare obtained. Under usual assumptions, the former is indeed maximum for output at equilibrium, but in fact this is not recognized, and from doctrine it is the latter which should be maximum. But the latter is only a phrase without an identified meaning, though it can gather the appearance of this from confusion with the former—wizardry with the differential calculus produces just this illusion. In consequence, equilibrium prices do not measure merely themselves but are proportional to 'marginal product'; they become distinguished not just as equilibrium prices but as 'efficiency prices' which lead the economy to maximum 'welfare'. A formidable structure has been built on circularities.

The market has value, even many values, in a sense which relates to its function and is alien from anything to do with magnitude. In theory, competition is enough to govern the market; so if, for instance, the single unswerving objective is elimination of dependence on any other form of government then it is indeed optimal, since such dependence is, at least in the model, completely eliminated. But here is quite another sense of value, in an unfortunate collision with others, and out of the wreckage of distinctions around it arises the mythical doctrine of maximality.

This digression, though it is important, is rather distant from the present subject. To be considered here is the distinction between the exchange-value of an income, stated by so-many £s, and the use-value which derives from what is done with it. The way this is developed depends on how the use-value is stated.

Consider a period 0 when prices are $p_0 \in \Omega_n$, and an income M_0 is spent on consumption of a bundle of goods $x_0 \in \Omega^n$. Income is understood to coincide with expenditure on the goods, equal to their cost at the prevailing prices, so

$$M_0 = p_0 x_0.$$

This limitation of what is meant by income fits the usual terminology in demand analysis, but it does not agree with income in any ordinary sense, about which there can be no neat theory of 'purchasing power'. Keynes remarks: "The importance of money essentially flows from its being a link between the present and the future." Dynamic involvements of income gathered in this remark entirely escape present considerations.

With Fleetwood (p. 12) the use-value of income M_0 in period 0 when the prices are p_0 would be simply the bundle of goods x_0. Then for an income M_1 to have the same use-value, or purchasing power, in period 1 when the prices are p_1, the condition is simply

$$M_1 = p_1 x_0.$$

This has validity when there is steadfast adherence to living-style, no entertainment of 'substitutes', and all that is wanted is to go on living as before. In this case there would be no buying of more coffee just because there is a rise in the price of tea; in brief, an easily accountable un-neoclassical condition of dignity prevails. But this is too simple and there is not much to say about it. Instead now, each bundle of goods is treated not as distinct individual use-value but as serving a general usefulness, in a use-system which is fixed and independent of time. But demand is history; there can be comment about it, on patterns present and forces which have effect, but no complete mechanical account. A utility ordering is supposed to persist through time, or be independent of it—while it determines historical events, the demands which take place in time. The pretence cannot be serious! An alternative position is that a utility ordering prevails in any moment of time, to determine demand in that moment, but it is changing with the time. But all that is observable in any moment is simply the demand. It can be said there is a utility ordering which determines the demand, a different one in every moment. But this means nothing, no refutation is possible, in other words there is no content to refute. Then certainly the assertion can be upheld—it does not matter since it makes no difference.

The utility hypothesis as a model of demand behaviour is just a model, to be played with—as it has been, extravagantly. But in the question of income purchasing power it does not have intention as a behaviour model; rather, it provides a basis for intelligibility of the question. It gives terms in which the question could be answered. Because the question involves the hypothesis just in its being understood, any dissatisfaction with the hypothesis must be redirected towards the question. However, the question itself escapes effective judgement about being sensible or not, because it is already imposed from practicalities in social-economic experience: prices change, and then any income must change if it is to maintain the same purchasing power—it is essential to know how much it should change. A similar question is with political decisions: there are many candidates and one must be chosen—which one? There is no single formula which tells how this must be settled; it is a matter of design with many possibilities. The same holds with the purchasing power question. Practice has fixed an approach, but theory would find this too simple for comment and takes up another—one quite familiar, an old help in the flight from disquieting unaccountabilities of history into the illusion of permanent mechanism—utility theory.

A postulate of utility theory is that consumption bundles are not distinct ends in themselves, each representative of a pattern of living, But instead there is a further end, in the general service of which they are all just alternative inputs. They are ranked together according to the extent in which they can serve it. In other words, there is an order R in the commodity space, that is a reflexive, transitive binary relation, where xRy signifies the bundle x is as good, or useful, for the purpose as the bundle y. The order R is fixed, independent of time or anything else. There is one non-committal element in this thinking: *the utility order R is not specified.*

Suppose an order R is specified. Let x be any bundle of good and p any price, and assume

$$\rho(p, x) = \min\{py : yRx\}$$

exists, as it must if Rx is closed and $p > 0$. For any bundle y such that yRx, an expenditure of money py suffices to buy consumption of at least standard of x, since it will buy y which is as good as x. The cost of a objective being the minimum expenditure adequate for attaining it, $\rho(p, x)$ is the cost at prices p for attaining the standard of consumption of x. Necessarily

$$\rho(p, x) \leq px$$

since R is reflexive; that is, the cost of attaining the standard of x does not exceed the cost of x itself. In ignorance of R, there is nothing more that can be said about ρ. But should a constraint be put on R, there will be a consequent constraint on ρ since it depends not only on p and x but also on R.

When orders R are considered which must satisfy certain constraints, there arises the question whether any such orders exist. A test has to be found, and discovering this is the first problem which will be considered. The test is shown in several different but equivalent forms. These serve the next considered problem, which is to determine all possible values of ρ corresponding to all possible orders R which satisfy the constraints. While

$$\rho = \rho(p, x)$$

could well be considered for any p and x, custom brings attention especially to

$$\rho_{10} = \rho(p_1, x_0).$$

The data on the consumer consists in the demands

$$(p_t, x_t) \quad (t = 0, 1).$$

This is all the data that are available, and if the order R which is to apply to the consumer is to be restricted by relation to the consumer, it can only be by relation to those demands. Then there is no obvious alternative but to require that the consumer appear to be governed by the order R in making those demands. For in the thought about the order R is the presumption that the calculations based on it will govern the consumer; and there is no available basis for supposing the consumer should be governed by any order R, except that it appears from observations that the consumer has already been governed by R. In the absence of a counter-proposal there is only this to follow.

To formulate the questions which will be dealt with, it remains to account the relation H applying between any order R and any demand (x, p). This expresses the idea of the order governing the demand, or generating it, or that the order and the demand together are compatible. Then consistency of any demands is defined by the existence of an order with which they are simultaneously compatible.

It is a premise in utility theory that a bundle of goods is not an irreplaceable individual object bought just for its own sake, but that the objective is its utility, which can be obtained also from many substitutes. The money px spent in the demand (x, p) has then to be viewed not as merely buying x but as buying the utility of x. While px is the cost of x, at prices p, $\rho(p, x)$ is the cost of the utility of x, necessarily at most px. If the consumer, in buying x, is truly buying just the utility of x at its cost, the money px spent on x must coincide with the utility–cost $\rho(p, x)$; that is,

$$\rho(p, x) = px.$$

An equivalent statement is that any bundle of goods y which has as much utility as x would cost at least as much, that is,

$$(H'') \quad yRx \implies py \geq px.$$

By this condition H'', the order R is such as to represent the demand (p, x) as *cost-efficient*, meaning it is impossible to achieve the same objective at a lesser cost.

But this condition, which asks that a given use-value be obtained with minimum sacrifice of exchange-value, is only part of the matter. It is the part compelled in order to give effect to the idea of *cost of living*. But also present is the idea of the *purchasing power of incomes*. While cost for a given gain in an objective, if it is to be unambiguous, can only mean the minimum possible cost for attaining it, similarly the gain from a given expenditure can only mean the maximum possible gain obtainable by means of it. With Fleetwood (p. 6)

... money is of no other use, than as it is the thing with which we purchase the necessities and conveniences of life ...

Here money instead purchases utility. Then the purchasing power of an income, or its use-value, is the highest level of utility attainable with it. There can be no comparison of the purchasing power of incomes without presumption that incomes realize their purchasing power. Accordingly, with a demand (p, x), it is required that no bundle better than x could have been bought with the same amount of money px. What is the same, x is as good as any bundle of goods y which costs no more, that is

$$(H') \quad py \leq px \implies xRy.$$

This condition H' shows the order R as representing the demand (p, x) as *cost-effective*, meaning that for the same cost it is impossible to achieve a superior objective.

The conjunction H of the conditions H' and H'' defines the relation of *compatibility* between an order R and a demand (p, x). Consumers' demands (x_t, p_t) at times $t = 0, 1$ are given, and any order R considered with which they are simultaneously compatible. This makes the consumer represented not only as fully deliberate and constant about wants, described by the relation R fixed through time, but also as a completely precise programmer, at least on the occasions $t = 0, 1$ when observed. In purchasing the bundle x_t at the prices p_t $(t = 0, 1)$ no bundle exists which is as good and costs less. Also, it is impossible with the money $p_t x_t$ spent, to buy a better bundle than x_t. The relation R is constrained simply by the requirement that it give this picture of the consumer as such a completely informed, deliberate, constant and precise individual.

For correspondence with experience, this picture is remote. But, fortunately, such correspondence is not here an issue. Rather, the picture serves to give a particular theoretical intelligibility to income 'purchasing power' and 'cost of living'. Then it gives rise to formal questions which, being purely formal, can be pursued separately and in disregard of original merit. Then they acquire another merit just in the pursuit—if the enormous attention given to utility theory is witness.

1 Consistency of demands

Let (x_t, p_t) $(t = 0, 1)$ be two given demands, associated with two periods $t = 0, 1$. They are associated with incomes $M_t = p_t x_t$, assumed positive, and then budget vectors $u_t = M_t^{-1} p_t$, for which $u_t x_t = 1$. Then, between them there are *cross-coefficients*

$$D_{st} = u_s x_t - 1 \quad (s, t = 0, 1),$$

for which $D_{tt} = 0$.

Let $H_t(R)$ assert the *compatibility* of demand t with a utility order R, this being the conjunction of conditions

$$H'_t(R) \equiv u_t x \leq 1 \;\Rightarrow\; x_t Rx$$
$$H''_t(R) \equiv xRx_t \;\Rightarrow\; u_t x \geq 1,$$

expressing *cost-efficiency* and *efficacy*. The simultaneous compatibility of the two demands with R is the conjunction $H(R)$ of $H_t(R)$ for $t = 0, 1$, and the assertion H of this for some R gives their *consistency*.

Consider also the condition

$$K \equiv u_0 x_1 \leq 1, \qquad u_1 x_0 \leq 1 \;\Rightarrow\; u_0 x_1 = u_1 x_0 = 1.$$

This just excludes the possibility

$$u_0 x_1 \leq 1, \qquad u_1 x_0 < 1$$

and the same with 0, 1 interchanged.

Theorem 1.1 $H \;\Rightarrow\; K$.

Suppose $H(R)$. Then, from $H'_0(R)$,

$$u_0 x_1 \leq 1 \;\Rightarrow\; x_0 Rx_1$$

and from $H''_1(R)$,

$$u_1 x_0 < 1 \;\Rightarrow\; x_0 \bar{R} x_1,$$

showing the required conclusion.

Another statement of K is that

$$D_{01} \leq 0, \quad D_{10} \leq 0 \;\Rightarrow\; D_{01} = 0, \quad D_{10} = 0$$

or that

$$(D_{01}, D_{10}) \leq 0$$

is excluded.

Any numbers $\lambda = (\lambda_0, \lambda_1)$ are *multiplier solution* if they satisfy the condition

$$L(\lambda) \equiv \lambda_0, \lambda_1 > 0, \qquad \lambda_0 D_{01} + \lambda_1 D_{10} \geq 0.$$

The assertion L of the existence of such numbers defines *multiplier consistency* of the demands.

Theorem 1.2 $K \Leftrightarrow L$.

Since

$$(D_{01}, D_{10}) \leq 0, \qquad \lambda_0, \lambda_1 > 0$$

implies

$$\lambda_0 D_{01} + \lambda_1 D_{10} < 0,$$

it follows that $L \Rightarrow K$.

To prove the converse, suppose K. Then either both D_{01}, D_{10} are zero or at least one, say D_{10}, is positive. In the former case L is verified, since $L(\lambda_0, \lambda_1)$ holds for all $\lambda_0, \lambda_1 > 0$. In the latter case it holds with $\lambda_0 = 1$ and $\lambda_1 > D_{01} D_{10}^{-1}$, so again L is verified, and the theorem is proved.

Any numbers $\lambda = (\lambda_0, \lambda_1)$, $\phi = (\phi_0, \phi_1)$ are a *multiplier-level solution* if they satisfy the condition

$$S(\lambda, \phi) \equiv \lambda_0, \quad \lambda_1 > 0, \quad \lambda_0 D_{01} \geq \phi_1 - \phi_0, \quad \lambda_1 D_{10} \geq \phi_0 - \phi_1.$$

The assertion S of the existence of such numbers defines *multiplier-level consistency*. Also for any λ let $S(\lambda)$ assert the existence of ϕ such that $S(\lambda, \phi)$.

Theorem 1.3 $L(\lambda) \Leftrightarrow S(\lambda)$.

Since

$$\lambda_0 D_{01} \geq \phi_1 - \phi_0, \quad \lambda_1 D_{10} \geq \phi_0 - \phi_1,$$

by addition, imply $\lambda_0 D_{01} + \lambda_1 D_{10} \geq 0$, it appears that $S(\lambda) \Rightarrow L(\lambda)$. For the converse, $L(\lambda)$ implies

$$\lambda_0 D_{01} \geq -\lambda_1 D_{10},$$

and hence the existence of ϕ_1 such that

$$\lambda_0 D_{01} \geq \phi_1 \geq -\lambda_1 D_{10}.$$

Then $S(\lambda, \phi)$ is verified with $\phi_0 = 0$.

Corollary $L \Leftrightarrow S$.

For any given λ, ϕ introduce functions

$$\phi_0(x) = \phi_0 + \lambda_0(u_0 x - 1), \quad \phi_1(x) = \phi_1 + \lambda_1(u_1 x - 1)$$

and

$$\phi(x) = \min[\phi_0(x), \phi_1(x)].$$

Let $C(\lambda, \phi)$ assert $H(R)$ where R is the utility order represented by $\phi(x)$, and let C assert this for some λ, ϕ. Thus immediately

$$C \Rightarrow H.$$

Theorem 1.4 $S(\lambda, \phi) \Rightarrow C(\lambda, \phi)$.

Since

$$\phi_0(x_0) = \phi_0, \quad \phi_1(x_0) = \phi_1 - \lambda_1 D_{10}$$

so

$$\phi(x_0) = \min[\phi_0, \phi_1 + \lambda_1 D_{10}]$$

it follows that

$$\phi(x_0) = \phi_0(x_0) \quad \Leftrightarrow \quad \lambda_1 D_{10} \geqq \phi_1 - \phi_0.$$

Also

$$u_0 x < 1 \quad \Rightarrow \quad \phi_0(x) < \phi_0(x_0) \quad \Leftrightarrow \quad \lambda_0 > 0.$$

Since in any case

$$\phi(x) \leq \phi_0(x)$$

it now follows that if

$$\lambda_0 > 0, \quad \lambda_1 D_{10} \geqq \phi_1 - \phi_0$$

then

$$u_0 x < 1 \quad \Rightarrow \quad \phi(x) < \phi(x_0),$$

and similarly with 0, 1 interchanged. This shows that

$$S(\lambda, \phi) \quad \Rightarrow \quad C(\lambda, \phi).$$

To consider the converse, suppose $C(\lambda, \phi)$, so

$$u_0 x < 1 \quad \Rightarrow \quad \phi(x) < \phi(x_0).$$

Since $\phi(x)$ is concave, with a support gradient g_0 at x_0, this implies

$$g_0 \leqq \mu u_0, \quad g_0 x_0 = \mu, \quad \mu > 0$$

for some μ. But either $g_0 = \lambda_0 u_0$ or $g_0 = \lambda_1 u_1$. In the second case, $\mu = \lambda_1 u_1 x_0$, so $\mu > 0$ requires $\lambda_1 > 0$, and then $u_1 \leqq u_1 x_0 u_0$. With $x_0 > 0$, this implies $u_1 = u_1 x_0 u_0$, that is, prices are proportional. Thus, positive quantities and exclusion of proportional prices requires $g_0 = \lambda_0 u_0$, and then $\phi(x_0) = \phi_0(x_0)$, that is $\lambda_1 D_{10} \geqq \phi_1 - \phi_0$. In this case $\mu = \lambda_0$, so $\lambda_0 > 0$. This shows the converse is valid at least under the qualification that all quantities be positive and prices in the two periods be not proportional.

Theorem 1.5 $H \Leftrightarrow K \Leftrightarrow L \Leftrightarrow S \Leftrightarrow C$.

This follows from the foregoing theorems together with $C \Rightarrow H$.

For a classical utility function $\phi(x)$ with any point $x \in \Omega^n$ there exists $g \in \Omega_n$, a support gradient of the function at that point, such that

$$\phi(y) - \phi(x) \leq g(y - x).$$

Then, given $ux = 1$, the compatibility condition

$$uy < 1 \implies \phi(y) < \phi(x)$$

is equivalent to

$$g \leq \lambda u, \quad gx = \lambda, \quad \lambda > 0.$$

Thus the particular function $\phi(x)$ constructed under the condition $S(\lambda, \phi)$ is classical. A support gradient g at any x is generally given by

$$g = \lambda_t u_t \quad \text{if } \phi_t(x) \leq \phi_s(x) \ (s, t = 0, 1).$$

But since, under the condition $S(\lambda, \phi)$,

$$\phi_t(x_t) = \phi_t \leq \phi_s + \lambda_s D_{st} = \phi_s(x_t)$$

it follows then that

$$g_t = \lambda_t u_t$$

is a support gradient at x_t.

With the indirect utility function, of any utility function ϕ, given by

$$\psi(u) = \max[\phi(y) : uy \leq 1],$$

$\psi(\rho^{-1}u)$ is in any case non-increasing quasi-convex in u and, provided ϕ is classical, it is non-decreasing concave in ρ, in which case also

$$\phi(x) = \min[\psi(v) : vx \leq 1].$$

The interpretation of the multiplier λ_t at x_t is that it is a support gradient of $\psi(\rho^{-1}u)$ at $\rho = 1$, that is

$$\psi(\rho^{-1}u_t) - \psi(u_t) \leq \lambda_t(\rho - 1).$$

Uniqueness of λ_t is equivalent to differentiability at $\rho = 1$, in which case

$$\frac{\partial \psi}{\partial \rho}(\rho^{-1}u_t)\bigg|_{\rho=1} = \lambda_t.$$

This shows the interpretation of the λ_t as marginal utilities, beside the interpretation of the ϕ_t as utilities, in any solution of $S(\lambda, \phi)$.

FIGURE 7

Classical Utility Construction

solution λ_r, ϕ_r: $\lambda_r > 0$, $\lambda_r(u_r x_s - 1) \geq \phi_s - \phi_r$
supports $\phi_r(x) = \phi_r + \lambda_r(u_r x - 1)$, function $\phi(x) = \min\limits_r \phi_r(x)$
graph t = $\phi(x)$; catagraph t $\leq$ $\phi(x)$

contour at level t: the x with $\phi(x)$ = t

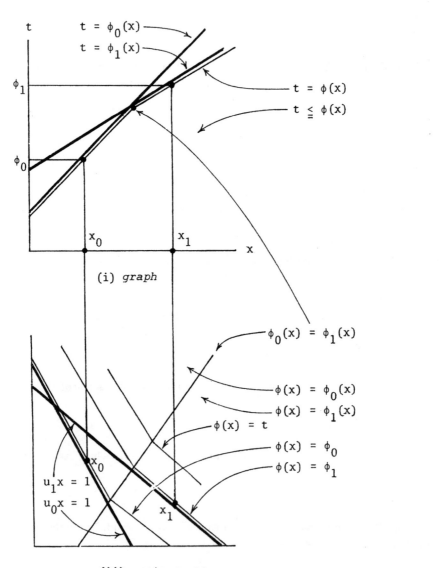

(i) *graph*

(ii) *contour map*

Now let $\phi(x)$ be any classical utility function compatible with the two demands. If ϕ_t is the value and g_t any support gradient at x_t, so

$$\phi(x) - \phi_t \leqq g_t(x - x_t),$$

then the compatibility condition

$$u_t x < 1 \quad \Rightarrow \quad \phi(x) \leqq \phi_t$$

is equivalent to

$$g_t \leqq \lambda_t u_t, \quad g_t x_t = \lambda_t, \quad \lambda_t > 0,$$

giving

$$\phi(x) - \phi_t \leqq \lambda_t(u_t x - 1).$$

With $x = x_s$, therefore

$$\phi_s - \phi_t \leqq \lambda_t D_{ts},$$

establishing the condition $S(\lambda, \phi)$, where the ϕ_t are the utility levels at ϕ_t, and the λ_t are the Lagrangian multipliers. This shows that these levels and multipliers constitute a multiplier-level solution as formerly defined. Earlier it appeared that any multiplier-level solution can be so expressed in relation to some compatible classical utility. Multiplier-level consistency S is thus identified with *classical consistency*, that is the possibility of simultaneous compatibility with some classical utility function. The condition C in Theorem 1.5 appears as a restricted form of classical consistency, relative to a function of the especially simple polyhedral type constructed under the condition S.

It has been concluded that various, and rather numerous, different forms of consistency condition which have been introduced for a pair of demands are in fact equivalent. The condition H has immediate intelligibility from usual terms of economic discussion, and K is of a type similar to the Houthakker condition in Samuelson's revealed preference approach to demand analysis. The others represent another departure, giving a technique for treating index questions as here and also more generally. But there is still another branch in the theory of consistency, treated next.

2 Revealed choice and preference

The importance of the demand data for the index problem is that they put a constraint on permitted utilities by the requirement of simultaneous compatibility. Consistency of the demands is the existence of such permitted utilities, and several equivalent expressions of it have been obtained, especially certain ones involving solution of linear inequalities. Further such expressions will now appear of a different type more connected with the "revealed" theory of Samuelson and general ideas about choice.

Given any demand (x, p), there is always the possibility though no necessity to view it as showing the choice of x from out of the set

$$S = [y : py \leqq px].$$

The possibility is simply because $x \in S$. The choice could instead have been, for example, that of $(-px, x)$ out of the set

$$T = [(-M, y) : M \geqq py],$$

or of any object a out of a set B where a and B are constructed from (x, p) so that $a \in B$. There is no necessity for associating (x, p) with the choice $(x; S)$, except that it happens to give language for translating an already existing theory without altering it in any way, though it might give a different way of thinking about it. A similar claim could be made for viewing (x, p) as showing the choice $[(-px, x)T]$. This in fact corresponds to a more general theory from which the $(x; S)$ theory results by imposing a limitation. But if there is resolution that (x, p) is to show the choice $(x; S)$, it can be declared by calling $(x; S)$ the *revealed choice* of the demand (x, p). Then there is the inevitable possibility, though again no necessity, of viewing any choice hypothetically as expressing preferences, by the relation of the chosen element to all the available elements. Thus the preferences in the choice $(x; S)$ are

$$(x, S) = [(x, y) : y \in S].$$

The preferences in the revealed choice of the demand can be called its *revealed preferences*. The term is usually arrived at immediately without any notice taken of the revealed choice. But if anything needs emphasis as peculiarly "revealed" it is the choice. For it is nothing new that any choice can freely be taken to show preferences, even if, to the extent knowable, it just happened and really might have nothing to do with preference (like the "best of all possible worlds" of Dr Pangloss, or the social optimum of economists—Dr Pangloss is on better ground, because it is the only world we have, and he is only pretending it is an element of recognized larger set and not really that there is a criterion available to him which settles a real issue, but economists with their model do not have the same reassuring vacuity but by abuse of language and persistent repetition, are making a serious and false innuendo).

If several given choices $(x_t; S_t)$ $(x_t \in S_t)$, are to be gathered as belonging to a single system of choice, this can be expressed by the presumption that the revealed preferences collected together, as in the set

$$[(x, y) : x = x_t, y \in S_t],$$

belong to the same hypothetical system of preferences. But a system of preferences is transitive, so also the transitive closure of the collection must then belong to the same hypothetical system. This gives the principle that the revealed preferences of a collection of choices form the order which is the transitive closure of the collection of their revealed preferences. Their would be nothing more to the matter, and no possible result to the exercise in hypothesis, were not some further "revelation" either slipped in or in any case brought into the matter.

This other component of revelation is that, beside a choice $(x; S)$ giving revealed preference (x, S), that is

$$[(x, y) : py \leq px],$$

it also gives *revealed non-preferences*. The hypothetically revealed non-preferences of Samuelson are

$$(S - x, x) = [(y, x) : py \leq px, y \neq x].$$

Here instead the revealed non-preferences will be fewer, and form the smaller set

$$[(y, x) : py < px].$$

It is from the conflict of hypothetically revealed preferences and non-preferences that contradictions can arise rejecting such hypothesis, and the exclusion of such contradictions gives consistency condition on the demands, identical with that considered formerly, which permits the hypothesis still to be entertained. Without the non-preferences there can be no contradictions and nothing more to be said one way or the other, and the "revealed preference approach" would be an empty ritual, just another ingredient in familiar economic metaphysics.

As with the revealed choice matter, this non-preference aspect of Samuelson's principle has been glossed over in the terminology and in the thought around it. But, by uncovering it, modifications such as the one adopted here and others suggest themselves and put the principle in a further perspective.

3 Preference–non-preference contradiction

Let relations $W, I, V \subset \Omega^n \times \Omega_n$ be defined by

$$xWu \equiv ux \leq 1, \quad xIu \equiv ux = 1, \quad xVu \equiv ux < 1,$$

and say the bundle x is *within, on* or *under* the budget u correspondingly.

Since $u_t x_t = 1$, so $x_t \in Wu_t$, $(x_t; Wu_t)$ is a choice determined by (x_t, u_t), defining the *revealed choice* of the demand. Then

$$R_t = (x_t, Wu_t)$$
$$= [(x_t, x) : xWu_t]$$
$$= [(x_t, x) : u_t x \leq 1]$$
$$= [(x_t, x) : p_t x \leq p_t x_t]$$

is the preference relation for the choice, defining the *revealed preference* relation of the demand. Then the revealed preference relation for the two demands simultaneously is the transitive closure

$$R_{01} = R_0 \overset{\cup}{\cup} R_1$$

of the union of their two revealed preference relations.

The *revealed non-preference* relation of demand t is

$$N_t = (Vu_t, x_t)$$
$$= [(x, x_t) : x Vu_t]$$
$$= [(x, x_t) : u_t x < 1]$$
$$= [x, x_t) : p_t x < p_t x_t].$$

For the two demands simultaneously, it is

$$N_{01} = N_0 \cup N_1.$$

The absence of *revealed contradictions*, that is of contradictions between revealed preference and revealed non-preferences, or the condition of revealed non-contradiction, requires

$$R_{01} \cap N_{01} = 0$$

or equivalently $R_{01} \subset \bar{N}_{01}$.

The relation R_{01} and N_{01} are, from their definitions, such that

$$x R_{01} y \iff (v_s, t = 0, 1) \quad x = x_s, \quad u_s x_t \leqq 1, \quad u_t y \leqq 1.$$
$$x N_{01} y \iff (v_t = 0, 1) \quad u_t x < 1, \quad y = x_t.$$

Thus the consistency condition $x R_{01} y \Rightarrow {\sim} x N_{01} y$ is equivalent to

$$u_s x_t \leqq 1, \quad u_t x_s \leqq 1 \Rightarrow u_t x_s \geqq 1$$

for all $s, t = 0, 1$. But this is equivalent to

$$u_0 x_1 \leqq 1, \quad u_1 x_0 \leqq 1 \Rightarrow u_0 x_1 = 1, \quad u_1 x_0 = 1,$$

which is the formerly considered condition K. Thus revealed consistency, as here introduced, is the same as all the consistencies which were formerly considered and shown to represent the same condition.

Had the revealed non-preference relation been taken instead to be

$$N_t = (Wu_t - x_t, x_t)$$
$$= [(x, x_t) : u_t x \leqq 1, x \neq x_t],$$

the consistency condition obtained would have been

$$u_0 x_1 \leqq 1, \quad u_1 x_0 \leqq 1 \Rightarrow x_0 = x_1,$$

which is Samuelson's revealed preference condition K^*.

The conclusion obtained is explained in Theorem 3.1.

Theorem 3.1 *If*

$$R_t = (x_t, Wu_t), \quad N_t = (Vu_t, x_t) \quad (t = 0, 1)$$

and

$$R_{01} = R_0 \,\vec{\cup}\, R_1, \quad N_{01} = N_0 \cup N_1$$

then

$$R_{01} \cap N_{01} = 0 \iff K.$$

That is, the condition K is necessary and sufficient for the absence of revealed contradictions.

The revealed preference relation R_t of the demand t is such that

$$x R_t y \iff x = x_t, \quad u_t y \le 1.$$

Then the cost-efficacy condition

$$H_t'(R) \equiv u_t x \le 1 \implies x_t R x$$

which is part of the condition $H_t(R)$ for compatibility between demand t and any utility order R, can be restated as

$$R_t \subset R.$$

Hence the condition $H'(R)$ required by simultaneous compatibility is equivalent to

$$R_0 \cup R_1 \subset R.$$

But with R transitive this is equivalent to

$$R_{01} \subset R.$$

Thus

$$H'(R) \iff R_{01} \subset R.$$

Also, the cost-efficiency condition is

$$H''(R) \equiv u_t x < 1 \implies x \bar{R} x_t$$

and this can be restated $N_t \subset \bar{R}$. It follows that

$$H''(R) \iff N_{01} \subset R$$

and hence that

$$H(R) \iff R_{01} \subset R, \quad N_{01} \subset \bar{R}$$
$$\iff R_{01} \subset R \subset \bar{N}_{01}.$$

Since, from Theorem 3.1,

$$K \iff R_{01} \subset \bar{N}_{01} \iff R_{01} \subset R_{01} \subset \bar{N}_{01},$$

this shows that

$$K \iff H(R_{01}).$$

But immediately,

$$H(R_{01}) \implies H.$$

That the revealed preference relation of the demands itself be compatible with them simultaneously, and thus assure their consistency, can define their *revealed consistency*. Since it has been seen that also $H \implies K$, the following is now proved.

Theorem 3.2 $H \iff H(R_{01})$. *That is, there exists a utility order simultaneously compatible with the demands if and only if their revealed preference relation is one such order, in other words revealed consistency is equivalent to general consistency.*

4   Cost-efficiency and non-satiation

It can be said there is *revealed cost-inefficiency* in period t ($t = 0, 1$), relative to the demand observations in periods 0 and 1, if

$$x R_{01} x_t, \quad u_t x < 1 \quad \text{for some } x,$$

which is to say, if there exists some bundle which is revealed as good as the bundle purchased in the period but which, at the same prices, costs less. The denial of this possibility defines *revealed cost-efficiency*. This is the condition

$$x R_{01} x_t \implies u_t x \geq 1$$

which immediately is identical with $H''(R_{01})$. But it has been seen, since $H'(R)$ for any R is equivalent to $R_{01} \subset R$ and in any case $R_{01} \subset R_{01}$, that $H'(R_{01})$ holds unconditionally. Accordingly,

$$H(R_{01}) \iff H''(R_{01}).$$

Thus, Theorem 4.1 gives still another view of the consistency condition.

Theorem 4.1   *Revealed consistency is equivalent to revealed cost-efficiency.*

Yet another view is obtained as follows. If for some x, y

$$x R_{01} y, \quad x < y,$$

it can be said there is *revealed satiation* at x and *revealed oversatiation* at y. The denial of such a possibility, defining *revealed non-satiation*, is stated by

$$x R_{01} y \implies x \not< y$$

or by

$$R_{01} \subset \bar{\bar{\oslash}}$$

Theorem 4.2 $R_{01} \subset \bar{\bar{\oslash}} \Leftrightarrow K$.

Since K has already been established as one of the many statements of consistency, this shows that revealed non-satiation is yet another.

Suppose the contrary of the left side. This is equivalent to

$$x_t R_{01} x, \quad x_t < x$$

for some t, x and then to

$$u_t x_s \leqq 1, \quad u_s x \leqq 1, \quad x_t < x$$

for some s, t, x. But since $u_s \geq 0$, so

$$x_t < x \implies u_s x_t < u_s x,$$

this implies

$$u_t x_s \leqq 1, \quad u_s x_t < 1$$

for some s, t and this is contrary to K. Also there is the converse, since $u_s x_t < 1$ implies

$$u_s x \leqq 1, \quad x_t < x \quad \text{for some } x.$$

This proves the theorem.

It has already been seen, in Section 1, that general consistency H is equivalent to classical consistency C. Since a classical utility function is semi-increasing and therefore without satiation, a conclusion from this is that H is equivalent to non-satiation consistency T defined by

$$T \equiv H(R), \quad R \subset \bar{\bar{\oslash}} \quad \text{for some } R.$$

But from here there is a more specific conclusion

$$H \Leftrightarrow H(R_{01})$$
$$\Leftrightarrow R_{01} \subset \bar{\bar{\oslash}}$$
$$\Leftrightarrow H(R_{01}), R_{01} \subset \bar{\bar{\oslash}}$$
$$\Rightarrow T$$
$$\Rightarrow H.$$

5   Critical costs

Consider the critical cost functions $\hat{\rho}$, $\check{\rho}$ applied to the revealed preference relation R_{01}, and for $r, s = 0, 1$ the values

$$\hat{\rho}_{rs} = \hat{\rho}(u_r, x_s), \quad \check{\rho}_{rs} = \check{\rho}(u_r, x_s)$$

defining *revealed critical costs*. Thus, from the definitions of these functions and of the relation, they are

$$\hat{\rho}_{rs} = \inf[u_r x : x R_{01} x_s]$$
$$= \min[u_r x_t : x_t R_{01} x_s]$$
$$= \min[u_r x_t : u_t x_s \leq 1]$$

and

$$\check{\rho}_{rs} = \inf[u_r x : x_s \bar{R}_{01} x]$$
$$= \inf[u_r x : u_s x_t \leq 1 \Rightarrow u_t x > 1]$$
$$= \min[u_r x : u_s x_t \leq 1 \Rightarrow u_t x \geq 1].$$

Since $u_t x_t = 1$ it follows that

$$\hat{\rho}_{rs} \leq u_r x_s,$$

in particular,

$$\hat{\rho}_{rr} \leq 1,$$

and also

$$\check{\rho}_{rr} \geq 1.$$

Theorem 5.1 $\hat{\rho}_{rs} = u_r x_s$ $(r \neq s)$.

Thus, with $r \neq s$,

$$\hat{\rho}_{rs} = \min[u_r x_t : u_t x_s \leq 1],$$

so if $u_r x_s \leq 1$, so that the range of t is $\{r, s\}$, then

$$\hat{\rho}_{rs} = \min[u_r x_r, u_r x_s]$$
$$= \min[1, u_r x_s]$$
$$= u_r x_s$$

and if $u_r x_s > 1$, so that the range of t is just r, then

$$\hat{\rho}_{rs} = \min[u_r x_s] = u_r x_s.$$

Thus in any case $\hat{\rho}_{rs} = u_r x_s$.

Theorem 5.2 $K \Leftrightarrow \hat{\rho}_{rr} = u_r x_r$.

Thus,

$$\hat{\rho}_{rr} = \min[u_r x_t : u_t x_r \leq 1],$$

so if $u_r x_s > 1 \ (s \neq r)$ then

$$\hat{\rho}_{rr} = \min[u_r x_r] = u_r x_r.$$

Also if $u_s x_r \leq 1$ then

$$\hat{\rho}_{rr} = \min[u_r x_r, u_r x_s],$$

in which case

$$\hat{\rho}_{rr} = u_r x_r \Leftrightarrow u_r x_s \geq 1.$$

Thus

$$u_s x_r \leq 1 \implies u_r x_s \geq 1$$

if and only if

$$\hat{\rho}_{rr} = u_r x_r.$$

But the first condition is equivalent to K.

Corollary $K \Leftrightarrow \hat{\rho}_{rs} = u_r x_s$.

This follows by combination with Theorem 5.1.
The present theorem gives a connection with Theorem 4.1. For

$$H_t''(R_{01}) \Leftrightarrow x R_{01} x_t \implies u_t x \geq 1$$
$$\Leftrightarrow \inf[u_t x : x R_{01} x_t] \geq 1$$
$$\Leftrightarrow \hat{\rho}_{tt} \geq 1,$$

and it has already been remarked that $\hat{\rho}_{tt} \leq 1$, unconditionally. Hence

$$H''(R_{01}) \Leftrightarrow \hat{\rho}_{tt} = 1$$
$$\Leftrightarrow K \text{ (Theorem 5.2)}$$
$$\Leftrightarrow H \text{ (Theorem 1.5)}$$
$$\Leftrightarrow H(R_{01}) \text{(Theorem 3.2)}$$

Theorem 5.3 $\check{\rho}_{rr} \leq \hat{\rho}_{rr} \Rightarrow K \Rightarrow \check{\rho}_{rs} \leq \hat{\rho}_{rs}.$

Thus, K implies

$$u_{sr} \leq 1 \Rightarrow u_r x_s \geq 1,$$

which implies

$$\check{\rho}_{rs} = \min[u_r x : u_s x_t \leq 1 \Rightarrow u_t x \geq 1]$$

$$\leq u_r x_s.$$

But, by Corollary of Theorem 5.2, K also implies $\hat{\rho}_{rs} = u_r x_s$. Thus K implies $\check{\rho}_{rs} \leq \hat{\rho}_{rs}$. Alternatively, K is equivalent to $R_{01} \subset \ominus$ by Theorem 4.2, and this implies $\check{\rho} \leq \hat{\rho}$, by the Theorem of Chapter I, Section 3. To prove the remaining part of the theorem, suppose K does not hold, say

$$u_s x_r \leq 1, \quad u_r x_s < 1.$$

Then

$$\hat{\rho}_{rr} = \min[u_r x_t : x_t R_{01} x_1]$$

$$= \min[u_r x_s, u_r x_r]$$

$$= u_r x_s < 1.$$

But then also

$$\check{\rho}_{rr} = \min[u_r x : u_r x_t \leq 1 \Rightarrow u_t x \geq 1]$$

$$= \min[u_r x : u_r x \geq 1, u_s x \geq 1]$$

$$\geq 1,$$

so $\hat{\rho}_{rr} < \check{\rho}_{rr}$, and the theorem is proved.

Alternatively, it is always the case that

$$\hat{\rho}_{rr} \leq 1 \leq \check{\rho}_{rr}.$$

But if K does not hold then, as just seen, $\hat{\rho}_{rr} < 1$ for some r, whence the required conclusion.

Concerning the general formula for $\check{\rho}_{rs}$ it should be noted that if $u_s x_r \leq 1$ it gives

$$\check{\rho}_{rs} = \min[u_r x : u_r x \geq 1, u_s x \geq 1]$$

and if $u_s x_r > 1$ it gives

$$\check{\rho}_{rs} = \min[u_r x : u_s x \geq 1].$$

But in the first case, if $u_s \leq u_r$, so that $u_s x \geq 1$ implies $u_r x \geq 1$, the second formula is again valid, and otherwise

$$\check{\rho}_{rs} = 1.$$

This shows the following.

Theorem 5.4   *If* $u_s x_r > 1$ *or* $u_s \leqq u_r$ *then*

$$\check{\rho}_{rs} = \min[u_r x : u_s x \geqq 1]$$

and otherwise

$$\check{\rho}_{rs} = 1.$$

6   Revealed bounds and classical limits

With the critical cost function $\hat{\rho}, \check{\rho}$ now determined in respect to any utility order R, define

$$\hat{\rho}_{rs}(R) = \hat{\rho}(u_r, x_s), \quad \check{\rho}_{rs}(R) = \check{\rho}(u_r, x_s),$$

so

$$\hat{\rho}_{rs} = \hat{\rho}_{rs}(R_{10}), \quad \check{\rho}_{rs} = \check{\rho}_{rs}(R_{10}).$$

For any R which is complete and without satiation $\check{\rho} = \hat{\rho}$, so in that case both functions can be denoted ρ. In particular $\check{\rho}_{rs}(R) = \hat{\rho}_{rs}(R)$, and these are denoted $\rho_{rs}(R)$.

Theorem 6.1   *With* (x_t, u_t) $(u_t x_t = 1)$ *given for* $t = 0, 1$ *and*

$$\hat{\rho}_{rs} = u_r x_s, \quad \check{\rho}_{rs} = \min[u_r x : u_s x_t \leqq 1 \Rightarrow u_t x \geqq 1],$$

for any utility order R

$$H(R) \quad \Rightarrow \quad \check{\rho}_{rs} \leqq \check{\rho}_{rs}(R), \quad \hat{\rho}_{rs}(R) \leqq \hat{\rho}_{rs},$$

so if R is complete and without satiation

$$H(R) \quad \Rightarrow \quad \check{\rho}_{rs} \leqq \rho_{rs}(R) \leqq \hat{\rho}_{rs}.$$

This follows from Theorem 5.2, and from the Theorem in Chapter I, Section 3, Corollary (iii), since $H(R) \Rightarrow R_{01} \subset R$.

Theorem 6.2   *For any* $\lambda = (\lambda_0, \lambda_1)$, $\phi = (\phi_0, \phi_1)$ *let*

$$\phi_t(x) = \phi_t + \lambda_t(u_t x - 1)$$

and

$$\phi(x) = \min_t \phi_t(x).$$

Also let

$$\rho_{rs}(\lambda, \phi) = \rho_{rs}(R),$$

where R is the relation represented by the classical utility function $\phi(x)$ thus determined from λ, ϕ and let $S(\lambda, \phi)$ be the condition

$$\lambda_t > 0, \quad \lambda_s D_{st} \geqq \phi_t - \phi_s,$$

so this implies $H(R)$. Then the values of $\rho_{rs}(\lambda, \phi)$ for all λ, ϕ subject to $S(\lambda, \phi)$ cover all points of the closed interval with upper and lower limits given by the numbers $\hat{\rho}_{rs}, \check{\rho}_{rs}$ with the possible exception of the lower limit.

With $\phi(x)$ determined as stated,

$$\rho_{rs}(\lambda, \phi) = \min[u_r x : \phi(x) \geq \phi(x_s)].$$

But $S(\lambda, \phi)$ implies $\phi(x_s) = \phi_s$, so

$$\phi(x) \geq \phi(x_s) \quad \Leftrightarrow \quad \phi(x) \geq \phi_s$$
$$\Leftrightarrow \phi_t + \lambda_t(u_t x - 1) \geq \phi_s$$
$$\Leftrightarrow u_t x \geq 1 + \frac{\phi_s - \phi_t}{\lambda_t},$$

and hence

$$\rho_{rs}(\lambda, \phi) = \min\left[u_r x : u_t x \geq 1 + \frac{\phi_s - \phi_t}{\lambda_t}\right].$$

There is no alteration of the matter if there is restriction to solutions with $\lambda_s = 1$, $\phi_s = 0$. Then $S(\lambda, \phi)$ becomes equivalent to

$$\lambda_r > 0, \qquad u_s x_r - 1 \geq \phi_r \geq -\lambda_r(u_r x_s - 1),$$

and

$$\rho_{rs}(\lambda, \phi) = \min\left[u_r x : u_s x \geq 1, u_r x \geq 1 - \frac{\phi_r}{\lambda_r}\right].$$

First it will be shown that a solution λ, ϕ can be chosen to make $\rho_{rs}(\lambda, \phi) = u_r x_s$. Thus, if any solutions λ, ϕ exist, as they must under the condition K, λ_r must satisfy

$$u_s x_r - 1 \geq -\lambda_r(u_r x_s - 1).$$

Then it is permissible to take

$$\phi_r = -\lambda_r(u_r x_s - 1),$$

so

$$1 - \frac{\phi_r}{\lambda_r} = u_r x_s,$$

and

$$\rho_{rs}(\lambda, \phi) = \min[u_r x : u_s x \geq 1, u_r x \geq u_r x_s].$$

Immediately

$$\rho_{rs}(\lambda, \phi) \geq u_r x_s.$$

But because $u_s x_s = 1$ also

$$\rho_{rs}(\lambda, \phi) \leq u_r x_s.$$

Hence

$$\rho_{rs}(\lambda, \phi) = u_r x_s.$$

But by Corollary of Theorem 5.2, K implies

$$\hat{\rho}_{rs} = u_r x_s.$$

Thus

$$\rho_{rs}(\lambda, \phi) = \hat{\rho}_{rs}.$$

Now it will be shown that a solution λ, ϕ can be chosen to make $\rho_{rs}(\lambda, \phi)$ arbitrarily close to $\check{\rho}_{rs}$. Cases permitted by K will be distinguished as follows:

$$u_s x_r \leq 1, \quad u_r x_s \geq 1, \tag{1}$$

otherwise

$$u_s x_r > 1 \tag{2}$$

with subcases

$$u_r x_s \geq 1 \tag{2.1}$$

$$u_r x_s < 1. \tag{2.2}$$

In case (1) the formula for $\check{\rho}_{rs}$ gives

$$\check{\rho}_{rs} = \min[u_r x : u_r x \geq 1, u_s x \geq 1].$$

and in case (2) it gives

$$\check{\rho}_{rs} = \min[u_r x : u_s x \geq 1].$$

In case (1) it is permissible to take $\phi_r = u_s x_r - 1$ and λ_r arbitrarily large. As $\lambda_r \to \infty$, $\rho_{rs}(\lambda, \phi)$ is non-increasing and converges to $\check{\rho}_{rs}$. More specifically, if $u_s x_r = 1$ it is constant and identical with $\check{\rho}_{rs}$, and if $u_s x_r < 1$ its behaviour is the same as

$$\rho_{rs}(\varepsilon) = \min[u_r x : u_s x \geq 1, u_r x \geq 1 + \varepsilon]$$

for $\varepsilon > 0$, as $\varepsilon \to 0$. This if $(1 + \varepsilon)u_s \leq u$ for some $\varepsilon > 0$ then $\rho_{rs}(\varepsilon) = \check{\rho}_{rs}$ for this and all smaller ε, so the value $\check{\rho}_{rs}$ is certainly attained. Otherwise $\rho_{rs}(\varepsilon) = 1 + \varepsilon$ while $\check{\rho}_{rs} = 1$, so $\rho_{rs}(\varepsilon) > \check{\rho}_{rs}$, and the value $\check{\rho}_{rs}$ is approached only in the limit.

In case 2.1 it is permissible to take $\phi_r = u_s x_r - 1$ and arbitrary $\lambda_r > 0$. Then it is possible to choose λ_r so that $0 < \lambda_r \leq \phi_r$, making $1 - (\phi_r/\lambda_r) \leq 0$, so there is the reduction

$$\rho_{rs}(\lambda, \phi) = \min[u_r x : u_s x \geq 1],$$

because of redundancy of the second constraint. But in case 2, also $\check{\rho}_{rs}$ is given by this formula, showing that $\rho_{rs} = \check{\rho}_{rs}$.

In case 2.2 it is permissible to take ϕ_r as before and then any λ_r such that

$$0 < \lambda_r \leqq \min[\phi_r, \phi_r/(1 - u_r x_s)].$$

Then again, because the same constraint becomes redundant, the formula reduces as before and gives the same conclusion.

It remains to remark that the solutions under the condition $S(\lambda, \phi)$ form a convex, that is linearly connected, set and $\rho(\lambda, \phi)$ is a continuous function on this set, so its values form a connected set. But the only connected sets of real numbers are intervals.

Theorem 6.3   *The values of $\rho_{rs}(R)$ for all complete and non-satiated R subject to $H(R)$ describe all the points in the closed interval with upper and lower limits $\hat{\rho}_{rs}, \check{\rho}_{rs}$ with the possible exception of $\check{\rho}_{rs}$.*

This follows by combination of Theorems 6.1 and 6.2. Thus Theorem 6.1 shows the values must all lie within this interval. Then Theorem 6.2 shows that even with further classical restriction on R, all values in the interval can be attained except possibly the lower limit. The exception is possible only if $u_s x_r \leqq 1$ and there is no $\varepsilon > 0$ such that $(1 + \varepsilon)u_s \leqq u_r$.

FIGURE 8

Cost of Living Limits

limits of cost of 0-utility at 1-prices

for all compatible utilities

consistent cases

(i) $u_0 x_1 < 1$, $u_1 x_0 > 1$: (a) $u_1 \nleqslant u_0$ (b) $u_1 > u_0$

(ii) $u_0 x_1 > 1$, $u_1 x_0 > 1$

(iii) $u_1 x_0 < 1$, $u_0 x_1 > 1$

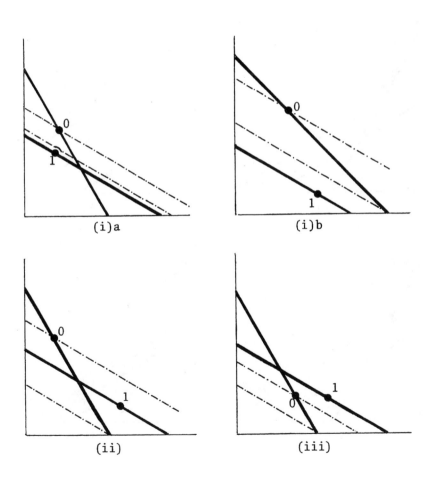

(i)a

(i)b

(ii)

(iii)

FIGURE 9

Utility for Upper Limits

limiting positions of 0-utility locus
for upper limits of cost of 0-utility at 1-prices
for all compatible utilities, cases as in figure 8

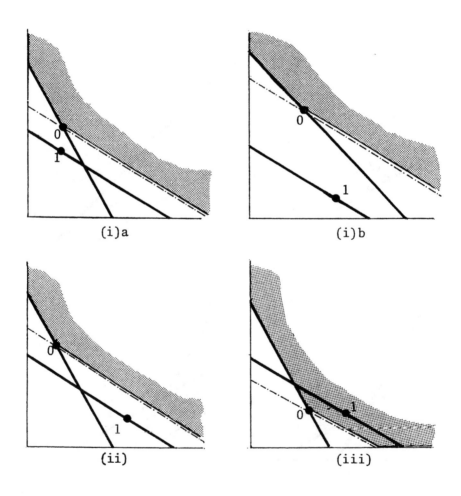

(i)a   (i)b

(ii)   (iii)

FIGURE 10

Utility for Lower Limits

limiting positions of 0-utility locus
for lower limits of cost of 0-utility at 1-prices
for all compatible utilities, cases as in figure 8

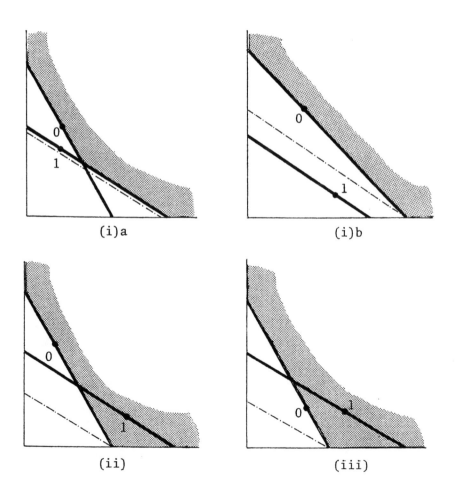

(i)a

(i)b

(ii)

(iii)

III The homogeneous problem
—Laspeyres and Paasche

Anywhere in economics, in everyday statistics or in volumes of theory, it is easy to meet price indices. They are introduced as such. But still, how could it be known if any identity happened to be a mistake, or how this should matter? No plain answer is given. But still, it is possible to make enquiries. Is 1.6 a price index? To some this is just a number. Then does it become a price index if it is called one? Perhaps. Then is any number a price index? At this point there is a stop and disengagement. But try again. Is $p_1 x_0 / p_0 x_0$ a price index? Yes, of course, that is the Laspeyres price index! But why is it a *price index*? . . . The story of this encounter is—though because of a scatter of formulae it has an air of better science—much the same as the previous one.

Irving Fisher lists (by my count) 126 price index formulae, which he describes, compares and classifies as a botanist might wild flowers. (Out of respect for the empirical it should be recorded that Dr Yrjo O. Vartia, of the Research Institute of the Finnish Economy, counts 145.) By "crossing", new price indices can be bred from others, some with especially desirable, even "ideal" properties, and their variety has no limit. But none was produced which met the "Tests" Fisher required for the "true" index; it can still be asked what would have been settled if one, or many, had been found.

The index-number-making which had a culmination with Irving Fisher still flourishes. But next to it is a theory which has become regarded as more modern, dealing with so-called 'constant utility' index numbers. These are index numbers derived on the assumption (which could be impossible with the data) that demand is governed by a utility function and, moreover, the function has some special form. Here there is a change. Formerly, it was as if an answer was proposed without first having had a question, and it was wondered if it could be an answer to a question, any question at all. Even, many answers to no question in particular were proposed—the names of their proposers are attached to some of them. Now a question comes first and the answer follows. It is easy, and even usual, to overlook a possible vacuity: the assumption which gives basis for the question asked of the data—for which an answer has been deduced on condition there is an answer—can be impossible with the data, so in fact there is no proper question and no answer. Nevertheless the order of question and answer is more natural—unless there never is notice whether one stands on clear ground or sinks in quagmires, as sometimes fits a well-conditioned economist. Byushgens, with his remark about Fisher's ideal index and homogeneous quadratic utility, the subject of Chapter IV, possibly initiated the 'constant-utility' approach to price indices; at least, he made a distinct contribution to it. The Cobb–Douglas utility function is similarly related to Palgrave's price index. The "New Formula" of Wald (1939), which involves quadratic utility, is a more general, direct descendant of Byushgens, as also is my related still more general Four-Point Formula, reported here in Part II. But these apply to the broader 'cost of living' problem, which was the concern in Chapter II and does not of necessity show anything about price indices. The Klein–Rubin cost of living index is related to Palgrave's price index in the same way that Wald's formula is related to Fisher's—or it would be were an account given of the parameter which appears in it as an indeterminate constant of integration.

Examples of the approach involving utility of a special algebraical form, and leading to an algebraical formula for an index in terms of the demand data alone, are so few as hardly to constitute an important general approach. Also, they are special in a way which is linked, on main appearances, more with accidents of algebra than with any central theoretical purpose. The example dealt with in Chapter IV, which involves quadratic utility, gives expression to the typical features of the approach. One feature which seems never to be noticed, but should nevertheless be recognized as outstanding, is that the basic hypothesis can be inadmissible on the data. The conclusion obtained with quadratics is striking enough and also unimportant enough not to be altogether spoilt by neglect of its possible vacuity. But, less satisfactorily, there has been neglect of the same matter for price indices generally, free of arbitrary restrictions on the form of utility and incorporating just the particular restriction which is characteristic of a price index as such. There is a remedy in my approach which involves solution of simultaneous inequalities instead of rational algebraical formulae.

A proposition which has been most central for the theory of price indices makes the Laspeyres and Paasche indices upper and lower 'limits' of the 'true index'. Two arguments offer this: one is well known from textbooks, and the other is familiar from Keynes. Then follows the so-called "theorem" that the Paasche index does not exceed that of Laspeyres. The inequality is not generally valid; rather, it is associated with a restrictive hypothesis, which needed to be excavated. The 'limits' are in the sense of bounds, not of best possible bounds for which there has yet been no argument. The meaning of 'true index' is, at least in the present context, still left loose; it can be allowed that the index either is unique, or capable of many, or even of no values; in any case, it describes a set of values, which must be a function of the pair of demands

$$(p_0, x_0), (p_1, x_1)$$

since everything has reference to these. The 'limits' proposition appears to say this set is bounded from above and below by the Laspeyres and Paasche indices. Should 'true index' be properly defined, the set should be describable better than this. There is even no assurance yet that it is ever non-empty. The description of the set is complete in at least one particular case: if the Paasche index exceeds that of Laspeyres it is empty; or, contrapositively, if a 'true index' exists then the Paasche index does not exceed the Laspeyres index. This last conclusion gives the form of a possible theorem, and it would be one were a definite meaning given to the hypothesis in it. And then there could be enquiry about the converse: if the Paasche index does not exceed the Laspeyres index then does a true index exist? The question is never asked. If no true index exists, still the 'limits' proposition, taught on limitless blackboards, does have that guarantee of veracity by which it is always permitted to say anything about nothing. But it could have a vacuity, and if this is to be avoided at least a 'true index' must be shown to exist. The possible values have been limited to lie somewhere between the Paasche and Laspeyres indices, that is on the closed interval with these as its lower and upper extremities. In the search for favourable candidates, it seems especially interesting to know whether either of the Paasche and Laspeyres indices themselves is a true index. For though they are always called price indices, it is not said why, or whether they are 'true' or not. These possibilities are extreme, and between them lies their geometric mean which is the Fisher ideal index. It has been said that this must be a "better approximation" to a true index than either extreme. No reason is given; nor can there be one before even the existence, let alone the actual identity, of what is being approximated is known.

An examination of familiar arguments for the 'limits' proposition will give evidences about the meaning of 'true index', and show hypotheses which produce first that proposition and then the usual Paasche–Laspeyres inequality.

In the textbook argument, or an approximation of it, an indifference curve is drawn through the point x_0 in such a way that it touches the budget line

$$p_0 x = p_0 x_0.$$

This signifies that there is consideration of some utility order R which is compatible with the demand (p_0, x_0). So, with

$$\rho(p, x) = \min\{py : yRx\}$$

as the associated utility-cost function, there is the condition

$$(0) \quad \rho(p_0, x_0) = p_0 x_0.$$

Thus R is constrained to represent $p_0 x_0$ as not merely the cost of x_0 but as the cost of the utility of x_0 at prices p_0. Then there is consideration of the cost $\rho(p_1, x_0)$ of the utility of x_0 at the prices p_1 and it is observed that

$$\rho(p_1, x_0) \leq p_1 x_0.$$

The observation usually is made by reference to the diagram, but all that is relevant is the reflexivity of R. For this assures that one way of purchasing the utility of x_0 is by purchasing x_0 itself, at the cost $p_1 x_0$ so the cost, that is the minimum cost $\rho(p_1, x_0)$, of purchasing that utility cannot exceed that cost. Then there is the conclusion

(10) $\rho(p_1, x_0)/\rho(p_0, x_0) \leq p_1 x_0 / p_0 x_0.$

Similarly, if R is constrained also by compatibility with the demand (p_1, x_1) so

(1) $\rho(p_1, x_1) = p_1 x_1,$

then, since in any case

$\rho(p_1, x_0) \leq p_1 x_0,$

there is the conclusion

(01) $\rho(p_0, x_1)/\rho(p_1, x_1) \leq p_0 x_1 / p_1 x_1$

Thus the *simultaneous compatibility* of R with the demands in the two periods 0 and 1 gives the conclusions (10) and (01). The argument is that $(0) \Rightarrow (10)$ and $(1) \Rightarrow (01)$, and hence

(0) & (1) $\Rightarrow$ (10) & (01).

That is as far as the argument can go without imposition of a further feature.

A statement of that needed further feature, usually without mention, is that R is supposed to be such as to make the proportion

$\rho(p_0, x) : \rho(p_1, x)$

independent of x; thus,

$\rho(p_1, x) = P_{10}\rho(p_0, x)$

and inversely

$\rho(p_0, x) = P_{01}\rho(p_1, x)$

P_{10} and P_{01} being independent of x and such that

$P_{10}P_{01} = 1.$

Here enters the idea of a price index P_{10} as giving the slope of a homogeneous linear relation

$M_1 = P_{10}M_0$

between incomes M_0, M_1 which at prices p_0, p_1 have the same purchasing power, that is, which purchase the same utility. In particular, with $x = x_0$,

$\rho(p_1, x_0)/\rho(p_0, x_0) = P_{10}$

and then with (10),

$$P_{10} \leq p_0 x_1 / p_0 x_0$$

Similarly

$$P_{01} \leq p_0 x_1 / p_1 x_1.$$

Then, because

$$P_{10} = P_{01}^{-1},$$

it follows that

$$p_1 x_1 / p_0 x_1 \leq P_{10} \leq p_1 x_0 / p_0 x_0.$$

The price index P_{10} thus has the Laspeyres and Paasche indices as upper and lower bounds.

The price index P_{10} is determined by the utility order R and the prices p_0, p_1. The condition on R which permits this determination, for arbitrary p_0 and p_1 is equivalent to the requirement that the utility–cost function admit the factorization into a product

$$\rho(p, x) = \theta(p)\phi(x),$$

of price and quantity functions. Then the price index, with 0 and 1 as base and current periods, is expressed as the ratio

$$P_{10} = P_1 / P_0$$

of 'price-levels'

$$P_0 = \theta(p_0), \quad P_1 = \theta(p_1).$$

Keynes had a different argument. It is assumed that any £ at prices p_0 purchases a bundle of good e_0 where $p_0 e_0 = 1$. Then £M_0 purchases M_0 of these, that is the bundle $e_0 M_0$. In other words, the expansion locus for prices p_0 is the ray through e_0, the demand with an income M_0 at these prices being the point $e_0 M_0$ on the ray. Similarly, any £ at prices p_1 purchases a bundle of goods e_1, where $p_1 e_1 = 1$, and £M_1 purchases the bundle $e_1 M_1$.

Let R be a utility order which is compatible with the given demands

$$(p_0, e_0 M_0), \quad (p_1, e_1 M_1)$$

for all M_0, M_1. In other words, R is compatible with the expansion loci for prices p_0, p_1 being rays through e_0, e_1. These rays could be specified by any points x_0, x_1

on them. Then

$$e_0 = x_0(p_0x_0)^{-1}, \quad e_1 = x_1(p_1x_1)^{-1};$$

so

$$p_1e_0 = p_1x_0/p_0x_0$$

is the Laspeyres index, with 0 and 1 as base and current periods, and

$$1/p_0e_1 = p_1x_1/p_0x_1$$

is the Paasche index.

Consider incomes M_0, M_1 which are decided by R to have the same purchasing power at prices p_0, p_1. Since, governed by R, the incomes purchase the bundles e_0M_0, e_1M_1 the condition is that these bundles be decided indifferent by R. Should

$$p_1e_0M_0 < M_1$$

it would follow (by 'revealed preference') that e_1M_1 is superior to e_0M_0, and not indifferent; so this is impossible. Hence

$$M_1/M_0 \le p_1e_0$$

and similarly

$$M_0/M_1 \le p_0e_1$$

giving

$$1/p_0e_1 \le M_1/M_0 \le p_1e_0$$

equivalently

$$p_1x_1/p_0x_1 \le M_1/M_0 \le p_1x_0/p_0x_0$$

where x_0, x_1 are any points on the rays through e_0, e_1.

The conclusions of the two arguments are different, and so are the assumptions. Keynes remarked his argument to be "more rigorous", but both, when all that is thought or half-thought is said, are certainly simple and rigorous. However, while the textbook argument explicitly deals with a utility order with the restrictive property which immediately permits definition of a price index, Keynes' argument does not. This makes the textbook argument more directly to the point, though both arguments have been inarticulate about that point.

In both arguments the utility order which is to be the criterion for purchasing power is restricted to have simultaneous compatibility with the given pair of demands for periods 0, 1. But each requires a different additional restriction. With one, the price index makes an immediate appearance as the ratio, which is fixed by assumption, between incomes in the two periods which have the same purchasing power. With the other, expansion loci in the two periods are assumed to be rays from the origin in the commodity space, and there is no explicit entry of the idea of a price index. The conclusion in the first argument is that the price index is bounded by the Paasche and Laspeyres indices, and of the second it is that the ratio of equivalent incomes is bounded in the same way.

The conclusion of the first, from the definition of the price index, implies that of the second. That of the second should there be a price index would imply that of the first. But the second argument tells nothing of there being a price index. There is a proper difference between the two arguments. But either gives the conclusion that if a utility order exists subject to the restrictions required in it then the Paasche index does not exceed the Laspeyres index. This conclusion, familiar as the index number "Theorem", can be stated $P \leq L$. Let the two hypotheses which have been seen to give this be denoted H_I, H_{II}; so

$$H_I \implies P \leq L, \quad H_{II} \implies P \leq L.$$

Consider a utility order R with the property

$$xRy \implies x\lambda Ry\lambda \quad (\lambda \geq 0),$$

by which it is homogeneous, or conical. For such an order it is immediate and elementary that the relation between equivalent incomes, at different prices, is described by a price index; that is, it is homogeneous linear; and also all expansion paths are rays. Thus the requirement that R be such a type of relation strengthens both of restrictions on R which appear in the two arguments as additional to the requirement of simultaneous compatibility with the given pair of demands. Let H_0 assert the existence of such a homogeneous R which is simultaneously compatible with the demands, defining their *homogeneous consistency*, so now

$$H_0 \implies H_I, \quad H_0 \implies H_{II}.$$

It is shown, in this chapter, that

$$H_0 \iff P \leq L,$$

and with this it follows here that

$$H_0 \iff H_I \iff H_{II} \iff P \leq L.$$

Thus three properly different conditions on the pair of demands, each requiring the existence of a compatible utility order having one of three different properties, are seen to be equivalent to each other and to the usual inequality between the Laspeyres and Paasche indices. Here is one special context where three properly different properties for a utility order lose their difference, and there are others. For one instance—one which is tractable by differential calculus methods—if a utility order is considered which determines a continuously differentiable demand function then these three properties are equivalent.

But anyway, without dependence on such outside propositions, R in being conical satisfies simultaneously the additional restrictions of both arguments. It is a greater restriction than either, and therefore the set of 'true' indices associated with it, bounded between Paasche and Laspeyres, can only be the same or smaller than in the other two instances. But it is shown later in this chapter that the set exhausts the entire closed interval between those extremities. The other two sets, being the same or larger, and bounded in the same interval, can only coincide with it, and with that interval.

Any ambiguity about 'true index' from there, being now three different identifications shows no effect in the unambiguous result that the set of values is in any case identical with the Paasche–Laspeyres interval. The 'true' points are just the points in that interval and no others; and none is more true than another. There is no sense to a point in the interval being a better approximation to 'the true index' than others. There is no proper distinction of 'constant utility' indices, often claimed for some index or other as if it made them in some way special, since all these points have that distinction.

1 Conical utility and expansion loci

A utility relation being given by a set $R \subset \Omega^n \times \Omega^n$, in the Cartesian product of the commodity space Ω^n with itself, the case of *homogeneous utility* is when this set is a cone. With conical R, if any point (x, y) is included then so is every point $(x, y)\lambda = (x\lambda, y\lambda)$ ($\lambda \geq 0$) on the ray through it,

$$x, y \in R \;\; \Rightarrow \;\; (x, y)\lambda \in R \quad (\lambda \geq 0).$$

With the notation $xRy \equiv (x, y) \in R$, this condition is

$$xRy \;\; \Rightarrow \;\; x\lambda Ry\lambda \quad (\lambda \geq 0).$$

Given any demand $(x, p) \in \Omega^n \times \Omega_n$ and utility relation $R \subset \Omega^n \times \Omega^n$, $H(R; x, p)$ is the assertion that R is an order (reflexive and transitive) compatible with the demand by the conditions

$$py \leq px \;\; \Rightarrow \;\; xRy, \qquad yRx \;\; \Rightarrow \;\; py \geq px.$$

From the definition of H,

$$H(R; x, p) \;\; \Rightarrow \;\; H(R; x, \lambda p) \quad (\lambda \geq 0).$$

Then with

$$E(R; p) = [x : H(R; x, p)]$$

defining the *expansion locus* of R for prices p, that is the locus of budles x, the demand of which at prices p is compatible with R, there is the property

$$E(R; p) = E(R; \lambda p) \quad (\lambda > 0).$$

FIGURE 11

The "Limits" Argument

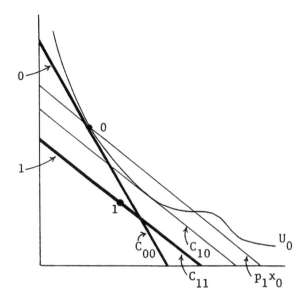

applying to demands for periods 0, 1
and any utility described by a utility-cost
function ρ

$p_0 x_0$ cost of 0-demand at 0-prices
$C_{00} = \rho(p_0, x_0)$ cost of 0-utility at 0-prices
$p_1 x_0$ cost of 0-demand at 1-prices
$C_{10} = \rho(p_1, x_0)$ cost of 0-utility at 1-prices

compatibility between 0-demand and utility
expressed by 0-cost line which simultaneously
touches 0-utility curve and passes through
0-demand point: $C_{00} = p_0 x_0$

in any case $C_{10} \leqq p_1 x_0$, so
$$C_{10}/C_{00} \leqq p_1 x_0 / p_0 x_0$$
and the same with 0, 1 interchanged gives
$$C_{01}/C_{11} \leqq p_0 x_1 / p_1 x_1$$

price-index introduced by the condition

$$\rho\,(p_1,\ x) = P_{10}\rho\,(p_0,\ x)\ \text{for all x}$$

in particular for $x = x_0,\ x_1$

$$C_{10} = P_{10}C_{00}, \quad C_{11} = P_{10}C_{01}$$

conclusion:

$$p_1x_1/p_0x_1 \lesseqgtr P_{10} \lesseqgtr p_1x_0/p_0x_0.$$

FIGURE 12

Keynes' "Method of Limits"

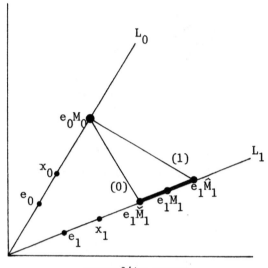

commodity space

$e_0,\ e_1$ bundles purchased by £1 at prices $p_0,\ p_1$ so

$$p_0e_0 = 1, \quad p_1e_1 = 1$$

$x_0,\ x_1$ arbitrary bundles purchased at prices $p_0,\ p_1$

$\hat{P}_{10} = p_1e_0$ Laspeyres, $\check{P}_{10} = 1/p_0e_1$ Paasche

for incomes $M_0,\ M_1$ with the same purchasing power

at prices $p_0,\ p_1$: $\check{P}_{10} \leq M_1/M_0 \leq \hat{P}_{10}$

FIGURE 13

The Paasche-Laspeyres Cone

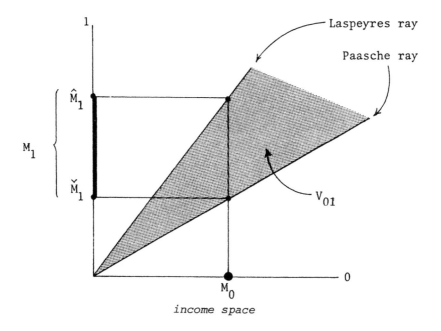

income space

M_0 any income at prices p_0

M_1 the equivalent income at prices p_1

indeterminate in the interval between

$$\hat{M}_1 = \hat{P}_{10}M_0, \quad \check{M}_1 = \check{P}_{10}M_0;$$

alternatively

$$M_1 = P_{10}M_0$$

where P_{10} is indeterminate in the interval

between $\hat{P}_{10}$, $\check{P}_{10}$; or again

$$(M_0, M_1) \in V_{01}$$

the graph of the correspondence being the

Paasche-Laspeyres cone V_{01}

Thus, the expansion locus depends only on the ray

$$\vec{p} = [\lambda p : \lambda \geq 0]$$

through p, and the same locus is obtained when p is replaced by any other point on the ray except 0. The *demand system* associated with R is

$$F(R; p, M) = [x : H(R; x, p), px = M]$$
$$= [x : x \in E(R; p), px = M],$$

and it has properties

$$x \in F(R; p, M) \ \Rightarrow \ px = M,$$
$$F(R; p, M) = F(R; \lambda p, \lambda M) \quad (\lambda > 0).$$

The effect of imposing the conical restriction on R is to obtain the property

$$H(R; x, p) \ \Rightarrow \ H(R; x\lambda, p) \quad (\lambda > 0),$$

not valid without it. Another statement is that the expansion loci $E(R; p)$ are conical, that is

$$x \in E(R; p) \ \Rightarrow \ x\lambda \in E(R; p) \quad (\lambda > 0);$$

or for the demand system

$$F(R; p, \lambda M) = \lambda F(R; p, M),$$

equivalently

$$F(R; \lambda^{-1} p, M) = \lambda F(R; p, M).$$

2   Homogeneous consistency

Demands (x_t, p_t) $(t = 0, 1)$ being given, let $\dot{H}(R)$ be the assertion that R is a utility order with which they are simultaneously compatible and moreover that R is conical. Then $\dot{H}$ asserts the existence of such R, or *homogeneous consistency* of the demands.

Let

$$\sigma_{rs} = p_r x_s / p_r x_r = u_r x_s$$

so $\sigma_{rr} = 1$. The condition on the two demands given by

$$\dot{K} \equiv p_0 x_1 p_1 x_0 \geq p_0 x_0 p_1 x_1$$

is then the same as

$$\sigma_{01} \sigma_{01} \geq 1.$$

A condition on any numbers $\phi = (\phi_0, \phi_1)$ is given by

$$\dot{S}(\phi) \equiv \phi_t > 0, \quad \sigma_{st} \geq \phi_t / \phi_s$$

and let S assert the existence of such ϕ.

For any ϕ_t $(t = 0, 1)$ let

$$\phi_t(x) = \phi_t p_t x / p_t x_t = \phi_t u_t x,$$

and let

$$\phi(x) = \min \phi_t(x).$$

The let $\dot{C}(\phi)$ assert simultaneous compatibility of the demands with the classical homogeneous utility represented by the function $\phi(x)$ thus constructed from $\phi = (\phi_0, \phi_1)$. Let $\dot{C}$ assert the existence of such ϕ so immediately $\dot{C} \Rightarrow \dot{H}$.

These conditions $\dot{H}$, $\dot{K}$, $\dot{S}$ and $\dot{C}$ can be readily be seen to be restrictions of the earlier defined H, K, S and C.

$$\dot{H} \;\Rightarrow\; H$$
$$\dot{K} \;\Rightarrow\; K$$
$$\dot{S}(\phi) \;\Leftrightarrow\; S(\phi, \phi), \quad \text{so } \dot{S} \Rightarrow S$$
$$\dot{C}(\phi) \;\Leftrightarrow\; C(\phi, \phi), \quad \text{so } \dot{C} \Rightarrow C.$$

Just as the earlier ones were proved equivalent, the same will appear for these.

Theorem 2.1 $\dot{H} \;\Rightarrow\; \dot{K}$.

Suppose $\dot{H}(R)$, that is

$$u_t x \leq 1 \;\Rightarrow\; x_t Rx, \qquad x Rx_t \;\Rightarrow\; u_t x \geq 1$$

for conical R. Then for $x = x_s t_s$ such that $u_t x_s t_s = 1$ it follows that $x_t Rx_s t_s$, equivalently $x_t t_s^{-1} Rx_s$ since R is conical, that is $x_t u_t x_s Rx_s$. Similarly $x_s Rx_t(u_s x_t)^{-1}$. Hence, by transitivity of R,

$$x_t u_t x_s Rx_t(u_s x_t)^{-1},$$

equivalently

$$x_t(u_t x_s)(u_s x_t) Rx_t.$$

But by $\dot{H}(R)$ this implies

$$u_t x_t(u_t x_s)(u_s x_t) \geq 1.$$

But $u_t x_t = 1$, so this gives

$$u_t x_s u_s x_t \geq 1,$$

that is $\dot{K}$.

Theorem 2.2 $\dot{K} \Rightarrow \dot{S}$.

Suppose $\dot{K}$, that is

$$u_0 x_1 u_1 x_0 \geqq 1.$$

Then

$$u_0 x_1 \geqq 1/u_1 x_0,$$

so there exists ϕ_1 such that

$$u_0 x_1 \geqq \phi_1 \geqq 1/u_1 x_0.$$

This with $\phi_0 = 1$ gives ϕ $(t = 0, 1)$ such that

$$u_s x_t \geqq \phi_t / \phi_s,$$

that is $\dot{S}(\phi)$, demonstrating $\dot{S}$.

Theorem 2.3 $\dot{s}(\phi) \Rightarrow \dot{C}(\phi)$.

For any ϕ_t let

$$\phi_t(x) = \phi_t u_t x,$$

and

$$\phi(x) = \min_t \phi_t(x),$$

so for all t

$$\phi(x) \leqq \phi_t(x)$$

and

$$\phi(x) = \phi_t(x) \quad \Leftrightarrow \quad \phi_t(x) \leqq \phi_s(x) \quad \text{for all } s.$$

Also

$$\phi_t(x_t) = \phi_t,$$

and so if $\phi_t > 0$

$$u_t x < 1 \Rightarrow \phi(x) \leqq \phi_t(x) < \phi_t$$
$$\Rightarrow \phi(x) < \phi_t.$$

Now if $\dot{S}(\phi)$, then

$$\phi_t(x_t) = \phi_t \leqq \phi_s u_s x_t = \phi_s(x_t),$$

and also

$$u_t x \leqq 1 \implies \phi(x) \leqq \phi_t,$$

and hence

$$\phi(x_t) = \phi_t.$$

Then also, since $\phi_t > 0$

$$u_t x < 1 \implies \phi(x) < \phi(x_t)$$
$$u_t x \leqq 1 \implies \phi(x) \leqq \phi(x_t).$$

This shows the utility is simultaneously compatible with the demands, that is $\dot{C}(\phi)$, as required.

Corollary $\dot{S} \implies \dot{C}$.

Theorem 2.4 $\dot{H} \iff \dot{K} \iff \dot{S} \iff \dot{C}$.

The Theorems 2.1–2.3 give

$$\dot{H} \implies \dot{K} \implies \dot{S} \implies \dot{C}.$$

But it is immediate from the definitions that $\dot{C} \implies \dot{H}$.

3   Revealed homogeneous preference

The revealed preference relation of demand t has been defined as

$$R_t = (x_t, Wu_t)$$
$$= [(x_t, x) : u_t x \leqq 1].$$

Now define the *revealed homogeneous preference relation* as the conical closure of this, that is

$$\dot{R}_t = [R_t \rho : \rho \geqq 0]$$
$$= [(x_t \rho, x\rho) : u_t x \rho \leqq \rho, \rho \geqq 0]$$
$$= [(x_t \rho, x) : u_t x \leqq \rho]$$

it being understood that $x \geq 0$. Thus

$$\dot{R}_t = [(x_t \rho, x) : u_t x \leqq \rho].$$

From this definition, $\dot{R}_t$ is conical and

$$R_t \subset \dot{R}_t.$$

For the cost-efficiency condition, required by compatibility between demand t and a utility R,

$$H'_t(R) \iff R_t \subset R.$$

Taking conical closures

$$R_t \subset R \implies \dot{R}_t \subset \dot{R}.$$

But if R is conical, so $\dot{R} = R$, since in any case $R_t \subset \dot{R}_t$, it follows that

$$\dot{R}_t \subset \dot{R} \implies R_t \subset \dot{R}_t \subset R.$$

Thus, with conical R

$$R_t \subset R \iff \dot{R}_t \subset \dot{R}.$$

Consequently,

$$\dot{H}'_t(R) \iff \dot{R}_t \subset R,$$

since $\dot{H}$ is H joined with the assertion that R is conical.

The revealed homogeneous preference relation of several demands is defined as the transitive closure of the union of their individual revealed homogeneous preference relations. Thus for the two given demands, their revealed homogeneous preference relation is

$$\dot{R}_{01} = \dot{R}_0 \vec{\cup} \dot{R}_1.$$

It is conical, and has the property

$$\dot{H}'(R) \iff \dot{R}_{01} \subset R.$$

With this it will be seen later that, besides

$$\dot{H}(R) \implies \dot{R}_{01} \subset R,$$

also

$$\dot{H} \iff \dot{H}(\dot{R}_{01}),$$

and these properties justify the definition of $\dot{R}_{01}$.

From the definition of $\dot{R}_t$,

$$x\dot{R}_t y \iff (v_t, \rho)x = x_t \rho, \quad u_t y \leqq \rho.$$

Then from the definition of $\dot{R}_{01}$, the cases of elements which have this relation are

$$x_0 \rho \dot{R}_{01} x_0 \sigma \iff (v_m)(u_0 x_1 u_1 x_0)^m \leqq \rho/\sigma,$$

and

$$x_0 \rho \dot{R}_{01} x_1 \sigma \iff (v_m)(u_0 x_1 u_1 x_0)^m u_0 x_1 \leqq \rho/\sigma.$$

Further

$$x_0 \rho \dot{R}_{01} x \iff (v_t, \sigma)x_0 \rho \dot{R}_{01} x_t \sigma, \quad u_t x \leqq \sigma.$$

Then to complete the description of $\dot{R}_{01}$,

$$x\dot{R}_{01} y \iff (v_t, \rho)x = x_t \rho, \quad x_t \rho \dot{R}_{01} y.$$

Theorem 3.1 $\dot{K} \Leftrightarrow \dot{R}_{01} \subset \bar{\bar{\ominus}}$.

Suppose

$$x\dot{R}_{01}y, \quad x < y$$

for some x, y or, equivalently,

$$x_t\rho\dot{R}_{01}y, \quad x_t\rho < y$$

for some t, ρ and y, or again

$$x_t\rho\dot{R}_{01}x_s\sigma, \quad u_sy \leqq \sigma, \quad x_t\rho < y$$

for some s, t, ρ, σ and y. If $s = t$ this is equivalent to

$$x_t\rho\dot{R}_{01}x_t\sigma, \quad \rho < \sigma$$

which implies

$$(v_m)(u_0x_1u_1x_0)^m \leqq \rho/\sigma < 1$$

which is impossible unless

$$u_0x_1u_1x_0 < 1$$

contradicting $\dot{K}$. In the case $s \neq t$, instead there is equivalence to

$$x_t\rho\dot{R}_{01}x_s\sigma, \quad u_sx_t\rho < \sigma,$$

which implies

$$(v_m)(u_0x_1u_1x_0)^mu_tx_s \leqq \rho/\sigma < 1/u_sx_t,$$

which again implies the contradiction of $\dot{K}$. This proves half the theorem. To prove the converse, now suppose $u_0x_1u_1x_0 < 1$, this being the denial of $\dot{K}$. Then

$$x_0\dot{R}_{01}x_1\sigma$$

where $\sigma = (u_0x_1u_1x_0)^{-1} > 1$. Then since $u_0x_0 = 1 < \sigma$, there exists $x > x_0$ such that $u_0x \leqq \sigma$. But then $x_0\dot{R}_{01}x$, giving a contradiction of $\dot{R}_{01} \subset \bar{\bar{\ominus}}$. The theorem is now proved.

Theorem 3.2 $\dot{H} \Leftrightarrow \dot{H}(\dot{R}_{01})$.

It suffices to see that

$$\dot{K} \Leftrightarrow x_s\rho\dot{R}_{01}x_t \Rightarrow u_tx_s\rho \geqq 1.$$

But this follows from

$$x_s\rho\dot{R}_{01}x_t \Leftrightarrow (v_m)(u_0x_1u_1x_0)^mu_sx_t \leqq \rho$$

$$x_s\rho\dot{R}_{01}x_s \Leftrightarrow (v_m)(u_0x_1u_1x_0)^m \leqq \rho.$$

4   Range of the price index

Consider any R such that $\dot{H}(R)$, so R is conical and simultaneously compatible with the demands (x_t, p_t). It is compatible also with any demand $(x_t\lambda, p_t)$ for $\lambda \geq 0$. The point $x_t\lambda$ on the ray through x_t corresponds to an income $M_t = p_t x_t \lambda$, so $x_t M_t / p_t x_t$ corresponds to the income M_t. Then the equivalent income at prices s is

$$M_s = \inf\,[p_s x : xRx_t M_t / p_t x_t]$$

$$= \frac{M_t}{p_t x_t}\inf[p_s x : xRx_t].$$

Thus

$$M_s / M_t = P_{st}(R)$$

where

$$P_{st}(R) = \frac{1}{p_t x_t}\inf[p_s x : xRx_t]$$

$$= \frac{p_s x_s}{p_t x_t}\inf[u_s x : xRx_t].$$

This is the price index between the periods as determined by the homogeneous utility R simultaneously compatible with the demands in them. It is required to determine its range for all complete and non-satiated such R. It is convenient to do this in terms of the critical cost functions, which in application to a conical relation will be denoted $\hat{\Pi}$, $\check{\Pi}$ and which for these R coincide in the function

$$\Pi_{st}(R) = \inf[u_s x : xRx_t],$$

from which the price index is determine as

$$P_{st}(R) = \frac{p_s x_s}{p_t x_t}\Pi_{st}(R).$$

The values

$$\hat{\Pi}_{st} = \hat{\Pi}_{st}(\dot{R}_{01}), \quad \check{\Pi}_{st} = \check{\Pi}_{st}(\dot{R}_{01})$$

when R is the revealed homogeneous preference relation $\dot{R}_{01}$ will be determined under the hypothesis $\dot{K}$. Since

$$\dot{K} \;\Leftrightarrow\; \dot{H} \;\Leftrightarrow\; \dot{H}(\dot{R}_{10})$$

and

$$\dot{H}(R) \;\Rightarrow\; \dot{R}_{01} \subset R,$$

it will follow, for R which is complete and non-satiated , so $\hat{\Pi}$, $\check{\Pi}$ coincide in Π, that

$$\dot{H}(R) \;\Rightarrow\; \check{\Pi}_{rs} \leq \Pi_{rs}(R) \leq \hat{\Pi}_{rs}.$$

5 Revealed bounds

Theorem 5.1 $\dot{K} \Leftrightarrow \hat{\Pi}_{rs} = u_r x_s, \; \bar{\dot{K}} \Leftrightarrow \hat{\Pi}_{rs} = 0.$

Thus,

$$\hat{\Pi}_{rs} = \inf[u_r x : x\dot{R}_{01} x_s]$$
$$= \inf[u_r x_t \rho : x_t \rho \dot{R}_{01} x_s]$$
$$= u_r x_s \inf[\rho : (v_m)(u_0 x_1 u_1 x_0)^m \leq \rho]$$
$$= u_r x_s \quad \text{if } u_0 x_1 u_1 x_0 \geq 0,$$

and otherwise the value is 0.

Theorem 5.2 $\dot{K} \Leftrightarrow \check{\Pi}_{rs} = 1/u_s x_r, \; \bar{\dot{K}} \Leftrightarrow \check{\Pi}_{rs} = \infty.$

Thus,

$$\check{\Pi}_{rs} = \inf[u_r x : x_s \bar{\dot{R}}_{01} x]$$
$$= \inf[u_r x : x_s \dot{R}_{01} x_t \rho \Rightarrow u_t x \geq \rho].$$

But

$$x_s \dot{R}_{01} x_s \rho \Leftrightarrow (v_m)(u_0 x_1 u_1 x_0)^m \leq 1/\rho$$
$$x_s \dot{R}_{01} x_r \rho \Leftrightarrow (v_m)(u_0 x_1 u_1 x_0)^m u_s x_r \leq 1/\rho$$

showing that if $\dot{K}$ does not hold then the value is ∞, and otherwise

$$\check{\Pi}_{rs} = \inf \left[u_r x : u_s x \geq 1, \quad u_r x \geq 1/u_s x_r \right].$$

From here immediately

$$\check{\Pi}_{rs} \geq 1/u_s x_r.$$

But also $x = x_r/u_s x_r$ is a feasible solution, showing that

$$\check{\Pi}_{rs} = u_r x = u_r x_r/u_s x_r = 1/u_s x_r.$$

Theorem 5.3 *For complete non-satiated R,*

$$\dot{H}(R) \Rightarrow 1/u_s x_r \leq \Pi_{rs}(R) \leq u_r x_s.$$

This follows from Theorems 5.1 and 5.2 together with the remarks at the end of the Section 4.

6   Classical limits

It is to be shown now that, even under further restriction on R that it be classical, the bounds shown in Theorem 5.3 are attained, so they are in fact limits, and also every value between these limits is attained.

Theorem 6.1   *For ϕ_t such that*

$$\phi_t > 0, \quad u_s x_t \geqq \phi_t / \phi_s$$

and

$$\phi_t x = \phi_t u_t x, \quad \phi(x) = \min_t \phi_t(x),$$

the range of

$$\Pi_{rs}(\phi) = \min[u_r x : \phi(x) \geqq \phi(x_s)]$$

is the closed interval with upper and lower limits $u_r x_s, 1 / u_s x_r$.

The conditions on ϕ_t assure that

$$\phi_s(x_s) = \phi_s \leqq \phi_t u_t x_s = \phi_t(x_s),$$

so that

$$\begin{aligned}
\phi(x_s) &= \min[\phi_s(x_s), \phi_t(x_s)] \\
&= \phi_s(x_s) \\
&= \phi_t.
\end{aligned}$$

Hence

$$\begin{aligned}
\Pi_{rs}(\phi) &= \min[u_r x : \phi(x) \geqq \phi_s] \\
&= \min[u_r x : \phi_s(x) \geqq \phi_s, \phi_r(x) \geqq \phi_s] \\
&= \min[u_r x : u_s x \geqq 1, u_r x \geqq \phi_s / \phi_r].
\end{aligned}$$

But if any such ϕ_t exist at all, for which the condition is $\dot{K}$, that is $u_r x_s u_s x_r \geqq 1$, then also it is possible to take

$$u_r x_s \geqq \phi_s / \phi_r \geqq 1 / u_s x_r$$

where

$$\phi_s / \phi_r = \theta / u_s x_r + (1 - \theta) u_r x_s$$

for $0 \leqq \theta \leqq 1$. Then

$$\Pi_{rs}(\phi) = \min\left[u_r x : u_s x \geqq 1, u_r x \geqq \theta / u_s x_r + (1 - \theta) u_r x_s\right].$$

From this immediately

$$\Pi_{rs}(\phi) \geqq \theta/u_s x_r + (1 - \theta)u_r x_s.$$

But also

$$x = x_r\theta/u_s x_r + x_s(1 - \theta)$$

is feasible and gives

$$u_r x = \theta/u_s x_r + (1 - \theta)u_r x_s,$$

showing that

$$\Pi_{rs}(\phi) = \theta/u_s x_r + (1 - \theta)u_r x_s.$$

This establishes that $\Pi_{rs}(\phi)$ takes the values $u_r x_s$ and $1/u_s x_r$, and every intermediate value.

Since the condition which the $\phi = (\phi_0, \phi_1)$ are subject to, is $S(\phi)$, and this implies the condition $C(\phi)$ that the polyhedral classical function $\phi(x)$ constructed from them represents a relation R such that $\dot{H}(R)$, there is the following.

Theorem 6.2   *The range of $\Pi_{rs}(R)$ for all complete non-satiated R such that $\dot{H}(R)$ is the closed interval with upper and lower limits $u_r x_s$ and $1/u_s x_r$.*

The proof follows from the Theorem 5.3 and Theorem 6.1, together with the remarks made at the beginning of the section.

Corollary   *The range of*

$$P_{rs} = \inf[p_r x : x R x_s]$$

for all complete non-satiated R such that $\dot{H}(R)$ is the closed interval with upper and lower limits given by the Laspeyres and Paasche indices

$$\hat{P}_{rs} = p_r x_s/p_s x_s, \quad \check{P}_{rs} = p_r x_r/p_s x_r.$$

IV Fisher and quadratics

For any pair of demands, a necessary and sufficient condition for the existence of a compatible homogeneous utility, and hence of a compatible (or 'true') price index, is the PL-*inequality*, which is that the Paasche index does not exceed that of Laspeyres. This is the condition for the PL-*interval*, or the set of points bounded above and below by the Laspeyres and Paasche indices, to be non-empty. A *compatible* price index being one determined in respect to some compatible homogeneous utility, its possible values are identical with the points of the PL-interval. When the interval is non-empty, the Fisher 'ideal' index is one of its points and therefore has this property of compatibility like any other. These are results coming directly from Chapter III.

Thus, whenever there exists any value at all which can be established as a price index on the basis of utility, the Fisher index provides one such value. But then *so also do all the points in the PL-interval*, these being the Paasche and Laspeyres indices themselves, together with every value between them. The Fisher index therefore is not uniquely distinguished by being derivable on the basis of utility, since it shares the distinction with all the points of the PL-interval. Also it has that distinction at all only when that interval is non-empty, which is to say when the PL-inequality holds.

S. S. Byushgens (1925) seemed to offer a special distinction for the Fisher index; at least, he showed what appeared to be a possible route leading towards this. Though the route was established, it was never travelled. The conclusion that the Fisher index is derivable on the basis of utility requires the existence of a quadratic utility compatible with the given demands, and this starting position was not even approached. Byushgens showed that if there were a compatible homogeneous quadratic utility, then the Fisher index would correspond to it. At the time a primary significance—which, with the foregoing results, has now evaporated—could have been that it seemed the 'ideal' formulae could become distinguished among the great variety of index formulae as being directly derivable on the basis of utility, making it more ideal than ever. That a specifically quadratic utility is involved then would have been a secondary part of the matter, though this is now the interest which remains. It had only seemed, the index might be thus derivable because, there was no notice that the hypothesis required might be impossible. The neglect does not diminish the nicety of the result that, if such a quadratic exists there is no need to actually identify it to find the index which derives from it: all that needs to be known is computed by the Fisher formula from the pair of demands with which it is required to be compatible. But still the existence question remains; it is not completely straightforward . . . .

That a homogeneous quadratic could be compatible with given demands is certainly true. We are quite accustomed to illustrating by the example with rectangular hyperbolae $x_1 x_2 = k$. This example falls under cases of both quadratic and Cobb–Douglas utility. It is safest to regard it as falling under the latter: any Cobb–Douglas looks like a good utility function, but not any quadratic. Here is a hint of the syndrome of unpleasantness in the quadratic existence question taken as it stands. But it will not be taken as it stands.

For the existence of any compatible homogeneous utility, the PL-inequality is necessary and sufficient. But required now is the existence of a utility with a restriction in addition to homogeneity. For this the PL-inequality must be necessary, but a sufficient condition could have to be stronger. If the additional restriction on utility is that it be quadratic, any sufficient condition does indeed have to be stronger, and it is in a way which is entirely without 'economic' significance or interest. Inspection shows this, and without an independent impulse for the effort there is no sense to investigate such a condition. However, a simple change in the quadratic requirement abolishes any unwanted intricacies.

Rather than asking for a utility which is quadratic, that is representable by a quadratic function, instead let the requirement be weaker and ask for a utility which is locally quadratic in the sense that it has a quadratic representation at least in the same neighbourhood containing the demand points x_0, x_1. With this definition there is a simple result: *the PL-inequality is both necessary and sufficient for the existence of a compatible locally quadratic utility.*

Byushgens' theorem remains true, and is enlarged, when the quadratic utility is replaced by one which is only locally quadratic. So now there is the theorem which enlarges this enlargement of it: for any pair of demands, *whenever compatible price indices exist, the Fisher index is one, and is distinguished as corresponding to a locally quadratic utility.*

A descendant of Byushgens' theorem, which inherits all its defects and adds to them from a more ample opportunity, is the "New Formula" of A. Wald (1939). Another relative is a formula of Afriat (1956) (referred to elsewhere here, and reproduced in Shubik (1968)), also not without a defect, which can still be remedied. But Wald's formula is so immediate a relative as to be a corollary.

Wald remarked that the expansion loci of a quadratic utility are lines. In fact, they break into linear parts which generally lie in linear manifolds. They lie in lines only when the quadratic is regular, having a unique centre, where the gradient vanishes and where the expansion lines are all concurrent, and are terminated – they cannot be complete lines but at most half-lines, or segments where the half-lines cut the commodity space.

Wald took a pair of expansion lines L_0, L_1 and associated prices p_0, p_1 to be given, and considered the hypothesis that they belonged to a quadratic utility. But if the lines are meant to contain complete expansion loci of a quadratic, the quadratic must be regular, and hence, for consistency with the hypothesis, the lines must intersect. Let c be their intersection, so with this, the lines are specified by any other points x_0, x_1 on them. Then the quadratic in x becomes a homogeneous quadratic in $z = x - c$, when the origin in the commodity space is changed to c. Also, a budget constraint $p_0 x = M_0$ is equivalent to

$$p_0(x - c) = M_0 - p_0 c_0$$

and becomes

$$p_0 z = N_0$$

with the change of origin, where

$$N_0 = M_0 - p_0 c_0;$$

the point x_0 on L_0 corresponds to $d_0 = x_0 - c_0$; the line L_0 becomes the ray through d_0; and similarly with 1 in place of 0.

Now to establish the equivalence of incomes M_0, M_1 with the general quadratic, it is as if incomes N_0, N_1 were to be equivalent for a homogeneous quadratic which is compatible with demands $(p_0, d_0), (p_1, d_1)$. For this equivalence, Byushgens' theorem applies to give the condition

$$N_1 = P_{10} N_0,$$

where

$$P_{10} = \sqrt{p_1 d_0 p_1 d_1 / p_0 d_0 p_0 d_1}. \tag{i}$$

Thus the relation between equivalent incomes M_0, M_1 is

$$M_1 - E_1 = P_{10}(M_0 - E_0) \tag{ii}$$

where

$$E_0 = p_0 c, \quad E_1 = p_1 c \tag{iii}$$

are the *income origins*. This, therefore, must be what Wald's "New Formula" asserts, in the case where the hypothesis is for a regular quadratic utility.

A similar, though more intricate argument applies to the case where the lines L_0, L_1 do not intersect, though now the hypothetical quadratic cannot be regular, and the lines cannot contain complete expansion loci of it, since these must be of higher dimension.

The lines generally have no common point c. Instead *critical points* c_0, c_1 are determined on them such that

$$p_0 c_0 = p_0 c_1, \quad p_1 c_0 = p_1 c_1. \tag{iv}$$

These exist and are unique provided

$$\begin{vmatrix} p_0 d_0 & p_0 d_1 \\ p_1 d_0 & p_1 d_1 \end{vmatrix} \neq 0. \tag{v}$$

Income origins are now determined from

$$E_0 = p_0 c_0, \quad E_1 = p_1 c_1. \tag{vi}$$

Just as well, giving the same values, they could be determined as before with a point c no longer the intersection of the lines, which no longer generally exists, but instead any point on the *critical transversal T* which is the join of c_0, c_1. This preserves precisely the form of the first derived formula. Should the lines intersect, the critical points coincide in their intersection, the critical transversal degenerates to this point, and the first formula is recovered from the second.

As formulae, these are nowhere visible in the dense uncouth algebra which originally made the "New Formula" of Wald. They should coincide with this simply because they have the same premise and are directed to the same question and so, one hopes, give the same answer.

The relation (ii) between incomes M_0, M_1 which, as decided by the hypothetical quadratic, have the same purchasing power at prices p_0, p_1 is a general linear relation, with slope P_{10} given by (i) and defining the *incremental price index*. It shows a departure from the price-index idea, which requires a homogeneous linear relation.

Should the lines L_0, L_1 be rays, that is lines through the origin, then the

$$c_0 = c_1 = o \tag{vii}$$

so

$$E_0 = E_1 = 0 \quad \text{and} \quad d_0 = x_0, \; d_1 = x_1, \tag{viii}$$

and hence the equivalent income relation (ii) reduces to the homogeneous linear relation

$$M_1 = P_{10} M_0, \tag{ix}$$

where

$$P_{10} = \sqrt{p_1 x_0 p_1 x_1 / p_0 x_0 p_0 x_1}, \tag{x}$$

this being the Fisher price index, a function of the rays through the points x_0, x_1 rather than of the points themselves, these being arbitrary points on the lines L_0, L_1 which in the present case are rays.

The introduction of the critical points not only enables the statement, and the derivation, of Wald's formula to be simplified. It also gives the terms required in a criterion for the applicability of the "New Formula" and, generally, of any formula for purchasing power comparison between incomes M_0, M_1 on the basis of the given data. This applicability criterion first makes a distinction between *hyperbolic* and *elliptical* cases, by the conditions

$$p_0 d_0 p_1 d_1 < p_1 d_0 p_0 d_1 \quad \text{and} \quad p_0 d_0 p_1 d_1 > p_1 d_0 p_0 d_1.$$

Then incomes $M_0, M_1 > 0$ which are comparable in the hyperbolic case must satisfy

$$M_0 \geq E_0, \quad M_1 \geq E_1,$$

and those which are so in the elliptical case must satisfy

$$M_0 \leq E_0, \quad M_1 \leq E_1.$$

It appears from here that there can be no entertainment of quite arbitrary comparisons between incomes, but the ranges of incomes to enter into comparisons must be made specific in advance and then it can be decided whether they are permissible or not. Emphasizing this, there are instances where no incomes can enter into comparison at all, such as in the elliptical case with $E_0, E_1 \leq 0$. With homogeneity, when $E_0, E_1 = 0$ only in the hyperbolic case are any incomes comparable. The hyperbolic condition then reduces to

$$p_0 x_0 p_1 x_1 < p_0 x_1 p_1 x_0,$$

which relaxed to allow equality (the parabolic case) is simply the requirement that the Paasche index does not exceed that of Laspeyres. Here, therefore, is a further perspective on that already familiar requirement.

FIGURE 14

Critical Points and the Incremental Price Index

(p_0, L_0), (p_1, L_1) the given linear expansions

c_0, c_1 the critical points lying on L_0, L_1

such that $p_0 c_0 = p_0 c_1$, $p_1 c_0 = p_1 c_1$

T   the critical transversal, their join

$E_0 = p_0 c$, $E_1 = p_1 c$ the critical incomes

fixed for all   c   on   T

x_0, x_1 any other points on L_0, L_1

$d_0 = x_0 - c_0$, $d_1 = x_1 - c_1$ "incremental bundles"

specifying the directions of L_0, L_1

$\hat{P}_{10} = p_1 d_0 / p_0 d_0$, $\check{P}_1 = p_1 d_1 / p_0 d_1$, $\overline{P}_{10} = (\hat{P}_{10} \check{P}_{10})^{\frac{1}{2}}$

incremental price indices

the "incremental" counterparts of the

Laspeyres, Paasche and Fisher price indices

Income Purchasing Power

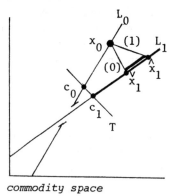

commodity space

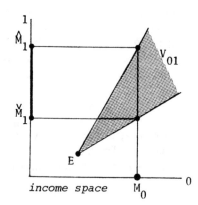

income space M_0

incomes M_0, M_1 which are
equivalent in purchasing power
as decided by any utility order
compatible with the given linear expansions
are in a correspondence $M_1 - E_1 = P_{10} (M_0 - E_0)$
the incremental price index P_{10} being
indeterminate in the interval $\underset{\smile}{P}_{10} \leq P_{10} \leq \overset{\frown}{P}_{10}$

Wald's "New Formula"

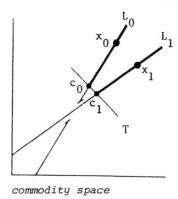

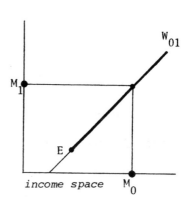

commodity space   income space M_0

Wald's "New Formula" is simply $P_{10} = \overline{P}_{10}$

Hyperbolic and Elliptical Cases

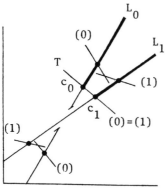

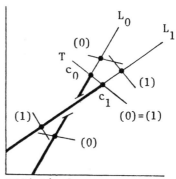

Hyperbolic
$p_0 d_1 p_1 d_0 > p_0 d_0 p_1 d_1$

Elliptical
$p_0 d_1 p_1 d_0 < p_0 d_0 p_1 d_1$

for compatibility with any utility order
the expansion lines must be truncated to
half-lines with the critical points as vertices
which halves are admitted being decided by
the case being hyperbolic or elliptical

$$p_0 x_0 p_1 x_1 < \text{ or } > p_0 x_1 p_1 x_0 .$$

consequently only restricted ranges of incomes M_0, M_1
can enter into purchasing power correspondence at all
in the hyperbolic case those with

$$M_0 \geq E_0, \ M_1 \geq E_1,$$

and in the elliptical case those with

$$M_0 \leq E_0, \ M_1 \leq E_1 .$$

omitted in this description is the non-central or
parabolic case

$$p_0 x_0 p_1 x_1 = p_0 x_1 p_1 x_0 .$$

(See Afriat, Karlsruhe Seminar, 1976.)

the illustrations here show the hyperbolic case with $E_0, E_1 > 0$.

1 Byushgens on Fisher

Robin Marris made a remark (see Preface) to the effect that Byushgens (1925) showed Fisher's index to be "exact" if utility is a homogeneous quadratic. Without having seen it, the following seems a likely content of the paper, based on the remark.

A homogeneous quadratic has the form

$$\phi(x) = \tfrac{1}{2}x'hx,$$

where h is a symmetric matrix, the Hessian of the function. The gradient is then

$$g(x) = x'h.$$

It has the property

$$g(x_0)x_1 = x_0'hx_1$$
$$= x_1'hx_0$$
$$= g(x_1)x_0,$$

since $h = h'$. Also

$$\phi(x) = \tfrac{1}{2}g(x)x.$$

Theorem 1.1 *If (x_0, p_0), (x_1, p_1) are a pair of demands which are simultaneously compatible with a homogeneous quadratic utility $\phi(x)$ then*

$$\phi(x_0) = \phi(x_1) \quad \Rightarrow \quad p_0x_0p_1x_0/p_0x_1p_1x_1 = 1$$

provided $x_0, x_1 > 0$.

Compatibility of $\phi(x)$ with (x_t, p_t) requires x_t to be a maximum of $\phi(x)$ subject to $p_t x = p_t x_t$, $x \geq 0$, and for this, with $x_t > 0$, it is necessary that

$$g(x_t) = \lambda_t p_t.$$

Compatibility also requires

$$p_t x < p_t x_t \quad \Rightarrow \quad \phi(x) < \phi(x_t)$$

and this implies $\lambda_t > 0$. Then

$$\lambda_0 p_0 x_1 = g(x_0)x_1$$
$$= g(x_1)x_0 = \lambda_1 p_1 x_0.$$

Also

$$\phi(x_t) = \tfrac{1}{2}g(x_t)x_t = \tfrac{1}{2}\lambda_t p_t x_t,$$

so $\phi(x_0) = \phi(x_1)$ is equivalent to

$$\lambda_0 p_0 x_0 = \lambda_1 p_1 x_1,$$

which with

$$\lambda_0 p_0 x_1 = \lambda_1 p_1 x_0$$

together with $\lambda_0, \lambda_1 \neq 0$ implies

$$p_0 x_0 / p_0 x_1 = p_1 x_1 / p_1 x_0.$$

Corollary (i)   *Under the same hypothesis, for any $t_0, t_1 > 0$,*

$$\phi(x_0 t_0) = \phi(x_1 t_1) \implies t_1^2/t_0^2 = p_0 x_0 p_1 x_0 / p_0 x_1 p_1 x_1.$$

For if the demand (x_r, p_r), is compatible with a given homogeneous quadratic then so is the demand $(x_r t_r, p_r)$ for all $t_r > 0$, so the required conclusion follows just by replacing x_r by $x_r t_r$ in the conclusion of the theorem.

Corollary (ii)   *Under the same hypothesis, if incomes M_0, M_1 are determined by $\phi(x)$ to have the same purchasing power at prices p_0, p_1 then*

$$M_1/M_0 = \bar{P}_{10}$$

where

$$\bar{P}_{10} = (p_1 x_0 p_1 x_1 / p_0 x_0 p_1 x_1)^{\frac{1}{2}},$$

this being Fisher's price index.

At prices p_r any income M_r purchases a bundle $x_r t_r$ where

$$p_r x_r t_r = M_r,$$

so

$$t_r = M_r / p_r x_r.$$

Then incomes M_0, M_1 have the same purchasing power at prices p_0, p_1 if $\phi(x_0 t_0) = \phi(x_1 t_1)$. By Corollary (i) this gives

$$(M_1 p_0 x_0 / M_0 p_1 x_1)^2 = p_0 x_0 p_1 x_0 / p_0 x_1 p_1 x_1,$$

as required.

The result about Fisher's index shown in Corollary (ii) is understood to be Byushgens Theorem.

2 Question about Byushgens

The Theorem is true even if no quadratic exists to validate the hypothesis, but in that case it makes a vacuous comment on Fisher's index. An interest arising from the theorem is therefore in the existence of such a quadratic.

The existence of a homogeneous quadratic utility simultaneously compatible with the demands can define their *homogeneous quadratic consistency*. From the definition, this condition implies homogeneous consistency, which has been seen equivalent to the "Index Number Theorem" condition

$$\check{P}_{10} \leq \hat{P}_{10}$$

between the Laspeyres and Paasche indices, which implies that moreover

$$\check{P}_{10} \leqq \bar{P}_{10} \leqq \hat{P}_{10}.$$

Thus for homogeneous quadratic consistency, certainly the Laspeyres–Paasche test is necessary. But since, at least on the homogeneous quadratic consistency is more restrictive than homogeneous consistency, for which this test is necessary and sufficient, it would appear that this test is not sufficient. Then it can be asked what additional test applied to the demands would give that sufficiency.

If the question is left as it is, the answer is not simple. It is better to modify the question. This can be done in a way which retains Byushgens' result, or rather amplifies it by removing an inessential part of the hypothesis, and then the answer is simple, and possibly surprising: *no additional test is required*.

Let *local compatibility* between a demand (x, p) and a utility order R signify compatibility which has reference to some neighbourhood of x instead of the entire commodity space. It requires the usual conditions

$$py \leqq px \ \Rightarrow \ xRy, \qquad yRx \ \Rightarrow \ py \geqq px$$

but for y near x, not for all $y \geq 0$. Everything, in Theorem 1.1 and Corollaries, remains valid when compatibility is replaced by local compatibility, or alternatively when instead of a homogeneous quadratic utility there is a homogeneous, or conical, utility relation R which near the points x_t admits representation by a quadratic. There might appear to be a difference between *homogeneous quadratic local consistency* defined by simultaneous local compatibility with some homogeneous quadratic, and *local homogeneous quadratic consistency*, defined by simultaneous compatibility with some utility with the required homogeneous quadratic local representation. But, it appears there is none.

The proposed modification makes a difference because, even when there exist no compatible homogeneous quadratics, there can exist locally compatible homogeneous quadratics, signifying that through homogeneous quadratic consistency implies homogeneous quadratic local consistency, the converse of this is not true.

While homogeneous quadratic local consistency readily implies homogeneous consistency, there could well be the surmise that the converse is not true, so there might be surprise that the converse is in fact true.

Reference to the more general problem with more than two demands gives an explanation which reduces any surprise. In this problem, the converse, as can be guessed, is not true, but there is the theorem that homogeneous quadratic local consistency is necessary and sufficient homogeneous consistency together with the Fisher cyclical test applied to the Fisher index

$$\bar{P}_{rs}\bar{P}_{st}\bar{P}_{tr} = 1.$$

The sufficiency part of this theorem is settled with some immediacy, and makes it sure that generally homogeneous consistency alone is not enough to give the required quadratic condition. But if there are just two demands, this additional condition needed is automatically satisfied, since it reduces to the Fisher reversal test $\bar{P}_{10}\bar{P}_{01} = 1$ which is automatically satisfied by the Fisher index. From this follows the corollary that, with just two demands, homogeneous consistency is necessary and sufficient for homogeneous quadratic local consistency.

The outstanding feature of Byushgens theorem on its own is that, without even constructing a quadratic, or even knowing if a suitable one exists, all that would be relevant about it is obtained from the given pair of demands just by the Fisher index. The "New Formula" of Wald (1939) is a generalization, and Afriat (1956) gives a different generalization, which is also a generalization of Wald, as was pointed out by Houthakker with the cryptic statement (*circa* 1960) that, twice two is four. When interpreted, this means that when the four demands used by Afriat have the price vectors equal in pairs and the corresponding pairs of quantity vectors are joined in lines, the two linear expansions used by Wald are obtained. It can be verified that with this specialization of the prices Afriat's interval-indeterminacy formula reduces to Wald's point-determination formula, and it can be added, when these lines pass through the origin there is reduction of Wald's formula to Fisher's formula.

3   Gradients and quadratics

Simultaneous local compatibility of demands (x_0, p_0), (x_1, p_1) and a utility $\phi(x)$ with gradient $g(x)$ requires

$$g_0 = \lambda_0 p_0, \quad g_1 = \lambda_1 p_1$$

for some $\lambda_0, \lambda_1 \neq 0$, where $g_0 = g(x_0)$, $g_1 = g(x_1)$. Then, for $\phi(x)$ to be a homogeneous quadratic, it is necessary that

$$g_0 x_1 = g_1 x_0,$$

that is,

$$\lambda_0 p_0 x_1 = \lambda_1 p_1 x_0.$$

But given any pair of demands, it is always possible to choose λ_0, λ_1 and to determine $g_0 = \lambda_0 p_0$, $g_1 = \lambda_1 p_1$ for which $g_0 x_1 = g_1 x_0$. It can be asked then if there exists a homogeneous quadratic for which $g(x_0) = g_0$, $g(x_1) = g_1$. It will appear now that this symmetry condition on the gradients is sufficient to obtain that existence, and also that such quadratics, though they then form an infinite variety, are essentially unique in the linear space spanned by x_0, x_1.

Theorem 3.1 *A necessary and sufficient condition that vectors g_0, g_1 be the gradients of some homogeneous quadratic at points x_0, x_1 is that*

$$g_0 x_1 = g_1 x_0, \tag{i}$$

provided

$$\begin{vmatrix} g_0 x_0 & g_0 x_1 \\ g_1 x_0 & g_1 x_1 \end{vmatrix} \neq 0. \tag{ii}$$

Then the values of all such quadratics at any point $x_0 \alpha_0 + x_1 \alpha_1$ in the space spanned by x_0, x_1 are the same, and equal to

$$\tfrac{1}{2}(\alpha_0 g_0 + \alpha_1 g_1)(x_0 \alpha_0 + x_1 \alpha_1). \tag{iii}$$

One such quadratic is

$$\Phi(x) = \tfrac{1}{2} x' H x \tag{iv}$$

where

$$H = G'(GX)^{-1}G$$

and

$$X = (x_0, x_1), \quad G = \begin{pmatrix} g_0 \\ g_1 \end{pmatrix}, \tag{v}$$

the matrix GX being symmetric by (i) and regular by (ii). This quadratic has the property

$$\Phi(x) = \Phi(ex) \tag{vi}$$

where

$$e = X(GX)^{-1}G \tag{vii}$$

is such that $e^2 = e$ and is the projector onto the space X spanned by x_0, x_1 parallel to the orthogonal complement of the space G spanned by g_0, g_1.

The necessity of (i) and the conclusion (iii) are immediate from general properties of a homogeneous quadratic.

The gradient of the quadratic $\Phi(x)$ given by (iv) is

$$G(x) = x'H.$$

It will be shown that

$$G(x_0) = g_0, \quad G(x_1) = g_1.$$

For any $\alpha = \begin{pmatrix} \alpha_0 \\ \alpha_1 \end{pmatrix}$, denote

$$x_\alpha = x_0\alpha_0 + x_1\alpha_1 = X\alpha,$$
$$g_\alpha = \alpha_0 g_0 + \alpha_1 g_1 = \alpha'G.$$

Then it suffices to show that

$$G(x_\alpha) = g_\alpha.$$

Thus, by (i) GX is symmetric, so

$$GX = (GX)' = X'G'.$$

and hence

$$G(x_\alpha) = x_\alpha'H$$
$$= \alpha'X'G'(GX)^{-1}G$$
$$= \alpha'GX(GX)^{-1}G$$
$$= \alpha'G$$
$$= g_{\alpha'}$$

as required.

It is immediate that e given by (vii) is idempotent, $e^2 = e$. Therefore, it is the projector onto its range R_e parallel its null space N_e. But

$$R_e = [x : x = ey]$$
$$= [x : x = X(GX)^{-1}Gy]$$
$$= [x : x = Xz] = X.$$

Thus $R_e \subset X$. But also

$$eX = X(GX)^{-1}GX$$
$$= X,$$

which shows that $X \subset R_e$. Hence $R_e = X$. Also

$$N_e = [x : ex = 0]$$

$$= [x : x(GX)^{-1}GX = 0]$$

$$\subset [x : Gx = 0] = \bar{G}$$

where $\bar{G}$ is the orthogonal complement of G. Thus $N_e \subset \bar{G}$. But R_e is of dimension 2, so N_e is of dimension $n - 2$, and $\bar{G}$ has the same dimension since G is of dimension 2. But a linear space has no proper subspaces of equal dimension, so it follows that $N_e = \bar{G}$.

Finally, with GX symmetric, it is verified directly that $e'He = H$ and from this (vi) follows.

4   Conditions for compatibility

For a utility function $\phi(x)$, with gradient $g(x)$, to be compatible with a demand (x, p) $(px > 0)$, the condition

$$g(x) = \lambda p, \quad \lambda > 0$$

is necessary, and if the function is quasi-concave this is also sufficient. Since $p \geq 0$, this condition requires $g(x) \geq 0$. If the function is $\phi(x) = \frac{1}{2}x'hx$, so $g(x) = x'h$ and $\phi(x) = \frac{1}{2}g(x)x$, the condition gives

$$2\phi(x) = \lambda px,$$

so also $\phi(x) > 0$.

There is no possibility of the function being established as quasi-concave by showing it concave. For the condition, for ϕ to be concave is that the Hessian h be non-positive definite. But this means $\phi(x) \leq 0$ for all x, contradicting $\phi(x) > 0$. Also the possibility $\phi(x) \geq 0$ for all x is excluded, because this makes ϕ convex. Thus for ϕ to be quasi-concave is a region where it is positive, it must necessarily be an indefinite quadratic form, taking both positive and negative values.

With $\phi(x) > 0$, it is possible to introduce $f(x) = (\phi(x))^{\frac{1}{2}}$, and this has the property

$$f(xt) = f(x)t.$$

A function with this property is quasi-concave if and only if it is concave. Thus ϕ is quasi-concave in a region where it is positive if and only if the Hessian of f is non-positive definite there.

The gradient of f is

$$G = \frac{1}{2}\phi^{-\frac{1}{2}}g$$

and the Hessian is

$$H = -\tfrac{1}{4}\phi^{-\frac{3}{2}}g'g + \tfrac{1}{2}\phi^{-\frac{1}{2}}h$$
$$= \tfrac{1}{2}\phi^{-\frac{3}{2}}(\phi h - \tfrac{1}{2}g'g).$$

Then, since

$$2\phi(x) = g(x)x, \quad g(y) = y'h$$

it follows that

$$y'H(x)y \leq 0$$

if and only if

$$D(x, y) \leq 0,$$

where

$$D(x, y) = g(x)x\,g(y)y - g(x)y\,g(y)x$$
$$= \begin{vmatrix} g(x)x & g(x)y \\ g(y)x & g(y)y \end{vmatrix}$$
$$= \left| \begin{pmatrix} g(x) \\ g(y) \end{pmatrix} (x\ y) \right|.$$

With this condition, if it holds for a pair of points x, y then it holds for every pair of points in the linear space spanned by x, y. For let

$$z = x\lambda + y\mu, \quad z' = x\lambda' + y\mu'.$$

Then

$$D(z, z') = \Delta^2 D(x, y)$$

where

$$\Delta = \begin{vmatrix} \lambda & \lambda' \\ \mu & \mu' \end{vmatrix}.$$

Also, the value of ϕ at $z = x\lambda + y\mu$ is

$$\phi(z) = g(x)x\lambda^2 + 2g(x)y\lambda\mu + g(y)y\mu^2,$$

so $\phi(z) = 0$ for

$$\frac{\lambda}{\mu} = \frac{-g(x)y \pm \sqrt{-D(x, y)}}{g(x)x}.$$

If $D(x, y) < 0$, this determines two real values of λ/μ. Between these values $\phi(z)$ is positive and outside them it is negative, showing that the quadratic form is indefinite. In any case, if

$$\phi(x), \phi(y) > 0$$

and also

$$g(x)y = g(y)x \geqq 0$$

as is necessary if

$$g(x), g(y) \geq 0, \quad x, y \geqq 0,$$

then

$$\phi(z) > 0 \quad \text{for } (\lambda, \mu) \geqq 0.$$

These remarks lead to the following.

Theorem 4.1 *For a homogeneous quadratic ϕ with gradient g, if*

$$x_0, x_1 \geqq 0, \quad g(x_0), g(x_1) \geq 0, \quad \phi(x_0), \phi(x_1) > 0$$

and

$$D(x_0, x_1) = g(x_0)x_0 g(x_1)x_1 - g(x_0)x_1 g(x_1)x_0 \neq 0,$$

then a necessary and sufficient condition for ϕ to be quasi-concave in a convex neighbourhood of x_0, x_1 is that

$$D(x_0, x_1) < 0.$$

For if this condition holds then $D(y_0, y_1) \leq 0$ for all y_0, y_1 since it must hold for all y_0, y_1 near x_0, x_1 and therefore, as shown earlier, in the span of such y_0, y_1 and this span is the entire space. Also $\phi(x) > 0$ for $x \in \langle y_0, y_1 \rangle$ and y_0, y_1 near x_0, x_1 so there is a convex neighbourhood of x_0, x_1 where $\phi(x) > 0$. But $D(x, y) \leq 0$ for x in this neighbourhood and all y, which, as already shown, assures ϕ is quasi-concave in this neighbourhood. Thus the condition is sufficient, and the necessity comes directly from the earlier remarks.

Theorem 4.2 *If*

$$x_0, x_1 \geqq 0, \quad g_0, g_1 \geq 0, \quad g_0 x_0, g_1 x_1 > 0,$$

$$g_0 x_1 = g_1 x_0, \quad \text{and} \quad g_0 x_0 g_1 x_1 \neq g_0 x_1 g_1 x_0,$$

so GX is regular, where

$$X = (x_0, x_1), \quad G = (g_0, g_1),$$

and if also

$$H = G'(GX)^{-1}G,$$

then a necessary and sufficient condition for the homogeneous quadratic

$$\Phi = \tfrac{1}{2}x'Hx$$

to be quasi-concave in a convex neighbourhood containing x_0, x_1 is that

$$g_0 x_0 g_1 x_1 < g_0 x_1 g_1 x_0.$$

For, by Theorem 3.1,

$$G(x_0) = g_0, \quad G(x_1) = g_1$$

so Theorem 4.1 gives the required conclusion.

Since only locally quadratic homogeneous utilities are being dealt with, there is need to consider their homogeneous, though not necessarily quadratic, extensions from a neighbourhood to the entire commodity space.

Theorem 4.3 *Any classical conical utility $\phi_0(x)$ ($x \in N_0$) defined in a convex neighbourhood N_0 in the commodity space has a classical conical extension to the entire commodity space. There exists two such extensions $\check{\phi}(x)$, $\hat{\phi}(x)$ such that any function $\phi(x)$ is another if and only if it is classical conical and*

$$\check{\phi}(x) \leqq \phi(x) \leqq \hat{\phi}(x)$$

for all x.

Since ϕ_0 is conical, it can be taken without loss in generality that N_0 is a convex cone. Then $\phi_0(x)$ is characterized by the convex set in N_0 given by

$$M_0 = [x : \phi_0(x) \geq 1, x \in N_0],$$

since

$$\phi_0(x) = \max[t : \phi_0(x) \geq t] \quad (x \in N_0)$$
$$= \max[t : \phi_0(xt^{-1}) \geq 1]$$
$$= \max[t : xt^{-1} \in M_0].$$

Let $\phi(x)$ be any homogeneous classical function that extends the definition of $\phi_0(x)$ to the entire commodity space. Then it determines the set

$$M = [x : \phi(x) \geqq 1, x \in \Omega^n],$$

from which it is recovered by the formula

$$\phi(x) = \max[t : xt^{-1} \in M].$$

Then

$$\phi(x) = \phi_0(x) \quad (x \in N_0),$$

if and only if

$$M_0 = M \cap N_0.$$

For $\phi(x)$ to be a classical function, M must be a closed ortho-convex set. It contains M_0 and has intersection M_0 with N_0 if and only if it lies between the set $\check{M}$ which is the ortho-convex closure of M_0, that is the smallest ortho-convex set containing M_0, and the largest ortho-convex set $\hat{M}$ whose intersection with N_0 does not exceed M_0. The functions $\check{\phi}$, $\hat{\phi}$ are defined by these sets.

5 Theorem on quadratic consistency

Theorem 5.1 *For any demands* (x_0, p_0), (x_1, p_1) *such that*

$$p_0 x_0 p_1 x_1 \neq p_0 x_1 p_1 x_0,$$

a necessary and sufficient condition that there exists a homogeneous utility with which they are simultaneously compatible and which has a quadratic representation near x_0, x_1 *is that*

$$p_0 x_0 p_1 x_1 < p_0 x_1 p_1 x_0,$$

that is, the Laspeyres index is at least the Paasche index.

The necessity is already shown, since it has been shown that this is just the condition for homogeneous consistency, the existence of a compatible homogeneous utility, so it remains to prove the sufficiency.

Assuming the condition, so necessarily $p_0 x_1$, $p_1 x_0 > 0$, it is possible to choose $\lambda_0, \lambda_1 > 0$ so that

$$\lambda_0 p_0 x_1 = \lambda_1 p_1 x_0.$$

Then let

$$g_0 = \lambda_0 p_0, \quad g_1 = \lambda_1 p_1,$$
$$\phi_0 = \tfrac{1}{2}\lambda_0 p_0 x_0, \quad \phi_1 = \lambda_1 p_1 x_1$$

so

$$g_0, g_1 \geq 0, \quad \phi_0, \phi_1 > 0$$

and

$$g_0 x_1 = g_1 x_0,$$

and also

$$g_0 x_0 g_1 x_1 - g_0 x_1 g_1 x_0 = \lambda_0 \lambda_1 (p_0 x_0 p_1 x_1 - p_0 x_1 p_1 x_0) < 0.$$

Then with

$$G = \begin{pmatrix} g_0 \\ g_1 \end{pmatrix}, \quad X = (x_0, x_1), \quad H = G'(GX)^{-1}G,$$

the homogeneous quadratic

$$\phi(x) = \tfrac{1}{2} x' H x'$$

is as required for local compatibility, by Theorem 4.2, and then with Theorem 4.3 the proof is complete.

Appendix

I TOTAL AND INCREMENTAL INFLATION RATES
AND INFLATION BIAS*

In base and current periods $0, 1$ when prices are $p_0, p_1, \in \Omega_n$ a bundle of
consumption goods $x \in \Omega^n$ has costs $M_0 = p_0 x$, $M_1 = p_1 x$. Then it is associated
with a *Fleetwood point* $(M_0, M_1) \in \Omega \times \Omega$ and an *inflation rate* $R_{10} = M_1/M_0$.
To assure that consumption can be maintained undisturbed by the price change,
a household consuming x in the base-period, so the income is M_0, must have
an inflation adjustment with this rage, giving $M_1 = R_{10} M_0$ as current income.
Fleetwood showed this principle in 1707.

The original *inflation map* for a collection of households, from which further
maps will be derived, is the set of all Fleetwood points, one for each household.
It determines an average point $(\bar{M}_0, \bar{M}_1)$. Then $\bar{R}_{10} = \bar{M}_1/\bar{M}_0$ is the average
inflation rate, associated with the average consumption bundle and it is identical
with the *total inflation rate* associated with the total bundle for the collection.

The CPI is identical algebraically with the total inflation rate $\bar{R}_{10}$ determined
from a sample of households. As such it is an estimate of that rate for the population, or the "target group". An everyday use of the CPI is to apply this rate
uniformly to every income, as a social norm for inflation adjustments. In other
words it is used *as if* it were a price index which, by the meaning of the concept,
provides a homogeneous linear relation $M_1 = \bar{P}_{10} M_{10}$ between incomes which
at the different prices have the same purchasing power, the index being the slope.
According to the criterion given by the original inflation map, this procedure gives
a correct total inflation adjustment, because $\bar{M}_1 = \bar{R}_{10} \bar{M}_0$. But since every household has its own generally different inflation rate, the distribution of this total is
generally incorrect. However, a criterion of correctness which distinguished every
household is not wanted. The principle already implicit in both theory and practice
is that the norm for the inflation adjustment of an income should depend continuously on just the income. Let the population be stratified into, say, 2^k income

---

* Based on a paper presented with John Kuiper at the Third World Congress of the Econometric
Society, Toronto, 20–26 August 1975.

classes of equal size ($k = 0$ or 1 or ...). The number k describes the *degree* of stratification, obtained by repeated bisections. When these strata are suitably narrow or the degree is high, the inflation rates within any one, are in principle close to each other and represented statistically by the average inflation rate in it. The stratification determines a partition of the Fleetwood points in the original inflation map with 2^k classes, and correspondingly determine 2^k average Fleetwood points, say (M_0^i, M_1^i) ($i = 1, \ldots, 2^k$). Then $R_{10}^i = M_1^i/M_0^i$ is an estimate of the average (and total) inflation rate for the ith stratum. It specifies a correct total adjustment for each of the 2^k income strata.

Thus from the original inflation map with one point for each household is derived a map with one point for each of 2^k income strata. One such map for some k (e.g. $k = 1, 2, 3,$ or 4, giving $2, 4, 8,$ or 16 classes) in constructed as a *basic inflation map*, providing a basic criterion for correct distribution of inflation adjustments. Then from this map, by consolidating the strata in consecutive pairs into 2^{k-1} strata of twice the size, with the simple operation of replacing the corresponding pairs of Fleetwood points by their mid-point, the next coarser map of degree $k - 1$ is obtained. By repeating this process, finally the maps with stratifications 1 and 0 are derived. The last consists of a single point $(\bar{M}_0, \bar{M}_1)$, giving $\bar{R}_{01} = \bar{M}_1/\bar{M}_0$ as an estimate of the average (and total) inflation rate in the entire population, this being the same same as the CPI.

Considering the usual homogeneous procedure in which the CPI is used as a price index, for this to give the correct results as specified by the basic k-map the condition is

$$R_{10}^i = \bar{R}_{01} \quad \text{for all } i.$$

But this is just the conditions for all the points (M_0^i, M_1^i) in the basic k-map to lie on the same ray. Usually, on the contrary, there will be different inflation rates, R_{10}^i in all the strata $i = 1, \ldots, 2^k$, lying generally anywhere between the maximum and minimum of the price-ratios p_{1r}/p_{0r} ($r = 1, \ldots, n$) for the individual goods.

The series of maps $k, k - 1, \ldots, 0$ provide a series of decreasingly fine distribution criteria for the inflation adjustment of income. The last, the 0-criterion, specifies just the total. Next to that the 1-criterion specifies also how this total should be divided between the upper and lower halves, where incomes are above and below the median. The procedure with the CPI corresponds to adopting $M_1 = \bar{R}_{10}M_0$ as the relation between equivalent incomes. The graph is a ray in the Fleetwood space through the average point $(\bar{M}_0, \bar{M}_1)$. It can called the average price index or API-ray (it being understood that API = CPI = average inflation rate = total inflation rate). From this, and as already seen, it meets the 0-criterion. In fact any line through the average point $(\bar{M}_0, \bar{M}_1)$, that is any relation

$$M_1 - \bar{M}_1 = S_{10}(M_0 - \bar{M}_0)$$

will meet the 0-criterion about the total inflation adjustment. But there is *just one*, for a particular values of S_{10}, which moreover meets the 1-criterion about how the total is divided between upper and lower halves of the population. This is obtained by joining the two Fleetwood points in the 1-map, which are the average points for incomes above and below the median. It can be called the marginal price index or MPI-line. Its slope S_{10} defines the *incremental inflation rate* ($=$ MPI).

The sense of this is that if incomes are to be adjusted from the base period to the current period by a linear relations meeting criteria about the total inflation adjustment and about the division of this total between the upper and lower halves of the population, this is done by adjusting the total by the total inflation rate R_{10}, and adjusting the spacing of the incomes by the incremental inflation rate S_{10}.

From another point of view, these two rates two independent parameters for examining income distribution, taxation, and related norms or policies, and so also, when refinement are needed, are these rates which are associated with each class in any stratification. Of cardinal interest is the computed difference between the overall total and incremental inflation rates. The sign of this gives a distinction between *high bias* and *low bias inflation*. The ratio $B_{10} = S_{10}/R_{10}$ can define the *inflation bias index*. In the high bias case, the usual homogeneous procedure with CPI will have a bias in favour of low incomes and against high incomes, and vice versa in the opposite case. For many indexation purposes it is incremental rate alone which is relevant. In a similar way, inflation maps can be constructed with reference to other distinctions beside income class, such as regional, occupational, family characteristics, cities, and so forth.

I am indebted to Irene Spry whose objection to the ambiguous "marginal" instead of "incremental", influenced a change in terminology. The average and marginal price indices, API and MPI, have become the total and incremental inflation rates. An immediacy in the sense of the terms entering social and political interests comes from a remark of E. J. van Goudoever about the incremental rate: while the total rate affects the total level of incomes, the incremental rate affects the spacing between them, or the increments between the ranks. This change in terminology, and the reference to a basic inflation map as the origin for all construction, assists a release from the habit of thinking in terms of homogeneous price indices. Nevertheless, the API and MPI terminology fits in with a usage which is familiar in theory of the firm and has a counterpart in the theory and of index numbers. The scheme described embodies its own theory and requires no further conceptual explanation. But it can still be explained and elaborated further by being placed in a framework where price index and MPI appear as particular concepts and the API and MPI are constructed specifically as such.

FIGURE 15

Inflation Maps : Income Groups

Successive enlargements of information:

    (i)   the API (= CPI)

    (ii) community average Fleetwood point F

  (iii) first disaggregation, giving also the MPI

    (iv) second disaggregation

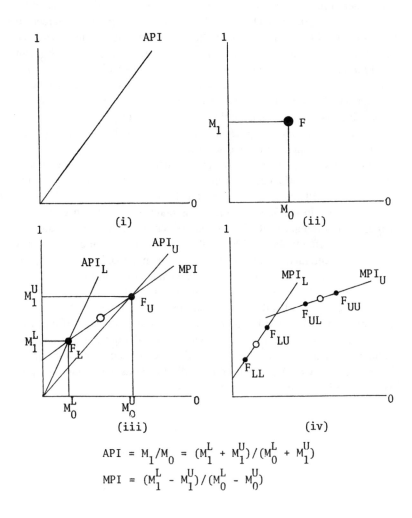

$$API = M_1/M_0 = (M_1^L + M_1^U)/(M_0^L + M_1^U)$$
$$MPI = (M_1^L - M_1^U)/(M_0^L - M_0^U)$$

II.   COMPUTATIONS : STATISTICS CANADA DATA

DATA:

(a)   Detailed average expenditures by 36 family income groups, covering entire income range, all Canada, urbanization classes, families and unattached individuals. 656 items including subtotals, 1969.

(b)   Consumer price indices for Canada, complete monthly series.   455 items, 1969 base.

COMPUTER:

IBM 360-65 at the University of Ottawa Computing Centre, using the MATOP package developed by John Kuiper (1974).

TABLES

INFLATION RATES, INCREMENTAL RATES

AND INFLATION BIAS

Tables for the entire expenditure range
for the following income stratifications:

I   *by approximate octiles*

II   "   "   *quartiles*

III   "   "   *median bisection*

IV   *overall*

comprising in each case tables for:

(a)   *total current consumption at the prices
in each year 1961-1974 for each income group
with 1969 standards*

(b)   *inflation rates across each year for
each income group*

(c)   *corresponding incremental rates*

(d)   *inflation bias*

NOTE

The *bias index,* in any income stratum, is given by

$$B = MPI/API .$$

The entries in the Tables (b) *and* (c) are

$$x = (API - 1)100 ,$$

$$y = (MPI - 1)100 ,$$

so

$$B = ((y/100) + 1)/((x/100) + 1)$$

$$= ((y/100) + 1)(1 - (x/100))$$

$$= ((y - x)/100) + 1$$

approximately, when x, y are small compared with 100. Thus, approximately,

$$(B - 1)100 = y - x,$$

and hence

$$z = (B - 1)100,$$

which is entered in Table (d), gives the approximation

$$z = y - x.$$

TABLE I

INCOME STRATIFICATION BY APPROXIMATE OCTILES

(a)   TOTAL CURRENT CONSUMPTION (1969 STANDARDS)

	GROUP 1	GROUP 2	GROUP 3	GROUP 4	GROUP 5	GROUP 6	GROUP 7	GROUP 8
1961	1795.43	2987.53	4059.16	4939.93	5686.79	6346.50	7313.85	9632.65
1962	1814.33	3017.99	4098.69	4986.89	5742.55	6409.93	7385.88	9731.86
1963	1841.08	3062.04	4157.46	5056.81	5825.37	6503.60	7494.59	9880.98
1964	1866.97	3107.99	4221.22	5134.25	5917.08	6609.34	7617.20	10047.16
1965	1904.25	3173.31	4312.69	5246.57	6047.87	6755.51	7783.87	10261.93
1966	1975.34	3292.10	4471.39	5436.00	6267.02	6999.31	8062.14	10622.20
1967	2036.10	3398.02	4617.84	5613.97	6474.76	7237.27	8341.71	11009.42
1968	2110.24	3520.19	4783.52	5814.49	6707.67	7500.46	8643.51	11416.05
1969	2197.58	3662.86	4975.28	6046.51	6977.67	7806.42	8993.83	11889.35
1970	2266.71	3775.00	5128.06	6234.00	7198.65	8056.87	9284.18	12287.14
1971	2325.79	3871.50	5262.15	6401.04	7397.80	8289.98	9552.64	12668.65
1972	2437.38	4050.62	5497.96	6685.95	7730.21	8663.55	9975.16	13230.22
1973	2627.88	4353.28	5891.58	7155.80	8275.86	9270.04	10657.20	14110.24
1974	2916.96	4832.20	6535.60	7932.41	9177.99	10278.21	11812.70	15631.40

(b)   INFLATION RATES

	GROUP 1	GROUP 2	GROUP 3	GROUP 4	GROUP 5	GROUP 6	GROUP 7	GROUP 8
1961-62	1.1	1.0	1.0	1.0	1.0	1.0	1.0	1.0
1962-63	1.5	1.5	1.4	1.4	1.4	1.5	1.5	1.5
1963-64	1.4	1.5	1.5	1.5	1.6	1.6	1.6	1.7
1964-65	2.0	2.1	2.2	2.2	2.2	2.2	2.2	2.1
1965-66	3.7	3.7	3.7	3.6	3.6	3.6	3.6	3.5
1966-67	3.1	3.2	3.3	3.3	3.3	3.4	3.5	3.6
1967-68	3.6	3.6	3.6	3.6	3.6	3.6	3.6	3.7
1968-69	4.1	4.1	4.0	4.0	4.0	4.1	4.1	4.1
1969-70	3.1	3.1	3.1	3.1	3.2	3.2	3.2	3.3
1970-71	2.6	2.6	2.6	2.7	2.8	2.9	2.9	3.1
1971-72	4.8	4.6	4.5	4.5	4.5	4.5	4.4	4.4
1972-73	7.8	7.5	7.2	7.0	7.1	7.0	6.8	6.7
1973-74	11.0	11.0	10.9	10.9	10.9	10.9	10.8	10.8

(c)   INCREMENTAL RATES

	GROUP 1	GROUP 2	GROUP 3	GROUP 4	GROUP 5	GROUP 6	GROUP 7	GROUP 8
1961-62	0.8	0.8	0.9	0.5	0.7	0.7	0.6	1.0
1962-63	1.2	1.4	1.2	1.2	1.3	1.3	1.2	1.6
1963-64	1.1	1.6	2.6	0.9	1.3	1.0	2.2	1.4
1964-65	2.1	2.3	2.6	1.4	1.9	1.5	2.1	1.8
1965-66	3.3	3.5	3.8	2.5	2.9	2.4	3.1	3.1
1966-67	3.1	3.7	3.4	3.5	3.7	3.7	4.1	4.0
1967-68	3.3	3.6	3.5	3.3	3.5	3.4	3.0	3.8
1968-69	3.9	3.7	3.7	3.8	3.7	3.5	3.5	4.2
1969-70	3.0	2.8	3.0	3.2	3.3	3.0	2.7	3.6
1970-71	2.9	2.4	1.9	2.9	3.2	3.2	2.3	3.8
1971-72	4.6	3.6	3.9	3.6	3.7	4.2	2.8	4.4
1972-73	7.3	5.9	7.2	4.9	5.3	5.8	4.6	5.8
1973-74	11.1	10.5	10.6	9.3	10.6	10.3	9.3	10.5

(d)   INFLATION BIAS

	GROUP 1	GROUP 2	GROUP 3	GROUP 4	GROUP 5	GROUP 6	GROUP 7	GROUP 8
1961-62	-0.2	-0.3	-0.1	-0.4	-0.3	-0.3	-0.3	0.0
1962-63	-0.3	-0.0	-0.2	-0.2	-0.1	-0.2	-0.2	0.1
1963-64	-0.3	0.1	1.1	-0.6	-0.3	-0.5	0.6	-0.1
1964-65	0.1	0.2	0.5	-0.7	-0.3	-0.6	-0.1	-0.4
1965-66	-0.4	-0.3	0.1	-1.1	-0.7	-1.3	-0.5	-0.6
1966-67	0.0	0.4	0.1	0.2	0.4	0.5	0.8	0.7
1967-68	-0.4	0.0	-0.1	-0.3	-0.1	-0.2	-0.6	0.2
1968-69	-0.3	-0.3	-0.3	-0.2	-0.4	-0.6	-0.5	0.2
1969-70	-0.1	-0.2	-0.1	0.1	0.1	-0.1	-0.4	0.4
1970-71	0.2	-0.2	-0.7	0.2	0.4	0.6	-0.4	1.1
1971-72	-0.2	-0.9	-0.5	-0.8	-0.7	-0.4	-1.5	-0.2
1972-73	-0.5	-1.4	0.0	-2.0	-1.7	-1.6	-2.3	-1.4
1973-74	0.1	-0.4	-0.3	-1.4	-0.2	-0.6	-1.4	-0.4

TABLE II

INCOME STRATIFICATION BY APPROXIMATE QUARTILES

(a) TOTAL CURRENT CONSUMPTION (1969 STANDARDS)

	GROUP 1	GROUP 2	GROUP 3	GROUP 4
1961	2442.37	4537.82	5986.02	8446.85
1962	2467.54	4581.38	6045.26	8532.15
1963	2503.68	4646.21	6133.00	8660.61
1964	2540.46	4717.41	6231.08	8804.51
1965	2592.95	4820.20	6368.84	8994.68
1966	2689.92	4995.61	6599.18	9313.02
1967	2775.19	5159.19	6820.63	9645.18
1968	2875.40	5343.80	7067.27	9998.21
1969	2992.76	5557.43	7353.58	10408.62
1970	3085.23	5729.08	7588.83	10751.46
1971	3164.63	5981.08	7802.48	11075.16
1972	3312.86	6143.57	8153.56	11565.62
1973	3564.23	6578.62	8726.81	12344.40
1974	3956.33	7294.69	9677.03	13678.56

(b) INFLATION RATES

	GROUP 1	GROUP 2	GROUP 3	GROUP 4
1961-62	1.0	1.0	1.0	1.0
1962-63	1.5	1.4	1.5	1.5
1963-64	1.5	1.5	1.6	1.7
1964-65	2.1	2.2	2.2	2.2
1965-66	3.7	3.6	3.6	3.5
1966-67	3.2	3.3	3.4	3.6
1967-68	3.6	3.6	3.6	3.7
1968-69	4.1	4.0	4.1	4.1
1969-70	3.1	3.1	3.2	3.3
1970-71	2.6	2.7	2.8	3.0
1971-72	4.7	4.5	4.5	4.4
1972-73	7.6	7.1	7.0	6.7
1973-74	11.0	10.9	10.9	10.8

(c) INCREMENTAL RATES

	GROUP 1	GROUP 2	GROUP 3	GROUP 4
1961-62	1.0	0.8	1.2	1.2
1962-63	1.4	1.3	1.6	1.7
1963-64	1.6	1.5	2.1	1.8
1964-65	2.3	2.3	2.2	2.0
1965-66	3.8	3.3	3.5	3.3
1966-67	3.4	3.3	4.1	4.2
1967-68	3.5	3.5	4.0	3.9
1968-69	3.9	3.9	4.5	4.4
1969-70	2.9	3.2	3.8	3.7
1970-71	2.5	3.0	3.7	3.8
1971-72	4.4	4.3	4.6	4.5
1972-73	7.0	6.4	6.5	6.1
1973-74	11.0	10.5	10.7	10.6

(d) INFLATION BIAS

	GROUP 1	GROUP 2	GROUP 3	GROUP 4
1961-62	-0.1	-0.1	0.2	0.2
1962-63	-0.0	-0.2	0.2	0.2
1963-64	0.2	-0.0	0.5	0.2
1964-65	0.2	0.1	0.0	-0.2
1965-66	0.0	-0.3	-0.1	-0.2
1966-67	0.3	-0.0	0.7	0.6
1967-68	-0.1	-0.1	0.3	0.3
1968-69	-0.2	-0.1	0.5	0.3
1969-70	-0.1	0.1	0.6	0.4
1970-71	-0.1	0.3	0.9	0.7
1971-72	-0.3	-0.1	0.1	0.0
1972-73	-0.6	-0.6	-0.5	-0.6
1973-74	0.0	-0.4	-0.2	-0.2

TABLE III

(a) APPROXIMATE MEDIAN INCOME STRATIFICATION

TOTAL CURRENT CONSUMPTION (1969 STANDARDS)

	GROUP 1	GROUP 2
1961	3442.28	7272.99
1962	3476.23	7345.87
1963	3526.06	7454.90
1964	3579.26	7576.94
1965	3655.76	7742.11
1966	3790.16	8018.47
1967	3912.80	8297.82
1968	4053.28	8600.10
1969	4216.59	8951.31
1970	4346.84	9242.84
1971	4460.88	9514.04
1972	4663.63	9938.01
1973	5002.65	10618.75
1974	5549.35	11769.77

(b) INFLATION RATES

	GROUP 1	GROUP 2
1961-62	1.0	1.0
1962-63	1.4	1.5
1963-64	1.5	1.6
1964-65	2.1	2.2
1965-66	3.7	3.6
1966-67	3.2	3.5
1967-68	3.6	3.6
1968-69	4.0	4.1
1969-70	3.1	3.3
1970-71	2.6	2.9
1971-72	4.5	4.5
1972-73	7.3	6.8
1973-74	10.9	10.8

(c) INCREMENTAL RATES

	GROUP 1	GROUP 2
1961-62	0.9	1.1
1962-63	1.4	1.6
1963-64	1.6	1.8
1964-65	2.3	2.0
1965-66	3.5	3.4
1966-67	3.4	4.1
1967-68	3.5	3.8
1968-69	3.9	4.2
1969-70	3.1	3.5
1970-71	2.7	3.5
1971-72	4.2	4.3
1972-73	6.5	6.0
1973-74	10.7	10.6

(d) INFLATION BIAS

	GROUP 1	GROUP 2
1961-62	-0.1	0.1
1962-63	-0.1	0.2
1963-64	0.1	0.2
1964-65	0.2	-0.1
1965-66	-0.1	-0.2
1966-67	0.2	0.6
1967-68	-0.0	0.1
1968-69	-0.1	0.1
1969-70	-0.0	0.3
1970-71	0.1	0.5
1971-72	-0.3	-0.2
1972-73	-0.7	-0.8
1973-74	-0.2	-0.2

TABLE IV

ALL INCOME GROUPS

(a) **TOTAL CURRENT CONSUMPTION (1969 STANDARDS)**

	TOTAL
1961	5277.91
1962	5330.51
1963	5408.71
1964	5494.90
1965	5613.89
1966	5816.31
1967	6014.05
1968	6232.06
1969	6485.41
1970	6692.94
1971	6882.29
1972	7191.05
1973	7693.81
1974	8530.09

(b) **INFLATION RATES**

	TOTAL
1961-62	1.0
1962-63	1.5
1963-64	1.6
1964-65	2.2
1965-66	3.6
1966-67	3.4
1967-68	3.6
1968-69	4.1
1969-70	3.2
1970-71	2.8
1971-72	4.5
1972-73	7.0
1973-74	10.9

(c) **INCREMENTAL RATES**

	TOTAL
1961-62	1.0
1962-63	1.5
1963-64	1.8
1964-65	2.2
1965-66	3.5
1966-67	3.7
1967-68	3.7
1968-69	4.1
1969-70	3.4
1970-71	3.2
1971-72	4.4
1972-73	6.5
1973-74	10.8

(d) **INFLATION BIAS**

	TOTAL
1961-62	0.0
1962-63	0.1
1963-64	0.2
1964-65	0.1
1965-66	-0.1
1966-67	0.3
1967-68	0.1
1968-69	0.1
1969-70	0.2
1970-71	0.4
1971-72	-0.1
1972-73	-0.5
1973-74	-0.1

Part II
The Cost of Living

I Price and quantity levels

The cost of a basket of goods x when the prices are p is the sum $px = \sum p_i x_i$, known by every shopper studying an account. There is no general possibility of expressing such as sum simply as a product PX, in effect, as if there were just one good, with quantity X and price P, P depending only on the prices of the goods and X on the quantities bought, say

$$P = e(p), \quad X = f(x).$$

Everyone should agree with that. But the possibility appears to be taken for granted whenever terms like price level or price index are used, as they are constantly in macroeconomic discussions, and everyday with regard to the CPI. It can be wondered what sense there should be to the phenomenon.

A price level must have role as a price, so applicable to a quantity, or level, such as the level or standard of living. If P is the price level then PX should be the cost of achieving the quantity level X. But many bundles x, any such that $f(x) \geq X$, achieve the level, and each of these has a cost px. Since any cost can be exceeded freely, cost has unambiguous sense only as minimum cost, and so this cost PX must be the cost of the cheapest bundle that achieves the level;

$$PX = \min[px : f(x) \geq X].$$

If this relation holds for all X, so that the expression on the right admits the factorization on the left, then the function f which determines quantity level has the homogeneity or constant returns to scale property

$$f(xt) = f(x)t, \quad \text{for all } t \geq 0.$$

Then the function e which determines price level is given by

$$e(p) = \min[px : f(x) \geq 1] = \min_x px/f(x)$$

Price and quantity levels (P, X) are associated with any demand (p, x), where $P = e(p)$ and $X = f(x)$. Then we have $PX \leq px$, since PX is the minimum cost of attaining the level X of x, while px is simply the cost of x and so at least this minimum; certainly x attains its own level, but there may be cheaper bundles that do also. Consequently the price and quantity functions e, f are such that

$$e(p)f(x) \le px \quad \text{for all } p, x.$$

Should the demand be cost-efficient, so that achieving the quantity level at a lesser cost is impossible, or no x' exists for which $f(x') \ge f(x)$ while $px' < px$, then, equivalently,

$$f(x') \ge f(x) \implies px' \ge px \quad \text{for all } x';$$

then also $PX \ge px$, and so now $PX = px$. Thus, an efficient demand (p, x) is distinguished as one that satisfies the condition

$$e(p)f(x) = px.$$

The function f which determines the quantity level, and with it the derived function e which determines price level, puts a constraint on the demand (p, x), if this is to be cost-efficient. Since the demand is, in principle, observable and the function hypothetical, it is suitable to put this relation the other way round and regard the demand as putting a constraint on the function. Then data of many demands will put many simultaneous constraints on the function to be allowed. An issue then is whether such a function exists at all, that is, whether the constraints are consistent. In the case where they are consistent, the functions admitted will be many, or there is an indeterminacy. Such indeterminacy produces an indeterminacy in any price and quantity levels. But the extent of this indeterminacy can be exactly determined.

1.1   Price–quantity duality

Let f be conical, having the property

$$f(xt) = f(x)t \quad (t \ge 0) \tag{i}$$

by which its graph is a cone. It could be a production function with constant returns to scale, meaning that, if the inputs x are doubled or scaled by any factor t, then so is the output; similarly, it could be a utility function.

For any input x the output is $f(x)$ and so the input for each unit of output, or unit input, is the vector $a(x) = x\{1/f(x)\}$, which by (i) has the property

$$a(xt) = a(x) \quad (t \ge 0) \tag{ii}$$

by which it is dependent only on the input proportions, and independent of the scale. If the input prices are p then the cost for each unit of output, or unit cost, is $pa(x) = px/f(x)$. This also depends only on the input proportions, and these can be chosen to make it minimum. The minimum value is a function e of p, the unit cost or price function associated with the production function f, given by

$$e(p) = \min_x px/f(x). \tag{iii-a}$$

From this definition, for all p,

$$e(p) \leq px/f(x) \quad \text{for all } x$$

$$e(p) = px/f(x) \quad \text{for some } x$$

or, what is the same,

$$e(p)f(x) \leq px \quad \text{for all } p, x \tag{iv}$$

together with

$$\text{for all } p, \quad e(p)f(x) = px \quad \text{for some } x. \tag{v-a}$$

In addition to (v-a), similar to it but with an exchange of roles between p and x, we have the possible but not generally necessary condition

$$\text{for all } x, \quad e(p)f(x) = px \quad \text{for some } p. \tag{v-b}$$

With the relation, K, of conjugacy between p and x, given by

$$pKx \equiv e(p)f(x) = px, \tag{vi}$$

(v-a) asserts that $pK \neq 0$ for all p and (v-b) asserts that $Kx \neq 0$ for all x. This relation depends only on proportions, so, for all $s, t > 0$, $pKx \Rightarrow spKxt$. This is the condition for the input factor proportions specified by x to be cost-efficient at the exchange rates specified by the prices p.

Just from the form of its definition (iii-a), regardless of properties of f, the function e is concave conical. Since f is given to be conical, it is concave if and only if it is superadditive: $f(x + y) \geq f(x) + f(y)$. If it is concave then, by the Support theorem, for any x there exists a p for which $f(y) - f(x) \leq p(y - x)$ for all y. Because f is conical, the replacement of y by $y\{f(x)/f(y)\}$ gives

$$0 \leq py\{f(x)/f(y)\} - px,$$

showing that

$$px/f(x) \leq py/f(y) \quad \text{for all } y,$$

showing that (iii-a) holds, for some p, and demonstrating (v-b). Then from (iv) and (v-b) we have, in addition to (iii-a),

$$f(x) = \min_p px/e(p). \tag{iii-b}$$

As with e in formula (iii-a), by which e is the conjugate of f, from this formula, f must be concave conical. We have seen now that, whatever f, the function e derived from it by (iii-a) is concave conical, and f is recoverable from e by formula (iii-b), or is the conjugate of e, if and only if it is concave conical. Functions related to each other symmetrically in this way, where each is the conjugate of the other, form a dual pair. Examples are given in Section 2.

We have seen the following:

Theorem I (conjugate function duality)   *For any function f, the function e derived from it by the formula*

$$e(p) = \min_x px/f(x)$$

is concave conical, and

$$e(p)f(x) \leq px \quad \text{for all } p, x$$

for all $p, e(p)f(x) = px$ for some x. Also,

$$f(x) \leq \min_p px/e(p),$$

and f is recovered from e by the formula

$$f(x) = \min_p px/e(p)$$

if and only if it is concave conical.

If f is differentiable, the gradient of $px/f(x)$ is

$$\nabla \{px/f(x)\} = \{1/f(x)\} \, p - \{px/\{f(x)\}^2\} \nabla f(x).$$

If this vanishes, as is required for the relation (vi) to hold, we have

$$\nabla f(x) = \{f(x)/px\} \, p$$

and hence, by (vi),

$$\nabla f(x) = \{1/e(p)\} \, p. \tag{vii-a}$$

The relation (vi) is similarly equivalent to

$$\nabla e(p) = x\{1/f(x)\}. \tag{vii-b}$$

From (vii-b), the derivatives of e give the inputs for each unit of output when these inputs are chosen in cost-efficient proportions. Similarly, the derivatives of f give the prices which would make the input proportions cost-efficient, the currency unit being the minimum cost of producing a unit at those prices.

Theorem II (price–quantity duality)   *If e, f are any conjugate price and quantity functions, so that*

$$e(p)f(x) \geq px \quad \text{for all } p, x$$

then the condition

$$e(p)f(x) = px$$

for any prices and quantities p, x to be conjugate is equivalent to

$$\nabla e(p) = x\{1/f(x)\}$$

and to

$$\nabla f(x) = \{1/e(p)\}\, p.$$

1.2   Dual function examples

Cobb-Douglas and Cobb-Douglas

A simple illustration of function duality, where functions are related to each other by the formulae 1.1 (iii-a) and 1.1 (iii-b), is provided by the Cobb-Douglas function

$$f(x) = A \prod_i x_i^{w_i} \tag{i}$$

where $w_i > 0$, $\sum w_i = 1$. With $X = f(x)$, the derivatives for $x_i > 0$ are given by

$$X_i = X w_i / x_i \tag{ii}$$

Then from 1.1 (vii-a) with $P = e(p)$ we have $X_i = (1/P)p_i$, and 1.1 (v) requires $PX = px$, so that

$$X w_i / x_i = (1/P)\, p_i \tag{iii}$$

and also

$$p_i x_i = (px) w_i. \tag{iv}$$

This last relation shows the constant shares property of the Cobb-Douglas function, the shares being given by the exponents w_i.

Also we have

$$x_i = P X w_i / p_i$$

and so

$$X = A \prod_i x_i^{w_i}$$

$$= A \prod_i \left(P X w_i / p_i^{w_i} \right)$$

$$= A P X \left(\prod_i w_i^{w_i} / \prod_i p_i^{w_i} \right)$$

giving

$$P = B \prod_i p_i^{w_i}, \quad \text{where } AB = \prod_i w_i^{-wi}. \tag{v}$$

A peculiarity of the Cobb-Douglas, shown here, is that its conjugate is also Cobb-Douglas, and moreover has the same exponents. This symmetry where the functions have the same form is not shared by other examples.

The inequality 1.1 (iv) states that $PX \leq px$ for all p, x. For these functions e, f and with shares denoted $s_i = p_i x_i$, this gives

$$\prod_i (s_i/w_i)^{w_i} \leq 1$$

for all $s_i \geq 0, \sum s_i = 1$, or that $\prod_i s_i^{w_i}$ under these constraints is maximum at $s_i = w_i$.

The assumption that f is concave can be verified as follows. Because f is conical, and differentiable, the condition for it to be concave is that $f(y) \leq \nabla f(x) y$ for all x, y. From (ii), this condition is

$$f(y) \leq \sum f(x) w_i y_i / x_i,$$

and so by (i) it is

$$\prod_i (y_i/x_i)^{w_i} \leq \sum w_i (y_i/x_i)$$

which is true by the Theorem of the Mean, which states that an arithmetic mean with any weights is at least the corresponding geometric mean.

Leontief and linear

For another example, the conjugate of a linear function $f(x) = bx$, where $b \in \Omega_n$, is

$$\begin{aligned}
e(p) &= \min[px : bx \geq 1] \\
&= \max[t : tb \leq p] \text{ by LP duality} \\
&= \max[t : t \leq p_i/b_i, b_i > 0] \\
&= \min[p_i/b_i : b_i > 0],
\end{aligned}$$

this function having the Leontief form. Alternatively, starting with

$$e(p) = \max[t : tb \leq p],$$

we have

$$\begin{aligned}
f(x) &= \min[px : e(x) \geq 1] \\
&= \min[px : p \geq b] \\
&= bx.
\end{aligned}$$

Because of the symmetry between prices and quantities, we could just as well have taken f with the Leontief form, and then the conjugate e would have been linear.

Polyhedral and polytope

A further example, of importance in the next section, is the concave conical polyhedral function

$$f(x) = \min b_i x$$
$$= \max[t : tI \le bx]$$

where $b \in \Omega_n$ has rows b_i, and the elements of $I \in \Omega^n$ are all 1. The conjugate is the concave conical polytope function

$$e(p) = \min[px : bx \ge I]$$
$$= \max[vI : vb \le p] \text{ by LP duality.}$$

Let

$$f^0(x) = \min\{px : e(x) \ge 1\}.$$

Though we know it, because f is concave conical, it is interesting to verify directly that f is recovered from e by the formula $f = f^0$. As $f \le f^0$ follows directly from the definition of e from f, it remains to show that $f^0 \le f$. Thus, substituting for e in the formula for f^0,

$$f^0(x) = \min[px : px' \ge 1, bx' \ge I]$$
$$\le b_i x \quad \text{for all } i,$$

because $p = b_i$ is feasible. But this is equivalent to

$$f^0(x) \le \min b_i x = f(x).$$

Again, if f, instead of being polyhedral, had been given the polytope form, its conjugate e would have been polyhedral.

1.3 Price and quantity levels

A pair of function e, f, symmetrically related as shown by 1.1 (iii-a) and 1.1 (iii-b), and so necessarily concave conical and satisfying the functional inequality 1.1 (iv) together with 1.1 (v-a) and 1.1 (v-b), are a *conjugate pair of price and quantity functions*. Such a pair of functions, interpreted in utility terms, serves to give an intelligibility to ideas of 'price level' and 'price index', at the same time showing the inherent restrictions in their use.

Suppose a demand (p_t, x_t) is given as data for each period $t = 1, \ldots, k$, showing the quantities demanded and the prevailing prices. Let (P_t, X_t) be the associated price and quantity levels as determined from any given conjugate functions e, f, so

$$P_t = e(p_t), \quad X_t = f(x_t). \tag{i}$$

For the demands in the various periods all to be represented as cost-efficient by the conjugate pair e, f, we require

$$P_t X_t = p_t x_t \quad \text{for all } t. \tag{ii}$$

By this condition the demands are compatible with e, f; and for present purposes they will be said to be consistent if they are compatible with some such e, f. In any case, (iv) of section 1.1 requires

$$P_s X_t \leq p_s x_t \quad \text{for all } s, t. \tag{iii}$$

Therefore, assuming (ii), and dividing (iii) by (ii),

$$P_s/P_t \leq p_s x_t / p_t x_t \quad \text{for all } s, t.$$

With the coefficients

$$a_{ts} = p_s x_t / p_t x_t, \quad b_{ts} = p_t x_s / p_t x_t, \tag{iv}$$

determined from the demand data, the solvability of the inequalities

$$a_{ts} \geq P_s/P_t \quad \text{for all } s, t \tag{v-a}$$

for the P_t has appeared to be necessary for the consistency of the demands, as mentioned earlier. It is also sufficient, as will be shown. With (ii), the inequalities (v-a) are equivalent to

$$b_{ts} \geq X_s/X_t, \tag{v-b}$$

and the argument could proceed just as well in terms of these.

Suppose the inequalities (v-a) are solvable, and let P_t be any solution. Then let $b_t = P_t^{-1} p_t$ and

$$f(x) = \min_t b_t x \tag{vi-a}$$
$$e(p) = \min[px : b_t x \geq 1], \tag{vi-b}$$

so these are conjugate functions, of the polyhedral and polytope type dealt with in Section 1.2. Because, by (v-a),

$$b_t x_s = p_t x_s / P_t \geq p_s x_s / P_s = b_s x_s,$$

we have

$$b_s x_s = \min_t b_t x_s.$$

Then, because also

$$b_s x_s = p_s x_s / P_s = X_s,$$

by (ii), it appear that

$$f(x_s) = X_s.$$

Next we want to show $e(p_s) = P_s$. Thus, because e, f are conjugates,

$$e(p_s)X_s = e(p_s)f(x_s) \le p_s x_s,$$

so that

$$e(p_s) \le p_s x_s / X_s = P_s.$$

Therefore to prove $e(p_s) = P_s$, it remains to show that $e(p_s) \ge P_s$. We also have

$$b_t x_s / X_s = p_t x_s / P_t X_s \ge 1,$$

by (iii), so that

$$e(p_s) = \min[p_s x : b_t x \ge 1] \le p_s x_s / X_s = P_s,$$

and now we have the required conclusion.

Thus, with any solution P_t of the inequalities (v-a), the existence of which was seen first to be necessary for the consistency of the demands, we have constructed a conjugate pair of function e, f which establishes that consistency. The solvability of these inequalities is, therefore, both necessary and sufficient for the consistency of the demands.

We now have the following:

Theorem III (constructability) *For any demands*

$$(p_t, x_t) \in \Omega_n \times \Omega^n \quad (t = 1, \ldots, k)$$

and coefficients

$$a_{rs} = p_s x_r / p_r x_r, \quad b_{rs} = p_r x_s / p_r x_r,$$

derived from them, let $(P_t, X_t) \in \Omega \times \Omega$ be such that

$$P_t X_t = p_t x_t \quad \text{for all } t.$$

A necessary and sufficient condition that there exists a conjugate pair of functions e, f such that

$$P_t = e(p_t), \quad X_t = f(x_t)$$

is that

$$a_{rs} \ge P_s / P_r \quad \text{for all } r, s$$

or, equivalently,

$$b_{rs} \ge X_s / X_r \quad \text{for all } r, s.$$

Then one pair of such functions is

$$f^*(x) = \min_t p_t x / P_t$$

$$e^*(p) = \min[px : p_t x \geq P_t \quad \text{for all } t],$$

and another is

$$f_*(x) = \min[px : px_t \geq X_t \quad \text{for all } t]$$

$$e_*(p) = \min_t px_t / X_t.$$

These functions are such that $e_* \leq e^*$, $f_* \leq f^*$.

1.4   Limits of indeterminacy

The given demands (p_t, x_t) with

$$b_{rs} = p_s x_r / p_r x_r, \quad a_{rs} = p_r x_s / p_r x_r,$$

have any (P_t, X_t) as admissible price and quantity levels if

$$P_t X_t = p_t x_t \quad \text{for all } t, \tag{i}$$

and

$$b_{rs} \geq P_s / P_r \tag{ii}$$

$$a_{rs} \geq X_s / X_r. \tag{iii}$$

Subject to (i), the conditions (ii) and (iii) are equivalent. Therefore, with any solution P_t of (ii), the X_t determined from (i) are a solution of (iii), and vice versa.

The demands have any pair of functions (e, f) as admissible price and quantity functions if they are a dual pair of functions such that

$$e(p_t) f(x_t) = p_t x_t \quad \text{for all } t.$$

A conclusion from theorem is that admissible price and quantity levels (P_t, X_t) are identical with levels $P_t = e(p_t)$, $X_t = f(x_t)$ determined from admissible price and quantity functions (e, f). From this, admissible levels exist if and only if admissible functions exist, so the level consistency of the demands can mean either of these conditions.

Given any admissible levels, many admissible level functions exist which have these as their values at the base point p_t, x_t. The different functions can have different values at non-base points, so even when levels at base points are fixed the levels at those points have an indeterminacy, but one already put in limits by the limit functions e^*, e_* and f^*, f_*. But still, the admissible levels themselves, if they are any, are many. Here, therefore, is a further source of indeterminacy in the levels at any points, including the base points. When the indeterminacy at base points is put in limits, the indeterminacy at all other points is also, through the limit functions, associated with limit levels. The problem that remains, therefore, concerns the evaluation of level indeterminacy at the base points only. In other words, it concerns the variety of the admissible levels (P_t, X_t) obtained from solutions of the inequalities (ii), or alternatively (iii), since solutions of one or other system are in a correspondence through relation (i).

A particular source of indeterminacy is just scale indeterminacy, which is removed by setting one level to value 1, say $P_1 = 1$. Price indices being ratios of price levels, in effect, then, the levels P_t will become price indices with $t = 1$ as base. The indeterminacy that remains is associated with the ratios $P_{rs} = P_s/P_r$, which can range in a closed interval with upper limit

$$\hat{P}_{rs} = \min[P_s/P_r : b_{ij} \geq P_i/P_j]$$

and lower limit

$$\check{P}_{rs} = 1/\hat{P}_{sr}.$$

As appears in Appendices 1 and 6, there is also the formula

$$\hat{P}_{rs} = \min_{ij\cdots k} b_{ri}b_{ij}\cdots b_{ks},$$

and the efficient way to calculate the matrix of upper limits is to raise the matrix to powers in a sense which is a modification of the usual, where addition instead means taking the minimum.

Any level has its full range of indeterminacy only when the other levels are not fixed, since fixing any one level puts a new restriction on all the others. In particular, if one level is given an extreme value, at a limit of the interval to which it is basically restricted, the others will be confined to narrower intervals possibly excluding their basic limits.

Systems of inequalities of the form (i), or (ii), by taking logarithms can be put in the form $a_{rs} \geq x_s - x_r$. Systems of inequalities in this form, treated in Appendix 1, first arose in the more general form of demand analysis, without the homogeneity restriction suitable to the present topic. They arose again in the theory of minimum paths in networks. The mathematics, which contains these different interpretations and applications but is identical in each case, is put best in that usual connection. An expository statement for the present application is in the next section.

II   The True Index

The price index is associated with a narrow concept of the cost of living problem, but it is most familiar and important, for both theory and practice. With its long history and large literature, and now quite elaborate theory, a sketch can give the essentials more readily than an extended account. An outline of the main ideas is described in this chapter. History is touched only where points are encountered directly, and theorems are brought in discursively and without proof. Other chapters deal with the same matters in more detail. The ground has been trodden so often that what one makes of it might be a personal accident. William Fleetwood, Irving Fisher, and S. S. Byushgens stand out from the past in this account. Writings of J. R. Hicks, R. G. D. Allen, and Paul Samuelson form a background, while interest was evoked from J. R. N. Stone, and from Robin Marris who drew attention to the theorem of Byushgens that has influenced the other theorems. The 'true index' is an early vague term that has later acquired the meaning dealt with here.

2.1   The cost of living

When prices change, one question concerns how an income should be adjusted in order to preserve its purchasing power. This has a theoretical interest, and also a relevance to everyday life, especially when prices are rising. The sense of the question is not immediate, nor is giving it an answer. The theory of index numbers offers some intelligibility to the question, and approaches a solution.

The data usually allowed for in dealing with this question are demand observations, usually the two for the reference periods themselves, and possibly more. With several consumption periods, identified as $t = 1, 2, \ldots, T$, let row and column vectors p_t, x_t give the prices of commodities and the quantities of them demanded in period t. Then the cost, $C_t = p_t x_t$, of the commodity bundle x_t at the prices p_t, determines the expenditure on consumption in period t, which for convenience of statement is equated with income. What is done in practice draws little from the theory, being governed mostly by social factors and statistical practicality. The cost of living index in practice is really somewhat in the nature of a democratic social institution, and should be seen in that light, in addition to any light coming from the theory. The theory often associated with the practical index and offered in its support, where it is identified as a Laspeyres index, has little to do with it; Fleetwood (1707) is much nearer.

One understanding of the cost of living question depends on the supposition that any bundle of goods x has a level of utility, realized through consumption of the goods, representing a standard of living, so that in buying x one is in effect buying a level of utility, or a standard of living. The cost of a standard of living, at any prices for the goods, is the cost of the cheapest bundle of goods that can provide it.

2.2   The price index

In addition to that understanding, and to some extent independent of it, is the commonly accepted form for giving an answer to the cost of living question, which involves a single number, the price index. The index is associated with any pair of periods, and it specifies a ratio between any incomes that, in those periods and at the pries that prevail, should be accepted as having the same purchasing power. With any periods r and s, a number P_{rs} is associated, with the effect that any incomes E_r and E_s, at the prices p_r and p_s, that should be accepted as having the same purchasing power, must have the relation

$$E_r = P_{rs} E_s. \tag{i}$$

The number P_{rs} is the *price index*, with s as the *base* and r as the *current period*. Generally one would allow a relation which is monotonic increasing, and not necessarily homogeneous linear as here. The price-index concept therefore carries with it a special restriction about the relation between equivalent incomes.

With this use of a price index goes the question of how it should be determined. There is then the further question of how any determination, and before that how just the restricted idea of the index itself, fits in with the utility understanding of the purchasing power question it is meant to resolve. In some respects, these questions can be considered both separately and together.

2.3   Formulae and Fisher's tests

The determination question taken on its own has revolved around a large assortment of formulae coming more from a history of use, than from any theory, or if not actual use, then from inclusion among suggestions thrown out by makers of index numbers. Irving Fisher, with his book, *The Making of Index Numbers* (Fisher, 1922), represents the culmination of this phase, which is still not quite dead. In the beginning were the formulae, each with as much right as any other, even though they were subject to favouritism. Fisher classified them and gave Tests to judge their legitimacy, to bring order and discrimination to the prolific host. Though by the standards he laid down they are all illegitimate, he settled on one as his Ideal Index. The reasons he gave for the choice contain a compromise, but a theoretical property discovered for it has interest. That has to do with the utility theory and so belongs to a phase beyond Fisher's usual type of consideration.

A rule about index numbers formulae that has been taken for granted (and must be broken in the generalization for several periods taken simultaneously), is that any one of them should be an algebraical formulae in demand data, and that it should depend on demand data only for the two periods to which it refers. The formulae should involve only elementary arithmetic operations—addition, multiplication and the inverses. Accordingly, P_{rs} should be such a function of the demands (p_r, x_r) and (p_s, x_s) observed for periods r and s. Fisher's Ideal formulae is

$$\bar{P}_{rs} = \sqrt{p_r x_r p_r x_s / p_s x_r p_s x_s}. \tag{i}$$

It satisfies various of his tests, such as the identity test, $P_{rr} = 1$, and the reversal test,

$$P_{rs} = 1/P_{sr}, \tag{ii}$$

which, by taking $r = s$ implies the former, but not the more stringent chain test

$$P_{rs} P_{st} = P_{rt}, \tag{iii}$$

which implies all the foregoing.

There is a simple sense to these particular tests, which are among a larger collection. If E_r is any income for period r, and E_s is the income with equivalent purchasing power for period s, then we must have

$$E_s = P_{sr} E_r, \tag{a}$$

and E_t is the income equivalent in purchasing power to this for period t, so also

$$E_t = P_{ts} E_s. \tag{b}$$

Then, by transitivity of equivalence, this also has the same purchasing power as E_r in period r, so then also

$$E_t = P_{tr} E_r. \tag{c}$$

Thus, for all E_r, (a) and (b) must imply (c); equivalently, (iii) holds. The underlying thought is that a price index is a ratio of price levels P_r associated with the reference periods. Thus

$$P_{rs} = P_r/P_s, \tag{iv}$$

and from this the conclusion (iii) follows again. Though the term is a part of language, there is still some obscurity about how prices, which are many, should have a single level.

2.4 The Paasche–Laspeyres interval

One undoubted way of attaining in period r exactly the standard of living that was enjoyed in period s is to have exactly the same consumption x_s, at the current cost $p_r x_s$. Therefore, the income E_r in period r that has the same purchasing power as the income $C_s = p_s x_s$ in period s cannot exceed that cost, because having the income to meet that cost is enough. Accordingly,

$$E_r \le p_r x_s = (p_r x_s / p_s x_s) C_s.$$

Therefore, if P_{rs} is the price index that in principle gives $E_r = P_{rs} C_s$, we have

$$P_{rs} \le M_{rs}, \tag{i}$$

where

$$M_{rs} = p_r x_s / p_s x_s \quad \text{(Laspeyres)}. \tag{ii}$$

In other words, the Laspeyres formulae gives an upper bound for the true price index, and this is the classic proposition about price indices. If there is such a thing as a true price index, anything different from it might be a false index or not a price index at all. Even

$$W_{rs} = 1/M_{sr} = p_r x_r / p_s x_r \quad \text{(Paasche)} \tag{iii}$$

is called a price index, and usually there is no claim that either is true. The theory then arrives at proposition that this second formulae is a lower bound of the true index; for the true index must obey the reversal law 2.3 (ii) and with that, together with (iii), the relations

$$W_{rs} \le P_{rs} \quad \text{and} \quad P_{rs} \le M_{rs}$$

become equivalent. Therefore, both must be true if one of them is, and therefore both are true since one has been proved. From that argument we have the proposition

$$W_{rs} \le P_{rs} \le M_{rs}, \tag{iv}$$

which is central to the theory of index numbers. Also it makes a dilemma, since it is quite possible to find that

$$W_{rs} > M_{rs}, \tag{v}$$

in which case it is impossible to take the Laspeyres and Paasche indices to be upper and lower bounds of anything.

The interval I_{rs} defined by (iv) can be called the Paasche–Laspeyres (P–L) interval, with s as the base and r the current period. The two periods are taken here in detachment from any others, and without any involvement with the demand data, associated with others.

There is another way of representing this interval: it is not useful here where the two periods are taken alone, but gains significance when several periods are taken together. It is suitable to use a different notation

$$L_{rs} = p_r x_s / p_s x_s \tag{vi}$$

for what here is the Laspeyres index, because later with many periods this does not have the same significance as now, and ceases to be the counterpart of the

Laspeyres index in its role as a limit, even though the L is used out of regard for the present connection. The set C_{rs} of positive solutions of the pair of homogeneous linear inequalities

$$L_{rs} P_s \geq P_r, \qquad L_{sr} P_r \geq P_s, \tag{vii}$$

is a convex cone in the two-dimensional price-level space. Then

$$I_{rs} = [P_r/P_s : (P_r, P_s) \in C_{rs}], \tag{viii}$$

this being the set of slopes of the rays in the cone. Alternatively, the P–L interval is the set of values for P_r obtained by cutting the cone by the line $P_s = 1$. Another way of cutting the cone, useful later with many periods when it will be by a hyperplane, is by the line $P_r + P_s = 1$. The section D obtained is in this case a line segment from which the P–L interval I derives again in the same fashion as from the cone C. The counterpart with many periods is a convex polytope lying in the simplex of normalized price-level vectors.

2.5   Existence test

If 2.4 (iv) is true for a true price index, then the existence of a true price index must imply the relation

$$W_{rs} \leq M_{rs} \tag{i}$$

between the Paasche and Laspeyres indices, by which the one does not exceed the other. For a restatement,

$$p_r x_r p_s x_s \leq p_r x_s p_s x_r, \tag{ii}$$

or, with the notation 2.4 (vi),

$$L_{rs} L_{sr} \geq 1, \tag{iii}$$

which shows the condition as holding symmetrically between the two periods. Another restatement, which is strange but puts the condition in a form that has a direct generalization to any number of periods, is that the matrix

$$\begin{pmatrix} 1 & L_{rs} \\ L_{sr} & 1 \end{pmatrix} \tag{iv}$$

be idempotent in a modified arithmetic where addition means taking the minimum. In other words, now the data must be subject to the test (i) if dealing with a true price index on the basis of the data is to be permitted, at least on a theoretical basis without an allowance for error. Then it can be asked if the test is sufficient for that. In fact, it is necessary and sufficient for the existence of a homogeneous utility that fits the demand data. Moreover, in order for a price index, giving the relation 2.2 (i) between equivalent incomes, to be dealt with on the basis of utility, the utility must be homogeneous, with the property where, if one bundle is at least as good as another, then any multiplies of them have the same relation. If a true index is to be understood as one determined by any such utility, then there are many such utilities if there are any, and hence many true indices. The true indices describe a closed interval whose end-points can be calculated. They are given by the Paasche and Laspeyres formulae. This is fortunate for the early theory, which gave an answer without having a question, and now we have a question and it gives the answer. The usually wanted relation between Paasche and Laspeyres is not in itself a theorem, but a test to be applied to the data. For a proper theorem, we have this test, both necessary and sufficient for the data to admit the existence of a true price index. Any point of the closed interval there is a true price index—*each quite as true as any other*, and that includes the much considered Paasche and Laspeyres end-points as well.

Fisher offered tests for formulae, not tests for the demand data that enter the formulae, that is, tests prior to thinking about a particular formulae but rather about the question that any formulae is supposed to answer. However, assumptions implicit in the concepts used require the data to be subject to tests if their use is to be admissible. Bringing in such tests makes dilemmas disappear. There is not even any occasion for formulae tests, and so no encounter with the simultaneous necessity and impossibility of Fisher's tests when applied to the usual type of formulae, touched on first by A. Wald (1936) and investigated systematically by W. Eichhorn and J. Voeller (1976). When indices are constructed, it should be because the data satisfy the consistency or existence test that permits their construction. Then without question they have the properties they are intended to have, inherited from their construction and the prior condition that permitted it, and so there is no need for a verification afterwards. A question is formulated first and then a formulae is found to answer it, instead of the approach *vice versa*. Of course, formulae tests can be made into data tests, since the data enter the formulae, but even then the distinction just made is still valid. It is incidental that Fisher's tests are tight equations, which moreover cannot generally be satisfied, while the data tests are slack inequalities, a more tolerant allowance, which can be expanded to greater tolerance by admitting consumer inefficiency and error, as in Chapter II.6.

2.6   Theory and practice

Having a homogeneous linear relation between equivalent incomes is the essence of the price index idea, in both theory and practice. That may be too obvious to deserve mention, since it never is mentioned—or a mistake, or a kind of discovery. That it be fitting, as a matter of observation and of definition, is in any case a fundamental thesis in this work.

The simplicity with a price index gives a convenience for common use that compels its adoption. The method by which the index is determined is not constrained by a fixed principle, as might be supposed were it dominated by the theory; it has a freedom associated with the entire circumstances of the matter. The use of a price index at all, and then the value assigned to it, arises out of the social framework. It has the nature of a social and political institution, democratic or otherwise. A dictator could impose the use of a price index, and its value at any time, and the laws for its use; it could make a useful policy instrument in such hands. In a democracy, ideas of equity and impartiality take precedence, as in the election process. The index is based on consumers' own expenditures, giving them a representation—a vote, so to speak. The way those votes are gathered together to arrive at the result need not give universal satisfaction, but it must demonstrate suitable impartiality and other properties, or there might be complaints.

In such respects a comparison can be made with K. J. Arrow's Social Choice and Individual Values theory. That theory, divorced form its unsuitable welfare interpretation, can be regarded as an investigation into an alternative way of conducting a democratic election. First, there would be an election to choose an order, which the group would give to the candidates, and then the order would choose the candidate, the top one in it being the winner. Each elector would state not just a choice of one candidate but ranked preferences between all candidates. It would be a heavy burden on voters, because no candidate could be simply rejected, but preferences would have to be stated between all, including the rejected ones. This is not practical, and even if it were, there is no advantage to it over the old-fashioned method. It has nothing to do with welfare, where the advantage should lie, since arbitrary groups, about which we are told nothing further, do not have a welfare criterion. Even with a special group that did in some way have a welfare criterion, this might not be the way to approach it. The unlikelihood of using the procedure has nothing to do with the Impossibility theorem, and that theorem has nothing to do with the self-contradiction of democracy seen by P. A. Samuelson. The theory, though not what it is supposed to be, does not lose interest, however. It draws attention to formal characteristics of the democratic choice process. The CPI as an institution shares some of those.

Understanding the procedure involved in arriving at the CPI can be confused by theory, as it has nothing to do with Paasche, Laspeyres and Fisher. It is closer to Fleetwood who, in a straightforward way without any theory, dealt with a bundle of goods associated with a life-style at no time in particular, and compared its cost in his period to that four centuries earlier. Now the bundle of goods, instead of being for a single individual, is an average for the community. He explained the matter to a student (Fleetwood, 1st edition, 1707) and illustrated that lift-style with '4 Hogsheads of Beer, 6 Yards of Cloth, and c'. His remark, 'money is of no other use, than as it is the thing with which we purchase the necessities and conveniences of life . . .', preceded the introduction of utility theory and indicated a need for it. Goods that could be bought are numerous, and bringing in utility reduces their number to one, thereby giving a less ambiguous way of putting his argument. With the CPI, from time to time a bundle of goods is determined and then, as with Fleetwood, its cost is calculated from year to year, so making three dates involved, not the two that occur in theory.

The service the CPI offers is obvious, and so are its flaws. It would be possible to remedy certain defects and improve acceptibility, but at the cost of convenience.

The democratic principle is one side of the matter; another is the feelings of those who notice an alteration in the standard of living when prices rise and incomes do not. The utility concept offers a yardstick that should be better than Fleetwood's fixed bundle of goods, which does not recognize the substitution effect in the impact of a price change. Though the utility concept is usually linked to consumer behaviour, this matter is not; it is simply that consumers' feelings, regardless of behaviour, demand a kind of measurement.

2.7   Many periods

A price index usually is determined for a pair of periods in isolation from others, involving demand data from those periods alone. Price indices so determined for several periods, with such pairwise isolation, are then required, by Fisher's tests, to have a certain consistency together. The tests are an unreasonable imposition considering the isolated determinations, and it is natural that they cannot be satisfied. The problem needs to be reopened from the start by admitting the simultaneous presence of all the data. All we have for two periods is then put in a setting where it is better appreciated. The following is an outline.

The price index concept is an imposition on the broader idea of cost of living. Standard of living has sense with a utility relation R, an order (reflexive and transitive binary relation) in the commodity space, where the statement xRy means a bundle of goods x has at least the standard, or the utility, of y. Provided the sets Rx are closed, the function

$$c(p, x) = \min[py : yRx] \qquad\qquad\qquad (i)$$

is defined for all $p > 0$, and gives the cost at prices p of attaining at least the standard represented by the bundle x. From this definition

$$c(p, x) = py, yRx \quad \text{for some } y \qquad\qquad (ii\text{-}a)$$

$$yRx \quad \Rightarrow \quad c(p, x) \le py \quad \text{for all } y \qquad (ii\text{-}b)$$

and, because R is reflexive,

$$c(p, x) \le px. \qquad\qquad\qquad\qquad\qquad (iii)$$

Another consequence is that $c(p, x)$ is concave conical in p.

A utility R is oversatiated at a point x if

$$y < x, yRx \quad \text{for some } y,$$

that is, some smaller bundle is at least as good. The contrary is that

$$y < x \quad \Rightarrow \quad \text{not } yRx \quad \text{for all } y. \qquad (iv)$$

If this holds for all x, R is said to be non-satiated. Also, R is complete if

$$xRy \quad \text{or} \quad yRx$$

for all x and y, that is, the relation holds one way or the other between any bundles, equivalently

$$\text{not } xRy \implies yRx. \tag{v}$$

The demand (p, x) is represented as cost-efficient by the utility R if

$$c(p, x) = px, \tag{vi}$$

that is, if the cost of x at the prices p is equal to the minimum cost of attaining at least the standard represented by x. An equivalent statement is that the condition

$$H' \equiv yRx \implies py \geq px$$

holds; that is, attaining at least the standard requires at least the cost. In the contrapositive form, that is

$$py \leq px \implies \text{not } yRx. \tag{vii}$$

This condition can be put alongside the cost-effectiveness, or utility maximization, condition:

$$H'' \equiv py \leq px \implies xRy.$$

The cost-efficiency and effectiveness conditions H' and H'' are generally independent, and their combination is

$$H \equiv H' \text{ and } H''.$$

But relations are produced between them under special conditions. They are equivalent if the sets xR are all closed and R is complete and non-satiated. In that case either condition stands for the combination.

The price index is a concept that in the utility context requires a utility which is homogeneous, or conical; that is,

$$xRy, t > 0 \implies xtRyt. \tag{viii}$$

An equivalent condition is that the utility cost function $\subset$ must admit the factorization

$$c(p, x) = e(p) f(x) \tag{ix}$$

into product of a function of p alone and a function of x alone. Then from (iii),

$$e(p) f(x) \leq px, \tag{x}$$

and the condition (vi) for a demand (x, p) to be represented as efficient becomes

$$e(p) f(x) = px. \tag{xi}$$

Introducing

$$P_r = e(p_r),$$

the costs at any given prices p_r, p_s of attaining a standard of living X are

$$E_r = P_r X, \quad E_s = P_s X.$$

Hence, eliminating X,

$$E_r = P_{rs} E_s$$

where

$$P_{rs} = P_r / P_s.$$

That shows P_{rs} in the role of the price index between situations with the given prices, and indicates how it is determined from any homogeneous utility R in terms of the price function e associated with it.

The cost of living is intelligible in terms of a utility R, and there would be no problem about it if R were given. The cost of living problem arises because usually R is not given. Then the demand data have a bearing on the problem by their being used to provide constraints on any utility R that should be considered, by the requirement that R represent all observed demands as efficient.

The definition of cost of living (i) states it as a minimum cost, so it is inapplicable without that efficiency. In just asking the cost of living question, consumers are making a commitment about how they should be regarded. This use of the data therefore is appropriate; without it, or some more tolerant modification that allows inefficiency and error but still preserves the efficiency framework, all bearings for the question would be lost.

Imposed on this use of the data is the additional requirement, accompanying the insistence on having a price index, that the utility be homogeneous. With the conjugate price and quantity functions e and f that characterize such utility, let us introduce

$$P_t = e(p_t), \quad X_t = f(x_t). \tag{xii}$$

Then the efficiency condition (xi) applied to the observed demands gives

$$P_s X_s = p_s x_s \quad \text{for all } s \tag{xiii}$$

while (x) gives

$$P_r X_s \le p_r x_s \quad \text{for all } r, s. \tag{xiv}$$

By division, therefore,

$$L_{rs} \le P_r / P_s \quad \text{for all } r, s \tag{xv}$$

where

$$L_{rs} = p_r x_s / p_s x_s. \tag{xvi}$$

The existence of numbers P_r that satisfy the inequalities (xv) therefore is necessary for the existence of a homogeneous utility that fits the demand data, and of price indices that are true on the data. The condition is also sufficient. Given any solution P_r, true price indices between all periods are given by

$$P_{rs} = P_r / P_s.$$ (xvii)

When these exist let

$$M_{rs} = \min_{ij\cdots k} L_{ri} L_{ij} \cdots L_{ks}.$$ (xviii)

The condition for existence is that

$$L_{ri} L_{ij} \cdots L_{kr} \geq 1$$ (xix)

for all $r, i, j, \ldots, k$.

While the L-numbers given by (xvi) might look like Laspeyres price indices, they do not have the same role as limits, except when only two periods are involved. The availability of more data has removed some indeterminacy and narrowed the limits. These numbers can fall outside limits now effective, and then they are not true indices themselves, unlike the Laspeyres index for two isolated periods. The new limits are obtained by a generalized formulae or algorithm involving all the data simultaneously, unlike the Laspeyres and all price index formulae of the type recognized by Fisher. The result is not even conventionally algebraical in the way usually required for a price index.

Powers of a matrix can be redefined as in Section 2.5 for a modified arithmetic, where addition means taking the minimum. In raising the L-matrix of order T to successive powers by repeated matrix multiplications in the modified sense, either some power before the Tth will repeat, so making all succeeding powers identical with it, or it will not. That happening is a test for the existence of solutions P_r of the inequalities (xv), equivalent to the condition (xix). Otherwise, the series of powers is unending. In the case of termination, the last power obtained determines the matrix M of upper limits. Then the matrix L of lower limits has elements

$$W_{rs} = 1 / M_{sr}.$$ (xx)

The solutions of (xv) are identical with the solutions of either of the derived systems

$$M_{rs} \geq P_r / P_s \quad \text{for all } r, s$$ (xxi)

and

$$W_{rs} \leq P_r / P_s \quad \text{for all } r, s$$ (xxii)

which exist whenever there are any solutions, which also is just the condition for the existence of these derived systems. With any solution, a price index matrix P is determined from (xvii). The elements of any P-matrix, so obtained, automatically satisfy the Fisher chain test 2.3 (iii). The L-numbers satisfy the multiplicative triangular inequality

$$M_{rs}M_{st} \leq M_{rt} \tag{xxiii}$$

and the W-numbers have the similar property with the inequality reversed.

Except in the case of just two periods, the M and W matrices themselves generally are not possible P-matrices. However, their elements do give attainable limits for individual elements of the P-matrices. This comes out of a general extension property of solutions of the system (xxi), or (xxii). Any solution of a subsystem, where the indices range over a subset of periods, can be extended to a solution of the complete system. In particular, starting with a subsystem for two periods r, s the value of P_{rs} can have the full range between W_{rs} and M_{rs}. This is elaborated in detail in Chapter V.4.

2.8   Price levels

With the relation 2.7 (xx), the systems 2.7 (xxi) and 2.7 (xxii) are equivalent, so we need only think of one of them, and can choose 2.7 (xxi). The original system 2.7 (xv) is

$$(L) \quad L_{rs}P_s \geq P_r \quad \text{for all } r, s. \tag{i}$$

Then the system 2.7 (xxi), obtained by 2.7 (xviii), subject to 2.7 (xix), is

$$(M) \quad M_{rs}P_s \geq P_r \quad \text{for all } r, s. \tag{ii}$$

This is equivalent to the sytem (L), the two systems having identical solutions, but the derived coefficient satisfy the multiplicative inequality 2.7 (xxi). Any positive solution P_r defines a permissible system of price levels, represented by a point in the price-level space V of dimension equal to the number of periods T. The set C of solutions is a convex polyhedral cone in this space.

When price levels are normalized to have sum 1, they describe a simplex U in the vector space V. This simplex U cuts the cone C in a bounded convex polyhedron, or convex polytope, D. The cone C is recoverable from its section D, being the cone through that section, projecting it form the origin.

Taking price levels to be normalized, and so represented by points in the simplex U, is convenient for computation, and for geometrical representation. We are only concerned with ratios of price levels and these are unaltered by normalization. Every point in the normalized solution set D of the system (M) is a convex combination of a finite set of basic solutions, and so the computational problem requires finding just these. Given any solution P_r we form the matrix of price indices P_{rs} given by 2.7 (xvii). Now there will be explorations for a geometrical diagrammatic understanding of the system (M). Dealing with any three periods r, s, t is illustrative of the essential features. Though the associated solution cone C_{rst} is hard to visualize, the normalized solution polytope D_{rst} is much easier and can be represented graphically.

We can refer to any constraint of the system (M) by the two periods involved, so let (M_{rs}) denote the general constraint. There has already been some discussion of the case with two periods, in Section 2.4 on the P–L interval. Vectors of price levels for any subset of periods $r, s, \ldots$, understood as representing only the ratios, can be denoted

$$P_{r:s:\cdots} = (P_r : P_s : \cdots). \tag{iii}$$

Because the M-coefficients are given by 2.7 (xviii), subject to 2.7 (xix), and $L_{rr} = 1$, when these derived coefficients exist we must have

$$M_{rr} \geq 1 \tag{iv-a}$$

$$M_{rs} \leq L_{rs}, \tag{iv-b}$$

giving also

$$1 \leq M_{rr} \leq L_{rr} = 1 \text{ and consequently } M_{rr} = 1. \tag{v}$$

Also, there is the triangle inequality 2.7 (xxiii), and so now

$$M_{rs}M_{sr} \geq M_{rr} \geq 1, \tag{vi}$$

which gives a generalized counterpart of the less strict P–L inequality 2.5 (ii). Any period r corresponds to the vertex of the simplex U where $P_r = 1$, and vertices can be labelled by the corresponding periods. Any point on the edge rs of the simplex corresponds to a ratio $P_r : P_s$, that is $P_{r:s}$ in the notation (ii). Similarly any point in a simplex face rst specifies the ratios $P_{r:s:t}$ and so forth for any dimension.

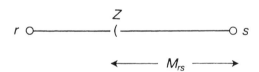

Figure 1

The constraint (M_{rs}) cuts the edge rs in a point Z and requires $P_{r:s}$ to lie in the segment Zs, where

$$rZ : Zs = 1 : M_{rs} = P_s : P_r. \tag{vii}$$

Without ambiguity, we can refer to the segment Zs on the edge rs as the segment M_{rs}, as in Figure 1. At the same time, the constraint (M_{rs}) requires $P_{r:s:t}$ to lie in the simplex Zst, and so forth to any dimension.

Considering now a pair of constraints (M_{rs}), and (M_{sr}), we have two segments M_{rs} and M_{sr} on the edge rs, and (viii) assures that they have a non-empty intersection D_{rs} shown in Figure 2. Because of (iv-b), this lies within the Paasche–Laspeyres interval, and is a generalization of that for when data from

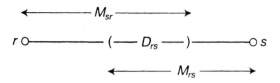

Figure 2

other periods are involved. It is generally narrower because any effect of extra data must be to reduce indeterminacy.

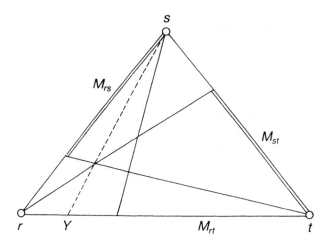

Figure 3

Now consider three constraints associated with the triangle inequality (Figure 3). Two of them produce intervals M_{rs} and M_{st} on rs and st and jointly produce the inrterval Yt on rt. The triangle inequality requires M_{rt} to be a subinterval of this.

If, instead of M_{rt}, we take M_{tr}, cyclically related to the other two, the resulting joint constraint determines a triangle lying within rst (Figure 4). The other three cyclically related constraints, associated with the opposite cyclical order, determine another triangle, so configured with the first that their intersection is a hexagon, D_{rst} (Figure 5).

It is seen in Figure 5 that D_{rs} is exactly the projection of D_{rst} from t onto rs. In other words, as $P_{r:s:t}$ describes D_{rst}, $P_{r:s}$ describes D_{rs}. Or again, for any point in D_{rs} there exists a point in D_{rst} that extends it, in the sense of giving the same ratios concerning r and s. That is the extension property described at the end of Section 2.7 (and in Chapter V.4 on minimum paths), and it continues into higher

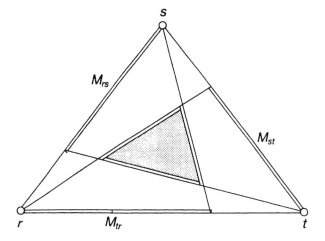

Figure 4

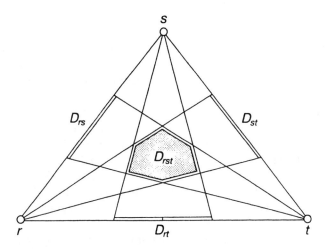

Figure 5

dimensions indefinitely:

$D_{rs\cdots t}$ is the projection of $D_{rs\cdots tq}$

from the vertex q of the simplex $rs\cdots tq$

on to the opposite face $rs\cdots t$.   (viii)

That shows how price levels for the periods can be determined sequentially, a further one at a time. Having found any price levels that satisfy the constraints that concern only them, they can be joined by another, so that this is true again. Starting with two periods and continuing in this way, a system of price levels finally will have been found for all the periods. When the data for a price index between two periods involve data also from other periods, and moreover when indices for any subset of periods are to be constructed consistently, these D-polytopes constitute a two-fold generalization of the Paasche–Laspeyres range of indeterminacy of a price index between two periods taken alone.

2.9   Fisher's formulae

This exposition concludes with a mention of the relevance of Fisher's tests to Fisher's index. Let $\bar{P}$ be the matrix of Fisher indices, the elements being determined by the formulae 2.3 (i). The question is whether these are true indices. This question can be put in three ways. For the first, one can think of any one element in isolation, and the constraints on utility produced just from the demand data for the two associated periods. The second involves the constraints from all the data, but the indices are still taken in isolation and each is allowed to correspond to a possibly different utility. In the third, the indices must be simultaneously determined from a single utility admitted by all the constraints.

The first is in the usual framework of just two periods, everything to do with the others being irrelevant. Often the argument is encountered that, with Paasche and Laspeyres as limits (in the sense of bounds) to the true index, Fisher, being their geometric mean, must be a better approximation to it than either. However, they are only bounds, and it is not known whether they are good ones, so the effect of taking the mean is not known. If one were a good approximation and the other not, the result might be not so good. In any case, the true index is not uniquely defined, or defined at all in the context of this argument, and so there are no grounds for speaking of approximations. A simple proposition answering the first question is that, if there exists a true price index at all, then the Fischer index is one. For the existence condition 2.5 (i) is that Paasche does not exceed Laspeyres, and then any point in the interval between them, including the end-points, is a true index, each as true as any other. In particular, the geometric mean of the end-points belongs to the interval, and that is the Fisher index.

For the second question, even if the existence test if fulfilled for any or all the periods, the constraints from the remaining data could narrow the range of true values lying within the Paasche–Laspeyres interval, so as to exclude the Fisher index. That puts the Fisher index, without an auxiliary condition, at a disadvantage in the third question.

S. S. Byushgens (1925) made a new kind of point when he showed that, if a homogeneous quadratic utility could be assumed to prevail, then Fisher's index is exact. The terms of this proposition are significant; in addition to marking the homogeneity inseparable from the price-index concept, which is absent in most accounts, it described the sense in which an index could be exact, or true, on the basis of a utility, and showed a link of the theoretical to the more purely statistical approach. The proposition raises the question about whether the quadratic utility hypothesis is admissible on given data. If not, though none the less still true, it becomes vacuous. However, it is admissible if and only if the general price index existence test (2.5 (ii), or 2.5 (i)) is satisfied. That is the broadest condition for thinking about a price index at all, and just that the Paasche index does not exceed that of Laspeyres.

This theorem, proved in Chapter III, is nice as it stands. But it is not true when there are more than two periods. Something must be added, and the minimum needed is, obvious, namely, the chain test. My point is that this addition is also enough, as concerns special treatment for Fisher. While with two periods nothing must be added beyond the minimal price index existence test, with more than two we must certainly have the existence test again, though now in the generalized form that has been stated, and obviously also Fisher's chain test, 2.3 (ii). In fact, here is all that is needed. The chain test reduces to te reversal test, 2.3 (iii), in the case of two periods, and Fisher's index satisfies that test anyway, so we have a generalization of the theorem. This generalization provides a way of answering the third considered question. For a matrix P of true price indices to exist, the existence test on the data is required and then, from the manner of construction that has been described, the chain test is automatically assured. Therefore, if $\bar{P}$ is to be an example of such a P-matrix, the existence test on the demand data is required, and $\bar{P}$ must satisfy the chain test. But, by the generalized theorem, that is enough to assure the existence of a utility for which the matrix P of price indices is identical with $\bar{P}$; in other words, the Fisher indices are true.

III Fisher and Byushgens

If we should ever encounter a case where a theory is named for the correct man, it will be noted.

George J. Stigler
The Theory of Price (3rd edition), 1966, p. 77

For Irving Fisher, index numbers where formulae of a certain type, and in *The Making of Index Numbers* (1922) he dealt with the many that had been proposed. Were these answers to a question, their correctness would depend on the question. But they were answers that had been provided without a definite question, so making the choice between them was difficult. However, a consistency in understandings about price indices requires a formula to have certain properties, and from these Irving Fisher produced his tests.

Though prices are many, and so there are many levels, the idea of a general 'price level' is often present in arguments, and it appears in models as if it were a definite number P, when one should like to know how to find the number. It seems unnecessary to have an absolute price level, and a relative price level, when one period is taken as base, would serve. The price index, understood to be a ratio of price levels, should be given by some formula depending on available data. It refers to two periods, distinguished as the *base* and *current periods*, say 0 and 1. Whatever the formula, from what it is supposed to represent and the way it is used, it has the form $P_{10} = P_1/P_0$, and therefore, with an exchange of role between base and current periods, it should be such that $P_{01} = 1/P_{10}$, which is Fisher's time *reversal test*. It is accepted that an index formula should involve the demand data (x_0, p_0), (x_1, p_1) for the two periods to which it has reference, and no more. Many formulae proposed do not satisfy the reversal test. Also, if one brings in a third period, 2, there is the *chain test* $P_{10}P_{21} = P_{20}$, and this usually is violated.

The more recent index thinking comes from the utility theory of the consumer, and it should have a bearing especially on the CPI. A main question concerns how much income M_1 is needed at the prices p_1 of the current period in order to live at the standard attained with some other income M_0 with the prices p_0 of the base period. A price index P_{01} is understood to provide the relation $M_1 = P_{10}M_0$ as an answer to this question. When utility is brought in to give intelligibility, the expenditure p_0x_0 in period 0 has bought the bundle of goods x_0 which provided a standard of living through its utility; and therefore an income equal to the cost $p_1 x_0$ of that same bundle at the current prices is at least enough to achieve the same standard. Therefore if the answer M_1 provided by the price index is correct for the particular case $M_0 = p_0 x_0$, we must have $p_1 x_0 \leq M_1$, that is $p_1 x_0 \leq P_{10} p_0 x_0$, or, what is the same, P_{10} where

$$\hat{P}_{10} = p_1 x_0 / p_0 x_0.$$

In the same way, $P_{01} \leq \hat{P}_{01}$. But $P_{01} = 1/P_{10}$, and so this is equivalent to $P_{10} \geq \check{P}_{10}$, where $\check{P}_{10} = 1/\hat{P}_{01}$; that is,

$$\check{P}_{10} = p_1 x_1 / p_0 x_1.$$

In a fashion like this, upper and lower bounds have been arrived at for the 'true' index. J. M. Keynes (1930) proceeds similarly, though with some difference (cf. *A Treatise on Money* Vol. I, 'The Method of Limits'). Then there is the familiar argument that, these being 'limits' to the 'true' index, their geometric mean,

$$\bar{P}_{10} = \sqrt{(\hat{P}_{10} \check{P}_{10})},$$

which lies between, must be a better 'approximation' to it than earlier. For this reason, in addition to his satisfaction of the reversal test, the formula

$$\bar{P}_{10} = \sqrt{(p_1 x_0 p_1 x_1 / p_0 x_0 p_0 x_1)}$$

became Fisher's Ideal Index.

Discussion of the argument so far is contained in the previous chapter, on 'The True Index'. This chapter is concerned with a finding of S. S. Byushgens (1925), 'On a class of hypersurfaces: concerning the 'ideal index' of Irving Fisher'. Robin Marris brought attention to this finding in 1955, and to Irving Fisher's reference to it in *The Making of Index Numbers* (1927 edition, where the author's name appears in the translated form, Buscheguennce). The point made is that Fisher's index is 'exact' if it can be assumed that demand is governed by a homogeneous quadratic utility function. The contents of the paper can be reconstructed from just this remark.

Everything admitted as relating to the theory of the price index up to that point has been described above, where the Laspeyres and Paasche formulae play a part as bounds of the 'true' index; Byushgens's theorem represents a new departure. In a manner of speaking, before, there was an answer without a question, and now there is a definite question for which it comprises the exact answer. Byushgens's theorem raises several questions, touched on in the last chapter; here we deal with one of those. It can be wondered if a utility function required in the hypothesis exists at all. If none does, the theorem remains nice and true, but becomes vacuous.

The homogeneity required in the theorem is essential of dealing with a price index. It represents a restricted understanding of the general cost of living problem, corresponding to the way it is dealt with in practice. To approach the general problem similarly in terms of quadratic utility, one would simply drop the homogeneity. This is done in Chapter IV on 'The Four-point Formula'; as complications go, it opens a Pandora's Box.

3.1 Byushgens' theorem

A utility function ϕ which is a homogeneous quadratic has the form

$$\phi(x) = x'hx/2$$

where h, the matrix of second derivatives, or Hessian, is symmetric, $h' = h$. The vector of first derivatives, or gradient, is $g(x) = x'h$. Therefore,

$$\phi(x) = g(x)x/2. \tag{i}$$

Also for any x_0, x_1 we have $x_0'hx_1 = x_1'hx_0$, because h is symmetric, and so

$$g(x_0)x_1 = g(x_1)x_0. \tag{ii}$$

The hypothesis that demand is governed by the utility ϕ requires any observed demand (x, p) to be compatible with it, and so there is the Lagrange condition

$$g(x) = \lambda p.$$

Because of the homogeneity, if ϕ admits any demand, (x, p) with $px > 0$ as compatible with it, then it does also every demand (xt, p) for $t \geq 0$, the expansion locus for the prices p being the ray through x. Any point xt on this ray is associated with an income $M = p(xt) = (px)t$, and so $x\{M/(px)\}$ is the point on the ray associated with any given income M, and its utility is

$$\phi\left(x\left(M/px\right)\right) = \phi(x)\{M/(px)\}^{1/2}.$$

Applied to the demands (x_r, p_r) observed in periods $r = 0,\ 1$ the condition for incomes M_r at the prices p_r to produce the same utility is that

$$M_1 = P_{10}M_0,$$

where, with $\phi_r = \phi(x_r)$,

$$P_{10} = (p_1x_1/p_0x_0)(\phi_0/\phi_1)^{1/2}$$

appears as the price index, with 0 and 1 as base and current peiods, as determined by the utility ϕ. Therefore, in order to learn this price index that is associated with such a ϕ, it is enough just to know the ratio ϕ_1/ϕ_0.

From the Lagrangean conditions $g(x_r) = \lambda_r p_r$ that are required by the hypothesis, by (i) we have $2\phi_r = \lambda_r p_r x_r$, and by (ii), $\lambda_0 p_0 x_1 = \lambda_1 p_1 x_0$, and so

$$\phi_1/\phi_0 = p_0x_1p_1x_1/p_0x_0p_1x_0.$$

Therefore,

$$P_{10} = \sqrt{(p_1x_0p_1x_1/p_0x_0p_0x_1)},$$

which is Fisher's formula.

The striking thing about this result, apart from the part Fisher's index plays in it, is that we do not need to know anything more about the quadratic utility in order to know the price index, let alone need to construct it. Subject to the hypothesis about the utility, the index is fully determined from the demand data for the two periods. If any utility function required by the hypothesis exists there might be many, even an infinity, of them, and so there would be an indeterminacy in the utility and, it might seem, possibly also in the associated price index. But even then, the price index is fully determinate.

It can still be wondered if any utility function such as is required by the hypothesis exists at all. If none does, the truth of the theorem is unaltered, but it becomes vacuous.

3.2   The existence question

The gradients of the hypothetical quadratic ϕ at the points x_r are given by $g_r = \lambda_r p_r$ subject to the requirement $g_0 x_1 = g_1 x_0$ which determines the ratio between the Lagrangean multipliers λ_r. The gradients are therefore determined but for an arbitrary multiplier, and the hypothetical quadratic can be taken to be specified to the extent of having these gradients at these points. The question now is whether one exists.

The *Paasche–Laspeyres inequality*, implied by the existence of price index and so certainly necessary, can be stated

$$p_0 x_0 p_1 x_1 \leq p_0 x_1 p_1 x_0.$$

Multiplying this by $\lambda_0 \lambda_1$, it becomes

$$g_0 x_0 g_1 x_1 - g_0 x_1 g_1 x_0 \leq 0.$$

The case of equality is excluded for the present and will be dealt with separately later.

Let

$$G = \begin{pmatrix} g_0 \\ g_1 \end{pmatrix}, \quad X = (x_0\ x_1),$$

so that GX is symmetric, since $g_0 x_1 = g_1 x_0$, with determinant $|GX| \leq 0$ by the P–L inequality. Let L be the linear space spanned by the x_r, described by points of the form $x = X\alpha$, which are linear combinations with coefficients given by a vector α. Also let

$$V = [X\alpha : \alpha \geq 0],$$

so this is the convex cone generated by the x_r. The gradient of the quadratic at any point $x = X\alpha$ of L, in particular of V, is $g(x) = \alpha'G$, and the value is

$$\phi(x) = \alpha'GX\alpha/2.$$

Therefore, provided $|GX| \neq 0$,

$$\phi(x) = \alpha'X'G'(GX)^{-1}GX\alpha/2 = x'h^*x/2.$$

where $h^* = G'(GX)^{-1}G$ is symmetric. Thus the function ϕ, already fully defined with restriction to L, has its definition there extended by the homogeneous quadratic ϕ^* with Hessian h^*, so we have $\phi(x) = \phi^*(x)$ for all $x \in L$. Since $X'h^* = G$, the gradient of this quadratic ϕ^* at x_r is g_r, as would be required were it to be the hypothetical quadratic ϕ.

Let $e = X(GX)^{-1}G$. This being such that $e^2 = e$, it is the projector on to its range, parallel to its null space, this being the linear space L spanned by the x_r and the orthogonal complement of the linear space spanned by the g_r. Evidently $h^*e = h^*$, and so by symmetry h^* also $e'h^* = h^*$, and hence $e'h^*e = h^*$. It follows that, for all $x, \phi^*(x) = \phi^*(ex)$, showing the cylindrical character of ϕ^*, with sections parallel to L. For any $x, ex = X\alpha$ where $\alpha = (GX)^{-1}Gx$, so ex belongs to the linear space L spanned by the x_r, and so the range of ϕ^* is identical with its range when restricted to L.

For any point $x = X\alpha$ of L, $2\phi(x) = \alpha'GX\alpha$. Therefore if $\alpha \geq 0$, so $x \in V$; then $\phi(x) \geq 0$, since $GX \geq 0$. Moreover, because $g_r x_r > 0, \phi(x) > 0$ if $x \neq 0$, so ϕ is positive definite on V. However, ϕ takes both positive and negative values, or is indefinite, in L; for the discriminant of the quadratic $\alpha GX\alpha$ is $|GX|$, and for this, being non-negative is equivalent to the P–L inequality. Therefore, it vanishes for real α with $\alpha_0, \alpha_1 \neq 0$, determining two values of α_0/α_1, distinct in the case of the strict P–L inequality when this determinant is positive, and coincident when it is zero.

The hypothetical function ϕ has been seen to be positive definite on V, but indefinite on L. Also, it must be quasi-concave at least near the points x_r, and the implications of that must be found. Moreover, there is no possiblity of the function being concave. The condition for a function to be concave is that its Hessian be non-positive definite. But in the case of a homogeneous quadratic, that property makes the function itself non-positive definite, which would contradict its being positive definite on V. Also the function, being non-negative definite, is excluded, since this would make it convex. For the hypothetical quadratic to be quasi-concave in a region where it is positive, it must necessarily be an indefinite quadratic, taking both positive and negative values.

Where $\phi(x) \geq 0$, as in some neighbourhood of V, it is possible to introduce $f = \phi^{1/2}$, and this function has the property $f(xt) = f(x)t$, by which it is homogeneous of degree 1, or conical, its graph in that case being a cone. Such a function is quasi-concave if and only if it is concave (Berge, 1963). Therefore, for ϕ to be quasi-concave, we require the Hessian of this function to be non-positive definite.

The gradient of f is $G = (1/2\phi^{3/2})g$, and the Hessian is

$$H = (1/\phi^{-3/2})(2\phi h - g'g).$$

Therefore, introducing

$$D(x, y) = g(x)xg(y)y - g(x)yg(y)x,$$

because $2\phi(x) = g(x)x$ and $g(y) = y'h$, we have

$$y'H(x)y \le 0 \iff D(x, y) \le 0.$$

It is readily seen that, if $D(x, y) \le 0$ for any x, y, then this holds also when x, y are replaced by any pair of points in the linear space spanned by them. Also, with

$$|GX| = D(x_0, x_1) < 0,$$

by the strict Paasche–Laspeyres inequality that has been assumed, $D(x, y) < 0$ for all independent $x, y \in L$. Thus, with any points $x = X\alpha, y = X\beta$ in L and $\Gamma = (\alpha, \beta)$, so also $g(x) = \alpha'G, g(y) = \beta'G$, we have

$$D(x, y) = |\Gamma'GX\Gamma| = |GX||\Gamma|^2,$$

so the sign of $D(x, y)$ is invariant and the same as that of

$$|GX| = D(x_0, x_1).$$

It appears from these considerations that, subject to the strict Paasche–Laspeyres inequality, the homogeneous quadratic ϕ^* with Hessian $h^* = G'(GX)^{-1}G$, provided it is taken to represent utility only in some neighbourhood of the convex cone V generated by the points x_r, can serve as the quadratic ϕ in the hypothesis of Byushgen's theorem. To that extent it provides one realization of the hypothesis, and any others must coincide with it in the cone V. It also appears that there is no generally broader way of realizing the hypothesis with a utility represented throughout the commodity space by a homogeneous quadratic. But, we have found a qualification for the hypothesis that makes it always realizable subject only to the strict Paasche–Laspeyres inequality.

The P–L inequality is anyway required, this being necessary and sufficient for the homogeneous consistency of the data, or the existence of a compatible homogeneous utility, required anyway for dealing with a price index at all. The exceptional P–L equality case, where the Paasche and Laspeyres indices are equal, still requires consideration. The case is instructive in a broader context apart from the following Theorem, and is dealt with in Section 3.3.

Theorem   *For any pair of demands $(x_r, p_r)(r = 0, 1)$ such that $p_r x_r > 0$, with $\lambda_r > 0$ such that $\lambda_0 p_0 x_1 = \lambda_1 p_1 x_0$ and $g_r = \lambda_r p_r$, and with*

$$G = \begin{pmatrix} g_0 \\ g_1 \end{pmatrix}, \quad X = (x_0 \; x_1),$$

the condition $|GX| \le 0$ is equivalent to the Paasche index being at most the Laspeyres index, and is necessary and sufficient for the existence of a compatible homogeneous utility, and for the existence of one moreover representable in a convex neighbourhood of the x_r by a quadratic function. Then, provided

$|GX| \neq 0$, *and with*

$$H = G'(GX)^{-1}G,$$

one such function is the homogeneous quadratic

$$\phi(x) = x'Hx/2$$

with Hessian H, this being positive definite and strictly quasi-convex in the convex conical closure V of the points x_r and having gradient g_r at x_r, and any other such quadratic must coincide with this in V.

3.3 Purchasing power correspondence

On the assumption that preferences determine choices, choices reveal the preferences. That should be so provided the assumption can be maintained and there are no contradictions, from the data or for other reasons, making the assumption untenable. With an absence of contradictions, the source of revelation may be exploited more freely, and when more is assumed about the preferences, the revelations can go still further. We will produce—to go alongside the usual revealed preferences—a *revealed homogeneous preference* principle. (We could just as easily call it a 'revealed separable preferences' or whatever, provided contradictions do not arise.)

Where homogeneity of utility is a part of the assumptions, any observed demand (x, p) reveals that the ray through x is the expansion locus for prices p, so the bundle $x(M/px)$ on this ray is the optimal bundle attainable with income M at those prices. Therefore, this bundle has at least the utility of any bundle y attainable with this income, that is, any one such that $py \leq M$. Thus, if R is the hypothetical utility order, with the homogeneity property

$$xRy \implies xtRyt \quad (t \geq 0),$$

we have

$$py \leq M \implies x(M/px)Ry,$$

for all y and M. Without the homogeneity we would have this just for $M = px$; that is,

$$py \leq px \implies xRy,$$

as usual, but with the homogeneity we have many more revealed preferences. That is so, provided no contradictions arise; otherwise, we may have to fall back to the ordinary revealed preferences, or even to having to revealed preferences at all.

Applying revelations from this expanded source to a pair of demands $(x_r, p_r)(r = 0, 1)$, we have

$$x_r(M_r) = x_r(M_r/p_rx_r)$$

as the optimal bundle attainable with any income M_r at the prices p_r, whose utility represents the purchasing power of the income at those prices. Therefore if S is the indirect utility order associated with the hypothetical R, so that

$$M_r^{-1} p_r S M_s^{-1} p_s$$

signifies that the income M_r at the prices p_r has at least the purchasing power of the income M_s at the prices p_s, we have

$$M_r^{-1} p_r S M_s^{-1} p_s \iff x_r(M_r) R x_s(M_s),$$

and also

$$p_r x_s(M_s) \le M_r \implies x_r(M_r) R x_s(M_s),$$

where the strict inequality implies the corresponding strict preference. For incomes M_0, M_1 which are to be admitted as equivalent in purchasing power at respective prices, we therefore must have

$$p_r x_s \, (M_s/p_s x_s) \ge M_r \quad (r, s = 0, 1);$$

that is,

$$p_1 x_0 / p_0 x_0 \ge M_1/M_0 \ge p_1 x_1 / p_1 x_0.$$

Another way of putting this is that $M_1 = P_{10} M_0$ where

$$\check{P}_{10} \le P_{10} \le \hat{P}_{10},$$

$\check{P}_{10}$ and $\hat{P}_{10}$ being Paasche and Laspeyres indices. In any case, we have a correspondence between M_0 and M_1 where any value of one corresponds to an interval of values of the other, and *every* value of P_{10} between the Paasche and Laspeyres limits determines a particular one–one subcorrespondence, which can be associated with some homogeneous utility compatible with the given pair of demands, and which so qualifies as a 'true' value. The geometric mean of the limits, which is Fisher's index, is one such value—therefore a true value, but also no truer than any other between these limits. A distinction that Byushgens' theorem gives to this particular value is that it is the one which would be obtained were the associated utility to have a quadratic representation.

The existence of such a utility has been considered, and it was found that, provided the Paasche index is strictly less than that of Laspeyres, a compatible homogeneous utility can be found which has a quadratic representation in a limited sense involving a convex neighbourhood of the points x_r. The threshold case, where the Paasche index equals the Laspeyres, remained to be considered. It will be found that in this case, assuming that the prices p_0 and p_1 are not proportional, any compatible homogeneous utility is essentially not differentiable and so certainly cannot be represented by a quadratic in any neighbourhood of the points x_r.

The P–L equality is necessary and sufficient for the existence of a unique ratio $t_0/t_1 > 0$ such that, for all $t_0, t_1 > 0$ in that ratio,

$$p_0 x_1 t_1 = p_0 x_0 t_0, \quad p_1 x_0 t_0 = p_1 x_1 t_1.$$

Such points $x_0 t_0$ and $x_1 t_1$ are therefore revealed indifferent, so they lie in the same utility surface, and so do all points of the line segment $\langle x_0 t_0, x_1 t_1 \rangle$ joining them, which therefore lies entirely in that surface. The two hyperplanes

$$p_0 x = p_0 x_0 t_0, \quad p_1 x = p_1 x_1 t_1$$

are both supporting hyperplanes to the surface with this segment in common with each other and the surface, and they are distinct hyperplanes, since the prices are not proportional, so denying differentiability of the surface at all points of the segment.

In the further case where the prices are proportional, if p is any price vector proportional to them, px is a homogeneous utility function compatible with the demands, and so the degenerate homogeneous quadratic (px) is compatible also and so realizes the hypothesis in Byushgens' theorem.

3.4   Many-period generalization

The homogeneous consistency of any demands (x_r, p_r) is defined by the existence of a homogeneous utility which is compatible with all of them. Now we can define *homogeneous quadratic consistency* by the existence of such a utility which, moreover, is representable by a quadratic in a convex neighbourhood of the demand points x_r. We have seen that, for a pair of demands, provided equality between the Paasche and Laspeyres indices is excluded, *homogeneous consistency is equivalent to homogeneous quadratic consistency*. (We can compare this result with the theorem on the equivalence of general and classical consistency, of Chapter II.3.) The neighbourhood qualification in our definition appears suitable because this theorem, which saves Byushgens' theorem from vacuity, would not be true without it.

Byushgens' theorem is as applicable to many periods as to two. But in that more general application, our result as stated, which makes the hypothesis realizable in the case of two periods, is certainly not true. Some further requirement is needed for the realizability, beside the neighbourhood qualification already brought in. It should make a proper restriction with more than two periods, and becomes empty in the special case of two.

One such requirement is obvious, and the question is whether it is all that is needed. It seems fair that Fisher's index should be subjected to Fisher's tests. Usually these tests have been regarded as tests of a formula, which on substitution should produce an identity. Another view is that they provide tests of the data that enter the formula. The reversal test is an identity with Fisher's formula so this is an empty requirement as concerns the data. The more general chain test is not an identity and represents a proper condition on the data when there are more than two periods. With two periods, it reduces to the reversal test and so in this case it becomes empty. Here is a case of non-compliance with a Fisher test that is not a disaster but a significant condition on the data.

A. Wald demonstrated a general inconsistency between certain of Fisher's tests, and such inconsistencies have been investigated systematically by W. Eichhorn and J. Voeller (1976). These are bound up with the convention about an index formula that it should involve the demand data for the two reference periods alone. Here we do not follow that convention and such issues cannot arise, since price indices for several periods are determined all together in a way that depends on the data for all the periods simultaneously, and they are automatically all that they should be. That applies also to Fisher's formula when it is exact in the sense of Byushgens' theorem, in providing values associated with a homogeneous utility compatible with the data. In that case, the values obtained must satisfy the chain test. The exactness depended on the utility admitting a certain quadratic representation, and the question now is whether the chain test requirement on the Fisher values, in addition to the homogeneous consistency required in the first place, is enough to assure the existence of such a utility. Should that be the case, with the same exclusion of the Paasche–Laspeyres equality, we would have a theorem that reduced in the case of two periods to just what we have already.

Given any numbers P_{rs}, the condition $P_{rs}P_{st} = P_{rt}$, which corresponds to Fisher's chain test for a formula, is necessary and sufficient for them to have the ratio form $P_{rs} = P_r/P_s$, so it can be called the *ratio test*. For, under this condition, we can take $P_r = P_{rt}$ for any fixed t, and then $P_{rs} = P_r/P_s$. Conversely, if the numbers have this form, then obviously the condition must be satisfied.

For the Fisher values

$$P_{rs} = \sqrt{(p_r x_r \, p_r x_s / p_s x_r \, p_s x_s)}$$

the ratio test is equivalent to the condition

$$p_r x_s \, p_s x_t \, p_t x_r = p_s x_r \, p_t x_s \, p_r x_t,$$

which is necessary and sufficient for the existence of number $\lambda_r > 0$ with unique ratios such that

$$\lambda_r p_r x_s = \lambda_s p_s x_r,$$

so that with $g_r = \lambda_r p_r$ and

$$G = \begin{pmatrix} g_1 \\ \vdots \\ g_m \end{pmatrix}, \quad X = (x_1 \cdots x_m),$$

the matrix GX is symmetric.

With $L_{rs} = p_r x_s / p_s x_s$, homogeneous consistency requires the existence of a simultaneous solution P_r to the *price-level system* of inequalities $L_{rs} \geq P_r/P_s$.

The condition for these inequalities to be solvable is the *cyclical product test*

$$L_{rs}L_{st} \cdots L_{qr} \geq 1$$

for all $r, s, t, \ldots, q$. A necessary condition for this is the *Paasche–Laspeyres test* that $L_{rs}L_{sr} \geq 1$, which is another statement of the Paasche–Laspeyres inequality that the one index does not exceed the other, now holding for all r, s. This condition *by itself is not sufficient for homogeneous consistency*, except for two periods taken alone. However, *its conjunction with the ratio test is sufficient*; for, the ratio test requires the Fisher values to have the form $P_{rs} = P_r/P_s$, and if $L_{rs}L_{sr} \geq 1$ then also $L_{rs} \geq P_{rs}$, showing that the price-level system of inequalities has a solution.

Suppose now that the data accept the ratio test and we have the symmetric positive matrix GX constructed as earlier, unique but for an arbitrary positive multiplier. A necessary condition for constructing the required quadratic is that $X\alpha = 0 \Rightarrow \alpha'G = 0$ for all α. This is assured, and the further discussion is simplified, if it is taken that GX is a regular matrix. Then we can consider the quadratic with Hessian $H = G'(GX)^{-1}G$; and, subject to the strict Passche–Laspeyres inequality, $L_{rs}L_{sr} > 1$, an argument along the lines of that used earlier for a pair of demands serves to show that this is a suitable quadratic. The present question paves the way for the question to follow in Chapter IV.

IV The Four-Point Formula

The *expansion locus* associated with any prices is the locus of consumption when income varies while the prices remain fixed. When demand is governed by utility, properties of the utility are reflected in the characteristics of the expansion loci. For instance, if the utility relation $R \subset C \times C$ is homogeneous, or conical, having the property

$$xRy \implies xtRyt \quad (t \geq 0),$$

by which its graph in $C \times C$ is a cone, then also the expansion loci in the commodity space C are cones, possibly just single rays, or lines through the origin. Correspondingly, the relation between incomes that have the same purchasing power at some different prices is homogeneous linear, and so is represented by a line through the origin, now in the *income space*, the space of two dimensions with the incomes as coordinates. We have also called this the *Fleetwood space*, because his method determines points in it, without the compulsion to take ratios of coordinates and otherwise abandon the points, as in effect is done with the CPI. The slope of the line, which in this case completely describes the relation of equivalent incomes, is the *price index* corresponding to the two different price situations. *The idea of a price index for both theory and practice is encompassed in the idea that this relation between equivalent incomes should be homogeneous linear, and so capable of description by a single number—its slope—that number being the price index.* At least, it seems, very suitable to think of it that way. In order for such a relation to be possible when expressed in terms of utility, the utility involved must be homogeneous or conical in the way just stated. Correspondingly, in the commodity space, expansion paths must be rays through the origin. Beyond that, no more can be said of the relation except that it should be monotonic. The price index thus represents a highly restricted idea about purchasing power, or cost of living, with implications about demand behaviour, and about utility when that is brought in.

For a less compromised but still simple approach to the same matter, the relation between equivalent incomes might be taken to be linear, not necessarily homogeneous, and so represented by a line which need not go through the origin. To describe such a relation two numbers are required, the slope and the intercept, instead of just one. Correspondingly, as concerns the expansion loci in the commodity space C, these would have to be lines, not necessarily through the origin in C. There are two different ways of stating the implications of the linear income relation as concerns utility. First, in terms of the cost function,

$$\varrho(p, x) = \min[py : yRx],$$

this must have the special form

$$\varrho(p, x) = \sigma(p)\phi(x) + v(p).$$

For the more restricted homogeneous case, $v(p) = 0$, so the cost function admits the factorization

$$\varrho(p, x) = \sigma(p)\phi(x)$$

into a product of a function of prices alone and a function of quantities alone, a *price function* and a *quantity function*. For the homogeneous case, all the utility surfaces have to be similar, so just one of them specifies the entire preference relation. In the general linear case, instead two surfaces are required, as elaborated in Chapter III.5.

For just one example of a utility that determines linear expansion loci, we have the general quadratic. For the homogeneous case that plays a part in Byushgens' theorem, these all go through the origin. With a general quadratic these are not necessarily through the origin, but through the centre of the quadratic, if it has one. It will be seen that in dealing with hypothetical quadratic utility on the basis of given demand data, the possible existence of a centre, where the gradient vanishes, is a critical matter, and so is its possible location. Such further complications are avoided in the homogeneous case, where the centre is at the origin, so that we know it exists and also where it is.

On the basis of homogeneous quadratic utility and the usual data provided by a pair of demands for the reference periods, it appears from Byushgens' theorem that price indices are fully determinate, and moreover that they are calculable from the data by Fisher's formula. It is plausible that a similar but less restricted approach to purchasing power could be made on the basis of general quadratics. In dropping the homogeneity of utility, the idea of a price index is abandoned. One would want to construct a general linear relation between equivalent incomes that is consistent with a quadratic that fits given data, and it should be obtained in terms of the data, without having to construct the quadratic. The procedure is suggested by Byushgens' theorem, but carrying it out is not simple and experience of the homogeneous case gives no anticipation of peculiar features encountered. The formulae obtained involve demand data from four periods, instead of the two usual with price-index formulae. Why that is so, and why the number is exactly four, will have to be seen. (A remark similar to this did not satify a journal editor, when I submitted a first note on the subject in 1956.) Also, the income purchasing power relation is not fully determinate, and so the formulae have to characterize all the many possibilities. For the special case where the four budgets are parallel in pairs, we do have determinacy, and the formulae become equivalent to Wald's 'New Formula'. The connection was appreciated by H. Houthakker (*c*.1960) with the observation that twice two is four. Here, therefore, is a generalization of Wald's formula, which itself is a generalization of Fisher's formula.

A comparison between the homogeneous and non-homogeneous cases, both in general and with quadratics in particular, will serve to indicate what we are about. This involves the finite demand analysis method shown in Part II, which was developed in dealing with this problem though now it is considered on its own. The formula to be obtained has complications, but they have been instructive and have produced that other work as a by-product.

For any demands (x_r, p_r), with associated expenditures $M_r = p_r x_r$ and budget vectors $u_r = M_r^{-1} p_r$, homogeneous consistency, or the existence of a homogeneous utility compatible with all of them, is equivalent to the existence of numbers P_r such that

$$p_r x_s / p_s x_s \geq P_r / P_s \quad \text{for all } r, s.$$

As concerns two periods r, s taken alone, these inequalities just require

$$p_r x_s \geq P_r / P_s \geq p_r x_r / p_s x_r;$$

that is, the ratio P_r / P_s must belong to the Paasche–Laspeyres interval

$$I_{rs} = [p_r x_r / p_s x_r, p_r x_s / p_s x_s].$$

When this interval is non-empty, the geometric mean of the end-points, which is the Fisher index, is one of its points, and therefore provides a particular solution. One can always pick this point in dealing with any two periods alone, but not in general for more than two at a time, since a special condition is required, as seen in Chapter III. The condition amounts to an acceptance of Fisher's chain test by Fisher's index. It happens that such a Fisher or *mean solution* can be associated with a quadratic utility, by the theorem in Section 3.2. But in any case it is a solution remote from the critical limits. Even when an exact solution is not available for more than two periods, one might want to pick one approximating the model.

A similar way of thinking can apply in the absence of the homogeneity that goes with price indices. It again produces a linkage with quadratics, though in this case they are not homogeneous. The general consistency of the given demands, or the existence of any utility whatsoever that is compatible with all of them, requires the existence of numbers, λ_r, ϕ_r which are a solution of the system of homogeneous linear inequalities

$$\lambda_r > 0, \quad \lambda_r D_{rs} \geq \phi_s - \phi_r \quad \text{for all } r, s$$

where the coefficients are given by $D_{rs} = u_r x_s - 1$. For a solution, the numbers are required to be such that the differences $\phi_s - \phi_r$ belong to the intervals

$$(\lambda_r D_{rs}, -\lambda_s D_{sr}).$$

As before, concerning ratios, though now with the arithmetic instead of geometric mean, a particularly well accepted solution might be taken to be one where these differences are not just in these intervals but coincide with their mid-points; that is, where

$$\phi_s - \phi_r = (\lambda_r D_{rs} - \lambda_s D_{sr})/2.$$

Such a *median solution* generally cannot be found for more than four periods, but for fewer than four there are many. For exactly four periods such a solution exists, and also is essentially unique, but for a positive multiplier of the λ_r and a linear transformation of the ϕ_r. As a kind of parallel to Byushgens' theorem, it is found that, if demand is governed by a quadratic utility, then the utilities and marginal utilities determined by it at the demand points x_r correspond to the ϕ_r and λ_r in a median solution, and so as such are essentially unique and can be calculated directly from the data. That is a reason why the formula to be obtained should involve the demand data from four periods, corresponding to the way in which Fisher's formula involves data from two.

The general and homogeneous cases have a correspondence that can be seen with reference to the two systems of inequalities, where the imposition of homogeneity makes a reduction of one to the other. For a utility function ϕ with gradient g, and with

$$\phi_r = \phi(x_r), \quad g_r = g(x_r),$$

we have the Lagrangean conditions $g_r = \lambda_r u_r$, with Lagrange multiplier $\lambda_r = g_r x_r$ since $u_r x_r = 1$. For a linearly homogeneous, or conical, utility we have $g_r x_r = \phi_r$, as Euler's identity, and so $\lambda_r = \phi_r$. Similarly for a homogeneous quadratic, $g_r x_r = 2\phi_r$, and so $\lambda_r = 2\phi_r$. By making these substitutions we obtain corresponding reductions. Thus for the general case we have the system of inequalities

$$\lambda_r(u_r x_s - 1) \geq \phi_s - \phi_r,$$

which with $\lambda_r = \phi_r$ becomes the system

$$u_r x_s \geq \lambda_s/\lambda_r$$

associated with the homogeneous case. Also for the median solution, where

$$\phi_s - \phi_r = \{\lambda_r(u_r x_s - 1) - \lambda_s(u_s x_r - 1)\}/2,$$

with $\lambda_r = 2\phi_r$ we obtain

$$\lambda_r/\lambda_s = u_s x_r/u_r x_s,$$

corresponding to the Fisher or mean solution for the homogeneous case, since now we have the square of a linearly homogenous function and the index is correspondingly squared.

For the general case, with any *multiplier-level solution* λ_r, ϕ_r we can construct a utility function ϕ, compatible with the given data, with indirect utility function ψ

in the budget space **B** which, from the compatibility, is such that $\phi(x_r) = \psi(u_r)$. Also $\phi(x_r) = \phi_r$, so the numbers ϕ_r in a solution appear as utility levels. Also, with $g_r = \lambda_r u_r$,

$$\phi(x) - \phi(x_r) \leq g_r(x - x_r) \quad \text{for all } x,$$

so λ_r appears as a Lagrange multiplier making g_r a support gradient of ϕ at the point x_r. Correspondingly, from convex programming theory,

$$\psi(M^{-1}p_r) - \psi(M_r^{-1}p_r) \leq (\lambda_r/M_r)(M - M_r),$$

for all incomes M, which in the differentiable case gives

$$\lambda_r/M_r = \partial\psi(M_r^{-1}p_r)/\partial M_r,$$

showing λ_r/M_r as the marginal utility of money in period r. In the homogeneous case we have

$$\psi(M^{-1}p) = M\psi(p),$$

and so

$$\lambda_r = \psi(u_r) = \phi(x_r) = \phi_r.$$

Then the price 'levels' are determined by $P_r = M_r/\lambda_r$, and price indices correspondingly.

The relation between any incomes E_r, E_s that have the same purchasing power at the prices p_r, p_s is determined from the condition

$$\psi(E_r^{-1}p_r) = \psi(E_s^{-1}p_s).$$

Without any qualification about underlying utility, this is simply a monotonic relation. For a homogeneous utility it takes the special homogeneous linear, or 'price index' form $E_r = P_{rs}E_s$ where P_{rs}, the price index, depends on the prices alone. The case we will be concerned with now is where this relation takes the general linear form and, as a case of consistency with that, utility has a quadratic representation, as in Byushgens' theorem, though without the homogeneity.

The result about determinacy of utilities and marginal utilities for a general quadratic utility from demand data for four periods was found in 1955. That in itself represents a generalization of Byushgens' theorem, dealt with in Chapter III. It was a response to the attention that Robin Marris (1955) drew to the theorem, in a consultation about the Paasche–Laspeyres 'spread', and is in my reports or papers (Afriat, 1956a,b,c, 1957b). The determinate values are obtained from what is now called a median solution for multipliers and levels. That terminology was introduced only after the general idea of multiplier-level solutions and their use for constructing utility, with data for any number of periods, was put forward in 1959. The report (Afriat, 1960c) on 'The system of inequalities $a_{rs} > x_s - x_r$' is auxiliary to the mathematics of multiplier-level solutions, including median solutions. This happens also to represent a phase in the theory of minimum paths, now well known. I was then unaware of the connection, as that subject, which comes to the fore with Ford and Fulkerson (1962), had hardly begun. The material is now absorbed into Appendix 1, and the aspect to do specifically with median solutions is in this chapter.

The passage from the determinacy theorem to the formula of this chapter was not immediate. On returning to the formula and its theory in order to give this account, thought it is dealt with more briefly with secondary aspects put aside, features that were not well developed in the earlier accounts have been elaborated. A stage was represented by three connected reports. (Afriat, 1961e), of which one is expository, and was reproduced in the volume in honour of Oskar Morgenstern (Afriat, 1967b), who had sponsored the work. The report on 'Gradient configurations and quadratic functions' (Afriat, 1961c) gives an account of the special questions that arise concerning quadratics, and in this chapter that material has been simplified and condensed. The formula remained as left in 1961, and there has not been a trace of attention to it. This is unlike the background theory of multiplier-level solutions, utility construction and the cost of living problem, which, finding the formula, provoked and which has had some rediscovery with other writers. Though it was considered eccentric to take time with the 'index number problem' in those days, now of course, with general inflation, it is quite popular, but the subject has an interest of its own.

4.1   Median multipliers and levels

The characteristic of a quadratic is that its Hessian, or matrix of second derivatives, is constant. Let $\phi(x)$ be a quadratic with gradient $g(x)$ and Hessian h, so h is a constant symmetric matrix, and form Taylor's theorem,

$$\phi(y) - \phi(x) = g(x)(y - x) + (y - x)'h(y - x)/2. \tag{i}$$

Then

$$g(y) - g(x) = (y - x)'h, \tag{ii}$$

and so also

$$\phi(y) - \phi(x) = \{g(x) + g(y)\}(y - x)/2. \tag{iii}$$

From this,

$$g(x)(y - z) + g(y)(z - x) + g(z)(x - y) = 0, \tag{iv}$$

which can be seen to be equivalent to

$$\{g(x) - g(y)\}(z - w) = \{g(z) - g(w)\}(x - y), \tag{v}$$

which also follows from (ii) with the symmetry of h. The consequence

$$\{g(x) - g(z)\}(y - z) = \{g(y) - g(z)\}(x - z), \tag{vi}$$

holding for any fixed z all x, y is sufficient to assure again (v) and (vi), for any vector field $g(x)$. This condition or these equivalents will define the *symmetry* of a vector field. The property is necessary and sufficient for a vector field to be the gradient field of a quadratic.

We will consider vectors g_r associated with given points x_r satisfying conditions corresponding to (iv), (v) and (vi), which in such an application are again equivalent, and the possible quadratics that have these gradients at these points, or admit such a *gradient configuration*.

Should any demands $(x_r, P_r)(r = 0, 1, 2, \ldots)$, with expenditures M_r and budget vectors $u_r = M_r^{-1} p_r$, be compatible with a utility that is represented by a quadratic ϕ in a neighbourhood of the points x_r, we would have $g_r = \lambda_r u_r$ for some Lagrange multipliers $\lambda_r > 0$, where $g_r = g(x_r)$. Therefore, with the utility levels $\phi_r = \phi(x_r)$, we should have

$$\phi_s - \phi_r = (g_r + g_s)(x_s - x_r)/2$$
$$= \{\lambda_r u_r(x_s - x_r) - \lambda_s u_s(x_r - x_s)\}/2$$
$$= (\lambda_r D_{rs} - \lambda_s D_{sr})/2,$$

where $D_{rs} = u_r x_s - 1$, since $u_r x_r = 1$.

Thus, the multipliers and levels λ_r, ϕ_r must satisfy the *median equations*

$$\lambda_r > 0, \quad \phi_s - \phi_r = (\lambda_r D_{rs} - \lambda_s D_{sr})/2,$$

and so be a *median solution*. The *interval inequalities*

$$\lambda_r D_{rs} + \lambda_s D_{sr} \geq 0$$

are then equivalent to

$$\lambda_r D_{rs} \geq \phi_s - \phi_r,$$

and so make a median solution also an ordinary multiplier-level solution for the demands, the existence of which is equivalent to their consistency. Thus, *the solvability of the median equations together with the interval inequalities implies the consistency of the demands.*

With any median solution, λ_r, ϕ_r and with $g_r = \lambda_r u_r$, we have

$$\phi_s - \phi_r = (g_r + g_s)(x_s - x_r)/2,$$

corresponding to (iii), which has the consequence (v), so we have

$$(g_r - g_0)(x_s - x_0) = (g_s - g_0)(x_r - x_0);$$

that is,

$$g_r(x_s - x_0) - g_s(x_r - x_0) = g_0(x_s - x_r).$$

Equivalently,

$$\lambda_r(D_{rs} - D_{r0}) - \lambda_s(D_{sr} - D_{s0}) = \lambda_0(D_{0s} - D_{0r}).$$

It can be seen now that any four demands $r = 0, 1, 2, 3$ have a median solution which is unique but for an arbitrary positive multiplier, provided that $(D_{12} - D_{10})(D_{23} - D_{20})(D_{31} - D_{30}) \neq (D_{21} - D_{20})(D_{32} - D_{30})(D_{13} - D_{10})$. For with arbitrary $\lambda_0 > 0$, here are three equations for λ_r $(r = 1, 2, 3)$ which have a unique solution subject to this condition. Then, with the λ_r so obtained and $g_r = \lambda_r u_r$, and with arbitrary ϕ_0, and

$$\phi_r = \phi_0 + (g_0 + g_r)(x_r - x_0) \quad (r = 1, 2, 3),$$

the λ_r, ϕ_r $(r = 0, 1, 2, 3)$ provide a median solution for the four demands. Then the matrices

$$G_0 = [g_r - g_0], \quad X_0 = [x_r - x_0]$$

with $g_r - g_0$ as rows and $x_r - x_0$ as columns, for $r \neq 0$, are such that the 3×3 matrix $G_0 X_0$, which is their product is symmetric.

The interval inequalities require $\lambda_r > 0$, so that $g_r \gtrsim 0$, and

$$0 \leq g_r(x_s - x_r) + g_s(x_r - x_s)$$
$$= -(g_r - g_s)(x_r - x_s),$$

and so $(g_r - g_s)(x_r - x_s) \leq 0$, in particular $(g_r - g_0)(x_r - x_0) \leq 0$, so making the diagonal elements of $G_0 X_0$ all non-positive. A further case, associated with a concave function, which will be dealt with further, is where $G_0 X_0$ is non-positive definite.

4.2   Centre locus

A *centre* of a quadratic is any point c where the gradient vanished; that is, $g(c) = 0$. Then by 4.1(ii), $g(x) = (x - c)'h$ for all x. Then c' is another if and only if $(c - c')h = 0$; that is, $c - c'$ belongs to the null space N of the Hessian h. Thus, for a central quadratic the *centre locus* is a linear manifold parallel to N. A *central quadratic* is one for which a centre exists. Any homogeneous quadratic is an example since it has the origin as a centre, and in this case the centre locus is identical with all null space N of the Hessian.

In the case of a *regular quadratic* for which the Hessian is a regular matrix with inverse k we have, again from 4.1(ii),

$$x - kg(x)' = y - kg(y)' \quad \text{for all } x, y$$

so we have a point c such that

$$x - kg(x)' = c \quad \text{for all } x.$$

This point is such that $g(x) = (x - c)'h$ and so $g(c) = 0$; so it is a centre, and moreover a unique centre, since with h regular $c - c' \in N \Rightarrow c = c'$. Thus, any regular quadratic has a unique point as centre. Also, for a central quadratic the centre is unique if and only if the quadratic is regular, that is, has a regular Hessian.

For a quadratic with centre c we now have, corresponding to similar properties in Section 4.1,

$$\phi(x) = \phi(c) + (x - c)'h(x - c) \tag{i}$$

$$g(x) = (x - c)'h \tag{ii}$$

$$\phi(x) = g(x)(x - c)/2 \tag{iii}$$

$$g(x)y - g(y)x = \{g(x) - g(y)\}c \tag{iv}$$

and

$$\{g(x) - g(z)\}z - g(z)(x - z) = \{g(x) - g(z)\}c. \tag{v}$$

Because h is symmetric, its range R is the orthogonal complement of its null space N. It appears from 4.1 (ii) that the *gradient locus* is a linear manifold parallel to R. In the case of a central quadratic this is identical with R, as seen from (ii) here.

There are complications with singular quadratics not present with regular ones. As seen already, while a regular quadratic always has a centre, in fact just one, a singular quadratic might or might not. We call a singular quadratic that does have a centre a *cylindrical quadratic*, with sections parallel to R and generators parallel to N.

Any displacement by a vector in N leaves the gradient unchanged. Resolving the gradient orthogonally into a component in R and a component in N, if there is one, the value is changed in such a displacement only by the component in N. In the case of a cylindrical quadratic, there is no component in N, and so again the value is unchanged. In that case the quadratic has identical values, and gradients, in every linear manifold parallel to R, at points which correspond by displacements parallel to N. Considered as a function in any sectional manifold, parallel to R, and taking any origin and Cartesian coordinates, its values are given by a regular quadratic in the coordinates. Thus a cylindrical quadratic becomes represented by an identical regular quadratic in every sectional manifold.

For a singular quadratic which is not cylindrical, the gradient locus is a linear manifold G, which is a parallel displacement of R, not identical with R and so not through the origin. If $\bar{g}$ is the foot of the perpendicular from the origin on to G, so necessarily $\bar{g}$ belongs to N; for any g in G, we have that $g - \bar{g}$ is both in R and perpendicular to $\bar{g}$, and G is described by all points of the form $\bar{g} + r$ where $r \in R$. The locus of points $\bar{x}$ where $g(\bar{x}) = \bar{g}$ is a linear manifold $\bar{N}$ which is a parallel displacement of N, the *parabolic axis* of the quadratic, cutting every sectional manifold in a unique point where the gradient is $\bar{g}$.

Consider again vector g_r associated with points x_r. If any quadratic with centre c has these gradients at these points, then, by (iv),

$$g_r x_s - g_s x_r = (g_r - g_s)c.$$

These are the *centre equations* for the gradient configuration (g_r, x_r), and the *centre manifold* is the linear manifold of points c which are solutions. If any solution exists, then necessarily

$$g_r x_s - g_s x_r + g_s x_t - g_t x_s + g_t x_r - g_r x_t = 0,$$

corresponding to 4.1 (iv); and, equivalently, corresponding to 4.1 (vi), the matrix $G_0 X_0$ introduced at the end of Section 4.1 is symmetric, this being the general gradient symmetry condition, equivalent to

$$G_0 x_r - (g_r X_0)' = G_0 x_0 - (g_0 X_0)'.$$

For an equivalent statement of the centre equations, subject to this symmetry, we have

$$G_0 x_0 - (g_0 X_0)' = G_0 c.$$

The centre equations have a solution $c = 0$ if and only if $g_r x_s = g_s x_r$, which is the homogeneous gradient symmetry condition; equivalently, $G_0 x_0 = (g_0 X_0)'$.

For any quadratic that admits the gradient configuration H with elements (x_r, g_r) its gradient any point $x_\alpha = x_0 + X_0 \alpha$ on the linear manifold through the x_r, or *base manifold*, must be given by the point $g_\alpha = g_0 + \alpha' G_0$ on the linear manifold through the g_r, or *gradient manifold* of the configuration. But the gradient at any point is unique, and so, for consistency with admission of H by some quadratic, we must have

$$x_\alpha = x_\beta \;\Rightarrow\; g_\alpha = g_\beta$$

for all vectors α, β and, equivalently,

$$X_0 \alpha = 0 \;\Rightarrow\; \alpha' G_0 = 0$$

for all vectors α.

Should we have $g_\alpha = 0$ for some α, every quadratic that admits H has $c = x_\alpha$ as a centre, and so is a central quadratic.

In any case, subject to the symmetry of $G_0 X_0$, at any point x_α which is a solution of the centre equations, and so in the intersection of the centre and base manifolds, the gradient g_α is such that $g_\alpha X_0 = 0$, and so if not null is perpendicular to the base manifold. For such a solution requires $-(g_0 X_0)' = G_0 X_0 \alpha$, which, with the symmetry of $G_0 X_0$, is equivalent to $g_\alpha X_0 = 0$.

For a *regular gradient configuration* H, $G_0 X_0$ is a regular symmetric matrix. In this case there is a unique point $\bar{c} = x_\alpha$, where the centre manifold cuts the base manifold. As just seen, the gradient $\bar{g} = g_\alpha$, at this point, if not null, is perpendicular to the base manifold. Thus, with the regularity, for a solution, x_α to the centre equations, we must have

$$\alpha = -(G_0 X_0)^{-1} X_0' g_0';$$

and therefore

$$\bar{c} = x_0 - X_0 (G_0 X_0)^{-1} X_0' g_0'$$

and

$$\bar{g} = g_0 - g_0 X_0 (G_0 X_0)^{-1} G_0 = g_0 (1 - e),$$

where

$$e = X_0 (G_0 X_0)^{-1} G_0$$

is idempotent, and therefore the projector on to its range parallel to its null space, these being the range of G_0 and the null space of X_0. Then $1 - e$ is the complementary projector, on to the null space, or the orthogonal complement to the range, of X_0, parallel to the range of G_0, and we have $\bar{g}$ as the image of g_0 by this.

For any quadratic that admits the gradient configuration H and has a point c as its centre, at any point x_α of the base manifold, where the gradient is g_α, that value must, by (iii), be given by

$$\phi_\alpha = C + g_\alpha (x_\alpha - c)/2,$$

where $C = \phi(c)$ is the value at the centre.

4.3 Linear purchasing power

Consider a regular quadratic ϕ. It must have a unique centre c and so have the form

$$\phi(x) = C + (x - c)' h (x - c)/2,$$

where h is the Hessian, symmetric and regular, and $C = \phi(c)$. The gradient is $g(x) = (x - c)' h$.

For the compatibility of a normalized demand (x, u), for which $ux = 1$, with a utility represented near x by ϕ, it is necessary that $g(x) = \lambda u$ for some $\lambda > 0$; that is,

$$(x - c)' h = \lambda u,$$

and so if k is the inverse of h, also symmetric, we have

$$x - c = ku'\lambda.$$

From $ux = 1$, therefore,

$$1 - uc = uku'\lambda,$$

and so

$$x - c = ku'(1 - uc)/uku'.$$

Hence with $u = M^{-1} p$ we have

$$x - c = kp'(M - pc)/pkp',$$

which shows that the locus of demand x as income M varies while prices p remain fixed, is a line through c, with direction kp'. Thus the expansion loci determined by a regular quadratic utility are all lines going through its centre.

The utility attained by an income M when the prices are p is

$$C + (M - pc)^2 / 2pkp',$$

that is, $\psi(M^{-1}p)$, where

$$\psi(u) = C + (1 - uc)^2 / 2uku'$$

is the indirect utility function obtained from ϕ.

If it is given that the quadratic is compatible with some four demands (x_r, p_r) $(r = 0, 1, 2, 3)$, with expenditures $M_r = p_r x_r$ and budget vectors $u_r = M_r^{-1} p_r$, then, as shown in Section 4.1 and subject to the stated regularity, the Lagrange multipliers λ_r corresponding to the normalized demands (x_r, u_r) are fully determined, but for an arbitrary multiplier of no importance, and then so are the ϕ_r, but for an additive constant which is fixed by assigning ϕ_0 arbitrarily.

The quadratic then admits the gradient configuration (x_r, g_r) where $g_r = \lambda_r u_r$, and so its centre c must satisfy the center equations

$$g_r x_s - g_s x_r = (g_r - g_s)c.$$

The compatibility of the quadratic with the given demands has further implications about the location of the centre, and so also about its value C at the centre consistent with the value given arbitrarily to ϕ_0. Here two cases become distinguished, as will be dealt with further. Also we have

$$1 - u_r c = u_r k u_r' \lambda_r.$$

Any incomes E_r, E_s that have the same purchasing power at the prices p_r, p_s as decided by the utility ϕ must be such that

$$\psi(E_r^{-1} p_r) = \psi(E_s^{-1} p_s);$$

equivalently,

$$(E_r - p_r c)^2 / p_r k p_r' = (E_s - p_s c)^2 / p_s k p_s'.$$

Now since

$$u_r = M_r^{-1} p_r, \quad g_r = \lambda_r u_r, \quad u_r k u_r' = (1 - u_r c)/\lambda_r,$$

this is equivalent to

$$(\lambda_r E_r / M_r - g_r c)^2 / g_r (x_r - c) = (\lambda_s E_s / M_s - g_s c)^2 / g_s (x_s - c).$$

But with $C = \phi(c)$ and $\phi_r = \phi(x_r)$,

$$\phi_r - C = g_r (x_r - c), \quad \lambda_r = g_r x_r,$$

and so with $\Delta_r = E_r/M_r - 1$ this is equivalent to

$$\{\lambda_r \Delta_r + 2(\phi_r - C)\}^2/(\phi_r - C) = \{\lambda_s \Delta_s + 2(\phi_s - C)\}^2/(\phi_s - C).$$

These relations holding for all r and s imply one or other of two possible cases:

$C > \phi_r$ for all r (elliptical case), $\hspace{3cm}$ (1)

$C < \phi_r$ for all r (hyperbolic case). $\hspace{2.7cm}$ (2)

The reason these are distinguished as elliptical and hyperbolic is given in more detail in Section 4.4. In case (1) take

$$\theta_r = -(C - \phi_r)^{1/2}, \hspace{4cm} (1')$$

and in case (2) take

$$\theta_r = (\phi_r - C)^{1/2}. \hspace{4.5cm} (2')$$

The reason for this procedure will be seen later. In either case the purchasing power relation comes into the form

$$(\lambda_r \Delta_r/\theta_r - \lambda_s \Delta_s/\theta_s)/2 = \theta_r - \theta_s.$$

For any value of the undetermined parameter C that provides one or other of the two cases, here is proper increasing linear relation between Δ_r and Δ_s and so between equivalent incomes E_r and E_s at prices p_r and p_s, for all $r, s = 0, 1, 2, 4$. For any permitted value of C, they are a consistent system of relations for all four periods, so that determining E_s from any E_r and then E_t from E_s gives the same result as determining E_t directly from E_r.

Let Δ_{rs} be the value of Δ_r obtained by taking $E_s = M_s$; that is, $\Delta_s = 0$, so

$$\lambda_r \Delta_{rs}/2 = \theta_r^2 - \theta_r \theta_s.$$

Then we have

$$(\lambda_r \Delta_{rs} - \lambda_s \Delta_{sr})/2 = \phi_s - \phi_r,$$

in the elliptical case, which should be compared with the median equations

$$(\lambda_r D_{rs} - \lambda_s D_{sr})/2 = \phi_s - \phi_r,$$

used initially to determine the λ_r and ϕ_r from the D_{rs}. Were the Δ_{rs} now given instead of the D_{rs}, the same λ_r and ϕ_r could be recovered from them in the same way. We also have

$$(\lambda_r D_{rs} + \lambda_s D_{sr})/2 = \theta_s^2 + \theta_r^2 - 2\theta_r \theta_s,$$
$$= (\theta_r - \theta_s)^2,$$

and so, corresponding to the interval inequalities, also

$$\lambda_r D_{rs} + \lambda_s D_{sr} \geq 0,$$

and consequently now, going further still with the parallel between the original D_{rs} and the determined Δ_{rs},

$$\lambda_r \Delta_{rs} \geq \phi_s - \phi_r,$$

which are the multiplier-level inequalities with the Δ_{rs} in place of the D_{rs}. The interval inequalities are required in the hyperbolic case also, as will be found in Section 4.5.

4.4   Critical locations

For a regular quadratic utility ϕ representing utility in some convex neighbourhood of the points x_r, the expansion loci are all lines concurrent in the quadratic's unique centre c. Gradients are positive, and in describing these lines in the direction of increasing income, and so of increasing utility, they all point either towards the centre or away from it. With C as the value at the centre, in the one case $\phi_r < C$ for all r and in other $\phi_r > C$ for all r. These cases have already been designated as elliptical and hyperbolic.

The first-order Lagrangean conditions required by compatibility of the hypothetical utility with the given demands have been the basis for developments so far. But the second-order conditions have implications also, from requiring the quadratic to be quasi-concave near the points x_r. In the first case $(x - c)'h(x - c)$ is negative and quasi-concave in a neighbourhood, and this can be so if and only is h is non-positive definite, which with h regular is equivalent to its being negative definite. In the other case this function is positive and quasi-concave in a neighbourhood. By the same argument used in Chapter III.3 for the homogeneous case, but with the quadratic centre taken as origin, the condition for this is that

$$g(x)(x - c)g(y)(y - c) \leq g(x)(y - c)g(y)(x - c)$$

for all x, y in the neighbourhood, and necessarily in this case h is an indefinite matrix, with a quadratic form taking both positive and negative values.

In the first case the utility surfaces are ellipsoids and in this they are hyperboloids, so here is the sense of the terminology for distinguishing the cases. In the homogeneous case dealt with earlier in connection with Fisher's index, and Byushgens' theorem about it, the elliptical case cannot arise and so only the hyperbolic case had to be dealt with, but now both must be investigated.

With the median equations for determining the multipliers and levels associated with quadratics, after the λ_r have been determined, the ϕ_r become fully determined after one of them has been assigned a value arbitrarily. Then the centre equations limit the possible locations of the hypothetical quadratic to a linear manifold. These further second-order considerations now put a further restriction on the possible locations of the centre, with the effect of putting a condition on the possible value C of the quadratic at its centre c consistent with its having the values ϕ_r at the points x_r. The implications are different in the two distinguished cases, which will be dealt with separately.

The parabolic case is where the centre is at infinity and so the expansion lines, having this as a common point, are parallel. This is a common limiting form for both the elliptical and hyperbolic cases, but with no need for a complete coincidence in the limit since the limiting expansion directions could be different in either case. In the one case where C has the ϕ_r as lower bounds it is approached when $C \to \infty$, and in the other case, where the ϕ_r are upper bounds, when $C \to -\infty$.

The purchasing power relation obtained in Section 4.3 contains C as an undetermined parameter, and becomes fully determined when C is assigned a value consistent with one case or the other. The object now is to find the legitimate values of C in the two distinguished cases. In the elliptical case we will find a lower limit $\bar{C}$ for C, greater than the lower bounds ϕ_r that it has already, and all $C > \bar{C}$ are admitted, so it is possible to make C arbitrarily large. We will evaluate the purchasing power relation in the limit as $C \to \infty$, and find a certain monotonicity characteristic for the approach. The hyperbolic case will have a similar treatment.

The following is involved in the evaluation for limits:

Lemma *For any numbers a, b and all $C > a, b$, the function*

$$F(C) = C - \{(C - a)(C - b)\}^{1/2}$$

has derivative $F'(C) < 0$ and so is monotonic decreasing if $a \neq b$, and in any case

$$F(C) \to (a + b)/2 \quad (C \to \infty).$$

The derivative is

$$F'(C) = 1 - \{(C - a)(C - b)\}^{-1/2}\{(C - a) + (C - b)\}/2$$
$$= \left[\{(C - a)(C - b)\}^{1/2} - (1/2)\{(C - a) + (C - b)\}\right]$$
$$/\{(C - a)(C - b)\}.$$

The numerator is the defect of the arithmetic mean of two positive numbers from the geometric mean. But this is always non-positive, and is zero if and only if the two numbers are equal, by the Theorem of the Mean.

The last part follows from the expression

$$F(C) = (a + b - ab/C)/(1 + \{(1 - a/C)(1 - b/C)\})^{1/2}.$$

Corollary *If $C < a, b$ and*

$$F(C) = -C - \{(a - C)(a - C)\}^{1/2}$$

then

$$F(C) > 0 \quad \text{if } a \neq b,$$

and in any case

$$F(C) \rightarrow -(a+b)/2 \quad (C \rightarrow -\infty).$$

4.5 Elliptical case

Any quadratic ϕ that admits the *gradient configuration* with elements (x_r, g_r), so that $g(x_r) = g_r$, must have gradient g_α at a point x_α of the base manifold, where

$$x_\alpha = x_0 + X_0\alpha, \quad g_\alpha = g_0 + \alpha'G_0,$$

and the matrices X_0 and G_0, with columns $x_r - x_0$ and rows $g_r - g_0 (r \neq 0)$, are such that their product G_0X_0 is symmetric.

If ϕ has centre c, this must lie on the centre manifold of the gradient configuration and so be such that

$$G_0x_0 - (g_0X_0)' = G_0c.$$

With the values ϕ_r determined from the median solution, with ϕ_0 assigned arbitrarily, we have a *function skeleton* with elements (x_r, g_r, ϕ_r). For any quadratic ϕ which admits this skeleton, so that $g(x_r) = g_r$ and $\phi(x_r) = \phi_r$, if $C = \phi(c)$ is the value at its centre c, the value ϕ_α at any point x_α of the base manifold is given by

$$\begin{aligned}
2(\phi_\alpha - C) &= g_\alpha(x_\alpha - c) \\
&= (g_0 + \alpha'G_0)(x_0 + X_0\alpha - c) \\
&= g_0(x_0 - c) + \alpha'(G_0x_0 - G_0c)' + g_0X_0\alpha + \alpha'G_0X_0\alpha \\
&= 2(\phi_0 - C) + 2g_0X_0\alpha + \alpha'G_0X_0\alpha.
\end{aligned}$$

Therefore

$$\phi_\alpha = \phi_0 + g_0X_0\alpha + \alpha'G_0X_0\alpha/2.$$

Provided G_0X_0 is regular, and with

$$H_0 = G_0'(G_0X_0)^{-1}G_0,$$

one particular quadratic that extends the function so determined on the base manifold to the entire commodity space is

$$\phi(x) = \phi_0 + g_0(x - x_0) + (x - x_0)'H_0(x - x_0)/2.$$

It has gradient $g(x) = g_0 + (x - x_0)'H_0$ with the value $g(\bar{c}) = \bar{g}$.

By taking any point c of the centre manifold which is not in the base manifold, and any value C, and adjoining the element $(c, 0, C)$ to the function skeleton and repeating this construction, we have another extension which has the point c as centre, and where the function value is C.

The case where a central quadratic ϕ admitted by the skeleton is concave, and so a maximum at its centre, requires $\phi_\alpha < C$ for all α, and so the matrix

$$H = \begin{pmatrix} 2(\phi_0 - C) & g_0 X_0 \\ (g_0 X_0)' & G_0 X_0 \end{pmatrix}$$

must be negative definite. For this, a necessary and sufficient condition is that $G_0 X_0$ be negative definite, and so regular and

$$|H|/|G_0 X_0| < 0.$$

But

$$|H| = |G_0 X_0| \{2(\phi_0 - C) - g_0 X_0 (G_0 X_0)^{-1} X_0' g_0'\}.$$

Therefore this condition is that $G_0 X_0$ be negative definite and $C > \bar{C}$ where

$$\bar{C} = \phi_0 + g_0 X_0 (G_0 X_0)^{-1} X_0' g_0'/2.$$

But with

$$\bar{c} = x_0 - X_0 (G_0 X_0)^{-1} X_0' g_0'$$

we have

$$\bar{C} = \phi_0 - g_0 (x_0 - \bar{c})/2$$
$$= C + g_0 (x_0 - c)/2 - g_0 (x_0 - \bar{c})/2$$
$$= C + g_0 (\bar{c} - c)/2,$$

so that

$$\bar{C} - C = g_0 (\bar{c} - c)/2.$$

The $C > \bar{C}$ is equivalent to $g_0 c > g_0 \bar{c}$.

Since $\bar{c}$ in any case lies on the centre manifold and c is also required it follows that $G_0 (c - \bar{c}) = 0$. Therefore with

$$\bar{g} = g_0 \{1 - X_0 (G_0 X_0)^{-1} G_0\},$$

we have $(\bar{g} - g_0)(c - \bar{c}) = 0$, and so the condition is also equivalent to $\bar{g} c > \bar{g} \bar{c}$.

Given that $G_0 X_0$ is negative definite, so is its inverse, and so from the formula for $\bar{C}$ it appears that $\bar{C} > \phi_0$. Since the original order of the given demands is arbitrary, ϕ_0 could just as well be ϕ_r; from this also, $\bar{C} > \phi_r$ for all r. Thus $\bar{C}$ is an improvement on the ϕ_r as lower bounds of C admissible in the elliptical case, and it is moreover the best lower bound or lower limit.

4.6   Hyperbolic case

Now we will deal similarly with the hyperbolic case. For a function ϕ to be concave at a point x, the gradient $g(x)$ must be a support gradient there; that is,

$$\phi(y) - \phi(x) \leq g(x)(y - x) \quad \text{for all } y.$$

This implies it is also a quasi-support there; that is,

$$g(x)y \leq g(x)x \;\Rightarrow\; \phi(y) \leq \phi(x) \quad \text{for all } y,$$

and this is the condition for ϕ to be quasi-concave at x. If ϕ is a homogeneous quadratic, so that $\phi(x) = g(x)x/2$, this condition in a region where the function is positive is equivalent to

$$g(x)xg(y)y \leq g(x)yg(y)x$$

for all x and y in the region. If ϕ is a quadratic with centre c, so that $\phi(x) = g(x)(x - c)$, the corresponding condition is that

$$g(x)(x - c)g(y)(y - c) \leq g(x)(y - c)g(y)(x - c).$$

For a compatible quadratic in the hyperbolic case, this condition is required for all points in the convex closure of the demand points x_r, in particular for these points themselves; that is,

$$g(x_r)(x_r - c)g(x_s)(x_s - c) \leq g(x_r)(x_s - c)g(x_s)(x_r - c).$$

This last condition is necessary but not sufficient. On the basis of it we can seek conditions on C for the hyperbolic case, but possibly not all those that are required.

We have $g_r(x_s - c) = g_s(x_r - c)$ and also

$$
\begin{aligned}
g_r(x_s - c) &= g_r(x_s - x_r) + g_r(x_r - c) \\
&= \lambda_r u_r(x_s - x_r) + 2(\phi_r - C) \\
&= \lambda_r D_{rs} + 2(\phi_r - C),
\end{aligned}
$$

and so the condition is equivalent to

$$\{\lambda_r D_{rs} + 2(\phi_r - C)\}^2 \geq 4(\phi_r - C)(\phi_s - C).$$

From the median equations,

$$\lambda_r D_{rs} + \phi_r - \phi_s = (\lambda_r D_{rs} + \lambda_s D_{sr})/2 = \lambda_s D_{sr} + \phi_r - \phi_s;$$

and with this, and

$$I_{rs} = (\lambda_r D_{rs} + \lambda_s D_{sr})/2,$$

so that $I_{rs} = I_{sr}$, and the interval inequalities are stated $I_{rs} \geq 0$, the condition becomes

$$(C - \phi_r)I_{rs} \leq (I_{rs} + \phi_s - \phi_r)/4.$$

If $I_{rs} = 0$ for all r, s, the conditions are satisfied for all C. If $I_{rs} < 0$ for any r, s, the condition implies $C > \phi_r$, contradicting $C < \phi_r$ required for the hyperbolic case. Otherwise, the conditions add nothing to the requirement $C < \phi_r$ that we have already.

In this last case, multiplier-level inequalities

$$\lambda_r D_{rs} \geq \phi_s - \phi_r$$

hold, since the median equations make them equivalent to the interval inequalities

$$\lambda_r D_{rs} + \lambda_s D_{sr} \geq 0;$$

that is, $I_{rs} \geq 0$. This case requires these to hold for all r, s and to hold strictly for some r, s.

It has appeared that for admission of a compatible quadratic in any case, elliptical or hyperbolic, it is necessary that the median multipliers be determined all positive and that the interval inequalities be satisfied, and so consequently the multiplier-level inequalities also.

Given this, for the elliptical case to be admitted it is necessary and sufficient that the matrix $G_0 X_0$ be non-positive definite. Then, for C to be the value at the centre of some compatible regular quadratic that admits the skeleton (x_r, g_r, ϕ_r), it is necessary and sufficient that $C > \bar{C}$.

The values of C so admitted for the elliptical case give determinations of the purchasing power relation, which carries C as a parameter. We will be able to find the limiting position of this linear relation as $C \to \infty$.

With all this, the analysis of the elliptical case is exhausted in a satisfactory way. The hyperbolic case has not yet been so yielding, and must be taken further.

The compatibility of a quadratic with centre c in the hyperbolic case requires the existence of a solution $t_r > 0$ of the inequalities

$$u_r(x_s - c)/u_r(x_r - c) \geq t_r/t_s \quad (r, s = 0, 1, 2, 3).$$

With $g_r = \lambda_r u_r$, and also $g_r(x_s - c) = g_s(x_r - c)$ since c must be on the centre manifold, these are equivalent to

$$g_s(x_r - c)t_s \geq g_r(x_r - c)t_r,$$

and, since $g_s(x_r - x_s) = \lambda_s D_{sr}$, also to

$$\{\lambda_s D_{sr} + g_s(x_s - c)\}t_s \geq g_r(x_r - c)t_r,$$

and, since $g_r(x_r - c) = 2(\phi_r - C)$, also to

$$\{\lambda_s D_{sr} + 2(\phi_s - C)\}t_s \geq 2(\phi_r - C)t_r.$$

But for a median solution,

$$\lambda_s D_{sr} + 2\phi_s = \lambda_{rs} D_{rs} + 2\phi_r.$$

Here, this is equivalent to

$$\lambda_r D_{rs}/2(\phi_r - C) + 1 \geq t_r/t_s.$$

With

$$K_{rs} = \lambda_r D_{rs}/2(\phi_r - C) + 1,$$

since $D_{rr} = 0$, necessary and sufficient conditions for the solvability of these inequalities are that

$$H_{ri} H_{ij} H_{jk} H_{kr} \geq 1 \quad (r, i, j, k = 0, 1, 2, 3).$$

What these mean for C seems not immediately obvious. However, collecting terms on the left, and clearing denominators, the coefficient of C^4 is zero, and that of C^3 is a negative multiple of

$$\lambda_r D_{ri} + \cdots + \lambda_k D_{kr}.$$

But this is positive as a consequence of the median equations together with the strict interval inequalities. It follows that there exists some C^* such that these conditions are satisfied for all $C < C^*$.

4.7   Parabolic limits

For determining the income E_r in period r that has the same purchasing power as any income E_s in period s, the purchasing power relation found in Section 4.3 gives

$$\lambda_r \Delta_r = \lambda_s \Delta_s \theta_r/\theta_s + 2(\theta_r^2 - \theta_r \theta_s),$$

where $\Delta_r = E_r/M_r - 1$. There is one such relation for every admissible value of C.

A proviso for any admissibility at all is that the median multipliers λ_r, say when λ_0, is arbitrarily assigned the positive value 1, all be determined positive and satisfy the interval inequalities $\lambda_r D_{rs} + \lambda_s D_{sr} > 0$. The matrix $G_0 X_0$ constructed from the median multipliers, necessarily symmetric, then has negative diagonal elements. This so far is the test for *quadratic consistency* of the given four demands, or for the existence of a compatible utility representable near the demand points x_r by a quadratic.

With that granted, two cases are distinguished. One, the elliptical case, requires an additional test for admissibility, which is that the matrix $G_0 X_0$ be negative definite. That being granted, the critical central value $\bar{C}$ is necessarily such that $\bar{C} > \phi_r$ for all r. Then any value $C > \bar{C}$ is admissible and determines $\theta_r = -(C - \phi_r)^{1/2}$ and therefore the associated purchasing power relation.

The remaining hyperbolic case requires no additional test. There is some $C^* \leq \min \phi_r$ such that any $C < C^*$ is admissible, and in this case we take $\theta_r = (\phi_r - C)^{1/2}$. Though we do not have an explicit formula for C^* as for C, we know, it exists and how to calculate it.

Thus, subject to quadratic consistency, we have the hyperbolic range $[-\infty, C^*]$ for C and, subject to $G_0 X_0$ being negative definite, also the elliptical range $[\bar{C}, \infty]$. Corresponding to any C so admitted, we have a consistent relation connecting equivalent incomes E_r in the four periods.

The limiting parabolic case is where the centre is at infinity, making the expansion lines all parallel, since they pass through the centre. We can evaluate the limiting purchasing power relations for both elliptical and parabolic cases as limits when $C \to \pm\infty$.

The factor θ_r/θ_s approaches the limit 1 monotonically as $C \to \pm\infty$. For the term $\theta_r^2 - \theta_r\theta_s$ we have limits $\pm(\phi_s - \phi_r)/2$ approached monotonically from above as $C \to \pm\infty$. In each case, $+$ is for the elliptical case and $-$ for the hyperbolic. Thus we have the limiting relations

$$\lambda_r \Delta_r \pm \phi_r = \lambda_s \Delta_s \pm \phi_s.$$

With $c(p, x)$ as the utility cost function for any compatible utility, while $M_{rs} = p_r x_s$ is simply the cost of the bundle x_s of period s at the prices of period r, $E_{rs} = c(p_r, x_s)$ is the cost at those prices of the utility of x_s, or the cost at the prices of period r of living at the standard of period s. Compatibility of the utility with the demand (x_r, p_r) requires the coincidence $M_{rr} = E_{rr}$. While the coefficient $D_{rs} = M_{rs}/M_{rr} - 1$ compares bundle costs, $\Delta_{rs} = E_{rs}/E_{rr} - 1$ compares utility costs. Since $M_r = M_{rr} = E_{rr}$, these numbers are $D_{rs} = M_{rs}/M_r - 1$ and $\Delta_{rs} = E_{rs}/M_r - 1$, and because $C(p, x) \leq px$ for all p and x we have $\Delta_{rs} \leq D_{rs}$.

The income M_s spend at the prices p_s in period s purchased the cost of living represented by the bundle x_s, and so the income E_{rs} at the prices p_r should have the same purchasing power as the income M_s at the prices p_s. To determine E_{rs} with respect to compatible quadratic utilities we take $E_s = M_s$, that is $\Delta_s = 0$, in the purchasing power relation obtained and so determine the corresponding Δ_r, that is

$$\Delta_{rs} = 2(\theta_r^2 - \theta_r\theta_s)/\lambda_r,$$

and then take $E_{rs} = M_r(1 + \Delta_{rs})$.

There is one such value of Δ_{rs} for every permissible value of C, and for all $\Delta_{rs} \leq D_{rs}$. For the elliptical case there is the value $\bar{\Delta}_{rs}$ corresponding to the critical value $\bar{C}$ of C. As C increases from $\bar{C}$ to ∞, Δ_{rs} decreases monotonically and approaches the limit $(\phi_s - \phi_r)/\lambda_r$. For the hyperbolic case where C decreases from its critical value C^* to $-\infty$, Δ_{rs} decreases from the corresponding value Δ_{rs}^* to the limit $-(\phi_s - \phi_r)/\lambda_r$.

4.8   Demonstration: Fisher's data

```
1 DATA The Four-point Formula
2 '
9 '
10 GOSUB 1000:GOSUB 100:END
```

```
11 '
79 '___ rotate
80 SWAP I,J:SWAP J,K:RETURN
89 '___ count
90 Z=1+(Z MOD 3):RETURN
91 '
99 '___ cycle coefficients
100 For I=1 TO 3:FOR J=1 to 3:A(I,J)=D(I,J)-D(I,0)
110 NEXT J,I:I=1:J=2:K=3:U=1:V=1
120 FOR R=1 TO 3:B(I)=D(0,K)-D(0,J):U=U*A(J,K):V=V*A(K,J)
130 GOSUB 80:NEXT:W=UV
199 '___ multipliers
200 PRINT#1,CR$,"Multipliers";CR$:M(0)=1:PRINT#1,1,:FOR R=1 TO 3
210 M=B(I)*A(J,I)*A(K,I)+B(J)*A(K,J)*A(J,I)+B(K)*A(J,K)*A(K,I)
220 M=M/W:M(I)=M:PRINT#1,M,:GOSUB 80:NEXT:PRINT#1,
299 '___ Levels
300 PRINT#1,CR$,"Levels";CR$:L(0)=0:PRINT#1,0,:FOR I=1 TO 3
310 L(I)=(M(0)*D(0,I)-M(I)*D(I,0))/2:PRINT#1,L(I),:NEXT
399 '___ gradients
400 FOR I=0 TO 3:FOR K=1 TO N:P(I,K)=M(I)*P(I,K):NEXT K,I
499 '___ relative
500 FOR I=1 TO 3:FOR K=1 TO N
510 X(I,K)=X(I,K)X(0,K):P(I,K)=P(I,K)-P(0,K):NEXT K,I
599 '___ critical matrix
600 PRINT#1,CR$;CR$,"Critical matrix";CR$:FOR I=1 TO 3:FOR J=1
TO 3
610 A=0:FOR K=1 TO N:A=A+X(I,K)*P(J,K):NEXT:A(I,J)=A
620 PRINT#1,A,:NEXT:PRINT#1,:NEXT
649 '___ determinant
650 I=1:J=2:K=3:E=1:D=0
660 FOR R=1 TO 3:D=D+E*A(1,I)*A(2,J)*A(3,K):GOSUB 80:NEXT
670 IF E=1 THEN E=1:I=2:J=1:GOTO 660
680 PRINT#1,CR$,"Determinant",D;CR$
699 '___ inverse
700 FOR I=1 TO 3:FOR U=1 TO 3
710 Z=I:GOSUB 90:J=Z:GOSUB 90:K=Z
720 Z=U:GOSUB 90:V=Z:GOSUB 90:W=Z
730 D(U,I)=(A(J,V)*A(K,W)-A(J,W)*A(K,V))/D:NEXT U,I
749 '___ critical value
750 FOR I=1 TO 3:B=0:FOR K=1 TO N
760 B=B+X(I,K)*P(0,K):NEXT:B(I)=B:NEXT
770 M=0:FOR I=1 TO 3:FOR J=1 TO 3
780 M=M+B(I)*D(I,J)*B(J):NEXT J,I:M=-M/2
790 PRINT#1,,"Critical value";M;CR$;CR$
798 '
799 '_____ utility-cost limits
800 PRINT#1,"Relative cross-costs:utility";CR$
809 '___ Lower
810 PRINT#1,"Lower limits";CR$:FOR I=0 TO 3:FOR J=0 TO 3
```

```
820 A(I,J)=1+(L(J)-L(I))/M(I):PRINT#1,A(I,J),:NEXT:PRINT#1,:NEXT
849 '___ upper
850 PRINT#1,CR$"Upper Limits";CR$:FOR I=0 TO 3
860 L(I)=SQR(2*(ML(I))):M(I)=-L(I)/M(I):NEXT
870 FOR I=0 TO 3:FOR J=0 TO 3:D(I,J)=1+M(I)*(L(J)-L(I))
880 PRINT#1,D(I,J),:NEXT:PRINT#1,:NEXT:PRINT#1,CR$:RETURN
998 '
999 '_____ initialize - read data
1000 DEFINT I,J,K,N:READ A$,B$,C$,N
1010 LF$=CHR$(10):FF$=CHR$(12):CR$=CHR$(13):ESC$=CHR$(27)
1020 DIM P(3,N),X(3,N),E(3,3),D(3,3),A(3,3),B(3),L(3),M(3)
1099 '
1100 PRINT FF$,A$;CR$:INPUT"screen, printer or disk (s/p/d)";o$
1110 IF o$="p" THEN o$="LPT1:" ELSE IF o$="d" THEN o$="A:FPF"
ELSE o$="SCRN:"
1120 CLS:OPEN o$ FOR OUTPUT AS #1
1199 '
1200 PRINT#1,A$;CR$;CR$;B$;CR$;C$;CR$
1210 PRINT#1,,"Periods";CR$:FOR I=0 TO 3:READ X$
1220 PRINT#1,I;" ";X$,:NEXT:PRINT#1,CR$
1299 '
1300 PRINT#1,"Price and Quantity Data - four
periods,";N;"commodities";CR$
1310 FOR I=0 TO 3:PRINT#1,,"Period";I;CR$
1320 FOR J=1 TO N:READ P(I,J):PRINT#1,P(I,J),:NEXT:PRINT#1,
1330 FOR J=1 TO N:READ X(I,J):PRINT#1,X(I,J),:NEXT:PRINT#1,
1340 PRINT#1,:NEXT:PRINT#1,
1399 '
1400 PRINT#1,,"Cross-costs: goods";CR$
1410 FOR I=0 TO 3:FOR J=0 TO 3:E=0:FOR K=1 TO N
1420 E=E+P(I,K)*X(J,K):NEXT:E(I,J)=E:PRINT#1,E,:NEXT:PRINT#1,:N-
EXT
1499 '
1500 PRINT#1,CR$,"Relative cross-costs: goods";CR$
1510 FOR I=0 TO 3:FOR J=0 TO 3:X=E(I,J)/E(I,I)
1520 D(I,J)=X1:PRINT#1,X,:NEXT:PRINT#1,:NEXT
1599 '
1600 FOR I=0 TO 3:FOR K=1 TO N:P(I,K)=P(I,K)/E(I,I):NEXT
K,I:RETURN
4998 '
4999 '_____ the data
5000 DATA Four kinds of fuel — 1913 & 1916-18
5010 DATA Irving Fisher — The Making of Index Numbers
5020 '
5030 DATA    4      :' N= number of commodities
5040 DATA  1913, 1916, 1917, 1918       :' 4 periods  0, 1, 2, 3
5090 '
5100 DATA         5.0636, 1.27,    3.03,   .1233     :' P0
5105 DATA         6.9,     477,    46.3,  10400      :' X0
```

```
5109 '
5110 DATA      5.2906, 2.07,    4.78,    .1217    :' P1
5115 DATA      6.75,   502,     54.5,    12640    :' X1
5119 '
5120 DATA      5.6218, 3.58,    10.66,   .1242    :' P2
5125 DATA      7.83,   552,     56.7,    14880    :' X2
5129 '
5130 DATA      6.5098, 2.4,     7,       .1695    :' P3
5135 DATA      7.69,   583,     55,      15680    :' X3
```

The Four-point Formula

Four kinds of fuel — 1913 & 1916-18
Irving Fisher — The Making of Index Numbers

                    Periods

0 — 1913   1 — 1916   2 — 1917   3 — 1918
Price and Quantity Data — four periods, 4 commodities

                    Period 0

5.0636   1.27   3.03   .1233
6.9   477   46.3   10400

                    Period 1

5.2906   2.07   4.78   .1217
6.75   502   54.5   12640

                    Period 2

5.6218   3.58   10.66   .1242
7.83   552   56.7   14880

                    Period 3

6.5098   2.4   7   .1695
7.69   583   55   15680

                 Cross-costs: goods

2063.338   2395.366   2747.193   2879.343
2510.889   2873.65   3265.987   3418.651
3531.689   3985.965   4472.697   4664.128
3276.618   3772.721   4294.832   4492.021

Relative cross-costs: goods

1	1.160918	1.331431	1.395478
.8737632	1	1.13653	1.189655
.7896106	.8911773	1	1.0428
.7294307	.8398718	.9561024	1

Multipliers

| 1 | .149656 | 1.295474 | 1.164477 |

Levels

| 0 | .1530234 | .3019927 | .3552749 |

Critical matrix

-1.578923E-02	-2.934116E-02	-3.231207E-02
-2.934071E-02	-5.887733E-02	-6.747752E-02
-3.231173E-02	-6.747791E-02	-8.040662E-02

Determinant   -1.093649E 07

Critical value .9776764

Relative cross-costs: utility

Lower Limits

1	1.153024	1.301993	1.355275
.8668962	1	1.129577	1.175924
.7668864	.8850079	1	1.04113
.694906	.8263155	.9542437	1

Upper Limits

1	1.159531	1.329807	1.395215
.8725571	1	1.136026	1.188278
.7883566	.8907308	1	1.041974
.729205	.8385131	.9551831	1

V   Wald's "New Formula"

A. Wald (1939) escaped from the then current insistence that the cost of living should be settled by a price index. When a utility function is given, it is possible to determine the relation between incomes that have the same purchasing power at different prices. Generally this could be any monotonic relation. Use of a price index requires it always to be a homogeneous linear relation, a line through the origin, for which the price index gives the slope.

With this price-index assumption it is implicit that expansion paths are lines through the origin of the commodity space. Therefore, when demands (x_r, p_r) $(r = 0, 1)$ to be associated with the utility are given as data, it is given that the ray L_r through x_r is the expansion path for the prices p_r. In effect we have expansion data (L_r, p_r) $(r = 0, 1)$ where L_r is the expansion path for the prices p_r given as a line through the origin. Wald instead took the given expansion paths L_r to be general lines in the commodity space. With that assumption, the price index expression of purchasing power is abandoned. Now the relation between incomes that have the same purchasing power must be a general linear relation, with an intercept as well as a slope, so two numbers are required to define it instead of just one. Wald observed that quadratic utility functions have linear expansion loci. He then showed that, with demand data in the form of a pair of linear expansions (L_r, p_r) $(r = 0, 1)$ and the hypothesis that these belong to some quadratic utility, the relation between incomes M_r that have the same purchasing power at the prices p_r, as decided by such a utility, is a fully determinate linear relation. His 'New Formula' is the procedure for arriving at that relation from the given data. He noted that, when the lines L_r happen both to go through the origin, this becomes a homogeneous linear relation, whose slope is given by Fisher's price index formula.

It is evident that Wald's theorem with its formula has a close relation to the theorem of S. S. Byushgens (1925) about Fisher's formula and homogeneous quadratic utility, which is the subject of Chapter III.3. It is possible to obtain Byushgens' theorem as a corollary of Wald's theroem, as Wald's note about the Fisher index, and the quadratic utility connection, immediately suggests. But also, it is possible to arrive at Wald's theorem as a corollary of Byushgens' theorem, and in doing that to produce an equivalent of Wald's formula which is very much simpler than the original, and also makes the connection with Fisher's formula completely transparent. For a proper generalization of these theorems and formulae, we have the Four-point formula and its theory of Chapter IV. The focus for Wald's formula is not generality, but the special form of its data.

A certain number D will be determined from the expansion data, the *discriminant*. Its sign and whether or not it is non-zero are central to issues about Wald's formula which will be dealt with. Certain points c_r are determined on the lines L_r, which are unique if the discriminant is non-zero. These are the *critical points* on the expansion lines, which are fundamental to our entire discussion. They give the formula a framework in which much more can be brought out about it.

We will be able to put Wald's formula in a new *marginal price index* framework, where price indices have non-homogeneous counterparts. Replacing commodity bundles in the formulae by *marginal bundles*, we have such counterparts for the Laspeyres, Paasche and Fisher indices. The 'Fisher marginal price index' so obtained is *identical* to that obtained from Wald's formula. Also, the Laspeyres and Paasche counterparts have a role as marginal price index limits, corresponding exactly to the role of the original formulae in the context of price indices. In the case where quantities and marginal quantities have the same ratios—which is the homogeneous case with the data, when the expansion lines are rays through the origin—the marginal price indices become simply price indices, given again by the usual formulae.

This marginal price index concept, beside being illuminating about the nature of price indices, also has a statistical workability. That is shown to some extent in *The Price Index* (Afriat, 1977b). There I used the usual expenditure data to calculate both average and marginal price indices, the average index coinciding, in principle, with the ordinary CPI. When the data confirm the homogeneous case, these would be identical. Otherwise, their comparison shows the departure from homogeneity, reflecting a possible *bias* inherent in the use of the average index.

5.1   Linear expansions

The demand data are now given in the form of a pair of *linear expansions* (L_r, p_r) $(r = 0, 1)$, L_r being a line in the commodity space which is the locus of consumption when the prices are p_r, different points of the line corresponding to different levels of income.

If a_r and b_r are any two points determining the line L_r, then, since different points correspond to different incomes, necessarily $p_r a_r \neq p_r b_r$, and we can suppose $p_r a_r < p_r b_r$. Then $d_r = b_r - a_r$ is a displacement on the line specifying its direction, such that $p_r d_r > 0$. The line is now described by points $x_r = a_r + d_r t_r$, t_r being a parameter. The income associated with the point x_r is $M_r = p_r x_r$.

Because $p_r d_r \neq 0$, there is one point of the line, the *income origin*, for which the associated income is zero. Since a_r is an arbitrary point of the line, it can for simplicity be taken to be this point, so we have $p_r a_r = 0$.

The displacement d_r describes the *marginal consumption pattern* when the prices are p_r, or the incremental proportions in which demand is affected by an increment of income. With linear expansion this is fixed for all increments, at all levels of income. The increment of demand for any unit increment of income, when the prices are p_r, is $e_r = d_r(p_r d_r)^{-1}$. This is the *unit incremental bundle* for the prices p_r. It has the same direction, or pattern, as d_r and is moreover such that $p_r e_r = 1$. Every additional unit of income goes towards buying one of these bundles (I discuss the sense of this assumption in Chapter II.1.2).

Any point of the line is now given by $x_r = a_r + e_r M_r$, where

$$p_r x_r = p_r a_r + p_r e_r M_r = 0 + 1 M_r = M_r,$$

since also $p_r a_r = 0$, so the parameter M_r of any point of L_r is identical with the income associated with it.

Wald offered the suggestion that the expansion loci associated with a quadratic utility are lines. Then, with demand data given in the form of a pair of linear expansion (L_r, p_r) $(r = 0, 1)$, he supposed these to be associated with some quadratic utility. He then showed that the relation between incomes M_0, M_1 that have the same purchasing power at the prices p_0, p_1 on the basis of such utility is determinate, by obtaining a formula for it in terms of the given data.

This result is straightforward as it stands but, without knowing that the hypothesis is realizable, it is also possibly vacuous. Whether the expansion lines are admitted in their entirety as providing demand data, or only some parts of them, will be found to be critical for the more basic consistency question of whether there is *any* utility that is compatible with the data. Even when that is settled, in whatever fashion that provides the consistency needed in order to proceed at all, there is the further question about the existence of some such compatible utility that is moreover representable by a quadratic.

Characteristics of the expansion loci of quadratics are glossed over in the offer that they are lines. Generally any one is a part—if not a whole then half—of a linear manifold, then, moreover, truncated in the commodity space. The dimension is 1 in the case of a regular quadratic, for which the Hessian is regular, and otherwise is greater by the nullity of the Hessian. Therefore, if the expansion loci of the quadratic are to be contained in the lines L_r and not in manifolds of higher dimension containing these, the quadratic must be regular. But a regular quadratic has a unique point, its centre, where the gradient vanishes, and all its expansion lines must go through this. In that case the lines L_r must intersect, in a point c which is the center of the regular quadratic to which they belong. If they do not intersect they cannot contain complete expansion loci of any quadratic utility. To save the theorem from vacuity, the lines, if they are the represent expansion loci of some compatible quadratic, need to be cut and then enlarged. Should the loci that result lie outside the commodity space, the vacuity is then inescapable.

5.2 Revealed purchasing power

The linear expansion (L_r, p_r) consists in the collection of demands (x_r, p_r) where $x_r \in L_r$. For any M_r there is just one for which $p_r x_r = M_r$, given by $x_r = a_r + e_r M_r$. Any restriction to a part of L_r is expressed by a restriction of M_r to some range.

Consistency of all the demands provided by the pair of linear expansions might be denied, so there might not exist any utility compatible with all of them. But consistency might be obtained when the ranges of the incomes M_r are suitably restricted. Now we can consider demands (x_r, p_r) with incomes M_r and relations between them that must be produced by any utility R that is compatible with them, or possibly with some range including them.

The purchasing power of the income M_r at the prices p_r is the utility of the bundle x_r that it buys at the prices. Then purchasing power relations between incomes on the basis of any compatible utility are concluded from any 'revealed preference' relation between the bundles they buy. Thus, from $p_r x_s \leq p_r x_r$ we have $x_r R x_s$, or the 'revealed preference' of x_r to x_s, and so M_r has at least the purchasing power of M_s at the respective prices. And from $p_r x_s < p_r x_r$ it is concluded that the purchasing power of M_r is strictly greater.

Since $p_r x_r = M_r$ and $x_r = a_r + e_r M_r$ where $p_r a_r = 0$ and $p_r e_r = 1$, the relation $_s \leq_r$ of *revealed relative purchasing power* at the prices of periods r and s, defined by

$$M_s \; _s\leq_r M_r \equiv p_r a_s + p_r e_s M_s \leq M_r,$$

reveals that income M_r at prices p_r has at least the purchasing power of M_s at prices p_s, and $_s<_r$ defined by

$$M_s \; _s<_r M_r \equiv p_r a_s + p_r e_s M_s < M_r$$

reveals that it is greater. For consistency, it is required that

$$M_r \; _r<_s M_s \quad \Rightarrow \quad {\sim}M_s \; _s\leq_r M_r,$$

this condition corresponding to Samuelson's revealed preference axiom.

We can also define the relation $_r=_s$ of *revealed purchasing power equivalence* by

$$M_r \; _r=_s M_s \equiv M_r \; _r\leq_s M_s \quad \text{and} \quad M_s \; _s\leq_r M_r.$$

This signifies necessary equivalence with respect to every compatible utility. The relation $_r{\sim}_s$, defined by

$$M_r \; _r{\sim}_s M_s \equiv {\sim}M_r \; _r<_s M_s \quad \text{and} \quad {\sim}M_s \; _s<_r M_r,$$

denies revealed inequivalence and so leaves open the possibility of equivalence with respect to some compatible utility. This relation establishes a many-many correspondence between points of L_r and L_s through the correspondence of their associated incomes. In general, a point of L_r corresponds to a segment of points of L_s, if it corresponds to any. Though now we have only a pair of linear expansions as data, and $r, s = 0$ or 1 only, the present concepts have scope when there is any number, also without the restriction that they be linear.

The requirement for revealed preference consistency is that inequalities

$$p_0 a_1 + p_0 e_1 M_1 \leq M_0, \quad p_1 a_0 + p_1 e_0 M_0 \leq M_1$$

imply the equalities. Should this be denied for any M_0 and M_1 then corresponding points on L_0 and L_1 cannot be simultaneously admitted as part of the data.

For possibly equivalent incomes M_0 and M_1, we have

$$p_0 a_1 + p_0 e_1 M_1 \geq M_0, \quad p_1 a_0 + p_1 e_0 M_0 \geq M_1.$$

These inequalities produce a correspondence between M_0 and M_1 in which any value of one in general corresponds to an interval of values of the other, and, by association with points of L_0 and L_1, any point of one corresponds to a segment of the other.

5.3 The critical points

Now we consider the possibility of finding a pair of points c_0, c_1 on L_0, L_1 which are revealed indifferent, without bearing the restriction that these belong to the commodity space. We require

$$p_0 c_1 = p_0 c_0, \quad p_1 c_0 = p_1 c_1.$$

But, with $C_0 = p_0 c_0$ and $C_1 = p_1 c_1$, these equations are

$$p_0 a_1 + p_0 e_1 C_1 = C_0, \quad p_1 a_0 + p_1 e_0 C_0 = C_1,$$

which can be stated

$$\begin{pmatrix} 1 & -p_0 e_1 \\ -p_1 e_0 & 1 \end{pmatrix} \begin{pmatrix} C_0 \\ C_1 \end{pmatrix} = \begin{pmatrix} p_0 a_1 \\ p_1 a_0 \end{pmatrix}.$$

Hence, introducing

$$D = \begin{vmatrix} 1 & -p_0 e_1 \\ -p_1 e_0 & 1 \end{vmatrix} = 1 - p_0 e_1 p_1 e_0$$

as the *discriminant* for the given data, the condition $D \neq 0$ is necessary and sufficient for the existence and uniqueness of a solution C_0, C_1 to the equations. This condition defines the *regular case*, and the unique points c_0, c_1 so determined under it are the *critical points* on the expansion lines L_0, L_1. The *singular case* where $D = 0$ will be considered later.

Subtracting the equations for the critical points from the inequalities determining incomes M_0, M_1 that are possibly equivalent in purchasing power, we obtain

$$p_0 e_1 (M_1 - C_1) \geq M_0 - C_0, \quad p_1 e_0 (M_0 - C_0) \geq M_1 - C_1.$$

Any compatible utility would determine a relation of purchasing power equivalence between M_0 and M_1 which gives a positive association between them, and which is a sub-relation on this. Consistency, which provides a compatible utility, therefore requires

$$p_0e_1 > 0, \quad p_1e_0 > 0.$$

With this given, the relation implies one or other of the two possibilities

$$M_0 \leq C_0 \quad \text{and} \quad M_1 \leq C_1 \tag{i}$$

$$M_0 \geq C_0 \quad \text{and} \quad M_1 \geq C_1. \tag{ii}$$

Another way of stating the relation between M_0 and M_1 so obtained is that

$$M_1 - C_1 = P_{10}(M_0 - C_0)$$

where in the first case

$$1/p_0e_1 \geq P_{10} \geq p_1e_0,$$

and in the second case

$$1/p_0e_1 \leq P_{10} \leq p_1e_0.$$

The existence of any M_0, M_1 different from C_0, C_1 having the relation obtained in the first case therefore implies $1/p_0e_1 > p_1e_0$, that is, $D < 0$. Similarly $D > 0$ if they have the relation obtained in the second case. It follows that only one of the two possible cases can occur, depending on the sign of the discriminant, the first or the second according to whether $D < 0$ or $D > 0$, respectively.

We distinguish *elliptical, parabolic* and *hyperbolic* cases by the possibilities $D < 0, D = 0$ and $D > 0$. Thus the regular case $D \neq 0$ just excludes the parabolic case, which will be dealt with later. The critical points, which exist and are unique in the regular case, cut the expansion lines each into two rays, going forwards to higher incomes and backwards to lower. It has appeared that points on the two lines which are possibly indifferent for some compatible utility always belong to the backward rays in the elliptical case and to forward rays in the hyperbolic case. It can also be seen that points on the opposite rays in either case are involved in revealed preference inconsistencies. Their exclusion is therefore required if the demand data are to be consistent.

On this basis, therefore, it is fitting to truncate the given expansion lines at their critical points, leaving the forward or backward rays according to the case. This process can be called *critical reduction* of the data. The demand data that so result, which consist of a pair of rays with vertices at the critical points, are always consistent, and to every point on one ray there corresponds a non-empty closed interval of points on the other which could be indifferent to it for some compatible utility.

Of course, critical reduction might eliminate all parts of the given expansion lines that lie in the commodity space, so that in effect there are no data left. That can happen only in the elliptical case, and then just when a critical point falls outside the commodity space.

For any quadratic ϕ with gradient g, it should be noted that if $g(x) = \lambda p, g(y) = \mu p$ then for any point $z = x\varrho + y\sigma$ where $\varrho + y\sigma = 1$, this being any point on the line L joining x and y, we have

$$g(z) = \varrho g(x) + \sigma g(y) = \nu p,$$

where $\nu = \varrho\lambda + \sigma\mu$. This is either always zero or is zero for just one point z of L, and it is constant if $\lambda = \mu$.

Theorem *For a pair of linear expansions (L_r, p_r) with unique critical points $c_r \in L_r$ $(r = 0, 1)$, if ϕ is a quadratic with gradient g such that $g(x_r) = \lambda_r p_r$ for some λ_r at two distinct points $x_r \in L_r$ $(r = 0, 1)$ then*

$$\phi(c_0) = \phi(c_1), \quad g(x_0) = g(c_1) = 0.$$

From the hypothesis, $g(c_r) = \mu_r p_r$ for some μ_r, and so

$$\phi(c_0) - \phi(c_1) = \{\mu_0 p_0 + \mu_1 p_1\}(c_0 - c_1)/2 = 0,$$

because the c_r are critical points, such that $p_r c_s = p_r c_r$. Then further, for any $x_r \in L_r, g(x_r) = \lambda_r p_r$ for some λ_r. Therefore

$$\phi(x_0) - \phi(c_0) = (\lambda_0 p_0 + \mu_0 p_0)(x_0 - c_0),$$
$$\phi(x_0) - \phi(c_1) = (\lambda_0 p_0 + \mu_1 p_1)(x_0 - c_1),$$

and with $d_0 = x_0 - c_0$ these now give $\mu_0 p_0 d_0 = \mu_1 p_1 d_0$, and hence $\mu_0 = \mu_1 p_1 e_0$. By the same argument $\mu_1 = \mu_0 p_0 e_1$. But $D \neq 0$ since the critical points are unique, and so it follows that $\mu_0 = \mu_1 = 0$, and hence $g(c_0) = g(c_1) = 0$.

This theorem shows the significance of the critical points as concerns compatible quadratics. If ϕ is compatible with some demand (x_r, p_r) where $x_r \in L_r$ then $g(x_r) = \lambda_r p_r$ for some $\lambda_r > 0$, and so c_r is the unique point on L_r where $g(c_r) = 0$. Note that, with x_r on one side of the critical point, $\lambda_r < 0$ for any $x_r \in L_r$ on the other side and so ϕ cannot be compatible also with the demand (x_r, p_r). This gives a reflection on the process of critical reduction of the data by which one-half of the expansion lines are rejected from it, to leave a pair of rays R_0, R_1 with vertices at the critical points.

The *critical transversal T* of the expansion lines joins their critical points. It is described by points $c = c_0\alpha_0 + c_1\alpha_1$ where $\alpha_0 + \alpha_1 = 1$. From $p_r c_s = p_r c_r$, it follows that $p_r c = p_r c_r$ for all $c \in T$. Also

$$g(c) = \alpha_0 g(c_0) + \alpha_1 g(c_1) = 0,$$

and

$$\phi(c) - \phi(c_0) = \{g(c) + g(c_0)\}(c - c_0)/2 = 0.$$

Thus, ϕ is constant and its gradient vanishes everywhere on T.

5.4   Marginal price indices and limits

Because the given data consist of linear expansions, there is no need to consider only compatible utilities for which the expansion loci are all linear. But it is natural to do so, and since quadratics have linear expansion loci these can be included as possible examples.

For utility functions that to have linear expansion loci, the purchasing power relation takes the linear form

$$M_1 - C_1 = P_{10}(M_0 - C_0),$$

for some constants C_0, C_1 and P_{10}, these being independent of the incomes, and depends only on the prices p_0, p_1. We call P_{10} the *marginal price index* determined by such a utility. With that known, the relation between M_0 and M_1 becomes fixed when the intercept $C_1 - P_{10}C_0$ is also known. We have seen that, with critical reduction of the data, replacing the lines L_0, L_1 by rays R_0, R_1 with vertices at the critical points, the resulting data are consistent, and then we can take $C_0 = p_0c_0$, $C_1 = p_1c_1$ with P_{10} indeterminate between certain upper and lower limits $\hat{P}_{10}$ and $\check{P}_{10}$. In the hyperbolic case, the relation has validity only for $M_0 > C_0$, and the formulae for these limits are

$$\hat{P}_{10} = p_1e_0 = p_1d_0/p_0d_0, \quad \check{P}_{10} = 1/p_0e_1 = p_1d_1/p_0d_1;$$

in the elliptical case, the formulae are exchanged, and $M_0 < C_0$ for validity. In either case,

$$\bar{P}_{10} = \sqrt{(\hat{P}_{10}\check{P}_{10})}$$

is a particular value of P_{10} which lies between the limits appropriate to the case. One could single out many such particular values between the limits, in fact any point between them. We will see that each corresponds to some compatible utility which has linear expansion loci. P_{10}, without other merit, just happens to be the marginal price index that would be obtained from any compatible quadratic utility, should one exist. Therefore, simply by picking it we have Wald's 'New Formula', which was derived on the basis of a hypothetical quadratic utility, but is now in a revealing disguise, with new qualifications about validity, depending on the sign of the discriminant, the reduction of the data necessary to make it consistent, and the restriction on income range.

The formulae for the marginal price index limits are impressively like the Paasche and Laspeyres formulae of price index theory, and their role as limits is similar also. Out of respect for that connection though the source is alien it seems suitable to call them the *Laspeyres and Paasche marginal price index formulae*. The connection that is immediately evident in this way should be taken further. Then the geometric mean of the limits not only looks like Fisher's formula but also has an association with quadratic utility, connecting it with the relation obtained by Wald. That is quite Byushgens' theorem about Fisher's formula and its association with homogeneous quadratic utility. In fact, the difference can be represented as corresponding simply to a change of origin for commodity bundles, from the origin in the commodity space to one of the critical points or, just as well when the expansion lines do not intersect so that these are distinct, to any point on the critical transversal T which joins them. We can see that, because we know that the gradient of any compatible quadratic must vanish at any point c of T, so that the quadratic has c as a centre, and is equivalent to—or translatable into—a homogeneous quadratic with c as origin.

A displacement on L_r is given by $d_r = x_r - c_r$, for any $x_r \in L_r$. Then, for and $c \in T$,

$$C_r = p_r c_r = p_r c$$

and

$$p_r(x_s - c_s) = p_r(x_s - c),$$

and so

$$p_r e_s = p_r(x_s - c)/p_r(x_r - c).$$

Then the 'Fisher' (or Wald) marginal price index counterpart is

$$\bar{P}_{10} = \sqrt{\{p_1(x_0 - c)p_1(x_1 - c)/p_0(x_0 - c)p_0(x_1 - c)\}},$$

and the relation based on this, which by implication from the quadratic association must coincide with Wald's 'New Formula', is

$$M_1 - p_1 c = \bar{P}_{10}(M_0 - p_0 c).$$

If the lines L_r intersect in the origin, then we have $c = 0$, and if they do not intersect but the critical transversal T passes through the origin, then we can take $c = 0$. Then the marginal price index counterpart of Fisher's index simply becomes Fisher's price index, and the equivalent income relation becomes the homogeneous relation

$$M_1 = \bar{P}_{10} M_0.$$

At the same time, the quadratic whose gradient vanishes at c must, now with $c = 0$, be a homogeneous quadratic, but for an additive constant, so we have Byushgens' theorem. The argument can be reversed, by taking a point $c \in T$ as origin so that Byushgens' theorem can be applied, and then we arrive at Wald's formula directly in the earlier form. Doing that depends on the critical point concept and the results associated with it, and so there is no suggestion here that Wald's formula was anything but 'New'.

A characteristic of the homogeneous case is that the elliptical case amounts to inconsistency. Critical reduction of the data leaves a pair of rays pointing from the origin outside the commodity space. Truncation of the expansion lines in the commodity space after critical reduction therefore leaves no data at all. So a consistency with homogeneity requires the hyperbolic case. The familiar roles of the Laspeyres and Paasche formulae as upper and lower limits which belong to this case are exchanged in the elliptical case. For a perspective with the Four-point formula of Chapter IV, there the centre of the quadratic has an indeterminacy, with a consequent indeterminacy in the purchasing power relation; whereas here, with a pair of expansion lines, the centre is determinate by identification with a critical point.

Appendices

1 **The system of inequalities** $a_{rs} > x_s - x_r$. *Research Memorandum* No. 18 (October 1960), Econometric Research Program, Princeton University. *Proc. Cambridge Phil. Soc.* 59 (1963), 125–33.

2 **The construction of utility functions from expenditure data.** *Cowles Foundation Discussion Paper* No. 144 (October 1964), Yale University. First World Congress of the Econometric Society, Rome, September 1965. *International Economic Review* 8, 1 (1967), 67–77.

3 **The concept of a price index and its extension.** Second World Congress of the Econometric Society, Cambridge, September 1970.

4 **The Theory of International Comparisons of Real Income and Prices.** In *International Comparisons of Prices and Output, Proceedings of the Conference at York University, Toronto, 1970*, edited by D. J. Daly. National Bureau of Economic Research, Studies in Income and Wealth Volume 37, New York, 1972 (Ch. I, 13–84).

5 **Measurement of the purchasing power of incomes with linear expansion data.** *Journal of Econometrics* 2, 3 (1974), 343–64.

6 **On the constructability of consistent price indices between several periods simultaneously.** In *Essays in Theory and Measurement of Demand: in honour of Sir Richard Stone*, edited by Angus Deaton. Cambridge University Press, 1981, 133–61.

7 **Index-number practice under conditions of hyperinflation— with particular reference to Peru.** International Development Research Centre (IDRC), Ottawa, 2 April 1991.

1
The system of inequalities $a_{rs} > x_s - x_r$

Research Memorandum No. 18 (October 1960), Econometric Research Program, Princeton University. *Proc. Cambridge Phil. Soc.* 59 (1963), 125–33.

Proc. Camb. Phil. Soc. (1963), **59**, 125

The system of inequalities $a_{rs} > X_r - X_s$*

Princeton University, Princeton, New Jersey, and
Rice University, Houston, Texas.

(*Received* 30 *November* 1961)

Introduction

In the investigation of preference orders which are explanations of expenditure data which associates a quantity vector x_r with a price vector p_r ($r = 1, \ldots, k$), in respect to some n goods, there is considered the class of functions ϕ, with gradient g, which are increasing and convex in some convex region containing the points x_r, such that $g_r = g(x_r)$ has the direction of p_r.[†] Let $u_r = p_r/e_r$, where $e_r = p'_r x_r$ so that $u'_r x_r = 1$. Then

$$g_r = u_r \lambda_r,$$

for some multipliers $\lambda_r > 0$, since ϕ is increasing. Also, if $\phi_r = \phi(x_r)$ then

$$(x_r - x_s)' g_s > \phi_r - \phi_s,$$

since ϕ is convex. Accordingly

$$\lambda_r > 0, \quad \lambda_s D_{sr} > \phi_r - \phi_s \quad (r \neq s), \tag{I}$$

where $D_{sr} = u'_s x_r - 1$. With the number D_{rs} given, there has to be considered all solutions $\Lambda = \{\lambda_r\}$, $\Phi = \{\phi_r\}$ of the system of inequalities (I). With this system, there is involved a consideration of systems of the form $a_{rs} > X_r - X_s$ (where $a_{rs} = \lambda_s D_{sr}, X_r = \phi_r$), the theory of which is going to be developed here. It is remarked, incidentally, that the existence of Λ, Φ satisfying (I) is equivalent to the existence of Λ satisfying

$$\lambda_r > 0, \quad \lambda_r D_{rs} + \lambda_s D_{st} + \cdots + \lambda_q D_{qr} > 0 \tag{II}$$

for all distinct $r, s, t, \ldots, q$ taken from $1, \ldots, k$.

Further, Λ satisfies (II) if and only if there exists a Φ such that Λ, Φ satisfy (I). Moreover, these two equivalent conditions on the number D_{rs} which are provided

* Revised version of Research Memorandum no. 18, Econometric Research Program, Princeton University, October 1960, issued with the partial support of the U.S. Office of Naval Research.

† S. N. Afriat. *Preference analysis: a general method with application to the cost of living index.* (Research Memorandum, no. 29, Econometric Research Program, Princeton University, August 1961.)

by the consistency of the system of inequalities (I) and (II) are equivalent to a condition, applying directly to these numbers, which is given by the familiar Houthakker[‡] 'revealed preference' axiom, which can be stated

$$D_{rs} \leqslant 0, \quad D_{st} \leqslant 0, \ldots, D_{qr} \leqslant 0 \qquad \text{(III)}$$

impossible, for all distinct $r, s, t, \ldots, q$ taken from $1, \ldots, k$.

Apart from any independent interest, the results which are now going to be obtained can be applied to a demonstration of these propositions, which are of fundamental importance for a method of empirical preference analysis in economics.

1. Open and closed systems

Let $n(n-1)$ numbers $a_{rs}(r \neq s; r, s = 1, \ldots, n)$ be given; and consider the system of simultaneous inequalities

$$S(a): a_{rs} > X_r - X_s \quad (r \neq s; r, s = 1, \ldots, n)$$

defining the *open system* $S(a)$, of *order* n, with *coefficients* a_{rs}. Any set of n numbers X_r $(r = 1, \ldots, n)$, forming a vector X, which satisfy these inequalities, define a *solution* X of the system $S(a)$; and the system is said to be *consistent* if it has solutions.

With the open system $S(a)$, there may also be considered the *closed system* $\bar{S}(a)$, defined by

$$\bar{S}(a): a_{rs} \geqslant X_r - X_s \quad (r \neq s; r, s = 1, \ldots, n).$$

Obviously, solutions of $S(a)$ are solutions of $\bar{S}(a)$, and the consistency of $S(a)$ implies the consistency of $\bar{S}(a)$, but not conversely.

2. Chain coefficients

Let $r, l, m, \ldots, p, s$ denote any *chain*, that is a sequence of elements taken from $1, \ldots, n$ with every successive pair distinct. Now from the coefficients a_{rs} of a system there can be formed the *chain coefficient* $a_{rlm\cdots ps}$, determined on any chain, by the definition

$$a_{rlm\cdots ps} = a_{rl} + a_{lm} + \cdots + a_{ps}.$$

Obviously

$$a_{r\cdots s\cdots t} = a_{r\cdots s} + a_{s\cdots t}.$$

Chains are considered associated with their coefficients, so that by a positive chain is meant one with positive coefficient, and so on similarly. A *simple chain* is one without loops, that is one in which no elements is repeated. There are

$$n(n-1)\cdots(n-r+1) = n!/r!$$

‡ H. S. Houthakker. Revealed preference and the utility function, *Economica*, 17 (1950), 159–74.

simple chains of length $r \leqslant n$, and therefore altogether

$$n! \left(1 + \frac{1}{1!} + \frac{1}{2!} + \cdots + \frac{1}{(n-1)!}\right)$$

simple chains.

A chain $r, l, m, \ldots p, s$ whose extremities are the same, that is, with $r = s$, defines a *cycle*. A simple cycle is one without loops. There are $(n - 1) \cdots (n - r + 1) = (n - 1)!/r!$ simple cycles of $r \leqslant n$ elements, and the total number of simple cycles is made up accordingly. The coefficients $a_{rs} + a_{sr}$ on the cycles of two elements define the *intervals* of the system.

Any chain can be represented uniquely as a simple chain, with loops at certain of its elements, given by cycles through those elements; and the coefficient on it is then expressed as the sum of coefficients on the simple chain and on the cycles. Also, any cycles can be represented uniquely as a simple cycle, looping in simple cycles at certain of its elements, which loop in simple cycles at certain of their elements, and so forth, with termination in simple cycles. The coefficient on the cycle is then expressed as a sum of coefficients on simple cycles. Thus out of these generating elements of simple chains and cycles, finite in number, is formed the infinite set of all possible chains.

3. Minimal chains

Theorem 3.1 *For the chains to have a minimum it is necessary and sufficient that the cycles be non-negative.*

If any cycle total should be negative, then by taking chains which loop repeatedly round that cycle, chains which have increasingly negative coefficients are obtained without limit; and so no minimum exists. However, should every cycle coefficient be non-negative, then by cancelling the loops on any chain, there can be no increase in the coefficient, so no chain coefficient will be smaller than the coefficient for some simple chain. But there is only a finite number of simple chains on a finite number of elements, and the coefficients on these have a minimum.

Theorem 3.2 *For the cycles to be non-negative it is necessary and sufficient that the simple cycles be non-negative.*

For the coefficient on any cycle can be expressed as a sum of coefficients on simple cycles.

Theorem 3.3 *If the cycles are non-negative then a minimal chain with given extremities always exists and can be chosen to be simple.*

For any chain is then not less than the chain obtained from it by cancelling loops, since the cancelling is then the subtraction of a sum of non-negative numbers.

4. Derived systems

According to Theorem 3.3, if the cycles of $S(a)$ are non-negative, that is

$$a_{rlm\cdots pr} \geqslant 0$$

for every cycle $r, l, m, \ldots, p, r$, or equivalently for every simple cycle, by Theorem 3.2, then the coefficients $a_{rlm\cdots ps}$ on the chains with given extremities r, s have a minimum, and it is possible to define

$$A_{rs} = \min_{l,m,\ldots,p} a_{rlm\cdots ps} \quad (r, s = 1, \ldots, n).$$

Then

$$a_{rlm\cdots ps} \geqslant A_{rs}$$

for every chain and, by Theorem 3.3, the equality is attained for some simple chain. In particular,

$$a_{rs} \geqslant A_{rs}.$$

The number A_{rr} is the minimum coefficient for the cycle through r, so that

$$a_{rlm\cdots pr} \geqslant A_{rr}$$

for every cycle, the equality being attained for some simple cycle. In particular, for a chain of two elements,

$$a_{rs} + a_{sr} \geqslant A_{rr}.$$

The hypothesis of non-negative cycles now has the statement

$$A_{rr} \geqslant 0.$$

The numbers A_{rs} ($r \neq s$), thus constructed from the coefficient of $S(a)$, define the coefficients of a system $S(A)$, which will be called the *derived system* of $S(a)$.

Any two systems will be said to be equivalent if any solution of one is also a solution of the other.

Theorem 4.1   *Any system and its derived system, when it exists, are equivalent.*

Let a system $S(a)$ have a solution X. Then, for any chain of elements $r, l, m, \ldots, p, s$ there are the relations

$$a_{rl} > X_r - X_l, \quad a_{lm} > X_l - X_m, \quad \ldots, \quad a_{ps} > X_p - X_s$$

from which, by addition, there follows the relation

$$a_{rlm\cdots ps} > X_r - X_s.$$

This implies that the derived coefficients A_{rs} exist, and

$$A_{rs} > X_r - X_s.$$

That is, X is a solution of $S(A)$.

Now suppose the derived coefficients A_{rs} of $S(a)$ are defined, in which case

$$a_{rs} \geqslant A_{rs}$$

and let X be any solution of $S(A)$, so that

$$A_{rs} > X_r - X_s.$$

Then it follows immediately that

$$a_{rs} > X_r - X_s$$

or that X is a solution of $S(a)$. Thus $S(a)$ and $S(A)$ have the same solutions, and are equivalent.

Theorem 4.2 *If the cycles of a system are non-negative or positive, then so correspondingly are the intervals of the derived system.*

Since A_{rs} is the coefficient of some chain with extremities r, s it appears that $A_{rs} + A_{sr}$ is the coefficient of some cycle through r, and therefore if the cycles of $S(a)$ are non-negative, or positive, so correspondingly are the intervals $A_{rs} + A_{sr}$ of the derived system $S(A)$.

5. Triangle inequality

From the relation

$$a_{r \ldots s} + a_{s \ldots t} = a_{r \ldots t}$$

it follows that the derived coefficients A_{rs} ($r \neq s$) satisfy the *triangle inequality*

$$A_{rs} + A_{st} \geqslant A_{rt}$$

the one side being the minimum for chains connecting r, t restricted to include s, and the other side being the minimum without this restriction.

Theorem 5.1 *Any system non-negative cycles is equivalent to a system which satisfies the triangle inequality, given by its derived system.*

This is true in view of Theorems 3.1, 4.1 and 4.2.

Theorem 5.2 *Any system which satisfies the triangle inequality has all its intervals non-negative.*

Thus, from the triangle inequalities applied to any system $S(a)$,

$$a_{tr} + a_{rs} \geqslant a_{ts}, \qquad a_{ts} + a_{sr} \geqslant a_{tr}$$

there follows, by addition, the relation

$$a_{rs} + a_{sr} \geqslant 0.$$

Theorem 5.3 *If a system satisfies the triangle inequality, then its derived system exists, and, moreover, the two systems are identical.*

From the triangle inequality, it follows by induction that

$$a_{rl} + a_{lm} + \cdots + a_{ps} \geqslant a_{rs}.$$

That is,

$$a_{rlm\cdots ps} \geqslant a_{rs},$$

from which it appears that the derived system exists, with coefficients

$$A_{rs} \geqslant a_{rs},$$

so that now

$$A_{rs} = a_{rs}.$$

This shows, what is otherwise evident, that no new system is obtained by repeating the operation of derivation, since the first derived system satisfies the triangle inequality.

6. Extension property of solutions

A *subsystem* $S_m(a)$ of order $m \leqslant n$ of a system $S(a)$ of order n is defined by

$$S_m(a): a_{rs} > X_r - X_s \quad (r,s = 1,\ldots,m).$$

Then the systems $S_m(a)$ $(m = 2,3,\ldots,n)$ form a nested sequence of subsystems of $S(a)$, each being a subsystem of its successor; and $S_n(a) = S(a)$.

Any solution $(X_1,\ldots,X_n)$ of $S(a)$ reduces to a solution $(X_1,\ldots,X_m)$ of the subsystem $S_m(a)$. But it is not generally true that any solution of a subsystem of $S(a)$ can be extended to a solution of $S(a)$. However, should this be the case, then the system $S(a)$ will be said to have the *extension property*.

Theorem 6.1 *Any closed system which satisfies the closed triangle inequality has the extension property.*

Let $X_1,\ldots,X_{m-1}$ be a solution of $\bar{S}_{m-1}(a)$, so that

$$a_{rs} \geqslant X_r - X_s \quad (r,s = 1,\ldots,m-1).$$

It will be shown that, under the hypothesis of the triangle inequality, it can be extended by an element X_m to a solution of $\bar{S}_m(a)$.

Thus, there is to be found a number X_m such that

$$a_{rm} \geqslant X_r - X_m, \quad a_{ms} \geqslant X_m - X_s \quad (r,s = 1,\ldots,m-1),$$

that is

$$a_{ms} + X_s \geqslant X_m \geqslant X_r - a_{rm}.$$

So the condition that such an X_m can be found is

$$a_{mq} + X_q \geqslant X_p - a_{pm},$$

where

$$X_p - a_{pm} = \max_r \{X_r - a_{rm}\}, \quad a_{mq} + X_q = \min_r \{a_{mq} + X_q\}.$$

But if $p = q$, this is equivalent to

$$a_{mq} + a_{qm} \geqslant 0,$$

which is verified, by Theorem 5.2, and if $p \neq q$, it is equivalent to

$$a_{pm} + a_{mq} \geqslant X_p - X_q,$$

which is verified, since, by hypothesis

$$a_{pm} + a_{mq} \geqslant a_{pq}, \quad a_{pq} \geqslant X_p - X_q.$$

Therefore, under the hypothesis, the considered extension is always possible. It follows now by induction that any solution of $S_m(a)$ can be extended to a solution of $S_n(a) = S(a)$.

This theorem shows how solutions of any system can be practically constructed, step-by-step, by extending the solutions of subsystems of its derived system.

Theorem 6.2 *Any closed system which satisfies the closed triangle inequality is consistent.*

For, by Theorem 5.2, $a_{12} + a_{21} \geqslant 0$; and this implies that the system

$$\bar{S}_2(a): a_{12} \geqslant X_1 - X_2, \quad a_{21} \geqslant X_2 - X_1$$

has a solution, which, by Theorem 6.1, can be extended to a solution of $\bar{S}(a)$. Therefore $\bar{S}(a)$ has a solution, and is thus consistent.

Theorem 6.3 *Any open system which satisfies the triangle inequality and has positive intervals has the extension property, and is consistent.*

The lines of proof follow those of Theorems 6.1 and 6.2. A system is defined to satisfy the *triangle equality* if

$$a_{rs} + a_{st} = a_{rt}.$$

Theorem 6.4 *If a system satisfies the triangle inequality and has null intervals then it also satisfies the triangle equality and has null cycles.*

For, from

$$a_{rs} + a_{sr} = 0, \quad a_{rs} + a_{st} \geqslant a_{rt}$$

follows also

$$a_{rs} + a_{st} \leqslant a_{rt}$$

so that

$$a_{rs} + a_{st} = a_{rt}.$$

By induction,

$$a_{rl} + a_{lm} + \cdots + a_{qp} = a_{rp}$$

and then

$$a_{rl} + a_{lm} + \cdots + a_{pr} = 0,$$

that is, the cycles are null.

7. Consistency

Theorem 7.1   *A necessary and sufficient condition that an open system be consistent is that its cycles by positive.*

If $S(a)$ is consistent, let X be a solution. Then, for any cycle $r, l, m, \ldots, p, r$ there are the relations

$$a_{rl} > X_r - X_l, \quad a_{lm} > X_l - X_m, \quad \ldots, \quad a_{pr} > X_p - X_r,$$

from which it follows, by addition, that

$$a_{rlm\cdots pr} > 0.$$

Therefore, if $S(a)$ is consistent, all its cycles must be positive.

Conversely, let the cycles of $S(a)$ be positive. Then the derived system $S(A)$ is defined, satisfies the triangle inequality, and has positive intervals. Hence, by Theorem 6.3, $S(A)$ is consistent. But, by Theorem 4.1, $S(A)$ is equivalent to $S(a)$. Therefore, $S(a)$ is consistent.

Similarly:

Theorem 7.2   *A necessary and sufficient condition that a closed system be consistent is that its cycles be non-negative.*

8. Cycle reversibility

A cycle is defined to be *reversible* in a system if the reverse cycle has the same coefficient, thus

$$a_{rl\cdots pr} = a_{rp\cdots lr}.$$

The condition of *k-cycle reversibility* for a system is that all cycles of k element be reversible with regard to it; and the general condition of *cycle reversibility* is the reversibility condition taken unrestrictedly, in respect to all cycles of any number of elements.

Theorem 8.1 *For the reversibility of cycles in a system, the reversibility of 3-cycles is necessary and sufficient.*

The proof is by induction, by showing that, given 3-cycle reversibility, the k-cycle condition is implied by that for $(k-1)$-cycles.

Thus, from

$$a_{l\cdots k} + a_{kl} = a_{k\cdots l} + a_{lk}$$

with

$$a_{ol} + a_{lk} + a_{ko} = a_{ok} + a_{kl} + a_{lo},$$

by addition, there follows

$$a_{ol} + a_{l\cdots k} + a_{ko} = a_{ok} + a_{k\cdots l} + a_{lo}.$$

Theorem 8.2 *If a system has positive intervals and reversible cycles, then it is consistent.*

Thus, if

$$a_{rs\cdots pr} = a_{rp\cdots sr}$$

and

$$a_{rs} + a_{sr} > 0,$$

then

$$2a_{rs\cdots pr} = a_{rs\cdots pr} + a_{rp\cdots sr}$$
$$= (a_{rs} + a_{sr}) + \cdots + (a_{pr} + a_{rp}) > 0,$$

so the cycles are positive, and hence, by Theorem 7.1, the system is consistent.

For any system $S(a)$, define

$$C_{rs\cdots t} = a_{rs\cdots tr} - a_{rt\cdots sr}$$

then $C_{rs\cdots t}$ is an antisymmetric cyclic function of the indices $r, s, \ldots, t$, depending just on the cyclic order of the indices and changing its sign when the cyclic order is reversed. The cycle reversibility condition for the system now has the statement

$$C_{rs\cdots t} = 0$$

and it has been shown to be necessary and sufficient just that

$$C_{rst} = 0.$$

Thus the reversibility conditions are not all independent, but are implied by those for the 3-cycles. Moreover, not all the 3-cycle reversibility conditions are independent; but, as appears in the following theorem, the reversibility of three of the four 3-cycles in any four elements implies that for the fourth.

Theorem 8.3   *For any four elements $\alpha, \beta, \gamma, \delta$ there is the identity*

$$C_{\beta\gamma\delta} + C_{\alpha\delta\gamma} + C_{\delta\alpha\beta} + C_{\gamma\beta\alpha} = 0.$$

This can be verified directly.

By the dependencies shown in this Theorem, the $\frac{1}{6}n(n-1)(n-2)$ conditions for 3-cycle reversibility, contained in and implying a much larger set of general reversibility conditions, reduce to a set of $\frac{1}{2}(n-1)(n-2)$ independent conditions.

Theorem 8.4   *There are $\frac{1}{2}(n-1)(n-2)$ independent cycle reversibility conditions in a system of order n.*

9. Median solutions

Any solution X of a system $S(a)$ must satisfy the condition

$$a_{rs} > X_r - X_s > -a_{sr},$$

that is, the differences $X_r - X_s$ must lie in the intervals $[-a_{sr}, a_{rs}]$, which are non-empty provided $a_{rs} + a_{sr} > 0$. In particular, a solution X such that these differences lie at the mid-points of these intervals will be called a *median* of the system. Thus, if X is a median of $S(a)$ then $X_r - X_s = \frac{1}{2}(a_{rs} - a_{sr})$. The condition that a system admit a median is decidedly stronger than that of consistency alone.

Theorem 9.1   *A necessary and sufficient condition that any system $S(a)$ admit a median is that*

$$a_{rs} + a_{st} + a_{tr} = a_{ts} + a_{sr} + a_{rt}, \quad a_{rs} + a_{sr} > 0.$$

The condition is necessary, since a median is a particular solution of the system, the existence of which implies that the intervals $a_{rs} + a_{sr}$ of the system are positive. Moreover, addition of the relations

$$X_r - X_s = \frac{1}{2}(a_{rs} - a_{sr}),$$
$$X_s - X_t = \frac{1}{2}(a_{st} - a_{ts}),$$
$$X_t - X_r = \frac{1}{2}(a_{tr} - a_{rt}),$$

gives

$$0 = a_{rs} - a_{sr} + a_{st} - a_{ts} + a_{tr} - a_{rt}.$$

Also it is sufficient. For it provides that, for any k, and all r, s

$$a_{rs} - a_{sr} = (a_{rk} - a_{ks}) - (a_{sk} - a_{ks}),$$

from which it follows that the numbers

$$X_r = \frac{1}{2}(a_{rk} - a_{kr})$$

satisfy

$$X_r - X_s = \tfrac{1}{2}(a_{rs} - a_{sr});$$

and, then since

$$a_{rs} + a_{sr} > 0,$$

they must be a solution of the system, which is, moreover, a median.

Now, combining with Theorem 8.1, we obtain

Theorem 9.2   *A necessary and sufficient condition that a system admit a median solution is that its intervals be positive and its cycles reversible.*

10. Simple systems

A system $S(a)$ which is such that, for some k, s

$$a_{rk} + a_{kr} > 0, \quad a_{rk} + a_{ks} \leqslant a_{rs},$$

for all r, s, will be called *simple*, with respect to the index k.

Theorem 10.1   *If $S(a)$ is simple, with respect to k, then it is consistent, and admits as solution all sets of number X_r such that*

$$a_{rk} > X_r > -a_{kr}.$$

For then, from relations

$$a_{rk} > X_r, \quad a_{ks} > -X_s,$$

there follows

$$a_{rs} \geqslant a_{rk} + a_{ks} > X_r - X_s.$$

2
The construction of utility functions from expenditure data

Cowles Foundation Discussion Paper No. 144 (October 1964), Yale University. First World Congress of the Econometric Society, Rome, September 1965. *International Economic Review* 8, 1 (1967), 67–77.

INTERNATIONAL ECONOMIC REVIEW
Vol. 8, No. 1, February, 1967

The construction of utility functions from expenditure data[*],[1]

In considering the behavior of the consumer, a market is assumed which offer some n goods for purchase at certain prices and in whatever quantities. A purchase requires an expenditure of money

$$e = \pi_1 \xi_1 + \cdots + \pi_n \xi_n = p'x$$

which is determined as the scalar product of the vector $x = \{\xi_1, \ldots, \xi_n\}$ of quantities, which shows the *composition* of the purchase, and the vector $p = \{\pi_1, \ldots, \pi_n\}$ of prevailing prices, where braces $\{\}$ denote a column vector, and a prime its transposition. The classical assumption about the consumer is that any purchase is such as to give a maximum of utility for the money spent. The consumer is supposed to attach a number $\phi(x)$ to any purchase, according to its composition x, which is the measure of the utility, to the effect that a purchase with composition x made at price p and, therefore, requiring an expenditure, $e = p'x$, is such as to satisfy the maximum utility condition

$$\phi(x) = \max\{\phi(y) : p'y \leqq e\}.$$

An equivalent statement of this condition is

$$\phi(x) = \max\{\phi(y) : u'y \leqq 1\},$$

where $u = p/e$ is the vector of prices divided by expenditure, that is with expenditure taken as the unit of money and is to be called the *balance* vector, corresponding to those prices and that expenditure. The fundamental property required for a *utility function* $\phi(x)$ is that, given a balance u, any composition x which is determined by the condition of maximum utility satisfies $u'x = 1$, so that

$$u'y \leqq 1 \implies \phi(y) \leqq \phi(x)$$

and

$$\phi(y) \geqq \phi(x) \implies u'y \geqq 1.$$

* Manuscript received December, 1964.
1 This work is part of a project on "The Analysis of Consumers' Preferences and the Construction of Index Numbers," conducted at the Econometric Research Program, Princeton University and at Rice University and the Cowles Foundation at Yale University with the support of the National Science Foundation.

Such an assumption cannot represent necessary deliberations on the part of the consumer. Any actual consumer is quite unaware of the attachment to such a function ϕ, and can even deny by intention and manifest behavior any such attachment. Then if ϕ is to have a proper existence, it would have to be in the stock of analytical construction of those who entertain the assumption, and based on data of observation. In the earliest form, as the one used by Gossen, Jevons, Menger and Walras, it was assumed that the utility of a composition of goods was the sum of utilities for the separate goods

$$\phi(x) = \phi_1(x_1) + \cdots + \phi_n(x_n).$$

Edgeworth then considered a general function

$$\phi(x) = \phi(x_1, \ldots, x_n),$$

and he also considered the indifference surfaces, the level surfaces $\phi = $ constant of the utility function. But the now familiar approach which is divorced from numerical utility and deals only with indifference surfaces was established by Pareto. Before this the utility analysis in demand theory dealt with utility and utility differences as measurable quantities. By rendering numerical utility inessential, Pareto brought relief to the discomfort of having to assume a measurable utility, the measurability of which was held in doubt.

Here the concern is with the utility function only as a measure of preference for deciding for better or worse between a collection of goods. But never through the long drawn out history of the hypothesis has such a function been generally shown. The revealed preference principle of Samuelson [5], elaborated by Houthakker [4], easily gives a condition for the rejection of the hypothesis of existence. But the principle has been absent by which the hypothesis can be accepted or rejected on the basis of any observed choice of the consumer, supposed to be finite in number; and, in the case of acceptance, a general method is needed for the actual construction of a utility fucntion which will realize the hypothesis for the data.

This problem will be discussed here. For the general problem which arises when the finiteness restriction is removed, one possible approach is by a limiting process, proceeding on the basis of the results which are going to be obtained. It is more general than the problem considered by Samuelson [5], Houthakker [4], Uzawa [6], Afriat [2] and others which involves a demand system and, therefore, quantities for every price situation; that is, a complete system of data. For the data could be assumed infinite but not necessarily complete. Also, even with completeness, the usual assumption of a single valued demand system could be omitted. Or, if a single valued function is assumed, the Lipschitz-type condition assumed by Uzawa [6] and, therefore, also the differentiability assumed by other writers can be dropped. In the familiar investigations, the assumptions have been such as to yield just one functionally independent utility function. In the finite problem, and even in the infinite problem with completeness assumed, there is no such essential uniqueness.

While the results for finite data do not immediately give results for complete data, such as for a demand system, it is also the case that the familiar investigations on demand systems seeking conditions for the existence of a utility function have no scope for the finite problem now to be considered. Those investigations depend on a continuous, even a differentiable structure, which can have no bearing here in the discrete finite case. They do not take into consideration the problem of establishing criteria by which any finite expenditure data can be taken as arising from some complete demand system which satisfies the appropriate conditions.

Let it be supposed that the consumer has been observed on some k occasions of purchase, and the expenditure data obtained for each occasion r $(r = 1, \ldots, k)$ provide the pair of vectors (x_r, p_r) which give the composition or purchase and the prevailing prices. Hence the expenditure is $e_r = p'_r x_r$ and the balance vector is $u_r = p_r / e_r$; and, by definition, $u'_r x_r = 1$. Let $E_r = (x_r | u_r)$ define the *expenditure figure* for occasion r, and $E = \{E_r \mid r = 1, \ldots, n\}$ the *expenditure configuration* constructed from the data. Only through this configuration does the utility hypothesis have bearing on the data.

The utility hypothesis applied to the configuration E asserts that there exists a utility function φ such that

$$\varphi(x_r) = \max\{\varphi(x) \mid u'_r x \leq 1\} \quad (r = 1, \ldots, n)$$

in which case the function φ can be said to exhibit the utility hypothesis for E or to be a utility function for E. The data E can be said to have the property of *utility consistency* if the utility hypothesis can be exhibited for it by some function, in other words if it has a utility function.

Now there is the problem of deciding, for any given expenditure configuration E, whether or not it has the property of utility consistency, and, if it has, of constructing a utility function for it.

If utility consistency holds for E, some utility function φ exists for it, and then

$$u'_r x_s \leq 1 \implies \varphi(x_r) \geq \varphi(x_s)$$

and

$$u'_r x_s \leq 1 \wedge \varphi(x_r) = \varphi(x_s) \implies u'_r x_s = 1$$

for all $r, s = 1, \ldots, k$. Hence, for all $r, s, \ldots, q = 1, \ldots, k$

$$u'_r x_s \leq 1 \wedge u'_s x_t \leq 1 \wedge \cdots \wedge u'_q x_r \leq 1$$
$$\implies \varphi(x_r) \geq \varphi(x_s) \geq \cdots \geq \varphi(x_q) \geq \varphi(x_r)$$
$$\implies \varphi(x_r) = \varphi(x_s) = \cdots = \varphi(x_q).$$

Hence

$$u'_r x_s \leq 1 \wedge u'_s x_t \leq 1 \wedge \cdots \wedge u'_q x_r \leq 1$$
$$\implies u'_r x_s = u'_s x_t = \cdots = u'_q x_r = 1.$$

This condition will define the property of *cyclical consistency* for E. It has been shown to be an obviously necessary condition for utility consistency, and it is going to be proved also sufficient. In order to do this, some other consistency conditions will be introduced for E, and finally they will all be proved equivalent. Define $D_{rs} = u'_r x_s - 1$, which may be called the *cross-coefficient*, from E_r to E_s. The cross-coefficients altogether define the *cross-structure* D for the expenditure configuration E.

The cyclical consistency condition now has the statement

$$D_{rs} \leqq 0, \quad D_{st} \leqq 0, \ldots, D_{qr} \leqq 0 \Rightarrow D_{rs} = D_{st} = \cdots = D_{qr} = 0$$

for all $r, s, t, \ldots, q = 1, \ldots, k$. Since a multiple cycle is just a conjunction of simple cycles, and since $D_{rr} = 0$, there is no restriction in assuming $r, s, t, \ldots, q = 1, \ldots, k$ all distinct.

Let a new consistency condition now be defined for E, again through its cross-structure D, by the existence of numbers λ_r $(r = 1, \ldots, k)$, to be called *multipliers* for E, satisfying the system of inequalities

$$\lambda_r > 0, \quad \lambda_r D_{rs} + \lambda_s D_{st} + \cdots + \lambda_q D_{qr} \geqq 0,$$

for all $r, s, t, \ldots, q = 1, \ldots, k$. The consistency of this system of inequalities, in other words the existence of multipliers for E, will define the condition of *multiplier consistency* for E. Again, the same condition is obtained if $r, s, t, \ldots, q = 1, \ldots, k$ are taken to be distinct.

It is obvious that multiplier consistency implies cyclical consistency. For

$$\lambda_r > 0 \wedge D_{rs} \leqq 0 \Rightarrow \lambda_r D_{rs} \leqq 0,$$

and

$$\lambda_r D_{rs} \leqq 0 \wedge \lambda_s D_{st} \leqq 0 \wedge \cdots \wedge \lambda_q D_{qr} \leqq 0$$

with

$$\lambda_r D_{rs} + \lambda_s D_{st} + \cdots + \lambda_q D_{qr} \geqq 0$$

implies

$$\lambda_r D_{rs} = \lambda_s D_{st} = \cdots = \lambda_q D_{qr} = 0,$$

which, with $\lambda_r > 0$, implies

$$D_{rs} = D_{st} = \cdots = D_{qr} = 0.$$

Therefore, multiplier consistency implies cyclical consistency. The converse is also true, as will eventually appear.

Now let still another condition be defined for E through its cross-structure, by the existence of numbers λ_r, φ_r $(r = 1, \ldots, k)$, to be called *multipliers* and *levels*, satisfying the system of inequalities

$$\lambda_r > 0, \quad \lambda_r D_{rs} \geqq \varphi_s - \varphi_r \quad (r, s = 1, \ldots, k).$$

The consistency of this system of inequalities will define the condition of *level consistency* for E.

It is obvious that level consistency implies multiplier consistency, and moreover that any multipliers which realize the level consistency condition also realize the multiplier consistency condition. For, from

$$\lambda_r D_{rs} \geqq \varphi_s - \varphi_r$$

follows

$$\lambda_r D_{rs} + \lambda_s D_{st} + \cdots + \lambda_q D_{qr} \geqq \varphi_s - \varphi_r + \varphi_t - \varphi_s + \cdots + \varphi_q - \varphi_r = 0.$$

It will be shown that, conversely, multiplier consistency implies level consistency, and moreover, that any set of multipliers which realized the multiplier consistency condition can be joined with a set of levels to realize the level consistency condition.

Theorem *The three conditions of cyclical, multiplier and level consistency on the cross-structure of an expenditure configuration are all equivalent, and are implied by the condition of utility consistency for the configuration.*

It has been seen that utility consistency for the configuration E implies cyclical consistency for its cross-structure D. Also it has been seen that level consistency implies multiplier consistency and that multiplier consistency implies cyclical consistency for D. Hence it remains to be shown that cyclical consistency implies multiplier consistency, and that multiplier consistency implies level consistency, and then the theorem will have been proved.

Introduce the relation W defined by

$$rWs \equiv D_{rs} \leqq 0,$$

it being reflexive, since $D_{rr} = 0$, and then $R = \vec{W}$, the transitive closure of W, this being transitive and such that $W \subset R$, from the form of its definition, and reflexive, since W is reflexive. Then $P = R \cap \bar{R}'$, the antisymmetric part of R, is antisymmetric, from the form of the definition, and transitive, since R is transitive. Hence it is an order. In case it is not a total order, there always exist a total order which is a refinement of it, that is $R \subset T$ where T is a total order, and $T \subset \bar{T}'$, since T is antisymmetric. Without loss is generality, it can be supposed that the occasions are so ordered that $rTs \equiv r < s$.

Now cyclical consistency is equivalent to the condition

$$D_{rs} \leqq 0 \wedge C_{st} \leqq 0 \wedge \cdots \wedge D_{pq} \leqq 0 \;\Rightarrow\; D_{qr} \geqq 0$$

which can be stated as

$$R \subset M',$$

Where M is the relation defined by

$$rMs \equiv D_{rs} \geqq 0$$

such that

$$rMs \;\Leftarrow\; D_{rs} > 0 \;\Leftrightarrow\; r\bar{W}s$$

so that

$$\bar{W} \subset M.$$

Now cyclical consistency gives $R \subset M'$; and the definition of R gives $W \subset R$, so that $\bar{R}' \subset \bar{W}' \subset M'$. Hence $R \cup \bar{R}' \subset M'$. But $R \cap \bar{R}' \subset T \subset \bar{T}'$ so that $T \subset \bar{R}' \cup R$. Hence $T \subset M'$, or equivalently

$$r < s \implies D_{sr} \geqq 0.$$

Now assume, as an inductive hypothesis, that, at an $(m-1)$-th stage, multipliers $\lambda_r > 0$ $(1 \leqq r < m)$ have been found such that

$$\lambda_r D_{rs} + \lambda_s D_{st} + \cdots + \lambda_q D_{qr} \geqq 0 \quad (1 \leqq r, \ldots, q < m).$$

Then, for the m-th stage to be attained, it is required to find a multiplier $\lambda_m > 0$ such that

$$\lambda_r D_{rs} + \lambda_s D_{st} + \cdots + \lambda_q D_{qm} + \lambda_m D_{mr} \geqq 0 \quad (1 \leqq r, \ldots, q \leqq m - 1).$$

But $D_{mr} \geqq 0$ if $r < m$. Hence let

$$\mu_m = -\min \left\{ \frac{\lambda_r D_{rs} + \lambda_s D_{st} + \cdots + \lambda_q D_{qm}}{D_{mr}} \,\middle|\, 1 \leqq r, \ldots, q < m; D_{mr} > 0 \right\}.$$

Then any $\lambda_m \geqq \max\{0, \mu_m\}$ is as required. Hence the m-th stage is attainable from the $(m-1)$-th. The second stage can obviously be attained, since, with any $\lambda_1 > 0$, there only has to be taken a $\lambda_2 > 0$ such that $\lambda_1 D_{12} + \lambda_2 D_{21} \geqq 0$, which is possible since $D_{12} < 0$ and $D_{21} < 0$ is impossible, by the hypothesis of cyclical consistency. It follows by induction that the k-th stage is attainable, that is, multipliers can be found which realize the multiplier consistency condition. The proof that cyclical consistency implies multiplier consistency is now complete.

To prove that multiplier consistency implies level consistency, assume a set of multiplier λ_r and let $a_{rs} = \lambda_r D_{rs}$. Then

$$a_{rs} + a_{st} + \cdots + a_{qr} \geqq 0,$$

for all distinct $r, s, t, \ldots, q$. It is now going to be proved that there exist numbers φ_r such that

$$a_{rs} \geqq \varphi_r - \varphi_s \quad (r \neq s), \tag{a}$$

whence the level consistency condition will have been shown. Let

$$a_{rlm \cdots ps} = a_{rl} + a_{lm} + \cdots + a_{ps},$$

and let

$$A_{rs} = \min_{l, m, \ldots, p} a_{rlm \cdots ps}.$$

Then

$$a_{rs} \geqq A_{rs}.$$

Also,

$$A_{rs} + A_{sr} \geqq 0 \quad \text{and} \quad A_{rs} + A_{st} \geqq A_{rt}.$$

Consider the system

$$A_{rs} \geqq \varphi_r - \varphi_s \quad (r \neq s). \tag{A}$$

Any solution φ_r of (A) is a solution of (a), since $a_{rs} \geqq A_{rs}$. Also, any solution φ_r of (a) is a solution of (A). For

$$a_{rl} \geqq \varphi_r - \varphi_l, \quad a_{lm} \geqq \varphi_l, \dots, a_{ps} \geqq \varphi_p - \varphi_s;$$

whence, by addition,

$$a_{rlm \cdots ps} \geqq \varphi_r - \varphi_l - \varphi_m + \cdots + \varphi_p - \varphi_s$$
$$= \varphi_r - \varphi_s,$$

and, therefore,

$$A_{rs} \geqq \varphi_r - \varphi_s.$$

It follows that the consistency of (a), which has to be shown, is equivalent to that of (A), which will be shown now.

The proof depends on an extension property of solution of the subsystems of (A). Thus, assume a solution φ_r $(r < m)$ has been found for the subsystem

$$A_{rs} \geqq \varphi_r - \varphi_s \quad (r \neq s; r, s < m). \tag{A, m – 1}$$

It will be shown that it can be extended by an element φ_m to a solution of (A, m).

Thus, there is to be found a number φ_m such that

$$A_{rm} \geqq \varphi_r - \varphi_m, \quad A_{ms} \geqq \varphi_m - \varphi_s \quad (r, s < m)$$

that is,

$$A_{ms} + \varphi_s \geqq \varphi_m \geqq \varphi_r - A_{rm}.$$

So the condition that such φ_m can be found is

$$A_{mq} + \varphi_q \geqq \varphi_p - A_{pm},$$

where

$$\varphi_p - A_{pm} = \max_r \{\varphi_r - A_{rm}\}, \quad A_{mq} + \varphi_q = \min_r \{A_{mq} + \varphi_q\}.$$

But if $p = q$, this is equivalent to

$$A_{mq} + A_{qm} \geqq 0,$$

which is verified by hypothesis; and if $p \neq q$, it is equivalent to

$$A_{pm} + A_{mq} \geqq \varphi_p - \varphi_q,$$

which is verified, since by hypothesis,

$$A_{pm} + A_{mq} \geqq A_{pq}, \quad A_{pq} \geqq \varphi_p - \varphi_q.$$

Since the system (A, 2) trivially has a solution, it follows by induction that the system $(A) = (A, k)$ has solution, and is thus consistent.

Theorem *If* $E = \{E_r | r = 1, \ldots, n\}$ *is any expenditure configuration, with figures* $E_r = (x_r | u_r)(u'_r x_r = 1)$ *and cross-coefficients* $D_{rs} = u'_r x_s - 1$, *and if* λ_r, φ_r *are any multipliers and levels, being such that*

$$\lambda_r > 0, \quad \lambda_r D_{rs} \geqq \varphi_s - \varphi_r \quad (r, s - 1, \ldots, n)$$

and if $g_r = u_r \lambda_r$, *and* $\varphi_r(x) = \varphi_r + g'_r(x - x_r)$, *then*

$$\varphi(x) = \min\{\varphi_r(x) \,|\, r = 1, \ldots, n\}$$

is a function which realizes the utility hypothesis for E.

Now

$$\varphi_r(x) = \varphi_r + g'_r(x - x_r)$$
$$= \varphi_r + \lambda_r(u'_r x - 1)$$

so that

$$\varphi_r(x_s) = \varphi_r + \lambda_r D_{rs} \geqq \varphi_s, \quad \varphi_s(x_s) = \varphi_s.$$

Hence

$$\varphi(x_s) = \min\{\varphi_r(x_s) : r = 1, \ldots, n\}$$
$$= \varphi_s.$$

Also, $\varphi(x) \geqq \varphi_s$ implies $\varphi_s(x) \geqq \varphi_s$, which, since $\lambda_s > 0$, equivalent to $u'_s x \geqq 1$. Therefore, $u'_s x < 1$ implies $\varphi(x) < \varphi_s$. Accordingly,

$$\max\{\varphi(x) : u'_s x \leqq 1\} = \varphi_s$$

and

$$u'_s x \leqq 1 \wedge \varphi(x) = \varphi_s \Rightarrow u'_s x = 1.$$

The function φ therefore realizes the utility hypothesis for the configuration.
Since level consistency is the condition for the existence of the λ_r, φ_r, there follows

Corollary *For an expenditure configuration to have the property of utility consistency it is sufficient that its cross-structure have the property of level consistency.*

But, by the previous theorem, level consistency is necessary for utility consistency and is equivalent to cyclical consistency, whence

Corollary *The cyclical consistency condition is necessary and sufficient for the utility consistency of a finite expenditure configuration.*

Some comments are now made on the form of the function $\varphi(x)$ which has been constructed. The functions $\varphi_r(x)$ are linear and, therefore, concave and they have gradients $g_r > 0$, so they are increasing functions. Therefore, $\varphi(x)$, since it is the minimum of increasing concave functions, in an increasing concave function. Its level surfaces $\{x : \varphi(x) = \varphi\}$ are the convex polyhedral surfaces which are the boundaries of the convex polyhedral regions $\{x : \varphi(x) \geqq \varphi\}$ defined by the inequalities $\varphi_r(x) \geqq \varphi$, or equivalently

$$u_r' x \geqq 1 + \frac{\varphi - \varphi_r}{\lambda_r} \quad (r = 1, \ldots, n).$$

The region $\Omega_s = \{x : \varphi(x) = \varphi_s(x)\}$, in which $\varphi(x)$ coincides with $\varphi_r(x)$, is a polyhedral region, which is the projection in x-spaces of the face in which $\varphi_s(x) = \varphi$ cuts the boundaries of the region in (x, φ)-space defined by these inequalities. Since $\varphi(x_s) = \varphi_s = \varphi_s(x_s)$, as has been seen, it appears that $x_s \in \Omega_s$. Also

$$\Omega_s = \{x : \varphi_r(x) \geqq \varphi_s(x); r = 1, \ldots, n\}.$$

Hence Ω_r is defined by the inequalities

$$\varphi_r + \lambda_r(u_r' x - 1) \geqq \varphi_s + \lambda_s(u_s' x - 1) \quad (r = 1, \ldots, n).$$

Thus for a point to belong to two of the cells, say $x \in \Omega_s \cap \Omega_t$, it is required that

$$\varphi_s + \lambda_s(u_s' x - 1) = \varphi_t + \lambda_t(u_t' x - 1).$$

Hence, in a regular case, these cells can only intersect on their boundaries. The regions Ω_r thus constitute a dissection of the x-space into polyhedral cells. In the relative interior of each cell Ω_r, the function $\varphi(x)$ is differentiable and has constant gradient $g(x) = g_r$ $(x \in \Omega_r)$.

Now an index-number formula will be shown which is made intelligible by the construction of this utility function. Given any utility function $\varphi(x)$, the cost of living index with r and s as base and current periods has the determination

$$\rho_{sr} = \min \left\{ u_s' x : \varphi(x) \geqq \varphi_r \right\},$$

where $u_s' x = p_s' x / p_s' x_s$, and $\varphi_r = \varphi(x_r)$. Hence, with determination relative to the function $\varphi(x)$ which has been constructed,

$$\rho_{sr} = \min \left\{ u_s' x : u_t' x \geqq 1 + \frac{\varphi_r - \varphi_t}{\lambda_t} ; t = 1, \ldots, k \right\},$$

showing a linear program formula which can be evaluated by the usual methods.[2]

It can be seen that the realization of the utility hypothesis by a utility function φ which is concave and has gradient g implies level consistency. For the concavity is equivalent to the condition

$$\varphi(y) - \varphi(x) \leqq g(x)'(y - x),$$

and Gossen's Law that preference and price directions coincide in equilibrium, gives $g = u\lambda$, where $\lambda = g'x$ since $u'x = 1$. Hence, with $\varphi(x_r) = \varphi_r, g(x_r) = u_r\lambda_r$, there follows

$$\varphi_s - \varphi_r \leqq \lambda_r u_r(x_s - x_r).$$

Thus

$$\lambda_r D_{rs} \geqq \varphi_s - \varphi_r.$$

By an easy enlargement, the present results can be made to encompass the point of view of Pareto of preference as a relation divorced from a numerical measure.

An expenditure figure $E_r = (x_r|u_r)$ is considered as the choice $(x_r|W_{u_r})$, of x_r from among all compositions in the set $W_{u_r} = \{x : u'_r x \leqq 1\}$; and the preferences *immediate* in this choice form the set

$$R_r = \{(x_r, x) : x \in W_{u_r}\} = (x_r, W_{u_r}).$$

If these belong to a relation R, for all r, then

$$\bigcup_{r=1,\ldots,k} R_r \subset R,$$

and if R is transitive, that is $\vec{R} \subset \vec{R}$ where $\vec{R}$ is the transitive closure, this is equivalent to

$$R_E \subset R,$$

where

$$R_E = \bigcup_{r=1,\ldots,n} \vec{R}_r$$

can define the preferences *implicit* in the configuration $E = \{E_r \mid r = 1, \ldots, n\}$. Any preference relation which can be a hypothesis for E, in that it is reflexive and

---

2 A further discussion of this and related approaches to index-number construction can be found in S. N. Afriat, "The Cost of Living Index," appearing in *Studies in Mathematical Economics, Essays in Honor of Oskar Morgenstern*, ed. Martin Shubik chapter 13 (to be published by the Princeton University Press).

transitive and contains all the preferences in the choices shown by E, is *revealed* to the extent of containing R_E.

Now let $\ominus$ stand for the relation by which one composition is greater than another. That is, $x \ominus y$ means every quantity in x is at least the corresponding quantity in y, and not all are the same. In any admissible preference hypothesis R, it is to be assumed that the greater is exclusively preferred to the lesser so that

$$xRy \implies \sim \cdot y \ominus x.$$

That is $R \subset \bar{\ominus}'$, and, with $R_E \subset R$, this gives

$$R_E \subset \bar{\ominus}'.$$

It will now be seen that this condition, which can be called the *preference consistency* condition and is obviously implied by utility consistency, implies cyclical consistency. For it implies that

$$x_r R x_q \implies \sim x_q \ominus x_r$$

which implies the same as cyclical consistency, namely that

$$D_{rs} \leqq 1 \wedge D_{st} \leqq 1 \wedge \cdots \wedge D_{qr} < 1$$

is impossible, since

$$x_q \ominus x_r \implies D_{qr} < 1. \tag{2}$$

Now if *normal utility consistency* is defined as utility consistency with realization by a concave utility function, and since, by virtue of the form of the function which has been shown constructible under level consistency and by the implication of level consistency from the existence of such a function, the following implications are established, those an the outside in the diagram having been quite immediate, and those on the inside having been proved with less immediacy.

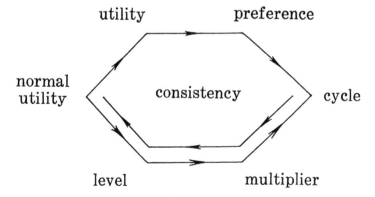

It follows therefore that all these six conditions are equivalent. The assumption in the utility consistency condition is weaker, and that in the normal utility consistency condition is stronger than the usual assumption that a utility function be continuous, increasing, and with concave levels. But now, in regard to the finite data, these three conditions appear equivalent. Also seen is the identity of the two approaches involving preference as a relation and utility as a magnitude. The finiteness of the configuration E has been essential for the methods used. Nevertheless it is possible to obtain analogous results without this restriction, though they must be without the present constructiveness.

References

[1]   Afriat, S. N., "The System of Inequalities $a_{rs} > X_r - X_s$," *Proceedings Cambridge Philosophical Society* (1963), LIX, 125–33.

[2]   ——, "Preference Scales and Expenditure Systems," *Econometrica*, XXX (April, 1962), 305–23.

[3]   Georgescu–Roegen, N., "Choice and Revealed Preference," *The Southern Economic Journal*, XXI (October, 1954), 119–30.

[4]   Houthakker, H. S., "Revealed Preference and the Utility Function," *Economica*, XVII (May, 1950), 159–74.

[5]   Samuelson, P. A., "Consumption Theory in Terms of Revealed Preference," *Economica*, XV (November, 1948), 243–53.

[6]   Uzawa, H., "Preference and Choice in the Theory of Consumption," *Mathematical Methods in the Social Sciences, 1959*, eds. K. J. Arrow, S. Karlin and P. Suppes (Stanford: Stanford University Press, 1960).

[7]   Wold, H., "A Synthesis of Demand Analysis," *Skandinavisk Akduarietidskrift*, 1943, 1944.

3
The concept of a price index and its extension

Second World Congress of the Econometric Society, Cambridge, September 1970.

Presented at the Second World Congress of the Econometric Society
Cambridge, England, Spetember 1970

The concept of a price index
and its extension

1.   The concept of a price index has origin in the notion that the scheme which applies for a single good, that the product of price and quantity determines exchange value in money, also has application to several goods. Let p and x denote non-negative row and column vectors. If quantities x are demanded at prices p then the total exchange value px is to have expression also as PX where $P = \theta(p)$, $X = \phi(x)$ are price and quantity "levels". This requires the cost function

$$\rho(p, x) = \min[py : yRx], \tag{1}$$

associated with the prevailing utility relation R, to admit the expression

$$\rho(p, x) = \theta(p)\phi(x), \tag{2}$$

which requires expansion paths to be lines through the origin. This means that the *pattern* of expenditures is fixed when prices are fixed, and thus is independent of the total, or that rich and poor distribute their expenditures identically.

From (1), and reflexivity of R,

$$\rho(p, x) \leqq px \tag{3}$$

for all p, x with equality in case of equilibrium.

Let (x_0, p_0), (x_1, p_1) be demands in the base and current periods 0, 1. Then, for compatibility with R, subject to (2),

$$\theta(p_0)\phi(x_0) = p_0x_0, \qquad \theta(p_1)\phi(x_1) = p_1x_1, \tag{4}$$

while by (3)

$$\theta(p_0)\phi(x_1) \leqq p_0x_1, \qquad \theta(p_1)\phi(x_0) \leqq p_1x_0. \tag{5}$$

Hence

$$p_1x_1/p_0x_1 \leqq P_{10} \leqq p_1x_0/p_0x_0, \tag{6}$$

where

$$P_{10} = \theta(p_1)/\theta(p_0) \tag{7}$$

is the *price index* between the reference periods, and dertermines equivalent incomes M_0, M_1 by the relation

$$M_1 = P_{10}M_0. \tag{8}$$

The limits for the price index in (6) are the Paasche and Laspeyres indices. A particular determination within these limits is

$$P_{10} = (p_1x_1 p_1x_0/p_0x_1 p_0x_0)^{\frac{1}{2}},$$

which is the Fisher index. Buscheguennce (1925)[1] remarked the correspondence of this determination to a homogeneous quadratic utility function.

Instead of (2), the assumption

$$\rho(p, x) = \theta(p)\phi(x) + \mu(p) \tag{9}$$

corresponds to expansion paths which are lines, not necessarily through the origin, nor even intersecting. This means the *marginal pattern* is fixed when prices are fixed, so that rich and poor spend an extra dollar identically. This does violence to important structure in reality, but not to the extent of the foregoing assumption. With this, in place of (6) and (8) there are relations

$$\frac{p_1x_1 - m_1}{p_0x_1 - m_0} \lessgtr P_{10} \lessgtr \frac{p_1x_0 - m_1}{p_0x_0 - m_0} \tag{10}$$

and

$$M_1 - m_1 = P_{10}(M_0 - m_0) \tag{11}$$

where the *original incomes* and the *marginal price index* are

$$m_0 = \mu(p_0), \quad m = \mu(p_1) \quad \text{and} \quad P_{10} = \theta(p_1)/\theta(p_0). \tag{12}$$

Let x_0, x_1 be taken now to be any pair of points on given expansion lines L_0, L_1. In the first case L_0, L_1 are determined by joining x_0, x_1 to the origin. But now they are determined with a further pair of points which, subject to a simple requirement on $(L_0, p_0), (L_1, p_1)$, given by the non-vanishing of a 2×2 determinant, can be chosen as the unique pair of *critical points* c_0, c_1 for which

$$p_0c_0 = p_0c_1, \quad p_1c_0 = p_1c_1. \tag{13}$$

The original incomes then have particular determinations

$$m_0 = p_0c_0, \quad m_1 = p_1c_1. \tag{14}$$

Then further, the marginal price index, limited by (10), has the particular determination

$$P_{10} = (p_1(x_1 - c_1)p_1(x_0 - c_0)/p_0(x_1 - c_1)p_0(x_0 - c_0))^{\frac{1}{2}} \tag{15}$$

1 Buscheguennce. 'Sur une classe des hypersurfaces'. A propos de 'l'index ideal' de M. Irv. Fisher. *Recueil Mathematique*, XXXII, 4 (1925), Moscow.

With these determinations, it is possible to identify (11) with the "New Formula" of Wald (1939),[2] obtained on the basis of a quadratic utility function, and thus to put that formula in the background of the general relation (11) where P_{10} has any determination within the limits (10). These limits, with original incomes determined by (14), are particular generalizations of the Paasche and Laspeyres indices, these indices being obtained when $c_0 = c_1 = 0$, that is when L_0, L_1 are rays through the origin. Correspondingly (15) is a marginal price generalization of Fisher's "ideal index" where the data consists of a general pair of expansion lines, instead of a pair concurrent in the origin.

Thus all essential features in standard theory of price indices have counterparts in a theory of marginal price indices. This is true also of the Divisia formula, which is based on a path instead of a discrete pair of demands. However, there are complications with general linear expansion which disappear in the homogeneous case.

A question which has been neglected is that of consistency of the data with the hypothetical utility model, at first the homogeneous linear cost model described by (2) and then the linear cost model described by (9). Then, for the theories of Buscheguennce and Wald, each of these must be taken with a further quadratic restriction. Then a further question is whether the directly implied bounds, such as are given by the Paasche and Laspeyres indices, in (6), and their extensions, in (10) with (14), are moreover the best possible, and therefore limits. An account is given of both these questions.

The theory can be extended to apply just as well to any number of references as to two, and distinctions between references can be taken to be in respect to time, national or geographical location, or both simultaneously. Still a further general development consists in relaxing strict consistency requirements by an economic concept of approximation, in terms of cost-efficiency.

2.   Now to be remarked is the extension of the Divisia formula which corresponds to the concept of a marginal price index.

Given a differentiable path $u(t)$ with $u(0) = u_0, u(1) = u_1, x_0 = f(u_0)$ and $\rho_{10} = \rho(u_1, x_0)$, where f is an expenditure system and ρ a utility cost function associated with the same utility relation, it has been established that $\rho_{10} = \rho(1)$ where $\rho(t)$ is a solution of the differential equation

$$\dot{\rho} = \dot{u} f(\rho^{-1} u), \quad \text{with } \rho(0) = 1. \tag{1}$$

In case of a cost function of the form

$$\rho(u, x) = \theta(u)\phi(x), \tag{2}$$

which is the case of homogeneous linear expansion, for which the condition is

$$f(\rho^{-1} u) = \rho f(u), \tag{3}$$

2 Wald, A. A New Formula for the Index of the Cost of Living. *Econometrica* 7, 4 (1939), 319–35.

and equivalently

$$f_u(u)u^1 = -f(u),\tag{4}$$

the differential equation becomes

$$\dot{\rho}/\rho = \dot{u}f(u),\tag{5}$$

and determines

$$\rho_{10} = e\int_0^1 \dot{u}f(u)\,dt.\tag{6}$$

With

$$U_t = \theta(u(t)), \quad X_t = \phi(x(t))\tag{7}$$

where $x(t) = f(u(t))$, so that

$$U_t X_t = 1,\tag{8}$$

and assigning

$$U_0 = 1, \quad X_0 = 1,\tag{9}$$

then

$$\rho_{10} = U_1 X_0 = U_1 = 1/X_1.\tag{10}$$

Also

$$U_{10} = U_1/U_0 = X_0/X_1 = X_{01}\tag{11}$$

thus

$$U_{10} = e\int_0^1 \dot{u}f(u)\,dt,\tag{12}$$

and reciprocally for X_{10}, which shows the Divisia formula for a price index, and the corresponding quantity index.

Thus the formula for ρ_{10} as $\rho_{10} = \rho(1)$ determined from (1) reduces to the Divisia formula under the considered hypothesis, described by the equivalent conditions (2)–(4). Now it will be seen what special formula is obtained under the less restrictive hypothesis, described by a utility cost function of the form

$$\rho(u, x) = \theta(u)\phi(x) + \mu(u).\tag{13}$$

This is the case of linear expansion, also described by the condition

$$f(\rho^{-1}u) = f(u) - (\rho - 1)f_u(u)u^1.\tag{14}$$

Provided (4) holds this coincides with (3), and (13) has $\mu(u) = 0$ so it coincides with (2). With this, (1) becomes

$$\dot{\rho} + (\rho - 1)\dot{u}f_u(u)u^1 = \dot{u}f(u).\tag{15}$$

Hence let

$$U_{t0} = e - \int_0^t \dot{u} f_u(u) u^1 \, dt = 1/U_{0t}, \tag{16}$$

and

$$X_t = - \int_0^t U_{0t} \dot{u} f(u) \, dt. \tag{17}$$

Then (15) can be stated

$$((\rho - 1)U_{0t}) = U_{0t}\dot{u} f(u), \tag{18}$$

and hence, with $\rho(0) = 1$, gives

$$(\rho - 1)U_{0t} = -X_t \tag{19}$$

equivalently

$$1 - \rho = U_{t0}X_t, \tag{20}$$

in particular

$$1 - \rho_{10} = U_{10}X_1. \tag{21}$$

To interpret this formula, consider (13) where $\phi(x)$ is fixed by setting

$$U_0 = \theta(u_0) = 1, \quad X_0 = \phi(x_0) = 0. \tag{22}$$

Then

$$n_0 = \mu(u_0) = 1, \tag{23}$$

since

$$U_0 X_0 + n_0 = 1. \tag{24}$$

Also

$$\begin{aligned} U_1 X_1 + n_1 &= 1, \\ U_1 X_0 + n_1 &= \rho_{10}, \end{aligned} \tag{25}$$

which shows that

$$n_1 = \rho_{10}, \quad U_1 = U_{10} \tag{26}$$

since $X_0 = 0, U_0 = 1$, so that (21) holds.

Since $t = 1$ can just as well be replaced by any t, X_t given by (17) is identified with

$$X_t = X_t - X_0 = \phi(x(t)), \quad U_t = U_t/U_0 = \theta(u(t)), \tag{27}$$

where $x(t) = f(x(t))$ and $\theta(u), \phi(x)$ are defined by the hypothesis (13) together with the specification (22). Generally

$$U_{ts} = \exp - \int_s^t \dot{u} f_u(u)^1 \, dt$$

$$X_t - X_s = - \int_s^t U_t \dot{u} f(u) \, dt \tag{28}$$

and, since

$$U_s X_s + n_s = 1, \quad U_t X_t + n_t = 1,$$

$$U_s X_t + n_s = \rho_{st}, \tag{29}$$

also

$$U_s(X_t - X_s) = \rho_{st}. \tag{30}$$

Though it is inevitable, it is as well to verify directly the reduction to Divisia's formula for the homogeneous case. In this case, because of (4), (16) becomes

$$U_{t0} = \exp \int_0^t \dot{u} f(u) \, dt. \tag{31}$$

Then (17) becomes

$$X_t [U_{0t}]_0^t = U_{0t} - 1, \tag{32}$$

so that (21) becomes

$$1 - \rho_{10} = U_{10}(U_{01} - 1)$$

$$= 1 - U_{10}, \tag{33}$$

that is

$$\rho_{10} = U_{10}, \tag{34}$$

where U_{10} is given by (31), which is the same as (6), as required. Thus (16) and (17) reconstruct the utility cost function under the hypothesis (13) together with the function $\theta(u), \phi(x)$ as fixed by the arbitrary normalization (22). This therefore is a system which stands between that of Divisia, which corresponds to homogeneous linearly, of utility cost or equivalently of expansion, and the generalization in (1) which is free of any restriction. It corresponds to linearity free of the further homogeneity, and to the concept of a marginal price index. Divisia gives the specialization of this corresponding to the standard concept of a price index.

4
Theory of International Comparisons of Real Income and Prices

In *International Comparisons of Prices and Output, Proceedings of the Conference at York University, Toronto, 1970*, edited by D. J. Daly. National Bureau of Economic Research, Studies in Income and Wealth Volume 37, New York, 1972 (Ch. I, 13–84).

Theory of International Comparisons
of Real Income and Prices

1.0 Concept of comparison

1.1 Framework

Two or more countries have similar commodities. But prices and quantities differ, and it is required to construct indexes which express a comparison. For a theory of such construction, it is essential to have a prior concept of the intended meaning of the comparison. From such a concept, together with a scheme for the data and a principle by which the data are related to the concept, the theory of construction should follow.

Comparison between two places in a single period is to be viewed in the same abstract framework as comparison between two periods in a single place. Though variables might occur in time and have a corresponding designation, temporal priority has no role. It makes no difference whether the distinctions be of time or place. What is in view is a variety of locations, temporal or geographical or possibly both, where prices and quantities differ, and which, when combined by analysis are to indicate differences of economic situation.

Let there be some k references which are to be compared and are indicated by $t = 1, \ldots, k$. But if there are two, these can be indicated by $t = 0, 1$ and distinguished as the *base* and *current* reference. The distinction between references can be taken to be as between different countries, or different periods of time, or both in conjunction. But in the question of international comparison, there often are k, or in particular two, different countries during the same period.

There are assumed to be some n goods involved. With n as the non-negative numbers, Ω_n and Ω^n are the spaces of nonnegative column and row vectors of n elements. The basic element of the data is a pair (x, p) formed by a vector $p \in \Omega_n$ of prices p_i and a vector $x \in \Omega^n$ of quantities x_i. Such a pair describes the *demand* of quantities x at prices p. The associated expenditure is $px = \sum_i p_i x_i$, and, with $M = px$, $u = M^{-1}p$ defines the associated *budget vector*. It forms with x the pair (x, u) such that $ux = 1$, which can be called the *associated budget*. Often an observed demand is meaningful only through its associated budget. The discussion is simpler in terms of budgets rather than original observed demands.

By an *expansion set* (S, p) is meant a set of demands $[(x, p) : x \in S]$ all associated with the same prices p. The set S could consist of a finite set of points, or it could be a path, in which case (S, p) indicates an *expansion path* associated with prices p. Inherent in the price level concept is the assumption that expansion paths are rays through the origin. In that case, the data for a demand (x, p) amount to data for an expansion path (S, p), where S is the ray $[x\lambda : \lambda \geq 0]$ through x. A more general model for an expansion path is the linear model, where the paths are lines not necessarily through the origin. In a common special form of this model, the expansion lines associated with different prices converge in a single point, not necessarily the origin.

For a basic scheme, it is postulated that the data consist of a set of demands (x_t, p_t) or, more elaborately, a set of expansions (S_t, p_t), associated with each country $t = 1, \ldots, k$. But in fact a single demand determines an expansion when analysis is based on the concept of a price index and hence on the assumption of homogeneity, which requires that expansion paths be rays through the origin, each determined by any one of its points. Thus again it is expansion data that are available, either explicitly or implicitly.

1.2   Nature of comparison

It is understood that the comparison is to be in real terms. This means, in the first place, that its reference must be exclusively to quantities of the basic goods, independent of the accident that money and prices are part of the data by means of which the comparison is made. The role of money and prices is just to express limitations of opportunities for possessing goods. But these limitations are of no significance if what is limited is not valued. Also value is meaningless if it is not pursued to a maximum within the limited opportunity available. With such optimality, data on choice under limitation communicates information about value which is relevant to comparisons. But value is an attribute of the chooser, and the chooser must therefore be clearly identified. Thus with national measurements it should be decided whether value derives directly from individuals or from the nation as a whole. In the latter case it should be asked in what sense, since national wants are not easily discovered and stated, and have dimensions which are without counterpart for the individual.

Some significant yardstick is presumed in making comparisons between situations. A yardstick that refers to bundles of goods is an ordering of them which expresses their relative value according to a system of wants. This immediately shows an obscurity in the meaning of comparisons between countries where wants are manifestly different, whether this be for the wants of the individual inhabitants or, in any sense conceivable, for that different type of individual represented by a single country. To speak of real national outputs or incomes implies a presupposition of national value, that is, a system of wants described by a utility relation. It this relation is not already on record and available in a form suitable for making the required comparisons, then it can only be inferred from price-quantity data, under the maximum hypothesis. Concerning the mechanism which provides this maximality, and there is only what Schumpeter termed the "maximum doctrine of perfect competition," which is an early concept. It was first criticized, seriously but cautiously, by Marshall and has now altogether lost its suggested meaning. Some such doctrine seems necessary if prices and price indexes are to be relevant to the measurement of a national output that differs from the summation of individual real incomes seemingly permitted by the assumption of homogeneity of utility which underlies the use of price indexes. Such a summation would appear to be permitted mathematically by the homogeneity assumption, but it would have no significance unless called for by some theory. Investigation of real national measures and comparisons seems to have little opportunity for development except for those that refer directly to individuals.

1.3   General principles

A problem to be considered is that of establishing a correspondence between individual incomes in different countries which represent the same real income or purchasing power, that is, which in choice of goods at the prices that prevail would obtain the same real output or utility. Such correspondence is to be established on the basis of a utility order $R \subset \Omega^n \times \Omega^n$ which compares bundles of goods $x, y \in \Omega^n$ according to value, or output of utility, so that the priority xRy signifies x is as good as, or produces at least as much utility as, y. The problem in such a comparison arises because though it is based conceptually on a utility scale no actual scale has been identified. However, the scale is validated by the holders of the incomes themselves. It is with that same scale that they are assumed to make optimal choices under limited budgets. The obverse of this is that data on choices impose a limitation on the scale that is to be applied. With fragmentary observations, this is a loose limitation, but essentially it is all there is with which to proceed.

So far as the idea of a definite structure of wants can be applied at all, it is recognized that wants are related to circumstances and differ between individuals, times, and countries. But the comparisons under consideration essentially involve the notion of a want structure that is common for all, and this universality is what makes the comparison intelligible. Such a yardstick is therefore a purely statistical concept. In such a case, complete generality of the basic model makes no sense. Indeterminacies can just as well be diminished, and in cases even removed, by imposing a special structure on the model. The structure most commonly imposed is homogeneity, which underlies the concept of a price index and with it almost the entire traditional theory of index numbers. It is an important form because it greatly simplifies procedures, and its lack of elaborate overrefinement is appropriate to some applications. But in other applications it effaces structural features which are of crucial significance.

In section 2.0, below, the basic analytical concepts bearing on index number construction are described. A special branch of this subject evolves from the homogeneity assumption, and leads to the theory of price index construction treated in section 3.0. Homogeneity of utility is equivalent to a homogeneous linear form for the expansion functions. Certain objections will be made to this in the present section, and to linear expansion in general. However, a limited generalization of the price index concept will be developed. This is the theory of marginal price indexes, which is presented later. It too is vulnerable to a serious objection, and it is shown how a further extension can overcome this, without sacrificing the practical features that belong to the earlier methods.

1.4   Analytical formulation

The basic concept of index theory is the value-cost function

$$\rho(p, x) = \min[py : yRx] \tag{1}$$

which derives from a utility relation R (see section 2.3). It determines the minimum cost at given prices p of a bundle of goods which ranks in R with a given bundle x. Since xRy, because of reflexivity of R,

$$\rho(p, x) \leqq px \tag{2}$$

for all p, x. Certain minimal properties are assumed for R (2.1), which in fact are not at all restrictive for the questions considered, with finite data (2.5), but give a simpler basis for discussion. While $\rho(p, x)$ derives from R, nothing of R is lost in it even when it is prescribed just for one value of p, since then as a function of x it is a utility function representing R:

$$xRy \iff \rho(p, x) \geqq \rho(p, y). \tag{3}$$

Such a particular utility function could be called a *cost gauge* of R. Any one can be constructed from any other:

$$\rho(p, x) = \min[py : \rho(p_0, y) \geqq \rho(p_0, x)]. \tag{4}$$

These are the natural yardsticks for the comparisons under consideration, since they deal with value and cost simultaneously, one of them being associated with any price situation; but they all represent a single system of measure by virtue of the transformations between them.

If R is specified for consumers (in practice, it is not), then $M_{10} = \rho(p_1, x_0)$ is the cost at current prices of living at the standard represented by the base consumption x_0. It goes without saying that the notion of costs has no meaning, and the equation has no unique determination, unless the calculation is at *minimum* cost. By (2),

$$M_{10} \leqq p_1 x_0, \tag{5}$$

this is, the "true" cost M, which is true in so far as R is the true utility relation, does not exceed the Laspeyres cost $p_1 x_0$. This is reassuring for traditional doctrine, which has proposed the Laspeyres index to be an upper bound of something. If more is intended than has just been said with (5), which is a vacuous consequence of definition, then it is necessary to be explicit.

Observed demands (x_0, p_0), (x_1, p_1) for the base and current periods, or countries, being available, a formula for M_{10} is required, traditionally in the form $M_{10} = P_{10} M_0$, where P_{10} is a "price index," and $M_0 = p_0 x_0$. Thus with the Laspeyres price index $P_{10} = p_1 x_0 / p_0 x_0$, $M_{10} = p_1 x_0$ as just remarked. But first the question will be considered without regard for the proposed significance of this form. What has mostly been lacking is an explicit recognition of a principle which relates the data to the question. One such principle is that R be such as to show observed cost $M_t = p_t x_t$ not to exceed minimum cost for the value obtained, $M_{tt} = \rho(p_t, x_t)$, that is, the observed demands must be expressed as satisfying a condition which is necessary for optimality, when R is the prevailing utility relation. Then

$$\rho(p_0, x_0) \geq p_0 x_0, \quad \rho(p_1, x_1) \geq p_1 x_1. \tag{6}$$

With (2) this is equivalent to

$$\rho(p_0, x_0) = p_0 x_0, \quad \rho(p_1, x_1) = p_1 x_1. \tag{7}$$

Any R for which (6) holds can be said to be *compatible* with the data. The further logic of the compatibility relation is shown in section 2.4. Possibly no compatible R exists. If any does the demands can be said to be *consistent*. (A more general theory of consistency is developed in section 2.5.) Then it can be asked, What is the range of values of $M_{10} = \rho_{10}(p_1, x_0)$ for all such R? The range of M_{10} appears to be an interval, which always includes the upper limit $(M_{10})_u$, but not necessarily the lower one $(M_{10})_l$. But the question of attainment of units is unimportant. What we really want to know is whether these are the proverbial bounds of index number lore. The Laspeyres value is identical with $(M_{10})_u$, but the Paasche value not only has no connection with $(M_{10})_l$, but even need not lie in the interval, presumed nonempty since the data are consistent. But it is evident in all arguments involving the Paasche index, and generally whenever the peculiar concept of a price index is dealt with, that an implicit special assumption has been made, namely, the homogeneity of utility. (It is examined in the next section.) Since there are serious objections to that assumption and, also, to limiting the data to base and current demands only, it is interesting to go outside the traditional framework and investigate the determination of $\rho(p_1, x_0)$ in a more general way.

It is simpler to discuss demands (x_t, p_t) through their derived budgets (x_t, u_t) where $u_t = M_t^{-1} p_t$, and $M_t = p_t x_t$, so that $u_t x = 1$. The requirement $M_{tt} = M_t$ for compatibility of R with any set of demands for $t = 1, \ldots, k$ is then

$$\rho_{tt} = 1, \quad t = 1, \ldots, k \tag{8}$$

where

$$\rho_{rs} = \rho(u_r, x_s), \quad r, s = 1, \ldots, k. \tag{9}$$

The next step is to determine the range of any ρ_{rs} for all R such that $\rho_{tt} = 1$ for all t. Again the range is an interval, whose limits can be determined. Let

$$D_{rs} = u_r x_s - 1, \tag{10}$$

and define a relation D by

$$rDs \equiv D_{rs} \leq 0, \tag{11}$$

and Q by

$$rQt \equiv rDsD \cdots Dt \quad \text{for some } s, \ldots \tag{12}$$

and let

$$(\rho_{rs})_u = \min[u_r x_t : tQs] \tag{13}$$

$$(\rho_{rs})_l = \min[u_r x : sQt \implies u_t x \geq 1]. \tag{13}$$

The condition for the consistency of the demands can be stated in three equivalent ways,

$$D_{rs} \leq 0, D_{st} \leq 0, \ldots, D_{qr} \leq 0 \implies D_{rs} = D_{st} = \cdots = D_{qr} = 0 \tag{14}$$

for all $r, s, \ldots, q$ or

$$rQs \implies u_s x_r \geq 0 \tag{15}$$

for all r, s or

$$(\rho_{rs})_l \leq (\rho_{rs})_u \tag{16}$$

for all r, s. Then, subject to consistency, so that the interval will be nonempty, $(\rho_{rs})_u$, $(\rho_{rs})_l$ are the desired limits. Consistency of the data implies the consistency of these as upper and lower limits, that is, that the one be not less than the other, for all r, s. In fact, by the equivalence of consistency to (16), the converse also is true.

In the special case of a pair of demands (x_0, p_0), (x_1, p_1), the consistency condition becomes

$$p_0 x_1 \leq p_0 x_0, \quad p_1 x_0 \leq p_1 x_1 \implies p_0 x_1 = p_0 x_0, \quad p_1 x_0 = p_1 x_1 \tag{17}$$

evidently implied by the Samuelson condition

$$p_0 x_1 \leq p_0 x_0, \quad x_1 \neq x_0 \implies p_1 x_0 > p_1 x_1 \tag{18}$$

which can be stated more symmetrically as

$$p_0 x_1 \leq p_0 x_0, \quad p_1 x_0 \leq p_1 x_1 \implies x_0 = x_1. \tag{19}$$

Further

$$(\rho_{10})_u = \min[u_1 x_t : u_t x_0 \leq 1] \tag{20}$$

so that, if $u_1 x_0 \leqq 1$,

$$(\rho_{10})_u = \min[u_1 x_1, u_1 x_0]$$
$$= \min[1, u_1 x_0] = u_1 x_0 \tag{21}$$

and if $u_1 x_0 > 1$,

$$(\rho_{10})_u = \min[u_1 x_0] = u_1 x_0. \tag{22}$$

Therefore, in any case, $(\rho_{10})_u = u_1 x_0$, which corresponds to the Laspeyres index, as already stated. Also

$$(\rho_{10})_l = \min[u_1 x : u_0 x_t \leqq 1 \implies u_t x \geqq 1]. \tag{23}$$

Therefore, if $u_0 x_1 \leqq 1$,

$$(\rho_{10})_l = \min[u_1 x : u_0 x \geqq 1, u_1 x \geqq 1] \geqq 1, \tag{24}$$

and if $u_0 x_1 > 1$,

$$(\rho_{10})_l = \min[u_1 x : u_0 x \geqq 1]$$
$$= \min[u_{1i}/u_{0i} : u_{0i} > 0], \tag{25}$$

so certainly $(\rho_{10})_l$ is not related to the Paasche index.

This approach, general though it is in that it depends on no special properties for utility, is nevertheless too rigid. Data may not satisfy the required consistency condition, and in that event the analysis can proceed no further. But the model is in any case unrealistic because there is no provision for error. An extension is shown in sections 2.4 and 2.5 where deviations are explained as error, measured in economic terms of inefficiency. No real economic agents have exact and invariable wants. But assuming any did, none would accurately allocate their expenditure down to the last penny. There would be perhaps a rough tendency toward equilibrium until any effort and cost for improvement would seem to outweigh any plausible benefit. Equilibrium in the larger framework, which takes into account the value and cost of every movement, its sacrifice and gain, would leave disequilibrium in the narrower framework to which analysis is confined. Since the wider framework is unknown, the method must be essentially statistical, dealing with fluctuations in a hypothetical model. Since economic error has the nature of inefficiency, it is appropriate that distance should be measured in an inefficiency sense, instead of, for instance, by a Euclidean sum of squares. A Euclidean distance, however vast, but which corresponded to a difference of a negligible penny would nevertheless be negligible. This argument, which is in opposition to some classical and other statistical techniques usual in econometrics, in particular in production and consumption analysis, is related to the argument in favour of approaching statistics from the viewpoint of decision theory.

To return to the demand consistency condition, in addition to the three equivalent conditions (14), (15), and (16), there are two further equivalents

$$\lambda_r D_{rs} + \lambda_s D_{st} + \cdots + \lambda_q D_{qr} \geqq 0, \quad \lambda_r > 0 \tag{26}$$

for all $r, s, \ldots$, for some λ_r, or

$$\lambda_r D_{rs} \geq \phi_s - \phi_r, \quad \lambda_r > 0, \tag{27}$$

for all r, s for some λ_r, ϕ_r. Moreover, for all λ_r and ϕ_r, (27) implies (26), and for all λ_r, (26) implies (27) for some ϕ_r. With any λ_r, ϕ_r let

$$\phi(x) = \min_t \phi_t + \lambda_t(u_t x - 1). \tag{28}$$

Then (27) is equivalent to the compatibility of the utility function $\phi(x)$ with the given demands, for it is equivalent to

$$\phi(x_t) = \phi_t, \min[u_r x : \phi(x) \geq \phi_s] = 1 \tag{29}$$

for all r, s, t. Thus, whenever the demands are consistent, that is, compatible with any utility function at all, then they are compatible with a utility function of the form (28), corresponding to a solution of (27). This method, as extended in sections 2.4 and 2.5 to allow different degrees of efficiency and approximation, shows how the utility hypothesis, which is basic to index numbers, can be given constructive realization with any data.

Any utility order R between consumption bundles determines an *adjoint utility order* S between consumption budgets. Thus $u S v$ means there exists x such that $ux \leq 1$ and for all y if $vy \leq 1$ then $x R y$; in other words, there exists a consumption attainable within the budget u which is as good as any attainable within v. Also, any utility function $\phi(x)$ determines an *adjoint utility function*

$$\psi(u) = \max[\phi(x) : ux \leq 1] \tag{30}$$

and if $\phi(x)$ represents R then $\psi(u)$ represents S.

Compatibility of R with (x_0, u_0), where $u_0 x_0 = 1$, is equivalent to $\phi(x_0) = \psi(u_0)$, and to

$$u_0 S v \iff vy \leq 1 \implies s_0 S y. \tag{31}$$

Given this,

$$\begin{aligned}
\rho_{10} &= \min[u_1 x : x R x_0] \\
&= \max[\rho : u_1 x \leq \rho \implies x_0 R x] \\
&= \max[\rho : u_0 S \rho^{-1} u_1].
\end{aligned} \tag{32}$$

Hence, with $\psi(u)$ representing S, it follows that $\rho = \rho_{10}$ is the solution of

$$\psi(u_0) = \psi(\rho^{-1} u_1). \tag{33}$$

Equivalently, $M = M_{10}$ is the solution of

$$\psi(M_0^{-1} p_0) = \psi(M^{-1} p_1). \tag{34}$$

With $\phi(x)$ concave, $\psi(M^{-1} p)$ is a concave function of M, so that, for some P_0,

$$\psi(M^{-1} p_0) - \psi(M_0^{-1} p_0) \leq (M - M_0)/P_0 \tag{35}$$

for all M. If $\psi(u_0)$ is differentiable at $u = M_0^{-1} p_0$, this implies

$$(\partial/\partial M_0)\psi(M^{-1} p_0) = 1/P_0, \tag{36}$$

so that P_0 appears as the marginal price of utility at the level of expenditure M_0 when commodity prices are p_0. Correspondingly, $1/P_0$ is the marginal utility of money. The average utility of money, or the reciprocal of the average price of utility, is $\psi(M^{-1} p_0)/M_0$. Identity between the average and marginal prices of utility, that is,

$$M\partial\psi(M^{-1} p)/\partial M = \psi(N^{-1} p), \tag{37}$$

implies that R is homogeneous. Conversely, if R is homogeneous, it can be represented by a linearly homogeneous utility function for which (37) holds. In fact, a necessary and sufficient condition that R be homogeneous, that is

$$xRy \;\Rightarrow\; x\lambda Ry\lambda \quad (\lambda \geqq 0), \tag{38}$$

is that the utility cost function be factorable thus:

$$\rho(p, x) = \theta(p)\phi(x) \tag{39}$$

and with this $\theta(p)$ is identified simultaneously with the average price and the marginal price of utility $\phi(x)$. The factorability of utility cost underlies the concept of a level of prices, and hence also that of a price index, which compares levels. There appears to be a lack of explicit recognition that the meaning of a price level, and therefore of all price indexes, depends on homogeneity of utility. Index constructions which depart from this, and which, so to speak, belong to a family which is one rung up the ladder of generality include the "new formula" of Wald (1939), and the "constant utility" index of Klein–Rubin (1947) which, appropriately put, exhibit utility price which is linear but not at the same time homogeneous. They can be seen as extensions of the Fisher and Palgrave formulas, respectively, and have corresponding limitations. Also the Paasche and Laspeyres indexes have correspondents in this family.

With $\phi(x)$, the utility function given by (28), and $\psi(u)$, its dual, compatibility, implied by (27), is equivalent to $\phi(x_t) = \psi(u_t)$. It appears, in (29), that $\phi(x_t) = \phi_t$. Thus ϕ_t appears as the utility at x_t, with a compatible utility function $\phi(x)$. Equivalent to (35) is

$$\psi(\rho^{-1} u_0) - \psi(u_0) \leqq \lambda_0(\rho - 1), \tag{40}$$

where $\rho = M/M_0$, $\lambda_0 = M_0/P_0$. Thus λ_t/M_t appears as the marginal utility of money for $\phi(x)$.

It is curious that (27) holds with $\delta_{rs} = \rho_{rs} - 1$ substituted for $D_{rs} = u_r x_s - 1$. For

$$\phi_t = \phi(x_t) = \psi(u_t), \quad \psi(\rho_{st}^{-1} u_t) = \psi(u_s),$$

which, with

$$\psi(\rho_{st}^{-1} u_t) - \psi(u_t) \leqq \lambda_t(\rho_{st} - 1), \tag{41}$$

gives

$$\lambda_t \delta_{st} \geq \phi_s - \phi_t. \tag{42}$$

Since, by (2),

$$\delta_{st} \leq D_{st} \tag{43}$$

(27) is recovered from (42). A certain duality between the D's and δ's becomes even more specific in further developments. The D's correspond to cross costs which apply to quantities, essentially Laspeyres indexes, which derive directly from data, and the δ's to cross costs which apply to their utility, which are the concern of index construction.

1.5   *Concept of the price level*

The price level concepts has its origin in the arithmetic of the market place, where the product of price and quantity equals exchange value in money, and in the notion that such as scheme of arithmetic can apply just as well for many goods treated as one, so that a product of price and quantity levels, determined from many prices and quantities, equals total exchange value, that is, the sum of products of individual prices and quantities. Thus, by simple market arithmetic

$$p_0 x_0 = M_0, \quad p_1 x_1 = M_1 \tag{1}$$

and then it is postulated that also

$$P_0 X_0 = M_0, \quad P_1 X_1 = M_1, \tag{2}$$

where the P's and X's correspond to levels of prices and quantities. Then

$$P_{10} X_{10} = M_{10}, \tag{3}$$

where $P_{10} = P_1/P_0$, and so forth. The idea is then taken further, and it is assumed that the composite price ratio P_{10} can be "approximated" by some kind of average of individual price ratios p_{1i}/p_{0i}. All standard price indexes are apparently expressible as averages—arithmetic, geometric, harmonic, and mixtures—of these, with various weights and exponents. Fisher examined about two hundred of them, and found that their divergences from each other were small compared to the errors inherent in the data. With P_{10} thus "approximated" by almost any formula, it is possible to "deflate" a money ratio M_{10} to determine $X_{10} = P^{-1} M_{10}$ as its "real" correspondent. This is the intelligible scheme for almost any index construction which has had application, starting with Fleetwood in 1708. The Laspeyres index has the merit of almost irreducible simplicity, and the theoretical distinction of being an "upper bound," though of what and to whom requires elaboration.

The essential concept here is that a utility relation R prevails and that is utility cost function $\rho(p, x)$, that is, the minimum cost at prices p of attaining the utility represented by x, can be factored:

$$\rho(p, x) = \theta(p)\phi(x). \tag{4}$$

But this is equivalent to the homogeneity of R, that is

$$xRy \implies x\lambda Ry\lambda \quad (\lambda \geqq 0), \tag{5}$$

and implies that both the price and quantity functions $\theta(p)$, $\phi(x)$ are linearly homogeneous,

$$\theta(\mu p) = \mu\theta(p), \quad \phi(x\lambda) = \phi(x)\lambda, \tag{6}$$

where λ, $\mu \geq 0$. Clearly all functions which can appear in the factorization (4) can differ only by a constant positive multiplier. The function $\phi(x)$ is fixed entirely by taking $\phi(x_0) = 1$ for any x_0. Thus the pair of *antithetic price and quantity functions* are, to this extent, uniquely determined. While R is represented by a wider class of utility functions, equivalent under increasing transformations, homogeneity in the sense of (5) requires there to exist a subclass of linearly homogeneous utility functions that are equivalent under multiplication by a positive constant; and these are the ones which are relevant.

From (4), and 1.4 (2),

$$\theta(p)\phi(x) \leq px \tag{7}$$

for all (p, x) and the condition for equilibrium is

$$\theta(p)\phi(x) = px, \tag{8}$$

which holds for a demand (x, p) which is compatible with R. Since for all p this holds for some x, it follows that the adjoint of $\phi(x)$ is

$$\psi(u) = [\theta(u)]^{-1} \tag{9}$$

so that

$$\psi(M^{-1}p) = M/\theta(p). \tag{10}$$

With $X = \psi(M^{-1}p)$ as the utility of money M at prices p, and the average price P of utility at that level given by

$$X/M = 1/P, \tag{11}$$

$P = \theta(p)$; so P is fixed when p is fixed and is independent of M. This implies that also

$$\partial X/\partial M = 1/P, \tag{12}$$

that is, the fixed average price necessarily coincides with the marginal price, which is then also fixed. But even if the average price is not fixed, it is possible to have a fixed marginal price. This shows the direction of the first step in generalizing the traditional price index concept, while preserving part of its practical simplicity.

The elementary prices, when they are taken as given in a perfect market, are themselves conceived of as fixed average prices coincident with marginal prices. The traditional price index concept corresponds to the idea that the average price of utility is fixed when elementary prices are fixed. It allows every unit of money to be treated separately and uniformly, aggregates to be treated by simple addition, the utility of a sum being the sum of the equal utilities of the equal units that compose it. Any unit of money in the base period is equivalent in general purchasing power to P_{10} units in the current period, and any M_0 base units are equivalent to

$$M_1 = P_{10} M_0 \qquad (13)$$

current units, since this is the condition that $X_{10} = 1$, in (3), and $X_0 = X_1$ in (2). It does not matter who or what the money is for; it could be a part or the whole of an individual income or a national income. All amounts of money have only to have a multiplier uniformly applied to them for a general correction for price change to be effected. Such a scheme has great statistical and social convenience because it is put into operation by publication of a single number. However, when the implications of the assumption which underlines the scheme are examined, it appears that no care in the choice of that number can overcome the radical defects. There is a similar, though more favourable, situation even with the next more general scheme, where it is required only that the marginal price of utility be fixed, as will be examined later.

Homogeneity of the utility relation brings about the cost separation (4). Then any x, p in a compatible demand have the relation E defined by

$$xEp \equiv \theta(p)\phi(x) = p(x). \qquad (14)$$

Since then

$$xEp \implies x\lambda Ep \quad (\lambda \geqq 0) \qquad (15)$$

for all p. Equivalently

$$x \in Ep \implies x' \subset Ep \qquad (16)$$

where $x' = [x\lambda : \lambda \geqq 0]$. It appears then that the expansion locus Ep for any price p is a cone, since if it contains a point then it contains every point on the ray it determines. If, for instance, $\phi(x)$ is quasi-concave then Ep is always a single ray if and only if $\phi(x)$ is strictly quasi-concave. Then, when prices are fixed at p, and as incomes vary, all consumptions lie on the ray Ep through the origin. That is, when prices are fixed the *pattern of consumption is fixed*, that is, the proportions between the goods which enter into consumption are fixed. But it is an overwhelmingly significant fact of experience that the rich, whether individuals or countries, have things that the poor do not have at all, let alone in corresponding proportion. Deliberately to overlook this in a system of calculation that seeks to make general comparisons leaves the significance of such calculation quite obscure, even as to the locus of injustice.

1.6 *National measurement*

The application of prices and price indexes to measure national output seems to be supported if not by arguments then by urgings from two sides, both objectionable.

One is more straightforward and will be remarked upon first. The other has something to do with the "maximum doctrine of perfect competition," so called by Schumpeter, or Adam Smith's teaching of the Invisible Hand, and whatever is to be made of such doctrine.

The homogeneity which is the essential characteristic of the standard index method based on the price level concept pictures a ray in the commodity space, determined only be prices, along which lie the consumptions of all individuals according to their different incomes. Hence the sum of all consumptions, since these lie on a ray, is also a point on that ray, and the income needed to purchase it is identical with the sum of all incomes, since $p \sum x = \sum px$. It is possible therefore to picture the sum of these incomes, or national income, as the income of a fictitious individual who has the same preferences as all other individuals and who, at the prevailing prices, would therefore spend it as would any others, that is, at the point on the ray corresponding to the consumption bundle that that income would purchase. Thus the nation is to be treated as an individual, and national income as the sum of individual incomes is to be treated like an individual income. National income deflated by a price index, determines the base period income which has the same purchasing power, and it gives a measure of current real national output. This seems to be the logic of the uses in the third category referred to by Chase (1960) in listing the major functions of price indexes, that is, the "deflation of [a] value aggregate to estimate physical quantities." Value means money value at prevailing prices, and physical quantity means quantity level in the utility sense of output.

Again, the average of all consumptions, since these lie on a ray, is also a point on the same ray, and moreover this average, or per capita, consumption corresponds to average or per capita income because $p(1/N) \sum x = (1/N) \sum px$. Hence it is possible to picture an "average individual," whose income is the average income, who again has the same preferences as any other individual, and who, at the prices given, would spend it as any one else would, that is, at the point on the ray corresponding to the consumption it can purchase. This puts average or per capita income, like total income, on the same footing as individual income. This seems to be the implicit logic of average comparisons.

The accident that permits individual incomes, average income, and total income all to be treated in the same fashion depends on both linearity and homogeneity. More explicitly, an average of points on a line is on the same line, but so also is a sum of points but generally only if the line passes through the origin. Thus it is necessary both that the locus of consumptions be a line and that the line pass through the origin. Should the locus of consumptions be a line but not pass through the origin, the argument for the "average individual" still holds, but that for the "total individual" loses the basis of its meaning.

This is not a general rejection of comparisons of totals but a description of the implicit logic of a standard procedure. If the concept of the procedure is still acceptable when this logic is made explicit, there can be a requirement that practical procedure be more strictly in accordance with it. There appears to be a reversion to the old concept of general purchasing power in a sense which does not even allow for the plurality of purchasing powers recognized by Keynes (1922). It asks that the economy resemble a molecular structure composed of homogeneous atoms, with reference to which the purchasing power of every penny, described by a particular bundle of commodities, is uniformly determined. But, as Ruggles (1967) says: "The concept of a price index as a measure of the level of prices no longer has significant support among economists." After dealing with the application to real national income, he adds: "Despite this disillusionment with the concepts of price level and economic welfare, the use of price indexes flourishes."

Overall comparison in terms of an "average individual" holds up better conceptually. Moreover, a description of the fictitious average individual, together with a statement of the number of individuals in the national population, conveys all the information that could be communicated about a "total individual," plus something more, namely, population size, and in a form which may have a more direct meaning.

The second approach to the relation of prices to national welfare measurement reinforces this first one, but is more objectionable. The first can be seen to be misleading because it requires that points for individuals lie on a ray and that a sum of points on a ray also lie on that ray, an event which could occur only by chance. It is compelling to view that sum point as associated with an individual, but without a theory to encourage such a summation, to make it conceptually and not only mathematically natural, it is meaningless. Here the Invisible Hand might come to the rescue. According to that doctrine, the freely operating adjustment mechanism of the competitive market automatically brings the economy to a state of maximum welfare or utility output. The prices are therefore proportional to marginal welfares, just like individual marginal utilities. Therefore, with homogeneity granted, the same indexes are applicable. This doctrine could have power beyond index numbers. But it is without quantitative content. Newton's second law of motion— that the force on a unit particle is identical with its acceleration—would be equally meaningless were there not separate ways for determining force and acceleration, such as gravitational or other force theory and kinematics. The maximum doctrine has no separate theory about the determination of welfare, whose maximum must then coincide with the position determined by the market. Its starting point seems to be in the observation that "we owe our bread not to the benevolence of the baker but to his self interest" (Adam Smith), so by adding non-sense to a truism an influential contribution has been made to an economic philosophy.

2.0 Analysis of value and cost

2.1 Utility

A relation $R \subset \Omega^n \times \Omega^n$ is reflexive and transitive, that is, it is an order in Ω^n, if

$$xRx, xRy, \ldots, Rz \;\Rightarrow\; xRz. \tag{1}$$

Equivalently

$$xRy \;\Leftrightarrow\; xR \supset yR \tag{2}$$

where $xR = [y : xRy]$, and similarly with Rx. It is complete if $xRy \vee yRx$, and continuous if it is a closed set in $\Omega^n \times \Omega^n$. If R is a complete order in Ω^n then it is continuous if and only if xR, Rx are closed sets in Ω^n. An order R is quasi-concave if the sets Rx are convex.

Any order R in Ω^n can be a *utility relation*. In that case, xRy means that consumption x is as good as, that is, produces as much utility as, y. The *law of disposal* for a utility relation is $x \geq y \Rightarrow xRy$. An x appears as a point of *oversatiation* if yRx and $y < x$ for some y, and the *law of want* excludes such points. If R is complete and continuous then this implies the law of disposal.

For simplicity, in the present discussion a utility relation is specifically limited to be a complete, continuous order in Ω^n subject to the law of want. It is distinguished as a *normal utility relation* if, moreover, it is quasi-concave.

Any function $\phi(x) \in \Omega$, where $x \in \Omega^n$, represents a complete order R in Ω^n where

$$xRy \equiv \phi(x) \geq \phi(y). \tag{3}$$

It is a *utility function* if R is understood to be a utility relation. The law of disposal for R requires

$$x \leq y \Rightarrow \phi(x) \leq \phi(y), \tag{4}$$

and that $\phi(x)$ be nondecreasing; the law of want requires

$$x < y \Rightarrow \phi(x) < \phi(y), \tag{5}$$

and that $\phi(x)$ be semi-increasing. Any complete, continuous order in Ω^n admits representation by a continuous function. An order R which is quasi-concave requires that any function which represents it be quasi-concave, having convex level sets $[y : \phi(y) \geq \phi(x)]$.

A *normal utility function* represents a normal utility relation and thus, beside being subject to the usually understood limitations, is quasi-concave. A utility function is concave if

$$\phi(x\lambda + y\mu) \geq \phi(x)\lambda + \phi(y)\mu \quad (\lambda, \mu \geq 0, \lambda + \mu = 1). \tag{6}$$

This implies that for all $x_0 > 0$ there exists $g_0 \geq 0$ such that for all $x \geq 0$,

$$\phi(x) - \phi(x_0) \leq g_0(x - x_0), \tag{7}$$

and $\phi(x)$ is differentiable at x_0 if and only if such g_0 is unique, in which case the g_0 is the gradient $g(x_0)$ of $\phi(x)$ at x_0. Now a classical utility function is defined by the existence of such $g_0 \geqslant 0$ for all $x_0 \geq 0$. This implies it is expressible in the form

$$\phi(x) = \min_{x_0}[\phi(x_0) + g_0(x - x_0)] \tag{8}$$

where a $g_0 \geqslant 0$ is determined from any $x_0 \geq 0$. It is therefore continuous, semi-increasing, and concave, and thus also a normal utility function. A *polyhedral classical utility function*, which is the most important type for empirical analysis, is expressible in the same form, but with x_0 ranging in a finite set, usually corresponding to finite observations, instead of possibly throughout Ω^n.

A utility relation R is *homogeneous* if

$$xRy \;\Rightarrow\; x\gamma Ry\gamma \quad (\gamma \geqq 0). \tag{9}$$

A utility function is homogeneous if it represents a homogeneous utility relation. Such a function is equivalent, under transformation by an increasing function, to one which is *linearly homogeneous*, that is, such that

$$\phi(x\gamma) = \phi(x)\gamma \quad (\gamma \geqq 0). \tag{10}$$

A function with this property is concave if and only if it is quasi-concave.

2.2 Adjoint utility

A *budget constraint* $px \leq M(x \in \Omega^n)$, associated with an expenditure limit $M > 0$ at prices $P \in \Omega_n$, is equivalent to a constraint $ux \leq 1$, where $u = M^{-1}p$. The budget constraints in Ω^n are thus coordinated with the points of Ω_n. Let the relation $W \subset \Omega^n \times \Omega_n$ be defined by $xWu \equiv ux \leq 1$. Then $Wu = [x : xWu]$ is the *budget set* associated with any $u \in \Omega_n$. In such association u can be called a *budget vector*, and otherwise an *exchange vector*. The *primal* space Ω_n has a symmetrical relation with the *dual* space Ω^n, a point of which is a *composition vector* which describes the composition of a consumption, each space being the space of nonnegative homogeneous linear functions defined on the other.

For any $x \in \Omega^n$, $u \in \Omega_n$, x can be said to be *within, on,* or *under* u according as $ux \leq 1$, $ux = 1$ or $ux < 1$, or, in a dual sense, the same can be said with x and u interchanged. Thus beside the within-relation just defined there are further relations (I, V) defined by $xIu \equiv ux = 1$, $xVu \equiv ux < 1$.

Any utility relation R in Ω^n has associated with it an *adjoint utility relation* $S = R^*$ in the adjoint space Ω^n, where

$$uSv \equiv (\vee ux \leqq 1)(\wedge vy \leqq 1)xRy, \tag{1}$$

that is uSv means there exist x within u which are, according to R, as good as every y within v. Thus uSu means there exists a consumption within the budget u which is as good as any other, that is, which is R maximal. This is always the case if $u > 0$, because of the compactness of Wu and the continuity of R. Thus S is reflexive at every point $u > 0$. Also, because R is a complete order, S is a complete order in the domain where it is reflexive. Thus S is a complete order at least in the interior of Ω_n. Because R is semiincreasing, S is semi-decreasing. From the form of the definition of S from R, regardless of properties of R, uS is a closed convex set. By this convexity the order S is quasi-convex. The order R is quasi-concave if Rx is convex, and a necessary and sufficient condition for this is that $R = S^*$, where S^* derives from S by the dual of the formula (1) by which R^* derives from R, that is, the identical formula where budget and composition vectors exchange their roles.

Let $\phi(x)$ be any utility function representing a utility relation R, that is,

$$xRy \quad \Leftrightarrow \quad \phi(x) \geq \phi(y).$$

Then the *adjoint utility function* $\psi(u) = \phi^*(u)$ is given by

$$\psi(u) = \max[\phi(y) : uy \leq 1], \tag{2}$$

for u wherever this is defined, which is where S is reflexive and is at least in the interior of Ω_n, by the compactness of Wu, if $u > 0$, and the continuity of R. Then the adjoint ψ of the function ϕ, where it is defined, represents the adjoint S of the relation R represented by ϕ, that is,

$$uSv \quad \Leftrightarrow \quad \psi(u) \geq \psi(v). \tag{3}$$

The function $\psi(u)$, which thus determines the maximum of the utility $\phi(x)$ attainable in the budget set Wu, is continuous, semi-decreasing, and quasi-convex. Since, from the definition

$$vx \leq 1 \quad \Rightarrow \quad \phi(x) \leq \psi(v) \tag{4}$$

it follows that

$$\phi(x) \leq \min[\psi(v) : vx \leq 1], \tag{5}$$

for all x, with equality if and only if

$$\phi(x) = \psi(u), \quad ux = 1 \quad \text{for some } u. \tag{6}$$

But this is true for all x if and only if $\phi(x)$ is quasi-concave and thus a normal utility function. Thus a utility function, subject to the given limitations, is quasi-concave, and thus normal, if and only if

$$\phi(x) = \min[\psi(v) : vx \leq 1] \tag{7}$$

for all x. The pair of relations (2) and (7) shows the reciprocal relation between a normal utility function and its adjoint. But in any case

$$\phi^{**}(x) = \min[\phi^*(v) : vx \leq 1] \tag{8}$$

is normal, even if $\phi(x)$ is not, and has the same adjoint $\psi(u) = \phi^*(u)$ as $\phi(x)$. It defines the *normalization* of $\phi(x)$. Any demand observation that admit $\phi(x)$ as compatible with them will also admit $\phi^{**}(x)$. Hence if a utility function is admitted, so also is a normal utility function. In this sense there is equivalent empirical scope between utility functions and normal utility functions and no empirical content to the assumption that a utility function be quasi-concave, that is, have concave contours.

The *profile* corresponding to exchange prices $u \geq 0$ of a utility function $\phi(x)$ with adjoint $\psi(u)$ is the function $F(\rho) = \psi(\rho^{-1}u)$, which is increasing since $\phi(x)$ is semi-increasing. Since a utility function and its normalization have the same adjoint, this is also the profile of the normalization. *A necessary and sufficient condition that a utility function be concave is that its levels and profiles be concave.* If $F(\rho)$ is concave, as when the utility function or its normalization is classical, then there exists a $\lambda > 0$ such that

$$\psi(\rho^{-1}u) - \psi(u) \leqslant \lambda(\rho - 1) \tag{9}$$

for all ρ; also $F(\rho)$ is differentiable at $\rho = 1$ if and only such λ is unique, and then $F'(1) = \lambda$. But, with $u = M^{-1}p$, $M(\partial\psi/\partial M)(M^{-1}p) = \lambda$; so λ/M appears as the marginal utility of money M at prices p, and $P = M/\lambda$ as the marginal price of utility.

Since, with p fixed, $\psi(M^{-1}p)$ is an increasing function of M, $t = \psi(M^{-1}p)$ has an inverse $M = \sigma(p, t)$, which determines the minimum cost at prices p of attaining the level of utility t. Then, with p fixed, $\Delta M/M \geqq \Delta t/\lambda$, or $\Delta M/\Delta t \geqq P$.

It follows immediately from the definition that $\sigma(p, t)$ is linearly homogeneous as a function of p. Therefore it is concave if and only if it is quasi-concave. But it is quasi-concave, because $\psi(u)$ has this property directly from its definition. Thus $\sigma(p, t)$ is a linearly homogeneous function of p. It is a convex function of t only if the normalization of $\phi(x)$ is concave.

Now setting $t = \phi(x)$, the function $\rho(p, x) = \sigma[p, \phi(x)]$ is obtained. But this function is most basic and is properly introduced directly from the utility relation R, without the auxiliary function ϕ, ψ, and σ as intermediaries.

2.3 Utility cost

For any utility relation R, with the given limitations,

$$\rho(p, x) = \min[py : yRx] \tag{1}$$

exists for all $p \in \Omega_n$, $x \in \Omega^n$ and defines the associated *utility cost function*. It gives the cost at prices p of attaining the standard of utility represented by x. From its definition, for all x, it is a linearly homogeneous concave function of p, determined by the set of homogeneous linear bounds py where yRx. Its linear supports at $p \geqslant 0$ are pz where

$$\rho(p, x) = pz, \quad zRx. \tag{2}$$

It is differentiable at p if and only if such z is unique, and then the gradient is

$$\rho_p(p, x) = z. \tag{3}$$

From the properties of R as a complete, semi-increasing, continuous order,

$$xRy \quad \Leftrightarrow \quad \rho(p, x) \geqq \rho(p, y), \tag{4}$$

showing that, for all p, $\rho(p, x)$ is a utility function which represents R. Since R is reflexive

$$\rho(p, x) \leqq px. \tag{5}$$

For all p the equality holds for some x, and for all x the equality holds for some p if and only if R is quasi-concave.

A necessary and sufficient condition that R be homogeneous is that $\rho(p, x)$ be factorable, that is, that

$$\rho(p, x) = \theta(p)\phi(x). \tag{6}$$

Then $\phi(x)$ is a linearly homogeneous utility function, unique but for a constant multiplier, which represents R, with adjoint $\psi(u) = [\theta(u)]^{-1}$, and cost function $\sigma(p, t) = \theta(p)t$.

The functions $\theta(p)$, $\phi(x)$ can be called *antithetic price and quantity functions*. Both are linearly homogeneous, and $\theta(p)$ is concave. If $\phi(x)$ is not concave, its normalization is concave and has the same antithesis, and is compatible with every demand that is compatible with $\phi(x)$. Hence nothing essential is lost if $\phi(x)$ is replaced by its normalization, or simply assumed to be concave, so that it is identical with its normalization.

From (5) and (6), antithetic functions satisfy the functional inequality

$$\theta(p)\phi(x) \leqq px \tag{7}$$

for all p, x where the equality holds for all p for some x and for x for some p. It follows that

$$\theta(p) = \min_x px[\phi(x)]^{-1} \tag{8}$$
$$\phi(x) = \min_p [\theta(p)]^{-1} px.$$

It follows from (8) that $\theta(p)$ and $\phi(x)$ are both linearly homogeneous and satisfy (7).

2.4 Compatibility

The condition $H = H(R; x, p)$ for a utility relation R and a demand (x, p) to be *compatible* is the conjunction of conditions

$$H' \equiv py \leqq px \implies xRy \tag{1}$$
$$H'' \equiv yRx \implies py \geqq px$$

signifying "maximum utility for the cost" and "minimum cost for the utility"; so H is the Pareto condition as applied to the competing objectives of gaining utility and saving money. But, with R semi-increasing, $H' \Rightarrow H''$, and with R continuous, $H'' \Rightarrow H'$. Thus, with the given limitation on R, H' and H'' are equivalent to each other and hence to H. A statement of H'' is

$$\rho(p, x) \geqq px. \tag{2}$$

But by 2.2(5), since R is reflexive, this is equivalent to

$$\rho(p, x) = px. \tag{3}$$

Then, if there is differentiability,

$$\rho_p(p,x) = x, \quad \rho_x(p,x) = \lambda p, \tag{4}$$

where, if there is homogeneity, $\lambda = 1$.

More generally, *e* compatibility, or *compatibility at a level of cost efficiency e* is the condition $H(R,e;x,p)$ given by

$$\rho(p,x) \geq epx. \tag{5}$$

Thus 0 compatibility is unconditional, 1 compatibility coincides with compatibility, and *e* compatibility implies e' compatibility for all $e' \leq e$. With the *cost efficiency* $\bar{e} = \bar{e}(R;x,p)$ of (x,p) relative to R given by

$$\bar{e} = \rho(p,x)/px, \tag{6}$$

e compatibility holds if and only if $e \leq \bar{e}$.

From the demand (x,p) is derived the budget (x,u) with $ux = 1$, where $u = M^{-1}p$ is the associated exchange vector, $M = px$ being the expenditure. With this,

$$\bar{e} = \rho(u,x). \tag{7}$$

2.2(5) is equivalent to

$$\rho(u,x) \leq 1. \tag{8}$$

The compatibility condition (3) is

$$\rho(u,x) = 1, \tag{9}$$

which, if there is differentiability, is equivalent to

$$\rho_u(u,x) = x, \tag{10}$$

and implies

$$\rho_x(u,x) = \lambda u \tag{11}$$

where $\lambda = \rho_x(u,x)x$, so that $\lambda = (u,x)$ if there is homogeneity, in which case (9) is equivalent to (11) with $\lambda = 1$,

$$\rho_x(u,x) = u. \tag{12}$$

Therefore, in this case, conditions (9), (10), and (12) are equivalent.

Consider a *demand configuration D* whose elements are demands $(x_t,p_t):t = 1,\ldots,k$, and the derived *exchange configuration E* with elements (x_t,u_t), where $u_t = M_t^{-1}p_t$ and $M_t = p_tx_t$. Compatibility of a utility relation R with D is defined by simultaneous compatibility with each element of D and is equivalent to compatibility with E. Thus it is the condition $H(R)$ given by

$$\rho(u_t,x_t) = 1, \quad t = 1,\ldots,k. \tag{13}$$

More generally, the condition $H(R, e)$ of e-compatibility of R with D is

$$\rho(u_t, x_t) \geqq e, \quad t = 1, \ldots, k. \tag{14}$$

If

$$\bar{e}(R) = \min \bar{e}_t(R), \tag{15}$$

where $\bar{e}_t(R) = \rho(r_t, x_t)$. Then

$$H(R, e) \Leftrightarrow e \leqq \bar{e}(R). \tag{16}$$

Thus $H(R, 0)$ holds for all R unconditionally, and

$$H(R) \Leftrightarrow H(R, 1) \Leftrightarrow \bar{e}(R) = 1 \Leftrightarrow \bar{e}_t(R) = 1. \tag{17}$$

2.5 Consistency

A demand configuration D or, equivalently, its derived exchange configuration E, is *consistent* if there exists a utility relation which is compatible with it, which is to say the condition H that there exists a utility relation R such that $H(R)$. More generally, e consistency, or consistency at the level of cost efficiency, e, is defined by the existence of an e-compatible utility relation, that is, the condition $H(e)$ that there exists a utility relation R such that $H(R, e)$. Thus $H(0)$ holds unconditionally and $H(1) \Leftrightarrow H$, and $H(e) \Rightarrow H(e')$ for all $e' \leqq e$. The *critical cost efficiency* is defined by

$$\bar{e} = \sup[e : H(e)], \tag{1}$$

so that $0 < \bar{e} \leq 1$. Then

$$H(e) \Rightarrow e \leqq \bar{e} \quad e < \bar{e} \Rightarrow H(e) \tag{2}$$

and

$$H(\bar{e}) \Leftrightarrow \bar{e} = 1 \Leftarrow H. \tag{3}$$

Let P denote any property for a utility function, such as homogeneity, or having a certain separation structure, or being on any special model. In particular, C can denote the classical property. Then let $H_P(R)$ be the condition that a utility relation R both have the property P and be compatible with D, and let $H_P(R, e)$ be the same with e compatibility instead. Then the condition H_P of P consistency is defined by the existence of R such that $H_P(R)$, and similarly for $H_P(e)$, or P consistency at the level of cost efficiency e. The P *critical cost efficiency* is defined by

$$e_P = \sup[e : H_P(e)]. \tag{4}$$

Thus, for any P and e,

$$H_P(R, e) \Rightarrow H(R, e) \tag{5}$$

so that

$$H_p(e) \;\Rightarrow\; H(e), \tag{6}$$

and hence $e_p \leqq \bar{e}$. The same things are defined in particular with $P = C$. Though obviously $H_C(R, e)$ is not implied by $H(R, e)$, it is nevertheless the case that

$$H_C(e) \;\Leftrightarrow\; H(e), \tag{7}$$

and hence $e_C = \bar{e}$. In other words, the classical restriction does not affect consistency. In particular $H_C \Leftrightarrow H$, that is, consistency is equivalent to classical consistency.

In fact these results essentially are stronger than is apparent in this formulation. They are true when a utility relation is understood to be any order relation in Ω^n without any further restrictions whatsoever, specifically without dependence on assumptions that R be continuous and semi-increasing. But in that case the basic condition $H = H(R; x, p)$ is not equivalent to H', since now H' and H'' are independent, but must again be identified with the conjunction of H' and H''. The same is true with the modification which permits a partial cost efficiency $e < 1$.

Defining *cross-differences*

$$D_{rs}^e = u_r x_s - e \tag{8}$$

and *e cyclical difference consistency*

$$K(e) \equiv D_{rs}^e \leqq 0, \, D_{st}^e \leqq 0, \dots , \tag{9}$$
$$D_{qr}^e \leqq 0 \;\Rightarrow\; D_{rs}^e = D_{st}^e = \cdots = D_{qr}^e = 0$$

it appears that

$$H(e) \;\Leftrightarrow\; K(e), \tag{10}$$

and thus $K(e)$ provides a finite test of e consistency. It follows then that

$$\bar{e} = \min_{r,s,\dots,q} \max[D_{rs}, D_{st}, \dots, D_{qr}]. \tag{11}$$

But $K(e)$ is necessary and sufficient for the existence of $\lambda_r > 0, \, \phi_r > 0$ such that

$$\lambda_r D_{rs}^e \geqq \phi_s - \phi_r. \tag{12}$$

Then with

$$\phi_t(x) = \phi_t + \lambda_t(u_t x - e) \tag{13}$$
$$\phi(x) = \min_t \phi_t(x)$$

it appears that $\phi(x)$ is a classical utility function, and that it is e-compatible with the demand configuration D. A consequence is (7), namely, that e consistency is equivalent to classical e consistency. The adjoint of $\phi(x)$ is

$$\psi(u) = \max[t : t \leqq \phi_t + \lambda_t(u_t x - e), ux \leqq 1]. \tag{14}$$

Numbers $\rho_{rs} = \rho(u_r, x_s)$ are determined as solutions of

$$\psi = (\rho_{rs}^{-1} u_r) = \psi(u_s) \tag{15}$$

and equivalently as

$$\rho_{rs} = \min[u_r x : \phi_t + \lambda_t(u_t x - e) \geq \phi_s]. \tag{16}$$

Then $1 \geq \rho_{tt} \geq e$, demonstrating e compatibility. In case $e = 1$, it appears that

$$\phi(x_t) = \phi_t = \psi(u_t) \tag{17}$$

and

$$\psi(\rho^{-1} u_t) - \psi(u_t) \leq \lambda_t(\rho - 1). \tag{18}$$

With $\delta_{rs} = \rho_{rs} - 1$, it appears from (15), (16), and (17) that

$$\lambda_r \delta_{rs} \geq \phi_s - \phi_r. \tag{19}$$

But since $\rho_{rs} \leq u_r x_s$, also $\delta_{rs} \leq D_{rs}, \lambda_r$ and ϕ_r having been chosen only so that $D_{rs} = D_{rs}^1 = u_r x_s - 1$ satisfy (12).

Analogously for homogeneous e consistency, which can be denoted $\dot{H}(e)$, with *cross-ratios*

$$L_{rs}^e = u_r x_s / e, \tag{20}$$

and *e cyclical ratio consistency*

$$\dot{K}(e) \equiv L_{rs}^e L_{st}^e \dots L_{qr}^e \geq 1 \tag{21}$$

which is necessary and sufficient for the existence of $\phi_r > 0$ such that

$$L_{rs}^e \geq \phi_s / \phi_r. \tag{22}$$

It appears that

$$H(e) \quad \Leftrightarrow \quad \dot{K}(e) \tag{23}$$

and, with ϕ_r as given,

$$\phi(x) = \min_t \phi_t u_t x \tag{24}$$

is a linearly homogenous classical utility function which is e-compatible with the given demands. A consequence is that homogeneous e consistency is equivalent to linearly homogeneous classical e consistency. Also it follows that the homogeneous critical cost efficiency is

$$\dot{e} = \max[e : u_r x_s u_x x_t \cdots u_q x_r \geq ee \cdots e]. \tag{25}$$

The antithetic price function for $\phi(x)$ is

$$\theta(u) = \min[ux : \phi_t u_t x \geq 1], \tag{26}$$

so $\theta(u)\phi(x) \leq ux$, but it appears that

$$1 \geq \theta(u_t)\phi(x_t) \geq e, \tag{27}$$

as required for e compatibility. In case $e = 1$, then moreover $\phi(x_t) = \phi_t, \theta(u_t) = 1/\phi_t$.

3.0   Price indexes

3.1   Theory of the price level

The idea of the existence of a *level of prices* is made intelligible by assuming that utility cost can be factored into a product of price and quantity levels,

$$\rho(p, x) = \theta(p)\phi(x),$$ (1)

which is equivalent to assuming that the utility relation R is homogeneous. Then for all p, x

$$\theta(p)\phi(x) \leq px,$$ (2)

and for utility cost efficiency of a demand (x, p),

$$\theta(p)\phi(x) = px.$$ (3)

Hence if $(x_0, p_0), (x_1, p_1)$ are a pair of demands compatible with R, say, corresponding to a *base* and a *current* observation,

$$\theta(p_0)\phi(x_0) = p_0 x_0, \quad \theta(p_1)\phi(x_1) = p_1 x_1$$ (4)

and

$$\theta(p_0)\phi(x_1) \leq p_0 x_1, \quad \theta(p_1)\phi(x_0) \leq p_1 x_0.$$ (5)

Then

$$P_{10} X_{10} = M_{10}$$ (6)

where

$$P_{10} = \theta(p_1)/\theta(p_0), \quad X_{10} = \phi(x_1)/\phi(x_0)$$ (7)

and

$$M_{10} = M_1/M_0,$$ (8)

where

$$M_0 = p_0 x_0, \quad M_1 = p_1 x_1.$$ (9)

Also

$$p_1 x_1/p_0 x_1 \leq P_{10} \leq p_1 x_0/p_0 x_0$$ (10)

and

$$p_1 x_1/p_1 x_0 \leq X_{10} \leq p_0 x_1/p_0 x_0.$$ (11)

From (6), $\phi(x_0) = \phi(x_1)$, that is, $X_{10} = 1$, if and only if $M_1 = P_{10} M_0$. This is the condition that an expenditure M_1 at prices p_1 be equivalent in purchasing power to an expenditure M_0 at prices p_0. All that must be specified to establish this purchasing power, or real value relation, is the *price index* P_{10}. Any current money M_1 can be *deflated* by the index to give the base equivalent $M_0 = M_1/P_{10}$.

In terms of derived budgets (x_0, u_0), (x_1, u_1) where

$$u_0 = M_0^{-1} p_0, \quad u_1 = M_1^{-1} p_1, \tag{12}$$

so that

$$u_0 x_0 = 1, \quad u_1 x_1 = 1 \tag{13}$$

and with

$$U_{10} = P_{10} M_0/M_1 = \theta(u_1)/\theta(u_0) \tag{14}$$

the foregoing relations are equivalent to

$$\theta(u_0)\phi(x_0) = 1, \quad \theta(u_1)\phi(x_1) = 1 \tag{15}$$

$$U_{10} X_{10} = 1 \tag{16}$$

and

$$\begin{aligned} 1/u_0 x_1 &\leq U_{10} \leq u_1 x_0, \\ 1/u_1 x_0 &\leq X_{10} \leq u_0 x_1. \end{aligned} \tag{17}$$

The condition for equivalent budgets is $U_{10} = 1$ or, equivalently $X_{10} = 1$. But compatibility of a budget (x, u) with a homogeneous utility relation implies the compatibility of $(\rho x, \rho^{-1} u)$ for all $\rho > 0$. Hence the condition that $(\rho_0 x_0, \rho_0^{-1} u_0)$, $(\rho_1 x_1, \rho_1^{-1} u_1)$ be equivalent is that $\rho_1/\rho_0 = U_{10}$.

3.2 Laspeyres and Paasche

From 3.1(17), for homogeneous consistency of the given budgets, that is, their simultaneous compatibility with some homogeneous utility relation, it is apparently necessary that the Paasche index not exceed that of Laspeyres. Equivalently,

$$u_0 x_1 u_1 x_0 \geq 1, \tag{1}$$

and in fact this is also sufficient. Also, if a homogeneous utility relation is constrained by compatibility with the budgets, then U_{10} is constrained to lie in the *Paasche-Laspeyres interval* defined by 3.1(17), which is nonempty by (1). In fact, the constraint set is identical with that interval. Without imposition of further constraints on utility, such as compatibility with further given budgets, or possession of special properties, there is no sharper specification of U_{10} than this. Various price index formulas single out various special points in the admissible set, which is nonempty subject to the homogeneous consistency condition (1). Thus the Paasche and Laspeyres formulas single out the extremes, and the Fisher formula singles out the geometric mean of these. But no principle is explicitly available here for discriminating between admissible points.

3.3   Fisher

Buscheguennce (1925) remarked that with the assumption of a homogeneous quadratic utility function the Fisher index is exact. In translation to present concepts, and with appropriate additional qualifications, given a pair of budgets $(x_0, u_0), (x_1, u_1)$ where $x_0, x_1 > 0$, if R is compatible and homogeneous and has quadratic representation in a convex neighborhood containing x_0, x_1 then

$$U_{10} = (u_1 x_0 / u_0 x_1)^{1/2}, \tag{1}$$

and reciprocally, and equivalently,

$$X_{10} = (u_0 x_1 / u_1 x_0)^{1/2}. \tag{2}$$

By *homogeneous quadratic consistency* of the pair of budgets can be meant the existence of such an R. Immediately, this is at least as restrictive as homogeneous consistency, which is equivalent to 3.2(1), and appearances suggest it is more restrictive. Therefore, there is some surprise that *for a pair of budgets, homogeneous quadratic consistency is equivalent to homogeneous consistency.* However, for more than two budgets, it is more restrictive.

Such a utility relation R corresponds to an antithetic pair of price and quantity functions of the form

$$\theta(u) = (u \, Bu')^{1/2}, \quad \phi(x) = (x' Ax)^{1/2} \tag{3}$$

where $BA = 1$, in a region where they are defined and satisfy the functional inequality

$$(u \, Bu')^{1/2} (x' Ax)^{1/2} \leq ux, \tag{4}$$

which is to say in the convex cone where $x' Ax$ is semi-increasing and quasi-concave, equality holding in equilibrium. Though such compatible R, if any, exist and are not unique, they all determine the unique value of U_{10} given by (1). But, as just remarked, a compatible homogeneous quadratic R exists if and only if a compatible homogeneous R exists. It follows that the Fisher index, where it is capable of interpretation at all, which is in the case of homogeneous consistency, is identifiable with the value of U_{10} determined with respect to a locally quadratic compatible homogeneous relation. Thus *the Fisher index cannot be divorced from the quadratic utility hypothesis.*

3.4   Palgrave

A demand (x, p) has a total expenditure

$$M = \sum_i p_i x_i = px \tag{1}$$

which is a sum of individual expenditures

$$M_i = p_i x_i \tag{2}$$

which represent a distribution of the total in shares

$$\sigma_i = M_i/M = p_i x_i/px = u_i x_i \tag{3}$$

where $u = M^{-1}p$. The Laspeyres index is expressible as an arithmetic mean of price ratios between the base and current period with the expenditure shares as weights. For

$$(U_{10})_u = u_1 x_0 = \sum_i u_{0i} x_{1i} = \sum_i u_{1i} x_{1i}(u_{0i}/u_{1i}) = \sum_i \sigma_{1i}(u_{0i}/u_{1i}). \tag{4}$$

The geometric mean which corresponds to this arithmetic mean, in which the same weights become exponents, is

$$(U_{10}^P)_u = \prod_i (u_{0i}/u_{1i})^{\sigma_{1i}} \tag{5}$$

This is Palgrave's formula, translated into present terms. By the general relation of an arithmetic mean to the corresponding geometric mean,

$$(U_{10}^P)_u \leqq (U_1)_u. \tag{6}$$

Similarly the Paasche index $(U_{10})_l = 1/(U_{01})_u$ has associated with it the companion to the Palgrave formula

$$(U_{10}^P)_l = \prod_i (u_{0i}/u_{1i})^{\sigma_{0i}} \tag{7}$$

It is obtained by replacing the current shares by the base shares as exponents. Similarly

$$(U_{10})_l \leqq (U_{10}^P)_l. \tag{8}$$

Just as the Fisher index cannot be divorced from the homogeneous quadratic utility function, so the Palgrave formula cannot be divorced from a quantity function of the extended Cobb-Douglas form.

$$\phi(x) = \prod_i (x_i)^{w_i}; \quad w_i \geq 0, \quad \sum w_i = 1. \tag{9}$$

The antithetic price function is

$$\theta(u) = \prod_i (u_i)^{\sigma_i}. \tag{10}$$

It is noticed that then, with $ux = 1$, $\sigma_i = u_i x_i$,

$$\theta(u)\phi(x) = \prod_i (u_i x_i)^c = \prod_i \sigma_i^c \leq 1, \tag{11}$$

with equality if and only if $\sigma_i = w_i$ (as can be verified by the Kuhn-Tucker argument). The equilibrium conditions

$$\theta(u_0)\phi(x_0) = 1, \quad \theta(u_1)\phi(x_1) = 1, \tag{12}$$

therefore require

$$\sigma_{0i} = w_i = \sigma_{1i}. \tag{13}$$

The consistency condition for this model of utility is therefore

$$\sigma_{0i} = \sigma_{1i}. \tag{14}$$

If this is satisfied, the companion pair of Palgrave indexes coincide, and, along with the Fisher index, provide just another point lying between the Laspeyres and Fisher indexes. However, the consistency conditions thus associated with Palgrave are more stringent than those associated with Fisher, which have been seen to be identical with the basic homogeneous consistency.

When Palgrave consistency is not satisfied, a Palgrave critical cost efficiency $e_P \leq \dot{e} \leq \bar{e} \leq 1$ can always be determined, and, for any $e < e_P$, a Cobb-Douglas utility function can be constructed which is e-compatible with each of the given two budgets.

The Laspeyres, Paasche, Fisher, and Palgrave formulas appear to be the only traditional price index formulas involving base and current budge data which have a supporting utility theory.

3.5   General price index construction

Ordinarily, the elements that are to enter into a construction of an index between a base (0) and current (1) location are regarded as data for the locations themselves. The conceptual basis for a price index is a homogeneous utility relation. Here it is understood that the purpose of budge data is to impose a constraint on the utility relation, by the compatibility requirement, and thereby to place a constraint on the admissible values of the index. There are two reasons why this framework is too simple. Any available budget data are pertinent by the same principle that the base and current data are pertinent. Therefore calculations should apply to a more general scheme of data, with two budgets as only a special case. This is particularly important and even essential when simultaneous comparisons are required between more than two locations. Then, with two or more budgets, there might not exist a homogeneous utility relation, or any other utility relation, with which they have simultaneous compatibility. That is, they might not be homogeneously consistent. In any case, exact consistency is too limiting a condition to insist on in practice, even if it is a basic theoretical requirement. Any budgets are homogeneously e-consistent, for some cost efficiency e, where $0 < e \leq 1$; and with this limitation, homogeneous 1-consistency. Thus a simple way of accommodating inconsistency is to permit partial cost efficiency. (The method is stated in section 2.5.)

Let $(U_{rs}^e)_u$, $(U_{rs}^e)_l$ be upper and lower limits of the interval described by $U_{rs} = \theta(u_r)/\theta(u_s)$ when determined with respect to all homogeneous utility relations which are *e*-compatible with a finite set of budgets (x_t, u_t), $t = 1, \ldots, k$. Then

$$e' \leqq e < \dot{e} \implies (U_{rs}^{e'})_l \leqq (U_{rs}^e)_l \leqq (U_{rs}^e)_u \leqq (U_{rs}^{e'})_u. \tag{1}$$

The intersection of all these intervals, for $e < \dot{e}$, is an interval with limits which coincide with $(U_{rs})_u = (U_{rs}^1)_u$, $(U_{rs})_l = (U_{rs}^1)_l$ if there is homogeneous consistency. Then in the special case where the available budgets are just the pair for $t = 0, 1$, these limits for U_{10} coincide with the Laspeyres and Paasche indexes,

$$(U_{10})_l = 1/u_0 x_1, \quad (U_{10})_u = u_1 x_0. \tag{2}$$

But more generally,

$$(U_{rs})_u = \min_{ij \cdots k} u_r x_i u_i x_j \ldots u_k x_s, \quad (U_{rs})_l = 1/(U_{rs})_u, \tag{3}$$

so

$$(U_{rs})_u (U_{st})_u \geqq (U_{rt})_u, \tag{4}$$

and

$$(U_{rr})_u \leqq 1 \tag{5}$$

since $u_r x_r = 1$. A necessary and sufficient condition for homogeneous consistency is that

$$(U_{rr})_u \geqq 1; \tag{6}$$

equivalently $(U_{rr})_u = 1$. In that case

$$(U_{rs})_u (U_{sr})_u \geqq 1. \tag{7}$$

Equivalently,

$$(U_{rs})_l \leqq (U_{rs})_u, \tag{8}$$

which generalizes the homogeneous consistency condition of 3.2. It requires that the generalized Laspeyres and Paasche indexes are consistent as upper and lower limits, the one being at least the other. Since

$$(U_{rt})_u = \min_s (U_{rs})_u (U_{st})_u$$

it follows that (6) holds for all r if and only if (8) holds for all r, s. Let

$$U_u = \min_v (U_{rv})_u$$

$$= \min_{r,s,\ldots,q} u_r x_s u_s x_t \cdots u_q x_r$$

so $U_u \leqq 1$. A necessary and sufficient condition for homogeneous consistency is $U_u \geqq 1$; equivalently $U_u = 1$. With U_u^e denoting U_u with each $u_r x_s$ replaced by $u_r x_s/e$, so that $(U^1)_u = U_u$, a necessary and sufficient condition for homogenous e consistency is $U^e \geqq 1$. Since U_u^e is a decreasing function of e, the homogeneous critical cost efficiency $\dot{e}$ is determined as the unique e such that $U_u^e = 1$.

3.6   *Extrinsic estimation*

Consider k countries and m levels of income in each which are judged by extrinsic criteria, that is, not on the basis of value and cost analysis of demands, but so as to correspond in purchasing power, at respective prices. Thus let M_{ti} be the ith level of income in country t ($i = 1, \ldots, m; t = 1, \ldots, k$). If the prices in country t are p_t, $P_t = \theta(p_t)$ is their level, and X_{ti} is the utility of M_{ti} at those prices, then a cost efficiency level of at least e requires that

$$M_{ti} \geqq P_t X_{ti} \geqq e M_{ti}. \tag{1}$$

But it is judged that, for all i, the X_{ti} are the same for all t, say, equal to X_i. Thus

$$M_{ti} \geqq P_t X_i \geqq e M_{ti}. \tag{2}$$

The value system and the efficiency being undetermined, it is proposed to determine P_t and e satisfying (2) with e as large as possible.

For $e = 1$ to be admissible in (2), equivalently for

$$M_{ti} = P_t X_i \tag{3}$$

to have a solution for P_t and X_i, it is necessary and sufficient that M_{si}/M_{ti} be the same for all i or, equivalently, that M_{ti}/M_{tj} be the same for all t. If this condition holds, then by choosing P_t in the ratio of M_{ti} for any i, and then determining X_i from (3) for any t, a solution of (3) is obtained and, hence, a solution of (2) with $e = 1$.

If this condition does not hold, then let

$$P_{rs} = \min_i M_{ri}/M_{si} \tag{4}$$

$$X_{ij} = \min_t M_{ti}/M_{tj}. \tag{5}$$

Then let $\bar{e}$ be the largest e such that

$$P_{rs} P_{st} \cdots P_{qr} \geqq ee \cdots e \tag{6}$$

and equivalently

$$X_{ij} X_{jk} \cdots X_{hi} \geqq ee \cdots e. \tag{7}$$

Then also $\bar{e}$ is the largest e such that

$$P_{rs}/e \geqq P_r/P_s. \tag{8}$$

Then (8) has a solution for P_t and, equivalently,

$$X_{ij}/e \geqq X_i/X_j \tag{9}$$

has a solution for X_i. Let P_t be any solution of (8) with $e = \bar{e}$. Then, with $e = \bar{e}$ and $P_t = \bar{P}_t$, (2) has a solution $X_i = \bar{X}_i$, necessarily a solution of (9) with $e = \bar{e}$.

Thus the largest possible e has been found such that (2) holds for some P_t, X_i; and such P_t, X_i have been found. Then $\bar{P}_{rs} = \bar{P}_r/\bar{P}_s$ are a set of price indexes between pairs of countries, which are consistent in that they satisfy the circularity test

$$\bar{P}_{rs}\bar{P}_{st}\bar{P}_{tr} = 1, \tag{10}$$

appropriate to a set of ratios, and which, with distance determined in the economic sense of cost efficiency, fit the constraints of the original data as closely as possible.

It should be noted that (1), with $P_{rs} = P_r/P_s$, implies

$$M_{ri}e_{ri} = P_{rs}M_{se}e_{se}, \quad e \leqq e_{ri} \leqq 1 \tag{11}$$

for some e_{ti}. In other words, efficient parts $M_{ri}e_{ri}$ of the income M_{ri}, with efficiencies e_{ri} at least e, are determined to be of equivalent purchasing power by the price indexes P_{rs}. It could have been required to determine the largest $\bar{e}$ such that there exist $\bar{P}_{rs}$ and e_{ri} which satisfy (10) and (11), and this would have had the same result as the foregoing determination. Necessarily some $e_{ti} = 1$ and some $e_{ti} = \bar{e}$, and generally $w_{ti} = 1 - e_{ti}$ is an imputed inefficiency associated with income M_{ti} in country t.

3.7 Rectification of pair comparisons

For any price index formula P_{st} between two points in time, s and t, Fisher's "time reversal" test requires that $P_{ts}P_{st} = 1$, which requires in particular, what apparently is true for all the formulas discussed here, that $P_{tt} = 1$. Fisher defined the "time antithesis" to be $P_{st}^* = P_{ts}^{-1}$. Fisher "rectified" a formula by "crossing" it with its time antithesis so as to obtain an associated formula which satisfied the time reversal test. Then the time antithesis of the Laspeyres formula is the Paasche formula. By crossing these according to the geometric mean, Fisher's "ideal" index is obtained, which is therefore the rectification of the Laspeyres index, and similarly of the Paasche. It satisfies the time reversal test and for that reason he considered it ideal. Here a more general rectification procedure will be considered.

In fact, the important logic behind the time reversal test is that any index P_{rs} which is expressible as a ratio $P_{rs} = P_r/P_s$ must satisfy the test. Since a price index theoretically, at least here, arises as a ratio of price levels, meeting the reversal test is a significant requirement. But so just as well is the "circularity test," which he considered, but which none of the one- or two-hundred formulas he examined appeared to satisfy.

All familiar price index formulas satisfy what might be called the *identify test* $P_{tt} = 1$. The circularity test implies the equivalence of this to the reversal test, and its combination with either constitutes what should be called the *ratio test*, since it is the condition for the expression $P_{rs} = P_r/P_s$. The combination of the circularity and reversal tests is equivalent to the combination of the identity test with the *chain test*

$$P_{rs}P_{st} = P_{rt}. \tag{1}$$

Also the chain test implies the equivalence of the identity and reversal tests and in combination with either is equivalent to the ratio rest. But an algebraic formula cannot satisfy the ratio test unless it immediately presents a ratio, and it cannot do this if as in most standard formulas, the data for different periods are not entered as separate factors, which could cancel in multiplication.

Another approach to "rectifying" a set of P_{rs} as closely as possible with respect to the ratio test is to reconcile them as closely as possible with a set of ratios P_r/P_s. Thus, with any given P_{rs}, and any e, 3.7(6) is necessary and sufficient for (8) to have a solution for P_t. The largest value $\bar{e}$ of e for 3.7(8) can be determined, and then a solution $\bar{P}_t$ of 3.7(8) with $e = \bar{e}$ can be found. With $\bar{P}_{rs} = P_r/P_s$

$$\bar{P}_{rs}/\bar{e} \leqq P_{rs} \leqq \bar{e}\bar{P}_{rs} \tag{2}$$

so that

$$P_{rs} = \bar{P}_{rs} \tag{3}$$

if and only if $\bar{e} = 1$, and generally $\bar{P}_{rs}$ is the best approximation to P_{rs} which satisfies the reversal and circularity tests. Here again approximation distance is in the economic sense of cost inefficiency, which is appropriate since an economic error is an inefficiency.

A difficulty which arises with multinational price comparisons by means of one of the standard price index formulas based on price-quantity data is that the circularity test is not satisfied; so a chain of comparisons is not consistent with the direct comparison, that is

$$P_{ri}P_{ij}\cdots P_{ks} \neq P_{rs}. \tag{4}$$

One way of resolving this difficulty is to combine the directly determined P_{rs} to determine $\bar{P}_{rs}$ as above. The latter do satisfy the circularity test, or, since $\bar{P}_{rr} = 1$, equivalently the chain test, and approximate the P_{rs} as closely as possible, in the manner described. It should be noticed that this difficulty is automatically avoided if the method of sections 2.5 and 3.6 is used, since those determinations each have explicit or implicit reference to some particular utility function.

With just two periods, the ratio test reduces to the reversal test, so the process just considered can be seen as a generalization of Fisher's general rectification procedure. But now it will be seen more closely as a generalization.

The Fisher "ideal" index, arrived at as the rectification $\bar{P}_{01} = (P_{01}P_{10}^{-1})^{1/2}$ of the Laspeyres index P_{01}, by geometric crossing with its time antithesis P_{10}^{-1}, so as to obtain an index which satisfies the time reversal test, can also be arrived at as the best approximation, with efficiency distance, which satisfies time reversal. Thus consider

$$\bar{P}_{01} = \bar{P}_{10}^{-1}, \tag{5}$$

equivalently

$$\bar{P}_{01} = \rho, \quad \bar{P}_{10} = \rho^{-1}, \tag{6}$$

such that

$$P_{ij}/e \geqq \bar{P}_{ij}, \tag{7}$$

equivalently

$$\rho/e \geqq P_{01} \geqq e\rho, \tag{8}$$

$$1/\rho e \geqq P_{10} \geqq e/\rho. \tag{9}$$

With P_{01}, P_{10} given, ρ is to be determined with e as large as possible. Equivalently

$$1/e^2 \geqq P_{01} P_{10} \geqq e^2, \tag{10}$$

$$\rho^2/e^2 \geqq P_{01}/P_{10} \geqq e^2\rho^2. \tag{11}$$

But with the largest e, and in fact any e, which satisfies (10), $\rho^2 = P_{01}/P_{10}$ automatically satisfies (11). The Fisher indexes $F_{01} = P_{01}/P_{10}$ and $F_{10} = F_{01}^{-1}$, among all numbers $\bar{P}_{01}$ and $\bar{P}_{10}$ such that $\bar{P}_{10} = \bar{P}_{01}^{-1}$, are closest to P_{01}, P_{10} in that they satisfy (8) and (9) with e as large as possible.

Since P_{ij} could here be given by any formula, this argument, which deals with a special case of the previous analysis, is mainly a comment on Fisher's procedure of rectifying a formula by geometric crossing with its time antithesis or even with any other formula.

4.0 Theory of marginal price indexes

4.1 Marginal price indexes

Let R be a utility relation for which the associated utilities cost function can be represented by

$$\rho(p,x) = \theta(p)\phi(x) + \mu(p). \tag{1}$$

By this property, R can be called a *linear cost utility*. With this classification, a homogeneous relation, which is characterized by the same utility property but with $\mu(p) = 0$, can be distinguished as a *homogeneous linear cost utility*. Thus here there is a particular generalization of homogeneity as applied to relations.

Since $\rho(p,x)$ is linearly homogeneous in p for all x, both $\theta(p)$, $\mu(p)$ in (1) must be linearly homogeneous, and $\phi(x)$ must be uniquely determined up to a linear transformation. Thus $\phi(x)$ is completely specified when its values are specified at two points which are not indifferent and then so are the other functions. A function associated with a linear cost relation in the same way that a linearly homogeneous function is associated with a homogeneous, or homogeneous linear, cost relation can be described as a *linear profile* function, for the reasons presented below. With this classification, a function which is linearly homogeneous appears as a *homogeneous linear profile* function.

From (1), for all p, x

$$\theta(p)\phi(x) + \mu(p) \leqq px \tag{2}$$

and for all p, equality holds for some x, and R is quasi-concave if and only if for all x equality holds for some p. Whenever a utility relation is considered, it will be because it is compatible with given demands. But compatibility is preserved when the relation is replaced by its normalization obtained by taking the adjoint of its adjoint. That relation is automatically quasi-concave, its superior sets being the convex closures of those of the original. It appears from this that there is no essential loss of generality, so far as present questions are concerned, and a simplification in exposition, in assuming all utility relations dealt with to be quasi-concave. This is a fortunate circumstance for standard theory, which seems always to assume indifference contours to be concave. But it does not mean they really are. It is just that, in the limited language of economic choice, it is impossible to communicate that they are not.

A further simplicity which follows from strict quasi concavity is that expansion loci are paths, with a unique consumption corresponding to every level of income. Sometimes it is as well to assume this, again for simplicity of exposition, and also because an arbitrarily small modification can replace concavity by strict concavity, so there is no significant difference when error is allowed.

Because, for any p, $\rho(p,x)$ is a utility function which represents R, so is $\phi(x)$. The adjoint is

$$\psi(u) = [1 - \mu(u)]/\theta(u), \tag{3}$$

and

$$\psi(M^{-1}p) = [M - \mu(p)]/\theta(p), \tag{4}$$

so that

$$\partial\psi(M^{-1}p)/\partial M = 1/\theta(p). \tag{5}$$

Thus $P = \theta(p)$ is the marginal price of utility $X = \psi(M^{-1}p)$ attained at elementary prices p with a level of expenditure M, and it is fixed when elementary prices are fixed.

The *profile*, for price p, of a utility function $\phi(x)$ with adjoint $\psi(u)$, is $\psi(M^{-1}p)$. Here it appears that the profiles are linear. Such a property is preserved under linear transformations, but not more general ones. An equivalent characterization of linear cost utility relations is that they admit representation by a utility function with linear profiles. It is to be seen that still another equivalent characterization is that the expansion loci are linear.

To see this, assume, as would be permitted on grounds already stated, that $\phi(x)$ is quasi-concave. Then, by a general proposition, since its profiles also are concave, it is concave. Let y and z be two different demands at prices p which are compatible, that is yEp, zEp which is to say $\theta(p)\phi(y) + \mu(p) = py$; $\theta(p)\phi(z) + \mu(p) = pz$. Then, with $\beta + \gamma = 1$, it follows that

$$\theta(p)[\phi(y)\beta + \phi(z)\gamma] + \mu(p) = p(y\beta + z\gamma).$$

But then with $\beta, \gamma \geq 0$, and $x = y\beta + z$, $\phi(x) \geq \phi(y)\beta + \phi(z)\gamma$, since $\phi(x)$ is concave, and, as usual, $\theta(p)\phi(x) + \mu(p) \leq px$. But this with the foregoing implies $\theta(p)\phi(x) + \mu(p) = px$, and shows that the demand of x at prices p is compatible, that is, xEp.

It has been shown that $y, z \in Ep \Rightarrow \langle y, z \rangle \subset Ep$, where $\langle y, z \rangle$ is the line segment joining y and z; that is, the expansion locus Ep is a convex set. But if it is a path, as it is if R is strictly quasi-concave, then it is a segment of a line. Since the line is in any case truncated within the commodity space, it cannot extend beyond a half-line. In fact, there may have to be a further interruption of a different nature, where the function becomes strictly quasi-convex, and where no demand is compatible, and this could leave at most a bounded segment. An intrinsic limitation of this kind is important in describing the range of incomes for which a comparison is valid.

It has been seen that if R is a quasi-concave utility order and (1) holds, then $\phi(x)$ has concave contours and profiles and hence is a concave function. Then it was deduced that the expansion sets Ep are convex, where xEp means $\rho(p, x) = 1$. Thus in particular, when the expansion sets are paths that cut every level of income (equivalently, every level of utility), in a single point, they must be straight lines to be convex.

Now a converse proposition will be shown. Suppose Ep are given as describing all levels of utility indicated by 0 and 1 and as convex. Then, between these levels R has the linear cost property (1).

For any u let $x_0(u), x_1(u)$ denote any elements of the expansion set Eu in utility levels indicated by 0 and 1. Then, by hypothesis,

$$x_t(u) = x_0(u) + [x_1(u) - x_0(u)]t$$

where $0 \leq t \leq 1$, is also in Eu. Also, since $x_0(u)Rx_0(v)$ for all u, v, then

$$ux_0(u) = \min[ux : xRx_0(u)] \leq ux_0(v).$$

Thus $ux_0(u) \leq ux_0(v)$ and similarly, $ux_1(u) \leq ux_1(v)$, for all u, v. It follows, multiplying these inequalities by $(t, 1-t)$ and adding, that $ux_t(u) \leq ux_t(v)$ for all $0 \leq t \leq 1$. But $x_t(u) \in Eu$, for all u. It follows that, for all such t, $x_t(u)Rx_t(v)$ for all u and v. Thus, for all such t, $x_t(u)$ for all u describes an indifference surface. Hence, defining $\phi[x_t(u)] = t$, $\phi(x)$ is a utility function which represents R. Also, if $\phi(x) = t$, $yRx \cdot \Leftrightarrow \cdot ux \geq ux_t(u)$ for all u. Hence

$$\rho(p, x) = \min[py : yRx] = \min[py : ux \geq ux_t(u)] = px_t(p)$$

$$= px_0(p) + p[x_1(p) - x_0(p)]t = \theta(p)\phi(x) + \mu(p),$$

where

$$\theta(p) = p[x_1(p) - x_0(p)], \quad \mu(0) = px_0(p),$$

as required.

The equilibrium relation E which holds between x, p in an R-compatible demand is given by

$$xEp \equiv \theta(p)\phi(x) + \mu(p) = px. \tag{6}$$

Thus, with compatible demands (x_0, p_0) and (x_1, p_1) in a base and current period, or country, if

$$
\begin{aligned}
M_0 &= p_0 x_0, & M_1 &= p_1 x_1 \\
m_0 &= \mu(p_0), & m_1 &= \mu(p_1) \\
P_0 &= \theta(p_0), & P_1 &= \theta(p_1) \\
X_0 &= \phi(x_0), & X_1 &= \phi(x_1)
\end{aligned}
\tag{7}
$$

then

$$
P_0 X_0 + m_0 = M_0, \quad P_1 X_1 + m_1 = M_1. \tag{8}
$$

But the m's and P's are determined by prices alone. Hence the condition $X_0 = X$ for *any* incomes M_0, M_1 to have the same purchasing power at prices p_0, p_1 is equivalent to

$$
M_1 - m_1 = P_{10}(M_0 - m_0) \tag{9}
$$

where $p_{10} = P_1/P_0$ is the *marginal price index* between p_0 and p_1. Therefore, with any incomes M_0, M_1 constrained to purchasing power equivalence,

$$
\Delta M_1 / \Delta M_0 = P_{10}. \tag{10}
$$

This shows the definition of a marginal price index by its characteristic role as applied to income differentials which preserve equivalence, instead of to incomes themselves, about which nothing can be said without knowledge of the *original values* m_0, m_1. This contrasts with an ordinary price index P_{10} which gives

$$
M_1 = P_{10} M_0 \tag{11}
$$

as the relation between equivalent incomes, and hence the same relation between income differentials which preserve equivalence. Thus in the use of marginal price indexes there is a distinction between total incomes and income differentials which is effaced by ordinary price indexes.

It would seem that (9) is an appropriate relation for adjusting wages for price change as required by an escalator clause in a labor-management contract, to maintain economic equity, but (10) could be appropriate for adjustment of any other moneys which do not have the nature of base incomes, such as rents, allowances, as so forth.

4.2   Method of limits

Continuing now, from 4.1(2),

$$
\begin{aligned}
P_0 X_1 + m_0 &\leqq p_0 x_1 \\
P_1 X_0 + m_1 &\leqq p_1 x_0
\end{aligned}
\tag{1}
$$

and from (8),

$$P_0 X_0 + m_0 = p_0 x_0$$
$$P_1 X_1 + m_1 = p_1 x_1. \tag{2}$$

Now from (11) and (12),

$$(p_1 x_1 - m_1)/(p_0 x_1 - m_0) \lesseqgtr P_{10} \lesseqgtr (p_1 x_0 - m_1)/(p_0 x_0 - m_0). \tag{3}$$

Thus, for any given pair of demands (x_0, p_0) and (x_1, p_1), if the hypothesis of their compatibility with R, for any values for m_0 and m_1, is accepted, then the bounds for P_{10} shown in (3) are determined. In the particular case with $m_0 = m_1 = 0$ these bounds coincide with the Paasche and Laspeyres price indexes. This circumstance can be amplified further later.

Now for any incomes M_0 and M_1, not necessarily $p_0 x_0$ and $p_1 x_1$ to be equivalent in purchasing power at respective prices p_0, p_1 it is necessary, by 4.1(9) and (3), that they be in the relation T_{01} depending on m_0, m_1 given by

$$M_0 T_{01} M_1 \equiv (p_1 x_1 - m_1)/(p_0 x_1 - m_0) \lesseqgtr (M_1 - m_1)/(M_0 - m_0)$$
$$\lesseqgtr (p_1 x_0 - m_1)/(p_0 x_0 - m_0). \tag{4}$$

Thus every M_0 corresponds to an interval of M_1 with upper and lower limits $(M_1)_u$, $(M_1)_l$ where

$$(M_1)_l - m_1 = [(p_1 x_1 - m_1)/(p_0 x_1 - m_0)] (M_0 - m_0)$$
$$(M_1)_u - m_1 = [(p_1 x_0 - m_1)/(p_0 x_0 - m_0)] (M_0 - m_0) \tag{5}$$

which can define the *extreme equivalents* of M_0, and similarly with 0 and 1 interchanged. Then a particular value $\bar{M}_1$ between these limits is given by

$$(\bar{M}_1 - m_1)^2 = [(M_1)_l - m_1][(M_1)_u - m_1)], \tag{6}$$

which can define the *principal equivalent* of M_0. There may seem to be no reason for introducing this concept for a particular correspondent $\bar{M}_1$ of M_0. It is just a way of singling out a point in the interval $M_0 T_{01}$ of correspondents of M_0. However, M_0 is the principal correspondent of its principal correspondent: The one-to-one subcorrespondence $\bar{T}_{01}$ the many-to-many correspondence T_{01} given by

$$M_0 \bar{T}_{01} M_1 \equiv [(M_1 - m_1)/(M_0 - m_0)]^2$$
$$= (p_1 x_1 - m_1)(p_1 x_0 - m_1)/(p_0 x_1 - m_0)(p_0 x_0 - m_0) \tag{7}$$

can define the *principal correspondence*. It holds between incomes M_0 and M_1 at prices p_0 and p_1 if any only if each is the principal correspondent of the other, in which case each is the principal correspondent of its principal correspondent. Note that if $m_0 = m_1 = 0$ then this is the correspondence associated with the Fisher price index.

The theory thus shows that the Laspeyres, Paasche, and Fisher indexes, understood in their role as price indexes, correspond to a special case, where the parameters m_0 and m_1 are zero.

A particular utility relation R which was presented earlier, has the property expressed by (1). With $\phi(x)$ fixed, by assigning values at two nonindifferent points, the other functions are fixed, and hence so are m_0 and m_1. For any M_0 there exists a unique M_1 such that

$$\psi(M_0^{-1}p_0) = \psi(M_1^{-1}p_1).\tag{8}$$

It has been shown that this together with $x_0 E p_0$, $x_1 E p_1$ for any x_0, x_1 implies $M_0 T_{01} M_1$. Thus it would be exceptional that also $M_0 \bar{T}_{01} M_1$. But the particular utility relation R makes (8) specific and also m_0, m_1. Usually in practice there is nothing available but fragmentary demand data, even when, as here, there are only two reference periods or countries.

4.3   *Expansion lines and critical points*

If at each of the prices p_0, p_1 just one demand is available x_0, x_1, then only a rather loose analysis can be developed, as has just been done, where the parameters m_0, m_1 are unspecified. Even this analysis can be taken further, but not here. Instead it will be supposed that a second demand is available at each of the prices, say, y_0, y_1. By implication then, since compatible linear cost utility is to be considered, for which expansion loci are line segments, or possibly half-lines, what is being considered is a pair of segments $K_0 = \langle x_0, y_0 \rangle$, $K_1 = \langle x_1, y_1 \rangle$ of demands associated with prices p_0, p_1.

Let L_0, L_1 denote the carrier of K_0, K_1. These are the lines joining the extremities. It can be shown that, if

$$\begin{vmatrix} p_0(x_0 - y_0) & p_0(x_1 - y_1) \\ p_1(x_0 - y_0) & p_1(x_1 - y_1) \end{vmatrix} \neq 0,\tag{1}$$

(and if this is not so then it can be made so, by distributing the data slightly, or at least within bounds of its conspicuous inaccuracy), then there exists a unique pair of *critical points* c_0, c_1 on L_0, L_1 such that $p_0 c_0 = p_1 c_1$, $p_1 c_0 = p_1 c_1$. These need not be on K_0, K_1 nor even in the commodity space. They are distinguished as being indifferent with respect to every compatible utility relation. Then a pair of half-lines L_0^*, L_1^* on L_0, L_1 with c_0, c_1 as vertexes are determined. Then pair is selected according to the sign of the elements and the determinants of the foregoing nonsingular 2×2 matrix. Then the expansions (K_0, p_0), (K_1, p_1) are generally consistent, that is, compatible with any utility relation, regardless of properties, if and only if $K_0 \subset L_0^*$ or $K_1 \subset L_1^*$. Thus, should L_0^*, L_1^* happen not lie in the commodity space at all then certainly the expansions are inconsistent. However, for *local linear cost consistency*, equivalently compatibility with a utility function which has linear expansion loci *in a convex neighborhood containing K_0, K_1*, it is necessary and sufficient that $K_0 \subset L_0^*$ and $K_1 \subset L_1^*$.

With c_0, c_1 as the pair of critical points on the carrier lines L_0, L_1, let x_0, x_1 now be any other pair of points $p_0(x_0 - c_0) > 0, p_1(x_1 - c_1) > 0$. Then for consistency it is necessary that also $p_0(x_1 - c_1) > 0, p_1(x_0 - c_0) > 0$. Then the *critical determinant*

$$\begin{vmatrix} p_0(x_0 - c_0) & p_0(x_1 - c_1) \\ p_1(x_0 - c_0) & p_1(x_1 - c_1) \end{vmatrix} \tag{2}$$

is nonzero by hypotheses (1). Then the *hyperbolic* and *elliptical* cases are distinguished by the sign, positive or negative, of (2). In the hyperbolic case, L_0^*, L_1^* correspond to $x_0 \in L_0, x_1 \in L_1$, where $p_0 x_0 \geqq p_0 c_0, p_1 x_1 \geqq p_1 c_1$. In this case, consistency of $(K_0, p_0), (K_1, p_1)$ requires

$$\begin{aligned} x_0 \in K_0 &\Rightarrow p_0 x_0 \geqq p_0 c_0 \\ x_1 \in K_1 &\Rightarrow p_1 x_1 \geqq p_1 c_1 \end{aligned} \tag{3}$$

Inequalities are reversed for the elliptical case.

Let $F_0(M_0), F_1(M_1)$ denote the points x_0, x_1 on L_0, L_1 with $p_0 x_0 = M_0$, $p_1 x_1 = M_1$.

With reference to the relation T_{01} given by 4.2(4), with the specification $m_0 = p_0 c_0, m_1 = p_1 c_1$ it can now be said that, at prices p_0, p_1, any incomes M_0, M_1 may be determined as of equivalent purchasing power with respect to some utility relation compatible with the expansions $(K_0, p_0), (K_1, p_1)$, if and only if, first, these expansions are consistent; second, in the hyperbolic case,

$$\begin{aligned} M_0 \geqq p_0 c_0, &\quad F_0(M_0) \geqq 0 \\ M_1 \geqq p_1 c_1, &\quad F_1(M_1) \geqq 0, \end{aligned} \tag{4}$$

and correspondingly in the elliptical case; and finally, $M_0 T_{01} M_1$.

With the appropriate qualifications about the range of M_0, M_1 it appears thus that the relation T_{01} determines, for any M_0, the best possible bounds, that is, the limits of M_1 that can be established as equivalent with respect to some compatible utility relation.

Two peculiarities may be noted. No restriction at all has been made for the utility relation in the foregoing, but now two restrictions will be considered. The first is that the utility relation be of the linear cost type, at least in a convex neighborhood containing K_0, K_1. However, even if this restriction is imposed on the utility relation just described, the description remains valid. This is remarkable only because on the face of the matter, it would seem that with this restriction the relation T should be contracted to a proper subrelation.

The other restriction to be considered is a stronger one. It requires the utility relation to be representable in a convex neighborhood containing K_0, K_1 by a general quadratic utility function. This implies qualification under the first restriction, since quadratic representation implies linear expansion. Again on the face of the matter, quadratic consistency is a stronger condition than linear expansion consistency. In regard to any number of expansions, it is. But it is surprising that for just a pair of expansions, it is equivalent. Then, under this common consistency requirement, it is natural to ask what is the subrelation, say T_{01}^*, of T_{01} corresponding to this further quadratic restriction. Certainly now it will be a proper subrelation, but since, if there are any, there are infinite compatible quadratics, it might be expected that T_{01}^* would not be one-to-one, but that, for every M_0, $M_0 T_{01}^*$ would be a subinterval of $M_0 T_{01}$, nonempty by consistency and with a variety of points because of the variety of compatible quadratics. However, it is established that $T_{01}^* = \bar{T}_{01}$, that is, the quadratically determined correspondence T_{01}^* coincides with the principle correspondence given by 4.2(7), and moreover this is one-to-one. Thus here there is a surprise opposite to the first. Introducing the values of m_0, m_1, that formula becomes

$$M_0 \bar{T}_{01} M_1 \equiv [(M_1 - p_1 c_1)/(M_0 - p_0 c_0)]^2$$
$$= p_1(x_1 - c_1)p_1(x_0 - c_0)/p_0(x_1 - c_1)p_0(x_0 - c_0). \tag{5}$$

It follows from the definition of the critical points c_0, c_1 on the carrier lines L_0, L_1 that c_0, c_1 in this formula could be replaced by any point c on the *critical transversal* to L_0, L_1 obtained by joining the L's, assuming L_0, L_1 are skew. But if L_0 and L_1 intersect in a point c, then both c_0 and c_1 coincide with c, and no such transversal is defined. It should be noted that if L_0, L_1 are skew, any compatible quadratic is singular, that is, its matrix of second derivatives, which is constant, is singular. In this case its expansion loci for p_0, p_1 do not lie in lines but in linear manifolds at least as large as the joins of c with L_0, L_1. For the expansion loci strictly to be lines, the quadratic must be regular, and in this case L_0 and L_1 must intersect.

If, in particular, the intersection is at the origin $c = 0$, the (5) becomes Fisher's formula. Then for consistency, the elliptical case is excluded entirely, since if $M_0 \leq 0$ then $F_0(M_0) \geq 0$ is impossible. Thus the consistency condition becomes simply $p_0 x_0 p_1 x_1 \geq p_0 x_1 p_1 x_0$, corresponding to the remaining hyperbolic case. Since c_0 and c_1 appear as points where the gradient of any compatible quadratic must vanish, $c_0 = c_1 = 0$ corresponds to the case of a homogeneous quadratic. This reproduces the observation of Buscheguennce that the Fisher index is exact if a homogeneous utility function can be assumed to prevail. But, related to this, as a generalization, Wald has shown that if a pair of expansion lines are given, with associated prices, and it can be assumed that a general quadratic utility function prevails, then it is possible to determine a unique one-to-one correspondence between equivalent incomes at these prices. This is by his "new formula," which, because of Buscheguennce's proposition must be essentially a generalization of Fisher's formula. Consistency conditions were not treated and, hence, neither were the necessary restrictions on the range of those incomes for such comparison. But with the introduction of the concept of critical points certainly his formula must be identical with (13), which is transparently a generalization of Fisher. A generalization of Wald's formula appears in Afriat (1964).

This theory of marginal price indexes extends every feature of the theory of price indexes based on the traditional concept. Instead of a pair of demands (x_0, p_0),

(x_1, p_1), which because of implicit homogeneity correspond in principle to a pair of linear expansions (x'_0, p_0), (x'_1, p_1), where x'_0, x'_1 are the rays through x_0, x_1, the data now consist of a general pair of linear expansions (K_0, p_0), (K_1, p_1), where K_0 and K_1 can arise from pairs of demands x_0, y_0 and x_1, y_1 not necessarily on the same ray. The Paasche-Laspeyres limits for a price index P_{10} become the limits given in (1) with $m_0 = p_0 c_0$, $m_1 = p_1 c_1$ for a marginal price index P_{10}. The index then has the role shown by 4.1(10), and m has the role shown by 4.1(9).

This theory of marginal price index construction, here restricted to data for two periods or countries, and dependent on consistency conditions, has a general extension for arbitrary data and with a relaxation of strict consistency to approximate consistency. But this development will be shown here only as it applies to the usual price indexes.

With all this, it still has to be claimed that marginal price indexes, as described here, are not yet general enough. They are not vulnerable to the objection made to price indexes, which was that the concept implies that the rich and poor have the same spending pattern. But they are vulnerable to the objection that the concept implies that rich and poor have the same *marginal pattern*. This is to say that an extra dollar given to a rich individual would be spent in identical fashion were it given to a poor one. This does not go so far as to say they enjoy all things in the same proportion and differ just in the scale corresponding to their different incomes, but it is a radical contradiction of reality nevertheless.

To escape this objection, a further method is possible, where the intervals of incomes to be compared can be dissected into consecutive corresponding subintervals, or steps, corresponding to different intervals of real income, where the foregoing scheme applies, but with different P_{10}, m_0, m_1 at each level. This corresponds to the concept of a utility relation determined by a finite set of indifference surfaces, each surface being the interface between consecutive intervals of real income. The interpolation between surfaces is by the unique linear cost utility relation they determine.

For arbitrary demand data, consistency of utility relations with such a form is not more restrictive than general consistency. Such a scheme for establishing equivalent real incomes, though it would not be put into operation by publication of a single number, as is the usual practice, would still have practical simplicity. It would establish corresponding income classes, and then different P_{10}, m_0, and m_1 for determining corresponding points in each pair of corresponding classes. Though a utility function conceptually underlies such information, there is no need to compute, let alone present, a particular one. In any case, such a scheme of information would present every thing about such a utility function that would be relevant to the desired comparison.

The real-income classes correspond to any partition of the range. When there is just one class, the method is identical with the original marginal index method. Transition from one class to another can correspond to a significant shift of marginal pattern.

A more elaborate general analysis can apply to several periods or countries, and express approximation in terms of cost efficiencies. Any income in any period would have an imputed cost-efficiency and an interval of corresponding incomes in every other period or country. Within each such interval of correspondents, a single point can be determined from the principal correspondence which is produced by the linear expansions across each real-income interval in the two periods or countries. This more elaborate method communicates information about underlying error and indeterminacy together with a one-to-one correspondence with represents a statistical resolution of both.

4.4 Multiple critical points

Let a set of expansion lines L_t, with associated prices p_t, be given ($t = 1, \ldots, k$). Let $x_t(M_t)$ be the point on L_t corresponding to an expenditure M_t,

$$x_t(M_t) \in L_t, \quad p_t x_t(M_t) - M_t. \tag{1}$$

Define the relation T_{rs} by

$$M_r T_{rs} M_s \equiv p_r x_s(M_s) \leqq M_r. \tag{2}$$

Then define

$$T_{rij\cdots ks} = T_{ri} T_{ij} \cdots T_{ks} \tag{3}$$

and

$$\vec{T}_{rs} = \bigcup_{ij\cdots k} T_{rij\cdots ks}. \tag{4}$$

Then define T_{rs}^* by

$$M_r T_{rs}^* M_s \equiv M_r T_{rs} M_s(M', -M'') \geq (M_r, M_s) \;\Rightarrow\; M' \vec{T}_{rs} M''. \tag{5}$$

Thus $M_r \vec{T}_{rs} M_s$ means $X_r(M_r)$ is revealed as good as $X_s(M_s)$, or that the purchasing power of M_r at prices p_r is as great as that of M_s at p_s. With $M_r T_{rs} M_s$, these relations are directly revealed, instead of through a chain. In the *critical revealed purchasing power relation* $M_r T_{rs}^* M_s$ is such that M_r is revealed as high as M_s, but no smaller M_r is revealed as high as M_s, and no greater M_s is revealed as no higher than M_r. A first requirement of consistency, of any segments $K_t \subset L_t$ whatsoever, is that T_{rs}^* be a one-to-one increasing relation between M_r, M_s. Thus, define $M_s = \check{F}_{rs}(M_r)$, and equivalently $M_r = \hat{F}_{rs}(M_s)$, by $M_r T_{rs}^* M_s$, so that

$$M_s \leqq F_{rs}(M_r) \;\Leftrightarrow\; M_r T_{rs}^* M_s \;\Leftrightarrow\; M_r \geqq F_{rs}(M_s) \tag{6}$$

and $\hat{F}_{rs}, \check{F}_{rs}$ are inverse increasing functions.

For any r, s and M_r define

$$\check{M}_{sr} = \check{F}_{rs}(M_r), \quad \hat{M}_{sr} = \hat{F}_{rs}(M_r). \tag{7}$$

Then for the compatible equivalence of M_s with M_r, that is equivalence determined in respect to some utility relation, it is necessary that

$$\check{M}_{sr} \leqq M_s \leqq \hat{M}_{sr}. \tag{8}$$

If a truncation of the L_t to appropriate segments is to be understood, this is al so sufficient. That appropriate truncation is going to be discovered. But (8) requires

$$\check{M}_{sr} \leqq \hat{M}_{sr}. \tag{9}$$

Since $M_r T_{rr} M_r$ and $T_{rr} \subset \vec{T}_{rr}$ if follows that $M_r \vec{T}_{rr} M_r$, and hence that

$$\check{F}_{rr}(M_r) \geqq M_r, \quad \text{equivalently } \hat{F}_{rr}(M_r) \leqq M_r, \tag{10}$$

for all r and M_r, that is

$$\hat{M}_{rr} \leqq M_r \leqq \check{M}_{rr}. \tag{11}$$

A consistency requirement is therefore that

$$\check{F}_{rr}(M_r) \geqq M_r, \tag{12}$$

and this is equivalent to

$$\check{F}_{rr}(M_r) = M_r. \tag{13}$$

It can be seen that $\check{F}_{rr}(M_r)/M_r$ is an increasing or decreasing function of M_r. The case where it is increasing can be distinguished as *elliptical* and the other as *hyperbolic*. There exists *critical* $\bar{M}_r$ such that (13) holds if and only if, in the elliptical case, $M_r \leqq \bar{M}_r$, and in the hyperbolic case $M_r \geqq \bar{M}_r$. It appears that

$$\check{F}_{rs}(\bar{M}_r) = \hat{F}_{rs}(\bar{M}_r) \tag{14}$$

for all s. Hence, for all s, define

$$\check{F}_{rs}(\bar{M}_r) = \bar{M}_s. \tag{15}$$

Thus unique critical $\bar{M}_t$ are defined for all t, such that (15) holds for all r, s.

Let $\bar{L}_t$ be the halfline of L_t corresponding to $M_t \leqq \bar{M}_t$ in the elliptical case and $M_t \geqq \bar{M}_t$ in the hyperbolic case. Truncation within the commodity space could be understood, but is not essential for this discussion, the effect of such truncation being clear.

The main proposition now is that the expansions $(\bar{L}_t, p_t)$ are consistent but they become not consistent if any $\bar{L}_t$ is prolonged beyond its vertex $c_t = x_t(\bar{M}_t)$. These vertices c_t define a set of *critical points* on the expansion lines L_t. They are all revealed indifferent to each other. Thus they are indifferent in respect to every relation compatible with $(\bar{L}_t, p_t)$. Again, for any segments $K_t \subset L_t$ which have linear continuations or while are comparable by revealed preference, the expansions (K_t, p_t), or such continuations are consistent if and only if $K_t \subset \bar{L}_t$.

This sketches the main features of the extension for several linear expansions of the critical point theory which has been developed more fully for a pair, and it can be developed further in corresponding fashion. (This extension originated in conversation with W. M. Gorman, March 1970.)

For empirical work, the further extension with approximation in terms of cost-efficiency would be appropriate.

4.5   Klein–Rubin

Klein and Rubin (1947) have considered index theory based on a utility function
of the form

$$\phi(x) = \prod_i (x_i - c_i)^{w_i}, \quad w_i \geq 0, \quad \sum_i w_i = 1 \quad (x \geq c) \tag{1}$$

which is the non-homogeneous extension of the utility function associated with
the Palgrave index. The associated expenditure system is

$$x_i = c_i + (M - pc)w_i/p_i \tag{2}$$

equivalently $x = f(u)$ where $u = M^{-1}p$ and

$$f_i(u) = c_i + (1 - uc)w_i/u_i. \tag{3}$$

The adjoint function is

$$\psi(u) = (1 - uc)/\theta(u) \tag{4}$$

where

$$\theta(u) = \Omega \prod_i u_i^{w_i}, \quad \Omega = \prod_i w_i^{-w_i}. \tag{5}$$

Then the cost function is

$$\rho(p, x) = \theta(p)\,\phi(x) + pc. \tag{6}$$

For $ux = 1$,

$$\theta(u)\,\phi(x) + uc \leq 1, \tag{7}$$

with equality just in case of equilibrium, that is $x = f(u)$.
   Thus, given a pair of budgets $(x_0, u_0), (x_1, u_1)$, compatibility with $\phi(x)$ requires

$$\theta(u_0)\,\phi(x_0) + u_0 c = 1$$
$$\theta(u_1)\,\phi(x_1) + u_1 c = 1, \tag{8}$$

Then $\rho_{10} = \rho(u_1, x_0)$ is given by

$$\theta(u_1)\,\phi(x_0) + u_1 c = \rho_{10}, \tag{9}$$

that is

$$\rho_{10} - u_1 c = U_{10}(1 - u_0 c) \tag{10}$$

where

$$U_0 = \theta(u_0), \quad U_1 = \theta(u_1) \tag{11}$$

and

$$U_{10} = U_1/U_0 \tag{12}$$

$$= \prod_i (u_{i1}/u_{i0})^{w_i}.$$

It can be asked if c and w_i exist such that (8) is satisfied, with $x_0, x_1 \geqq c$, $w_i \geqq 0, \sum w_i = 1$. Any such would then give a determination of ρ_{10} from (10), and many sould give many determinations, in which case it can be asked what is their range.

For notational simplicity, denote $(x_0, n_0), (x_1, u_1)$ by $(x, u), (y, v)$. Then (8) is equivalent to

$$u_i(x_i - c_i) = (1 - uc)w_i$$
$$v_i(y_i - c_i) = (1 - vc)w_i \tag{13}$$

and implies

$$u_i(x_i - c_i)v_j(y_j - c_j) = u_j(x_j - c_j)v_i(y_i - c_i). \tag{14}$$

But (14) is equivalent to the existence of w_i for (13), and also to

$$u_i(x_i - c_i)v_s(y_s - c_s) = u_s(x_s - c_s)v_i(y_i - c_i) \tag{15}$$

for any fixed s, for all i. That is

$$(v_s - u_s)c_s = (v_i - u_i + v_s c_s u_i - u_s c_s v_i)c_i. \tag{16}$$

But, from (16) with any assigned c_s, c_i is determined for all i. This means (14) has a path C of solutions for c, on which c is fixed when any element is fixed arbitrarily. Let $\bar{C}$ be the set of $\bar{c}$ on C for which

$$x, y \geqq c.$$

For any such $c = \bar{c}$, unique $w_i = \bar{w}_i$ are determined which satisfy (13) and $w_i \geq 0, \sum w_i = 1$. Thus the consistency of the pair of budgets, on the considered model is just that $\bar{C}$ be non-empty, equivalently that C has points lying below both $x_0 = x$ and $x_1 = y$.

Problem 1   *To find an algebraical test of consistency.*

Problem 2   *To find a formula for the range of ρ_{10} corresponding to all $c \in \bar{C}$ and the associated w_i.*

The analogues of both these problems have been solved for the special homogeneous model, with $c = 0$, which provides theory of the Palgrave index, and for several other models, general, homogeneous, quadratic and so forth. But here, though a scheme for their solution is established, an explicit algebraical formula is not in evidence. With Klein and Rubin a "constant of integration" appeared, but it remained undetermined.

A different development derives from the case where an expansion line L is specified in the base period. Then the w_i are determined. For if a, b are any points on L then

$$p_i(a_i - b_i) = p(a - b)w_i.$$

The indeterminacy now consists just in the position of c on L_0. The direction of any expansion line at prices q is determined as the direction d of w_i/q_i. All such lines which cut L describe a plane T. Thus, for consistency, any demand y at prices q must lie in this hyperplane. Then a point c is determined as the intersection with L of the line through y in the direction d.

Given several budgets (x_t, u_t), for any c let

$$a_{ij}^t = \frac{u_{it}(x_{it} - c_i)}{u_{jt}(x_{jt} - c_j)}$$

Then it can be asked to determine a solution of

$$a_{ij}^t \geqq ew_i/w_j$$

with $c \leqq x_t$ and e a maximum. A solution with $e = 1$ is the case of exact consistency. Otherwise c and w_i are determined which are best possible, according to efficiency distance.

4.6   *Real tax structure*

An idea, which seems possibly interesting, but neglected, of adjustment of an income-tax structure to maintain a fixed structure in real terms, can be illustrated here. An income tax structure is described by a determination $T = T(M)$ of tax as a function of income M before tax. Disposable income is therefore a function $D(M) = M - T(M)$ of M. Tax structures $T_0(M_0), T_1(M_1)$ in two periods could be considered to represent the same structure in real terms on condition that if M_0, M_1 are equivalent incomes in the two periods then so are

$$D_0(M_0) = M_0 - T_0(M_0), \quad D_1(M_1) = M_1 - T_1(M_1).$$

In other words, individuals in the two periods who would have been at the same standard of living without tax are at the same standard of living after tax. For such individuals, the money tax may differ but the real tax is the same.

The condition is that if

$$M_1 - m_1 = P_{10}(M_0 - m_0)$$

then

$$D_1(M_1) - m_1 = P_{10}(D_0(M_0) - m_0),$$

that is

$$D_1(m_1 + P_{10}(M_0 - m_0)) = P_{10}(D_0(M_0) - m_0),$$

or

$$D_0(M_0) = m_0 + P_{01}D_1(m_1 + P_{10}(M_0 - m_0))$$

where $P_{01} = P_{10}^{-1}$. Inversely

$$D_1(M_1) = m_1 + P_{10}D_0(m_0 + P_{01}(M_1 - m_1)).$$

This gives the relation between two income tax structures, by which either one is determined from the other, which assures they represent the same tax structure in real terms.

Bibliography

Afriat, S. N. "Theory of Economic Index Numbers." Mimeographed. Cambridge, Engl., Department of Applied Economics, Cambridge University, May 1956.

——. "Preference Scales and Expenditure Systems." *Econometrica* 30 (1962): 305–323.

——. "A Formula for Ranging the Cost of Living." Abstract in R. L. Graves and P. Wolf, eds. *Recent Advances in Mathematical Programming: Proceedings of the Chicago Symposium, 1962.* New York, McGraw-Hill, 1962.

——. "The System of Inequalities $a_{rs} > X_r - X_s$." *Proceedings of the Cambridge Philosophical Society* 59 (1963): 125–133.

——. "An Identity Concerning the Relation Between the Paasche and Laspeyres Indices." *Metroeconomica* XV, I (1963): 38–46.

——. "On Bernoullian Utility for Goods and Money." *Metroeconomica* XV, I (1963), 38–46.

——. "The Construction of Utility Functions from Expenditure Data." *International Economic Review* 8, 1 (1967): 66–77.

——. "The Cost of Living Index." In M. Shubik, ed. *Studies in Mathematical Economics in Honor of Oskar Morgenstern.* Princeton, N.J., Princeton University Press, 1967, Chap. 23.

——. "The Construction of Cost Efficiencies and Approximate Utility Functions from Inconsistent Expenditure Data." Paper presented at the winter meeting of the Econometric Society, New York, 1969.

——. "The Method of Limits in the Theory of Index Numbers." *Metroeconomica* (1970).

Allen, R. G. D. (1949) "The Economic Theory of Index Numbers." *Economica,* New Series XVI, 63 (August 1949): 197–203.

Antonelli, G. B. *Sulla Teoria Matematica della Economia Pura* (1886). Reprinted in *Giornale degli Economisti* 10 (1951), 233–263.

Bowley, A. L. (1923) Review of *The Making of Index Numbers,* by Irving Fisher. *Economic Journal* 33 (1923): 90–94.

—— "Notes on Index Numbers." *Economic Journal* (June 1928).

Buscheguennce. "Sur une classe des hypersurfaces. A propos de 'l'index idéal' de M. Irv. Fisher." *Recueil Mathematique* (Moscow) XXXII, 4 (1925).

Chase, Arnold E. "Concepts and Uses of Price Indices." Paper presented at the American Statistical Association meeting, August 1960.

Cournot, Augustine. *Researches into the Mathematical Principles of the Theory of Wealth* (1838). Translated by Nathaniel T. Bacon with an essay on Cournot and mathematical economics and a bibliography on mathematical economics by Irving Fisher (1924). Reprint: New York, Kelley, 1960.

De Finetti, Bruno. "Sulle stratificazioni convesse." *Ann. Mat. Pura Appt.* 4 (1949): 173–183.

Divisia, F. *Economique Rationelle*. Paris, 1928.

Dupuit, J. "De la mesure de l'utilité des travaux public" (1844). Reprinted in English translation as "On the Measurement of the Utility of Public Works," in *International Economic Papers*, No. 2. London, Macmillan, 1952.

Edgeworth, F. Y. "A Defense of Index Numbers." *Economic Journal* (1896): 132–142.

Fisher, Irving. *The Purchasing Power of Money*. New York, Macmillan, 1911.

——. *The Making of Index Numbers*. Boston, Houghton Mifflin, 1922.

——. "Professor Bowley on Index Numbers." *Economic Journal* 33 (1923): 246–251.

——. "A Statistical Method for Measuring Marginal Utility and Testing the Justice of a Progressive Income Tax." In *Economic Essays in Honor of John Bates Clark*. New York, 1927.

Fleetwood, William. *Chronicon Preciosum: or, an Account of English Money, The Price of Corn, and Other Commodities, for the last 600 Years—in a Letter to a Student in the University of Oxford*. London, 1707.

Foster, William T. Prefatory Note, to *The Making of Index Numbers*, by Fisher (see above).

Frisch, Ragnar. "Annual Survey of General Economic Theory: The Problem of Index Numbers." *Econometrica* 4, 1 (1936): 1–39.

Georgescu-Roegen, N. "Choice and Revealed Preference." *Southern Economic Journal* 21 (1954): 119–130.

Gorman, W. M. "Separable Utility and Aggregation." *Econometrica* 27, (1959): 469–487.

——. "Additive Logarithmic Preferences: A Further Note." *Review of Economic Studies* 30 (1963): 56–62.

Haberler, Y. *Der Sinn der Indexzahlen*. Tubingen, 1924.

Hicks, J. R. *A Revision of Demand Theory*. Oxford, Clarendon Press, 1956.

Hotelling, H. "Demand Functions with Limited Budgets." *Econometrica* 3 (1935): 66–78.

Houthakker, H. S. (1950) "Revealed Preference and the Utility Function." *Economica*, N. S. 17 (1950): 159–174.

——. "La forme des courbes d'Engel." *Cahiers du Seminarie d'Econometrie* 2 (1953): 59–66.

——. "An International Comparison of Household Expenditure Patterns, Commemorating the Centenary of Engel's Law." *Econometrica* 25 (1957): 532–551.

——. "Some Problems in the International Comparison of Consumption Patterns." In *L'évaluation et le rôle des besoins de consommation dans les divers régimes économiques*. Paris, Centre National de la Recherche Scientifique, 1963.

International Labour Office. *A Contribution to the Study of International Comparisons of Costs of Living*. Studies and Reports, Series N, 17. Geneva, 1932.

Keynes, J. M. *A Treatise on Money*, Vol. I, *The Pure Theory of Money*. New York, Harcourt, Brace, 1930.

Klein, L. R., and H. Rubin. "A Constant Utility Index of the Cost of Living." *Review of Economic Studies* 15 (1947): 84–87.

Konus, A. A. "The Problem of the True Index of the Cost of Living." *Economic Bulletin of the Institute of Economic Conjecture* (Moscow, 1924).

Lange, O. "The Determinateness of the Utility Function." *Review of Economic Studies* 1 (1934): 218–224.

Laspeyres, E. "Die Berechnung einer mittleran Waarenpreissteigerung." *Jahrbücher für nationaloekonomie und Statistik* (Jena) XVI, 1871: 296–314.

Lerner, A. P. "A Note on the Theory of Price Index Numbers." *Review of Economic Studies* (1935): 50–56.

Little, I. M. D. *A Critique of Welfare Economics.* New York, Oxford University Press, 1957.

Liviatan, Nissan, and Don Patinkin. "On the Economic Theory of Price Indices." *Economic Development and Cultural Change* IX (1961): 501–536.

Mathur, P. N. "Approximate Determination of Indifference Surfaces from Family Budget Data." *International Economic Review* 5 (1964): 294–303.

Midgett, B. D. *Index Numbers.* New York, Wiley, 1951.

Morgenstern, Oskar. *On the Accuracy of Economic Observations.* Princeton, N.J., Princeton University Press, 1963.

National Bureau of Economic Research. *Problems in the International Comparison of Economic Accounts.* Studies in Income and Wealth, Vol. 20. Princeton University Press for NBER, 1957.

Paasche, H. "Über die Priesentwickelung der letzten Jahre, nach den Hamburger Börsennotierungen." *Jahrbücher für Nationaloekonomie und Statistik* (Jena) XXIII (1874): 168–178.

Palgrave, R. H. I. "Currency and Standard of Value in England, France and India, and the Rates of Exchange between These Countries." *Memorandum Laid Before the Royal Commission on Depression of Trade and Industry,* 1886, Third Report, Appendix B, pp. 213–390.

Pareto, V. "Économie Mathématique." *Encyclopedie des sciences mathématiques,* 1911. Reprinted in English translation as "Mathematical Economics," in *International Economic Papers,* No. 5. London, Macmillan, 1955.

Prais, S. J. "Non-Linear Estimates of the Engle Curves." *Review of Economic Studies* 20, (1952–53): 87–104.

Prais, S. J., and H. S. Houthakker. *The Analysis of Family Budgets.* Cambridge, Engl., Cambridge University Press, 1955.

Rajoaja, V. "A Study in the Theory of Demand Functions and Price Indexes." *Commentationes physico-mathematicae, Societas Scientiarum Fennica* (Helsinki) 21 (1958): 1–96.

Report of the President's Committee on the Cost of Living. Office of Economic Stabilization. Washington, D.C., 1945.

Report of the Price Statistics Review Committee. *Government Price Statistics, Hearings.* Subcommittee on Economic Statistics of the Joint Economic Committee. Part I, pp. 5–99. 87th Cong., 1st sess., January 1961.

Rose, Hugh. "Consistency of Preference: the Two-Commodity Case." *Review of Economic Studies* 25 (1958): 124–125.

Roy, R. "La distribution du revenu entre les divers biens." *Econometrica* 15 (1947): 205–225.

Ruggles, Richard. "Price Indices and International Price Comparisons." In *Ten Economic Studies in the Tradition of Irving Fisher.* New York, Wiley, 1967.

Samuelson, P. A. "Evaluation of Real National Income." *Oxford Economic Papers* N. S. 2, 1 (1950): 1–29.

——. "Structure of a Minimum Equilibrium System." In R. W. Pfouts, ed., *Essays in Economics and Econometrics.* Chapel Hill, University of North Carolina Press, 1960.

Schumpeter, Joseph A. *History of Economic Analysis*. New York, Oxford University Press, 1954.

Slutsky, E. E. "Sulla teoria del biancio del consumatore" *Giornale degli Economisti* (1915). Reprinted as "On the theory of the budget of the consumer," translated by O. Ragusa, in G. J. Stigler and K. E. Boulding, eds. *Readings in Price Theory*. Chicago, Irwin, 1952.

Staehle, Hans. "A General Method for the Comparison of the Price of Living." *Rev. Econ. Papers*, New Ser., 2, 1 (1950): 1–29.

Stone, Richard. "Linear Expenditure Systems and Demand Analysis; an Application to the Pattern of British Demand." *Economic Journal*, 64 (1954): 511–524.

Stone, Richard, assisted by D. A. Rowe, W. J. Corlett, R. Hurstfield, and M. Potter. *The Measurement of Consumers' Expenditure and Behavior in the United Kingdom, 1920–1938*, Vol. I. Cambridge, Engl., Cambridge University Press, 1966.

Stone, Richard, and D. A. Rowe. *Ibid.*, Vol. II.

Theil, H. "The Information Approach of Demand Analysis." *Econometrica* 33 (1963): 67–87.

Ulmer, M. J. *The Economic Theory of Cost of Living Index Numbers*. New York, Columbia University Press, 1949.

Ville, J. "Sur les conditions d'existence d'une orphelimite total ed d'un indice du niveau des prix." *Annales de l'Université de Lyon* (1946). Reprinted in English translation as "The Existence Conditions of a Total Utility Function," in *Review of Economic Studies* 19 (1951–52): 128–132.

Viner, J. "The Utility Concept in Value Theory and Its Critics." *Journal of Political Economy* 33 (1925): 369–387, 638–659.

Volterra, V. "L'economia matematica." Review of *Manuale di Economia Politica*, by V. Pareto. *Giornale degli Economisti* 32 (1906): 296–301.

Wald, A. "A New Formula for the Index of the Cost of Living." *Econometrica* 7, 4 (1939): 319–335.

——. "The Approximate Determination of Indifference Surfaces by Means of Engel Curves." *Econometrica* 8 (1940): 144–175.

——. "On a Relation Between Changes in Demand and Price Changes." *Ibid.* 20 (1952): 304–305.

Walsh, C. M. *The Measurement of General Exchange-Value*. New York, Macmillan, 1901.

Wold, H. O. A. "A synthesis of pure demand analysis." *Skandinavisk Aktuarietidskrift* 26 (1943): 85–118, 221–263; *Ibid.* 27 (1944): 69–120.

Wright, Georg Henrik von. *The Logic of Preference*. Edinburgh, Scotland, Edinburgh University Press, 1963.

5
Measurement of
the purchasing power of incomes
with linear expansion data

Journal of Econometrics 2, 3 (1974), 343–64.

Journal of Econometrics 2 (1974) 343–364. © North-Holland Publishing Company

Measurement of
the purchasing power of incomes
with linear expansion data

Received May 1973, revised version received February 1974

1. Introduction

Purchasing power is attributed to an income taken as an indivisible whole. It does not bear on money which is not thus specifically identified. The object of purchasing power measurement is to decide the relation between incomes which are to be considered as having the same purchasing power in two periods in which prices are different. In principle this could be any monotonic increasing relation. But in usual practice it is established as a homogeneous linear relation, determined by a single number, the 'price index', which gives the slope of the relation.

The question of comparison is understood in terms of a hypothetical utility relation which regulates expenditures. An income is spent for the effect of maintaining a standard of living. This standard of living is the final value of the income, and represents its purchasing power. But money does not purchase a standard of living directly. Rather, it purchases a bundle of goods. Then the bundle of goods, in being consumed, produces the use-value or utility which provides the standard of living.

Income and prices together determine the set of bundles of goods which are attainable, this being the budget set. It is assumed that income is spent efficiently, so as to obtain the best bundle in that set, that is, the one which is of greatest utility. With some provisors about utility (it is continuous, and represents that greater quantities of goods give higher utility) this is equivalent to the supposition that the utility attained could not be attained with any less money. If prices change, the budget set is altered and consequently so is the utility purchasing power of the income. A different income is needed to attain the same standard of living, and this is determined from the utility order.

This states the theoretical concept of comparison of income purchasing powers at different prices. However, the method used in practice does not come from this immediately. Instead it proceeds on a basis, not offered by the general comparison concept, that prices have a 'level'. It is taken that a ratio of price 'levels' is expressed by a 'price-index' given by some kind of average of individual price ratios. In order to keep constant purchasing power as prices change, incomes must be adjusted in proportion to the price level. With this scheme there is a homogeneous linear relation between equivalent incomes.

The supposition of a homogeneous linear relation between equivalent incomes at different prices has several equivalent expressions. In terms of utility, it is that the utility relation be a cone, and in terms of demand behaviour it is that any expansion path be a ray through the origin. The last statement shows that when prices are fixed the pattern of consumption, defined by the proportions of quantities demanded, is also fixed and independent of income.

A consequent defect in the use of a price-index is that it permits no recognition of variation in the pattern of consumption at different levels of income. The simplest remedy for this defect is to adopt a more general hypothesis, allowing a general linear relation between equivalent incomes. This corresponds to a more general form of utility and allows expansion paths to be general lines not necessarily passing through the origin. Thus when prices are fixed, the pattern of consumption varies with income. However, the marginal pattern, defined by proportions of quantities added to demand for a small addition of income, is still fixed. This can be recognized as a remaining defect, since in reality not only the pattern but also the marginal pattern significantly varies in movement from low to high incomes, turning away from necessities towards luxuries. But it is a lesser defect, and it preserves the practical simplicity of a linear relation between equivalent incomes.

This non-homogeneous extension of the price-index method can be called the *marginal price-index* method. It produces a general linear relation between equivalent incomes, the slope of which defines the marginal price-index. The relation itself is determined by both the slope and also one point of it, for instance an intercept on one of the axes, or generally any one pair of incomes which it represents as equivalent. Thus essentially two numbers are involved, instead of just one as in the usual homogeneous method.

Though the marginal price-index does not by itself establish a comparison between incomes, it gives a comparison between income increments by giving the ratio of increments which when applied to equivalent incomes will leave them still equivalent. Thus like the homogeneous price-index, it provides a general valuation of money but the significance is specifically more limited. It is not an index of general purchasing power of money in the way that a homogeneous index admits interpretation by virtue of homogeneity. Rather it consolidates the repudiation of that idea, and with that the idea that prices can always be treated as having 'level'.

This paper reviews standard practice based on the usual homogeneous Laspeyres price-index, and then studies a modification employing the same data which shows the corresponding non-homogeneous method.

Other standard price-index formulae beside that of Laspeyres have non-homogeneous counterparts, shown in Afriat (1972). The general concept of a price-index and its extensions are discussed in Afriat (1970, 1972).

2. Price-indices

Consider two periods of consumption, distinguished as the base and current period 0 and 1, where the prices are given by vectors $p_0, p_1 \in \Omega_n$. Since prices are different in the periods, equal incomes in them generally have different purchasing powers. The question is to determine the correspondence between incomes M_0, M_1 in the two periods which have the same purchasing power, as decided on the basis of a scheme of demand data, with the hypothesis involving a structure of wants and efficiency of cost by which the question is made intelligible.

It is assumed there are no free goods so only price vectors $p > 0$ will occur. Also, quantities of commodities are constructed statistically as averages, over a sample individuals in a range of incomes, at least some of which will purchase any given commodity, so only vectors $x > 0$ in the commodity space Ω^n will occur.

In standard practice there is data of average quantities demanded at the prices in the periods, given by vectors $x_0, x_1 \in \Omega^n$. These could be average quantities over the entire population, or over some special class, geographical, occupational or any other type of class which might be in view as the object population.

The scheme of data $(p_0, x_0), (p_1, x_1)$ is then used to construct a price-index, such as the Laspeyres price-index,

$$P_{10} = p_1 x_0 / p_0 x_0. \tag{1}$$

As a price-index its use is to form the relation

$$M_1 = P_{10} M_0, \tag{2}$$

the relation between incomes M_0, M_1 which, at the prices p_0, p_1 in the reference periods, are taken to be equivalent in purchasing power.

It can be seen that nothing is altered in the price-index formula (1), and hence in the relation (2), if x_0 is replaced by $x_0 t$ for any $t > 0$, that is, by any point on the ray to x_0 from origin. Similarly with the variety of other formulae for price-indices which have been offered, none of them is altered when x_0, x_1 are replaced by any points on the rays they determine. Such formulae therefore are functions significantly not of p_0, x_0 and p_1, x_1 but rather of p_0, p_1 and of the rays through x_0, x_1 in the commodity space Ω^n. Having theoretical connection with this, the graph of the relation (2) for equivalent incomes is a ray through the origin in (M_0, M_1) space. The role of the price-index P_{10} is just to determine its slope. However, in theoretical principal this relation could be any monotonic relation. It could for instance be linear, and thus determined by a slope and an intercept, this giving the case to be treated here. That it is homogeneous linear, and thus determined simply by its slope, is a further special case which is in view when a price-index is used.

With the hypothesis that quantities demanded by any individual are a function of the budget constraint, determined by the ratios of prices and the money spent, the locus of demand when prices are fixed and expenditure varies through different levels defines the *expansion locus* associated with the prices. If the expansion

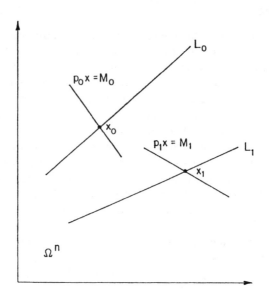

Figure 1 Linear expansion data $(p_0, L_0), (p_1, L_1)$.

locus is given, quantities demanded with a given expenditure are determined as its points of intersection with the corresponding budget constraint.

Thus let L_0 be the expansion locus for prices p_0. Assuming continuous variation, this will be a curve, cutting the budget constraint $p_0 x = M_0$, for any M_0, in a single point. In the particular case required for price-indices, L_0 is the ray through x_0, described by $x = x_0 t$ for $t > 0$. The point where this cuts the budget constraint has parameter $t = t_0$ determined from $p_0 x_0 t_0 = M_0$.

The point x_0 which determines the ray L_0 is obtained statistically as an average of consumption points in a sample S_0 of individuals in the population, in period 0 when they are faced with the prices p_0. In case all points in S_0 lie on a ray, L_0 will coincide with that ray. But otherwise L_0 will be the average of the rays through the points of S_0, in the sense that the point in which it cuts any budget hyperplanes will be the average of the points in which the rays through the points of S_0 cut that hyperplane. It can be considered a statistical estimate of the expansion locus with the data S_0, on the model that it is a ray.

Similarly let L_1 be the expansion ray for period 1 when the prices are p_1, as determined by a point x_1. While the Laspeyres price-index (1) is a function of (p_0, L_0) and p_1, the Paasche price-index, given by

$$P_{10} = p_1 x_1 / p_0 x_1 \qquad (3)$$

is similarly a function of p_0 and (p_1, L_1), and the Fisher index,

$$P_{10} = (p_1 x_0 p_1 x_1 / p_0 x_0 p_0 x_1)^{\frac{1}{2}}, \qquad (4)$$

is a function of (p_0, L_0) and (p_1, L_1), as also other price-index formulae.

3. Marginal price-indices

The use of price-indices for purchasing power measurement corresponds to the idea that the relation between equivalent incomes at different prices is a line through the origin, determined just by its slope. It depends on the hypothesis that expansion loci in the commodity space associated with various prices are all rays, that is lines through the origin.

But the hypothesis that expansion loci are rays permits no recognition that the pattern of consumption varies, in fact drastically, between different levels of income. It postulates that rich and poor alike enjoy all things in the same proportion. That is, their consumptions lie on the same ray, and only the scale differs, in proportion to income. The income just determines the point on the ray. This violates that rich and poor each purchase some things known only slightly to the other. There are purchases of the poor which the rich avoid as inferior goods, while the rich have luxuries which are completely out of reach to those with lesser incomes. Each can put a very different construction on the purchasing power effect of a price change.

A given price change might even have opposite effects on purchasing powers of high and low incomes. This last possibility is completely excluded by the linear expansion hypothesis, let alone the homogeneous linear expansion hypothesis of the price-index method.

A modified method will now be shown which incorporates a recognition of the difference in the pattern of consumption at different levels of income. It still depends on linearity in the expansion loci, but no longer on the homogeneity which requires them to be rays, that is lines through the origin. The method establishes a relation between equivalent incomes having the form

$$M_1 - E_1 = P_{10}(M_0 - E_0). \tag{5}$$

The graph of this is a line in (M_0, M_1)-space determined by any one of its points and its slope. Here E_0, E_1 which can be called a pair of *original incomes* in the relationship are a pair of equivalent incomes, providing one such point, and P_{10} is the slope, defining the *marginal price-index*. While this index is not equal to the ratio M_1/M_0 of equivalent incomes, as with a conventional price-index, it is equal to the ratio $\Delta M_1/\Delta M_0$ of increments to equivalent incomes which preserves their equivalence. As the ratio of equivalence-preserving increments it can be understood to give an index of the rate of inflation between the two periods 0, 1.

In the price-index construction, the sample S_0 of consumption points of the object population, in period 0 when the prices are p_0, is the average of the rays on the sample points. If the sample lies on a ray then this ray coincides with it. Moreover, if the sample lies on a line, then x_0 will be one point of that line, since averages of any subsets of points on the line also will be points of the line. A way of associating S_0 with a line L_0, which if S_0 happens to lie on a line will then coincide with that line, and which will in any case pass through the average point x_0 of S_0, is to construct the averages x_0', x_0'' in upper and lower subsets S_0', S_0''

in S where income is in the two strata above and below the median. The line L_0 which joins these points also passes through $x_0 = (x_0' + x_0'')^{\frac{1}{2}}$, which is average in S_0. With this scheme, the difference in the method to follow over the foregoing price-index method depends on the difference between the line joining x_0', x_0'' and the ray through their mid-point x_0. Should this line go through the origin, and therefore coincide with the ray, there will be no difference in the results. Other ways are readily presented for constructing the expansion line, but this way has claims for its simplicity and adequacy. Instead of joining the average point in the sample to the origin as formerly, the sample is split in two into equally numerous upper and lower income classes, and the averages in these, whose mid-point must then be the complete sample average, are joined in a line. Thus, still a line through the average point in obtained, but its direction has been adjusted in a way which expresses the average movement in pattern in passing from low to high income.

It should be noted that even the hypothesis that expansion loci are general lines makes an important violation of experience. It requires that an extra dollar of income given to a poor individual or a rich one will be spent in exactly the same way, on an extra bundle of goods where the proportions of quantities correspond to the direction of the line, in other words that the *marginal pattern* of consumption be fixed. In reality the marginal pattern changes continually in transition from low to high incomes, moving so as to incline away from inferior goods and more towards luxuries. Expansion loci must be considered in reality to be definitely curved. But there, rather than such reality, it is a special problem of social measurement with practical purposes and limitations that has to be considered. A line has been chosen which passes through the average consumption point and has the direction following the average marginal consumption pattern.

Suppose now that expansion lines L_0, L_1 are thus determined in the base and current periods 0, 1 by joining average consumptions above and below the median income, x_0', x_0'' and x_1', x_1''. The data scheme

$$\begin{pmatrix} p_0 & x_0' & x_0'' \\ p_1 & x_1' & x_1'' \end{pmatrix} \tag{6}$$

is then the initial input for the following procedures. The average consumption points for all incomes are then derived as

$$x_0 = (x_0' + x_0'')^{\frac{1}{2}}, \quad x_1 = (x_1' + x_1'')^{\frac{1}{2}}.$$

The method with price-indices relied just on the scheme

$$\begin{pmatrix} p_0 & x_0 \\ p_1 & x_1 \end{pmatrix}. \tag{7}$$

Comparison can be made between the results obtained by the two methods.

Average incomes above and below the medians are

$$M_0' = p_0 x_0', \qquad M_0'' = p_0 x_0'',$$
$$M_1' = p_1 x_1', \qquad M_1'' = p_1 x_1'',$$

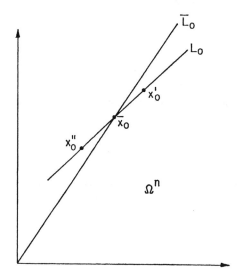

Figure 2 Discrepancy between estimation of expansion locus as a ray and a general line $(p_0, \bar{L}_0)$ and (p_0, L_0), where $\bar{x}_0 = (x'_0 + x''_0)^{\frac{1}{2}}$, x'_0, x''_0 being consumption averages for incomes above and below the median.

and average incomes over all levels are

$$\bar{M}_0 = p_0 x_0 = \tfrac{1}{2}(M'_0 + M''_0),$$
$$\bar{M}_1 = p_1 x_1 = \tfrac{1}{2}(M'_1 + M''_1).$$

These can make reference points for tabulations and comparisons.

4. Problem of purchasing power

In the hypothetical framework by which the idea of purchasing power is made intelligible, there is a structure of wants expressed by a preference order R in the commodity space, where for bundles of goods $x, y \in \Omega^n$, xRy states x is as good as y. This order is to determine

$$\rho(p, x) = \inf[py : yRx] \tag{8}$$

as the lower limit of cost at prices p of attaining a standard of consumption which is as good as that represented by x. Since R is reflexive, the inequality

$$\rho(p, x) \leqslant px \tag{9}$$

holds for all $p \in \Omega_n, x \in \Omega^n$.

If an income M_0 at prices p_0, purchases x_0, then

$$M_1 = \rho(p_1, x_0) \tag{10}$$

is the lower limit of income which has as much purchasing power at prices p_1. By eq. (9),

$$M_1 \leqslant p_1 x_0. \tag{11}$$

The utility order R is undetermined, and this gives rise to the measurement problem. But the available demand data is brought to bear by using it to bring a constraint on R and hence on the relation between M_1 and M_0 obtained from eq. (9).

Thus, if a line L_0 in the commodity space is given as the expansion locus for prices p_0, then R will be considered under the constraint of *compatibility* with this data.

The relation H of compatibility is first defined between any utility order R and demand (p, x). It requires that the order represents the demand as satisfying the efficiency conditions

(H′) $py \leqslant px \;\Rightarrow\; xRy,$

(H″) $yRx \;\Rightarrow\; py \geqslant px.$

Thus H′ asserts that according to R, x is as good as any y which costs no more at the prices p, and H″ that any y as good as x costs at least as much. In the language of cost-benefit analysis, these are conditions which require the demand to be *cost-effective*, that is the benefit be the greatest possible with the cost, and *cost-efficient*, that is cost be the smallest possible with the benefit, benefit here being the level of utility of the quantities demanded.

Compatibility with a set of demands is simultaneous compatibility with each of them. Thus compatibility of R with the expansion data (p_0, L_0) means compatibility with demands (p_0, x_0) for all $x_0 \in L_0$. Similarly R could be required to be compatible with a pair of expansions $(p_0, L_0), (p_1, L_1)$, or any other scheme of demand data D.

The problem of purchasing power measurement can be formulated as follows:

Given a set of demands D and prices p_0, p_1 to determine the correspondence between incomes M_0, M_1 for which

$$M_1 = \inf[p_1 x : xRx_0]$$

for some R and x_0 such that R is compatible with D and (p_0, x_0) and $p_0 x_0 = M_0$.

This problem is to be considered for when D consists in a linear expansion (p_0, L_0). In Afriat (1967, 1972) it is considered when D is a pair of linear expansions $(p_0, L_0), (p_1, L_1)$. Elsewhere [Afriat (1956, 1967, 1969, 1972)] there is treatment of cases with other forms for D.

5. Method of limits

First a method will be examined which, as with current practice with the Laspeyres index, involves only price data in the current period. In the base period there is price data together with an expansion line. Thus the date scheme is

$$\begin{pmatrix} p_0 & x_0' & x_0'' \\ p_1 & . & . \end{pmatrix}. \tag{12}$$

In the usual method with the Laspeyres index there is the scheme

$$\begin{pmatrix} p_0 & x_0 \\ p_1 & . \end{pmatrix} \tag{13}$$

to determine

$$P_{10} = p_1 x_0 / p_0 x_0, \tag{14}$$

and then the income

$$M_1 = P_{10} M_0, \tag{15}$$

which is to be current equivalent of the base income M_0. The principal in this is that a base income M_0 will purchase quantities $x_0 t_0$ on the ray through x_0, where $p_0 x_0 t_0 = M_0$, so $t_0 = M_0 / p_0 x_0$. Then the current cost of the same quantities determines a current income which is certainly enough to maintain the same standard of living. This cost is

$$M_1 = p_1 x_0 t_0,$$
$$= p_1 x_0 M_0 / p_0 x_0, \tag{16}$$

that is (15), where P_{10} is given by (14).

What is established is, more explicitly, that

$$M_1 \leqslant P_{10} M_0, \tag{17}$$

for any current M_1 which can be considered equivalent to any given base M_0, so by taking equality there is assurance that the M_1 obtained is at least equivalent in respect to any R comparable with the data. The assurance is conditional on the data which specifically involves the expansion locus L_0 as a ray, of which x_0 is one of the points. When L_0 is not established as a ray the assurance is not valid. Now the matter is to be examined again for when L_0 is permitted to be a general line.

Let a_0 be a point and d_0 a displacement on L_0, so any point on L_0 is

$$x_0 = a_0 + d_0 t_0, \tag{18}$$

for some value of t_0. The budget constraint $p_0 x = M_0$ for any income M_0 cuts L_0 in a point with parameter t_0 determined from

$$p_0(a_0 + d_0 t_0) = M_0. \tag{19}$$

Since this point is to be unique, necessarily $p_0 d_0 \neq 0$. It can be taken that

$$p_0 d_0 > 0, \tag{20}$$

for otherwise d_0 can be replaced by $-d_0$.

From (19)

$$t_0 = (M_0 - p_0 a_0)/p_0 d_0. \tag{21}$$

Any R is compatible with the data (p_0, L_0) if it is compatible with every demand (p_0, x_0) with $x_0 \in L_0$. According to the formulation in section 3, for any M_0 it is required to compute

$$M_1 = \inf[p_1 x : x R x_0'] \tag{22}$$

for x_0' such that $p_0 x_0' = M_0$, and R compatible with (p_0, L_0) and (p_0, x_0'). But if R is compatible with (p_0, L_0), and also (p_0, x_0') where $p_0 x_0 = M_0$, then also it is compatible with the $x_0 \in L_0$ for which (p_0, x_0). Then $x_0' R x_0$ and $x_0 R x_0'$, so that $R x_0' = R x_0$, and hence

$$M_1 = \inf[p x_1 : x R x_0]. \tag{23}$$

Then, by reflexivity of R,

$$M_1 \leqslant p_1 x_0 \tag{24}$$

where

$$p_0 x_0 = M_0 \quad \text{and} \quad x_0 \in L_0, \tag{25}$$

in which case x_0 is given by (18) with (21). Accordingly

$$p_1 x_0 = p_1 a_0 + (p_1 d_0/p_0 d_0)(M_0 - p_0 a_0), \tag{26}$$

so (24) becomes

$$M_1 - p_1 a_0 \leqslant (p_1 d_0/p_0 d_0)(M_0 - p_0 a_0) \tag{27}$$

Again, since R is compatible with (p_0, x_0), and $p_0 x_0 = M_0$,

$$x R x_0 \quad \Rightarrow \quad p_0 x \geqslant M_0, \tag{28}$$

so that

$$\inf[p_1 x : x R x_0] \geqslant \min[p_1 x : p_0 x \geqslant M_0]$$
$$= M_0 \min[p_1 x : p_0 x \geqslant 1], \tag{29}$$

the restriction $x \geqslant 0$ being understood. Then by linear programming duality

$$\min[p_1 x : p_0 x \geqslant 1] = \max[u : u p_0 \leqslant p_1]$$
$$= \min[p_{1i}/p_{0i} : p_{0i} > 0]. \tag{30}$$

It follows that

$$M_1 \geqslant M_0 \min[p_{1i}/p_{0i} : p_{0i} > 0]. \tag{31}$$

Thus, with (27) and (31), for any M_0, upper and lower bounds have been established for the M_1 which are determined as equivalent in purchasing power, in

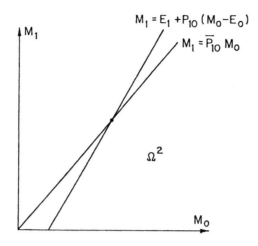

Figure 3 Corresponding discrepancy in relations for equivalent incomes: relation with price-index $\bar{P}_0 = p_1\bar{x}_0/p_0\bar{x}_0$, and relation with marginal price-index $P_{10} = p_1(x_0'' - y_0')/p_0(x_0'' - x_0')$ and original incomes $E_0 = p_0x_0'$, $E_1 = p_1x_0'[x_0 = (x_0', +x_0'')^{\frac{1}{2}}]$.

respect to any R which is compatible with (p_0, L_0). To show these bounds cannot be improved, so moreover they are limits, it will be shown they can be attained, so in fact they are a maximum and a minimum.

Consider the utility function

$$\phi(x) = \max[t : a_0 + d_0t \leqslant x]. \tag{32}$$

With (18) and (20), evidently

$$\phi(x_0) = t_0, \tag{33}$$

for all points x_0 of L_0. It will be shown that

$$\phi(x) \leqslant \phi(x) = p_0x_0 \leqslant p_0x, \tag{34}$$

and since ϕ is continuous this will establish with compatibility relation H with (p_0, L_0).

With (32) and (33), (34) is equivalent to

$$t_0 t, \leqslant a_0 + d_0t \leqslant x = p_0x_0 \leqslant p_0x. \tag{35}$$

But the left side here is equivalent to

$$x_0 + d_0(t - t_0) \leqslant x, \quad t - t_0 \geqslant 0, \tag{36}$$

and this, with $p_0 \geqslant 0$, implies

$$p_0x_0 + p_0d_0(t - t_0) \leqslant p_0x, \quad t - t_0 \geqslant 0, \tag{37}$$

which, with (20) implies $p_0x_0 \leqslant p_0x$, as required.

Now, with $p_1 \geqslant 0$,

$$\min[p_1 x : \phi(x_0) \leqslant \phi(x)] = \min[p_1 x : t_0 \leqslant t, a_0 + d_0 t \leqslant x]$$
$$= \min[p_1(a_0 + d_0 t) : t_0 \leqslant t]$$
$$= p_1(a_0 + d_0 t_0)$$
$$= p_1 x_0, \tag{38}$$

provided

$$p_1 d_0 \geqslant 0. \tag{39}$$

An interpretation of this proviso will appear later. But here it seen to assure that M_1 can attain the considered upper bound.

To see that the lower bound is attained, consider the utility function

$$\phi(x) = p_0 x. \tag{40}$$

Immediately, it is compatible with (p_0, L_0).

Also it yields the value

$$M_1 = \min[p_1 x : \phi(x) \geqslant \phi(x_0)]$$
$$= \min[p_1 x : p_0 x \geqslant M_0], \tag{41}$$

identical with the considered lower bound.

But for one feature, the following has been proved.

Theorem   *Let (p_0, L_0) be a linear expansion, L_0 being a line determined by a point a_0 and displacement d_0, with*

$$p_0 d_0 > 0, \tag{i}$$

and let p_1 be such that

$$p_1 d_0 > 0. \tag{ii}$$

Then for all M_0, and the $x_0 \in L_0$ such that $p_0 x_0 = M_0$, and for all M_1, a necessary and sufficient condition that

$$M_1 = \inf[p_1 x : x R x_0], \tag{iii}$$

for some order R compatible with (p_0, L_0) is that

$$\check{M}_1 \leqslant M_1 \leqslant \hat{M}_1, \tag{iv}$$

where

$$\check{M}_1 = M_0 \min[p_{1i}/p_{0i} : p_{0i} > 0], \tag{v}$$
$$\hat{M}_1 = p_1 a_0 + (p_1 d_0/p_0 d_0)(M_0 - p_0 a_0). \tag{vi}$$

Since, for all M_0, $\hat{M}_1$ and $\check{M}_1$ have been established as maximum and minimum of such M_1, for the proof to be complete it remains to see that the set of such M_1 is connected, or is an interval exhausting all values between the maximum and minimum.

A way of doing this, which in fact gives an alternative proof of the theorem, is as follows:

For any M_0 and θ define

$$M_1^\theta = \check{M}_1\theta + \hat{M}_1(1 - \theta),\tag{42}$$

where $\check{M}_1$, $\hat{M}_1$ are given by (v) and (vi). Provided $p_1 d_0 > 0$, and $0 < \theta < 1$, M_1^θ is an increasing function of M_0, and, assuming $\check{M}_1 < \hat{M}_1$, since otherwise there is nothing to prove, moreover $\check{M}_1 < M_1^\theta < \hat{M}_1$. This assures that the utility function

$$\phi(x) = \max[M_0 : p_0 x \geqslant M_0, \ p_1 x \geqslant M_1^\theta]\tag{43}$$

is non-decreasing quasiconcave. Also

$$x_0 \in L_0, \quad p_0 x_0 = M_0 \ \Rightarrow \ \phi(x_0) = M_0,\tag{44}$$

and since

$$p_1 x_0 = \hat{M}_1 > M_1^\theta,\tag{45}$$

it appears that

$$\phi(x) = \max[M_0 : p_0 x \geqslant M_0]$$
$$= p_0 x,\tag{46}$$

for x near x_0. But immediately, the utility function $p_0 x$ is compatible with (p_0, L_0). Since $\phi(x)$ is continuous and quasiconcave, this local compatibility assures the same condition globally. Also

$$\min[p_1 x : \phi(x) \geqslant \phi(x_0)] = \min[p_1 x : \phi(x) \geqslant M_0]$$
$$= \min[p_1 x : p_0 x \geqslant M_0, p_1 x \geqslant M_1^\theta]$$
$$= M_1^\theta,\tag{47}$$

since $p_0 x = M_0, p_1 x = M_1^\theta$ for some x, because, subject to $p_0 x = M_0, p_1 x$ takes all values between $\check{M}_1$ and $\hat{M}_1$, and M_1^θ is such a value. But with $0 < \theta < 1$ M_1^θ is any such value, and this proves the theorem.

Corollary   *Let (p_0, L_0) be a homogeneous linear expansion, L_0 being a ray determined by a point a_0, and let p_1 be arbitrary. Then for all M_0, and the $x_0 \in L_0$ such that $p_0 x_0 = M_0$, and for all M_1, a necessary and sufficient condition that*

$$M_1 = \inf[p_1 x : x R x_0],\tag{i}$$

for some order R compatible with (p_0, L_0), *is that*

$$\check{M}_1 \leqq M_1 \leqq \hat{M}_1, \tag{ii}$$

where

$$\check{M}_1 = M_0 \min[p_{1i}/p_{0i} : p_{0i} > 0], \tag{iii}$$

$$\hat{M}_1 = M_0 p_1 a_0 / p_0 a_0. \tag{iv}$$

It is of course understood in the theorem that L_0 is the truncation of a line in the commodity space Ω^n, and p_0, p_1 are vectors in the price space Ω_n and M_0, M_1 belong to the non-negative numbers Ω.

Now in the corollary, with L_0 a ray, that is a line from the origin, a_0 simultaneously represents both a point and a displacement on L_0. Thus with L_0 an interior ray of Ω^n, it is taken that $a_0 > 0$, and $d_0 = a_0$, so automatically (i) and (ii) are satisfied. Then the formula (vi) becomes

$$\hat{M}_1 = p_0 a_0 + (p_1 a_0 / p_0 a_0)(M_0 - p_0 a_0)$$
$$= M_0 p_1 a_0 / p_0 a_0, \tag{48}$$

and this proves the corollary. It is seen that the coefficient of M_0 here is simply the Laspeyres price-index. It is determined by the pattern of consumption, represented by a_0 or any point on the ray L_0, and is hypothetically fixed for all levels of incomes. In that case the pattern and the marginal pattern coincide. But with the general linear expansion hypothesis of the theorem, though the pattern varies, the marginal pattern is fixed, for all levels of income, and is represented by the direction of any displacement d_0. It is seen that the coefficient of M_0 in (vi) is determined by the marginal pattern, by a similar formula, so it might be called the *Laspeyres marginal price-index*. It appears as the non-homogeneous counterpart of the homogeneous linear concept presented by the familiar Laspeyres price-index which, to express its distinction and connection with this, can be identified as the *Laspeyres average price-index*.

The condition on d_0, which appears in the hypothesis of the theorem, and becomes vacuous in the case of the corollary, now requires an interpretation.

There is no question of consistency for the demand date presented by (p_0, L_0), because in any case the utility function $\phi(x) = p_0 x$ is compatible with it. But given (p_0, L_0) and a p_1, it can be asked if there exists a line L_1 such that the data formed by $(p_0, L_0), (p_1, L_1)$ is consistent. This condition, without regard for the usual confinement to the parts of the lines lying within the commodity space, can be called the *virtual consistency* of the scheme formed by (p_0, L_0) with p_1. The considered condition on d_0 is necessary and sufficient. For if it holds take $L_1 = L_0$, and then

$$\phi(x) = \max[t : p_0 x \geqslant p_0 a_0 + p_0 d_0 t, \ p_1 x \geqslant p_1 a_0 + p_1 d_0 t] \tag{49}$$

is a compatible utility function. This shows the condition is sufficient. Also it is necessary. For let $(p_0, L_0), (p_1, L_1)$ be consistent. The condition on d_0 holds in any case if $p_0 \parallel p_1$. Therefore let $p_0 \nparallel p_1$, and let y_0 be any point of L_0, x_1 any point such that

$$p_0 y_0 = p_0 x_1, \quad p_1 y_0 \neq p_1 x_1, \tag{50}$$

and z_0 any point of L_0 such that

$$p_1 x_1 = p_1 z_0, \tag{51}$$

so $y_0 \neq z_0$. Consider the demands

$$(p_0, y_0), \quad (p_0, z_0), \quad (p_1, x_1). \tag{52}$$

Given (50) and (51), for their consistency it is necessary that

$$p_1 y_0 \geqslant p_1 x_1, \quad p_0 y_0 \geqslant p_0 z_0. \tag{53}$$

But with (50) and (51) this is equivalent to

$$p_1(y_0 - z_0) \geqslant 0, \quad p_0(y_0 - z_0) \geqslant 0. \tag{54}$$

But

$$y_0 - z_0 = d_0 t, \tag{55}$$

for some $t \neq 0$, since $y_0 \neq z_0$. Then (20) with (54) and (55) show that $t > 0$, and then that (39) holds, as required.

It can be noticed that though the relationship (vi) in the theorem, that is

$$\hat{M}_1 = p_1 a_0 + (p_1 d_0 / p_1 d_1)(M_0 - p_0 a_0), \tag{56}$$

is constructed with reference to a particular point a_0 and displacement d_0 on the line L_0, it is invariant when these are replaced by any other point $a_0' = a_0 + d_0 t$ and displacement $d_0' = d_0 s$ ($s \neq 0$) on that line. This is known in advance from the principle by which the relationship was constructed, but also it can be directly verified algebraically. It is thus a well defined relationship determined entirely from the scheme $(p_0, L_0), p_1$.

Assuming $d_0 \geqslant 0$, which is the case of no inferior goods, when the line L_0 is semi-infinite in Ω_n, a further matter to be noticed is that the slope of the $\hat{M}_1, M_0$-line given by the marginal price-index

$$\hat{P}_{10} = p_1 d_0 / p_0 d_0, \tag{57}$$

always exceeds the slope of the $\check{M}_1, M_0$-line given by

$$\check{P}_{10}^* = \min[p_{1i} / P_{0i} : P_{0i} > 0]. \tag{58}$$

For

$$\hat{P}_{10} = \sum_i p_{1i} d_{0i} / p_0 d_0 \tag{59}$$

$$= \sum_i (p_{1i} / p_{0i})(p_{0i} d_{0i} / p_0 d_0)$$

$$= \sum_i (p_{1i} / p_{0i}) \mu_{0i},$$

where

$$\mu_{0i} = p_{0i}d_{0i}/p_0d_0, \tag{60}$$

and

$$p_0d_0 = \sum p_{0i}d_{0i}, \tag{61}$$

so that the μ_{0i}, which are the *marginal expenditure shares*, the shares in which any additional income is distributed over the commodities, are such that

$$\mu_{0i} \geqslant 0, \quad \sum_i \mu_{0i} = 1. \tag{62}$$

Thus $\hat{P}_{10}$ is the arithmetic mean of the price ratios p_{1i}/p_{0i} with weights μ_{0i}, and therefore it must be at least the minimum of these ratios, which is $\check{P}^*_{10}$.

This relation between the slopes is necessary for the relation

$$\check{M}_1 \leqslant \hat{M}_1 \tag{63}$$

to hold for all M_0, especially for large M_0. But evidently without a lower restriction on M_0 the lines might still cross, and give

$$\check{M}_1 > \hat{M}_1. \tag{64}$$

On this matter it needs to be recognized that a confinement to the commodity space is implicitly understood in all discussions, to the effect that the lowest value of M_0 which is considered is

$$M_0^* = p_0x_0^*, \tag{65}$$

where

$$x_0^* = a_0 + d_0t_0^* \tag{66}$$

and

$$t_0^* = \min[t_0 : x_0 + d_0t_0 \geqslant 0], \tag{67}$$

so x_0^* is the point where the line L_0 cuts the boundary of the commodity space Ω^n, and M_0^* the corresponding income. It is guaranteed that $\check{M}_1 \leqslant \hat{M}_1$ holds for $M_0 = M_0^*$ and, because of the relationship of the slopes, also for all larger M_0. That there is this guarantee moreover for any $M_0 = p_0x_0$ with $x_0 \in L_0$, and $x_0 \in \Omega^n$, is seen immediately from the relation

$$p_0x_0 \geqslant \min[p_1x : p_0x \geqslant M_0, \quad x \geqslant 0] = \check{P}^*_{10}M_0, \tag{68}$$

which holds for all x_0 such that $p_0x_0 = M_0$ and $x_0 \geqslant 0$.

Thus, for all $M_0 \geqslant M_0^*$, the formulae for $\hat{M}_1, \check{M}_1$ which are to serve as upper and lower limits always have the relation $\check{M}_1 \leqslant \hat{M}_1$ required for consistency with this role. This is in definite contrast to 'The Index Number Theorem' of traditional theory, which requires the Laspeyres and Paasche price-indices to be upper and

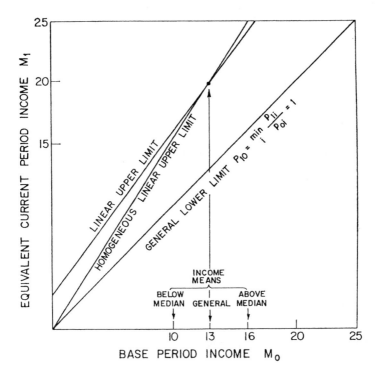

Figure 4

lower bounds of something, and thus one is not to exceed the other, while in fact there is no general necessity that this should be the case.

This discussion has been under assumption of the case $d_0 \geqslant 0$, which covers the corollary as a further special case. In the contrary case the part of L_0 in Ω^n is a bounded segment, say with extremities x_0', x_0'' on the boundary of Ω^n. The range of M_0 for which the theorem is valid is then between the limits

$$M_0' = p_0 x_0', \quad M_0'' = p_0 x_0''. \tag{69}$$

The slopes of the two lines in (M_0, M_1)-space in the theorem then have no generally decided relation. Nevertheless for M_0 between these limits the $\hat{M}_1$-line lies above the $\check{M}_1$-line,

$$M_0 \in \langle M_0', M_0'' \rangle \quad \Rightarrow \quad \check{M}_1 \leqslant \hat{M}_1. \tag{70}$$

6. Simple example

Consider a market of two commodities, and in the base and current periods 0, 1 let the prices be

$$p_0 = (2, 1), \quad p_1 = (2, 2).$$

Suppose a survey in the base period has produced averages of quantities for incomes above and below the median given by

$$a'_0 = \binom{4}{8}, \quad a''_0 = \binom{2}{6},$$

so the averages for all incomes are

$$\bar{a}_0 = \binom{3}{7}.$$

Thus the averages of incomes above and below the median are

$$M'_0 = 16, \quad M''_0 = 10,$$

and the overall average is

$$\bar{M}_0 = 13.$$

Also

$$d_0 = a'_0 - a''_0$$

$$= \binom{2}{2}.$$

Price-index method would determine

$$\bar{P}_{10} = p_1 \bar{a}_0 / p_0 \bar{a}_0$$

$$= 20/13,$$

and also

$$P^*_{10} = \min_i [p_{1i}/p_{0i}]$$

$$= \min [2/2, 2/1]$$

$$= 1,$$

to give the upper and lower limits

$$M_1 = \bar{P}_{10} M_0, \quad M_1 = P^*_{10} M_0,$$

for current income M_1 to be considered equivalent to any base income M_0.

The corresponding non-homogeneous method would determine instead

$$P_{10} = p_1 d_0 / p_0 d_0$$

$$= 4/3,$$

and

$$E_1 = p_1 \bar{a}_0 = 20,$$

$$E_0 = p_0 \bar{a}_0 = 13,$$

to give the upper limit

$$M_1 = E_1 + \hat{P}_{10}(M_0 - E_0)$$
$$= 20 + (4/3)(M_0 - 13)$$
$$= 8/3 + (4/3)\, M_0,$$

and lower limit

$$M_1 = P_{10}^* M_0$$
$$= M_0.$$

The coincidence of the two upper limits is where

$$20/13 M_0 = 8/3 + (4/3)\, M_0,$$

that is

$$M_0 = 13, \quad M_1 = 20.$$

The two methods offer the same lower limit relation. For the upper limit relation, they agree just on the equivalent of the average income $M_0 = 13 = \bar{M}_0$. But, relative to what the non-homogeneous method with the Laspeyres index deprives holders of incomes below the average in the base period on what constitutes an equivalent excess to incomes above the average. This indicates the nature of the relative bias between the two methods: *The 'homogenization' of conventional practice with price-indices understates the effect of inflation for low incomes, and overstates it for high incomes.*

7. Bias between rich and poor

The foregoing example illustrated a possible bias in the use of a price-index, whereby in compensation for a price change the rich receive an excess and the poor are deprived. Though it holds in the example, this particular bias is not inevitable, and the conditition which decides it needs to be examined.

With a_0', a_0'' the average consumptions above and below the median income there is determined the line L_0 joining them and also the ray $\bar{L}_0$ through the general average

$$a_0 = (a_0' + a_0'')^{\frac{1}{2}}. \tag{71}$$

A displacement on L_0 is given by

$$d_0 = (a_0' - a_0''). \tag{72}$$

The homogeneous and non-homogeneous methods with this data give upper limits

$$M_1 = (p_1 a_0/p_0 a_0) M_0, \tag{73}$$
$$= p_1 a_0 + (p_1 d_0/p_0 d_0)(M_0 - p_0 a_0), \tag{74}$$

for current equivalent to any base income M_0. Hence with base income at the average $M_0 = p_0a_0$, these two limits agree, and give $M_1 = p_1a_0$. Their relative bias for incomes above and below the average now depends on the sign of the intercept

$$p_1a_0 - (p_1d_0/p_0d_0)\, p_0a_0 \tag{75}$$

corresponding to $M_0 = 0$, or equivalently on the relation of the slopes

$$p_1a_0/p_0a_0, \quad p_1d_0/p_0d_0. \tag{76}$$

For the intercept to be non-negative, or for the homogeneous relation to have higher slope, in view of (71) and (72), the condition is

$$p_1a_0''\, p_0a_0' \leqslant p_1a_0'\, p_0a_0''. \tag{77}$$

In this case, relative to the non-homogeneous method, the homogeneous method gives an excess for incomes above the average and a defect for those below.

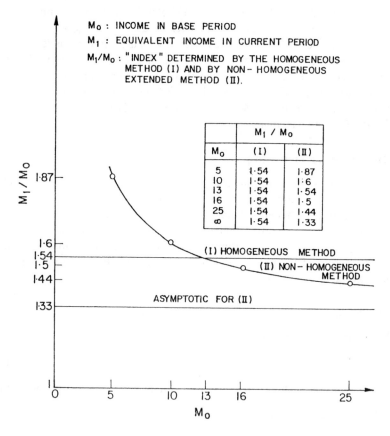

Figure 5

Evidently if a_0', a_0'' lie on the same ray, equality holds in (77), so the two methods perfectly agree. In fact, in this case L_0 is itself a ray and coincides with $\bar{L}_0$, so there is no distinction at all between the methods. Also if p_0, p_1 lie on the same ray, that is all prices change proportionately, then again equality holds in (77). In this case, though there is distinction between the methods, they agree in their results. Generally it might seem the bias favouring rich or poor could hold either way. It depends on the preponderance of price increase being more heavily on goods purchased by the poor or the rich, on necessities or luxuries.

The Laspeyres price-index

$$p_1 x_0 / p_0 x_0$$

determined for every $x_0 \in L_0$, is invariant if L_0 happens to be a ray, but otherwise it varies monotonically. Let $P_{10}(M_0)$ denote its value for the $x_0 \in L_0$ with $p_0 x_0 = M_0$. Evidently,

$$P_{10}(M_0) \rightarrow p_1 d_0 / p_0 d_0 \quad (M_0 \rightarrow \infty),$$

that is, it converges monotonically to the marginal price-index, as incomes M_0 increases indefinitely. The question is whether it increases or decreases. This is decided by the Laspeyres average and marginal price-indices in (76). If the average index exceeds the marginal index, it can be taken that luxuries, or goods which are bought more intensively at higher levels of incomes, receive a relatively lighter burden of price increase than the goods more necessary for lower income holders.

References

Afriat, S.N., 1956, Theory of economic index numbers, mimeo (Department of Applied Economics, Cambridge University).

Afriat, S.N., 1963, An identity concerning the relation between the Paasche and Laspeyres indices, Metroeconomica 15, 38–46.

Afriat, S.N., 1967, The cost of living index, in: M. Shubik, ed., Studies in mathematical economics in honor of Oskar Morgenstern (Princeton University Press, Princeton, N.J.) ch. 23.

Afriat, S.N., 1969, The method of limits in the theory of index numbers, Metroeconomica 21, 141–165.

Afriat, S.N., 1970, The concept of a price index and its extension, presented at the 2nd World Congress of the Econometric Society (Cambridge, England).

Afriat, S.N., 1972, The theory of international comparisons of real income and prices, in: D.J. Daly, ed., International comparisons of prices and output, Studies in income and wealth, vol. 37, Proceedings of the Conference at York University, Toronto, 1970 (National Bureau of Economic Research, New York) 13–84.

Afriat, S.N., 1973, A general defect with price indices and a simple remedy, Lecture delivered at the University of Ottawa, 1 May 1973, mimeo.

Allen, R.G.D., 1949, The economic theory of index numbers, Economica, New Series SVI, 63, 197–203.

Buschequennce, A., 1925, Sur une classe des hypersurfaces, A propos de l'index ideal de M. Irv. Fisher, Recueil Mathematique (Moscow) XXXII, 4.

Chase, A.E., 1960, Concepts and uses of price indices, Paper presented at the American Statistical Association Meeting.

Fisher, I., 1911, The purchasing power of money (Macmillan, New York).

Fisher, I., 1922, The making of index numbers (Houghton Mifflin, Boston).

Frisch, R., 1936, Annual survey of general economic theory: The problem of index numbers, Econometrica 4, 1–39.

Klein, L.R. and H., Rubin, 1947, A constant utility index of the cost of living, Review of Economic Studies 15, 84–87.

Lerner, A.P., 1935, A note on the theory of price index numbers, Review of Economic Studies 50–56.

Paasche, H., 1874, Über die Preisentwicklung der letzten Jahre, nach den Hamburger Börsennotierungen, Jahrbücher für Nationaloekonomie und Statistik (Jena) XXIII, 168–178.

Report of the President's Committee on the Cost of Living, 1945 (Office of Economic Stabilization, Washington, D.C.).

Report of the Price Statistics Review Committee, 1961, Government price statistics, Hearings, Subcommittee on Economic Statistics of the Joint Economic Committee, 87th Congress, 1st session, Part I, 5–99.

Wald, A., 1939, A new formula for the index of the cost of living, Econometrica 7, 319–335.

Wald, A., 1949, The approximate determination of indifference surfaces by means of Engel Curves, Econometrica 8, 144–175.

6
On the constructability of consistent price indices between several periods simultaneously

In *Essays in Theory and Measurement of Demand: in honour of Sir Richard Stone*, edited by Angus Deaton. Cambridge University Press, 1981, 133–61.

On the constructability of consistent price indices between several periods simultaneously

Introduction

A price index refers to a pair of consumption periods, and price-index formulae usually involve demand data from the reference periods alone. When there are many periods, a price index can be determined from any one period to any other, in each case using the data from just those two periods. But then consistency questions arise for the set of price indices so obtained. Especially, they must have the consistency that would follow from their being ratios of 'price levels'. The well-known tests of Irving Fisher have their origin in such questions. When these tests are regarded as giving identities to be satisfied by a standard formula and are taken in combination, it is impossible to satisfy them. Such impossibility remains even with partial combinations. Eichhorn and Voeller (1976) have given a full account of the inconsistencies between Fisher's tests. Reference is made there for their results and for the history of the matter.

Fisher recognizes the consistency question also in his idea of the 'rectification of pair comparisons'. In this the price indices are all calculated, as usual, separately and regardless of any consistency they should have together, and then they are all adjusted in some manner so that they can form a consistent set. For instance, by 'crossing' a formula with its 'antithesis' you got one that satisfied the 'reversal' test. Here he takes one of the tests separately as if any one could mean anything on its own, and contrives a formula to satisfy it. This is how he arrived at his 'ideal' index. It is 'ideal' because it satisfies the 'reversal' test but not so when those other tests are brought in. The search for a really ideal index seemed a hopeless task.

In any case these tests are just negative criteria for index-number-making, showing how a formula can be rejected and telling nothing of how one should be arrived at. Something is to be measured and it is not yet considered what, but whatever it is it must fit a certain mould. Here is not measurement but a ritual with form. In the background thought, what is to be measured is the price level, though prices are many so no one quite knows what that means, and a price index is a ratio of price levels. Therefore the set m^2 price indices P_{rs} $(r, s = 1, \ldots, m)$ between

m periods $1, \ldots, m$ must at least have the consistency required by their being ratios $P_{rs} = P_s/P_r$ of m 'price levels' P_r $(r = 1, \ldots, m)$. Therefore $P_{rr} = 1$, $P_{rs} = P_{sr}^{-1}$, $P_{rs} P_{st} = P_{rt}$ and so forth. There are other parts to Fisher's tests and here we have the part that touches just the ratio aspect.

In a seemingly more coherent approach, utility makes the base for what is being measured. There would be no problem there at all if only the utility function or order to be used could be known. But it is not known and therefore it is dealt with hypothetically. Its existence is entertained and inferences are made from that position. With utility in the picture the natural object of measurement is the 'cost of living', and at first we know nothing of the price-level or of a price-index. Giving intelligibility to the price index in the utility framework involves imposing a special restriction on utility.

Let M_0 be any income in a period 0 when the prices are given by a vector p_0. Hypothetically, the bundle of goods x_0 consumed with this income has the highest utility among all those which might have been consumed instead. Then it is asked what income M_1 in a period 1 when the prices are p_1 provides the standard of living, or utility, attained with the income M_0 in period 0. With p_0, p_1 fixed and the utility order given, M_1 is determined as a function $M_1 = F_{10}(M_0)$ of M_0, where the function F_{10} depends on the prices p_0, p_1 and the utility order. Without making any forbidding extra assumptions it can be allowed that this is a continuous increasing function, and that is all. However, turning to practice with price-indices, we find that to offer a relationship between M_0 and M_1 is the typical use given to a price index. The relationship in this case has the form $M_1 = P_{10} M_0$, P_{10} being the price index. In other words, using a price-index corresponds to the idea that there is a homogeneous linear relation between M_0, M_1 or that the relation is a line through the origin, the price-index being the slope.

To give the function F_{10}, just this form has implications about the utility from which it is derived. That utility must have a conical structure that is a counterpart of linear homogeneity of that function: if any commodity bundle x has at least the utility of another y then the same holds when x and y are replaced by their multiples xt and yt by any positive number t. To talk about a price-index and at the same time about utility, this assumption about the utility must be made outright.

If a conical utility is given, relative to it a price-index P_{10} can be computed for any prices p_0, p_1. Then, as explained further in section 11, it has the form $P_{10} = P_1/P_0$ where $P_0 = \theta(p_0)$, $P_1 = \theta(p_1)$ are the values of a concave conical function θ depending on prices alone. Price indices so computed for many periods automatically satisfy various tests of Fisher. The issue about those tests therefore becomes empty in this context, and pair-comparisons so obtained need no 'rectification'. But a remaining issue come from the circumstance that a utility usually is not given. Should one be proposed arbitrarily as a basis for constructing price indices, there can be no objection to it merely on the basis of the tests, at least with those that concern the ratio-aspect of price indices.

With each price-index formula P_{10} of the very many he surveyed, Fisher associated a quantity-index formula X_{10} in such a way that the product is the ratio of consumption expenditures $M_0 = p_0 x_0$, $M_1 = p_1 x_1$ in the two periods. For instance with the Laspeyres price index $P_{10} = p_1 x_0 / p_0 x_0$, the corresponding quantity-index is $X_{10} = p_1 x_1 / p_1 x_0$, and then

$$P_{10} X_{10} = (p_1 x_0 / p_0 x_0)(p_1 x_1 / p_1 x_0) = p_1 x_1 / p_0 x_0 = M_1 / M_0.$$

As a possible sense to this scheme, it is as if, beside the price-index being a ratio $P_{10} = P_1 / P_0$ of price-levels, also the quantity-index is a ratio $X_{10} = X_1 / X_0$ of quantity levels, and price-level multiplied with quantity level is the same as price-vector multiplied with quantity-vector, that is

$$P_0 X_0 = p_0 x_0 = M_0, \qquad P_1 X_1 = p_1 x_1 = M_1$$

to give

$$P_{10} X_{10} = (P_1 / P_0)(X_1 / X_0) = (P_1 X_1) / (P_0 X_0) = M_1 / M_0.$$

Here there is the simple result that all prices are effectively summarized by a single number and all quantities by a single quantity number, and instead of doing accounts by dealing with each price and quantity separately, and also with their product that gives the cost of the quantity at the price, the entire account can be carried on just as well in terms of these two summary price and quantity numbers, or levels, whose product is, miraculously, the cost of that quantity level at that price level. Though there are many goods and so-many prices and quantities, still it is just as if there was effectively just one good with a price and obtainable in any quantity at a cost which is simply, as with a simple goods, the product of price times quantity. Any mystery about the meaning of a price index vanishes, because it becomes simply a price. Were this scheme valid we could ask for so much utility, enquire the price and pay the right amount by the usual multiplication. When applied to income M_0 in period 0 when the price level is P_0, the level of utility is purchases is $X_0 = M_0 / P_0$. Then the income that purchases the same level of utility in period 1 when the price level is P_1 is given by $M_1 = P_1 X_0$. Hence, by division, $M_1 / M_0 = P_1 / P_0 = P_{10}$, giving the relation $M_1 = P_{10} M_0$ as usual.

Whether or not this scheme has serious plausibilities, it is implicit whenever a price index based on utility is in view. However, though such a scheme has here been imputed as belonging to Fisher's system, or conjured up as though that seems to belong to it or at least gives it an intelligibility, it cannot be considered to have clear presence there. For Fisher's system does not have a basis in utility and this scheme does. While this circumstance is not evidence of a union it still might not seem to force a separation. However, a symptom of a decided separation is that, even when many periods are involved, Fisher still followed standard custom in regarding an index formula as one involving the demand data just from its pair of reference periods, and really his system is about such formulae. Then he worried about the incoherence of the set of price indices for many periods so obtained. The utility formulation cares nothing about the form of the formula. When many periods are involved and all the price indices between them are to be calculated, the calculation of one and all should involve the data for all periods simultaneously. In the utility approach immediate thought is not of the demand data and of formulae in these at all, but rather it is of the utility order which gives the basis of the calculations, and necessarily gives coherent results. Instead, Fisher forces incoherence by rigidly following the standard idea of what constitutes an index formula. The main issue with the utility approach is about the utility function or order. When that utility is settled all that remains to be dealt with is a well-defined objective of calculation based on that utility. The role of the demand data is just to put constraints on the permitted utility order, and consequently price indices based on utility become based on that data. Having such constraints, the first question then is about the existence of a utility order that satisfies them. If none exists then no price indices exist and there the matter ends. Though that is so in the present treatment, by making the constraints more tolerant it is possible to go further (see Afriat, 1972b and 1973).

In the standard model of the consumer, choice is governed by utility, to the effect that any bundle of goods consumed has greater utility than any other attainable with the same income at the prevailing prices. With this model, the obvious constraint on a utility for it to be permitted by given data is, firstly, that it validate the model for the consumer on the evidences provided by that data. Then further, since price-indices are to be dealt with, the conical property of utility should be required.

With this method of constraint and the other definitions that have been out-lined, everything is available for developing the questions that are in view. But first there will be a change in formulation that has advantages. Instead of requiring that a chosen bundle of goods be represented as being the unique best among all those attainable for no greater cost at the prevailing prices, or as being definitely better than any others in utility, it will be required that it be just one among the possibly many best, or one at as least as good as any other. This alters nothing if certain prior assumptions are made about the utility order, for instance that it is representable by an increasing strictly quasiconcave utility functions. With the latter assumption a utility maximum under a budget constraint must in any case be a unique maximum, and so adding that the maximum is unique just makes a redundance. But we do not want to introduce additional assumptions about util-ity. A utility is wanted that fits the data in a certain way, and if all that is now wanted in such a fit is that some commodity bundles be represented as having at least the utility of certain others then we can always count on a utility function that is constant everywhere to do that service. In making what could at first seem a slight change in the original formulation of the constraint on permitted utilities, the result is no constraint at all: whatever the data there always exists a permitted utility, for instance the one mentioned which will give zero as the cost of attaining any given standard of living. That change is drastic and no such change is sought. All that is in view is a change that alters nothing important in the results, the effect being something like replacing an open interval by a closed one, while it is better to work with and in any case is conceptually fitting. One possibility is to add a monotonicity condition as an assumption about utility expressing that 'more is better'. But, as said, we do not want any such prior assumptions. Instead consider again the original strict condition, that the chosen bundle be the unique best attainable at no greater cost. It implies the considered weaker condition in which the uniqueness has been dropped. But also it implies a second condition: the cost of the bundle is the minimum cost for obtaining a bundle that is as good as it. These two conditions are generally independent, even though relations between them can be produced from prior assumptions about utility, of which we have none, and their combination is implied by the stricter and analytically more cumbersome original condition.

They are just what is wanted. They have equal warrant as economic principles. In the context of cost–benefit analysis they are familiar as constituting the two main criteria about a project, that it be *cost-effective* or gives best value for the cost, and *cost-efficient* or the same value is unattainable at lower cost.

Now the wanted constraint on an admissible utility can be stated by the requirement that every bundle of goods given in the demand data be represented by it as cost-effective and cost-efficient. Such a utility can be said to be *compatible* with the demand data. Then that data is *consistent* if there exists a compatible utility. It is *homogeneously consistent* if there exists a compatible utility that moreover has the property of being conical, or homogeneous, required whenever dealing with price-indices. A *compatible price-index*, or a 'true' one, is one derived on the basis of a homogeneous utility that is compatible with the given data.

The first problem therefore is to find a test for the homogeneous consistency of the data. In the case where there are just two periods, the test found reduces to a relation that is quite familiar, in a context where it is not at all connected with this test but is offered as a 'theorem', though certainly it is not that. The relation is simply that the Paasche index from one period to the other does not exceed that of Laspeyres. The relation is symmetrical between the data in the two periods, and so there is no need to put in this unsymmetrical form where one period is distinguished as the base. But this is the form in which it is familiar and known as the 'Index-Number Theorem'. That the 'Theorem', or relation, *is necessary and sufficient for homogeneous consistency* of the demands in the two periods is a theorem in the ordinary sense. It is going to be generalized for any number of periods.

Related to the Index-Number Theorem is the proposition that the Laspeyres and Paasche indices are upper and lower 'limits' for the 'true index'. From the foregoing consistency considerations it is recognized that even the existence of a price index, at least in the sense entertained here, can be contradicted by the data, so certainly some additional qualification is needed in the 'limits' proposition. Also, what makes an index 'true' has obscurities in early literature. An interpretation emerging in later discussions is that a true index is simply one derived on the basis of utility. This could be accepted to mean one that, in present terms, is compatible with the given demand data.

With demand data given for any number of periods and satisfying the homogeneous consistency test, a price index compatible with those data can be constructed from any period to any other. It has many possible values corresponding to the generally many compatible homogeneous utilities. These values *describe a closed interval* whose endpoints are given by certain formulae in the given demand data.

A special case of this result applies to the situation usually assumed in index-number discussions. In this, the only data involved in a price-index construction between two periods are the data from the two reference periods themselves. For this case *the formulae for the endpoints of the interval of values for the price index reduce to the Paasche and Laspeyres formulae*. Here therefore is a generalization of those well-known formulae for when demand data from any number of periods can be permitted to enter the calculation of a price-index between any two. *The values* of these generalized Paasche and Laspeyres formulae *are well defined just in the case of homogeneous consistency* of the data, under which condition they have the price-index significance just stated. Then a counterpart of the 'Index-Number Theorem' condition in the context of many periods is that *the generalized Paasche formula does not exceed the generalized Laspeyres formula*. There seems to be one such condition for each ordered pair of periods, making a collection of conditions. However, all are redundant because they are *automatically satisfied* whenever the formulae have well-defined values, as they do just in the case of homogeneous consistency of the data.

For price-indices P_{rs} between many periods to be *consistent* they should have the form $P_{rs} = P_s/P_r$ for some P_r. Let $\hat{P}_{rs}$, $\check{P}_{rs}$ be the generalized Laspeyres and Paasche formulae. These, when they have well-defined values, are connected by the relation $\hat{P}_{rs}\check{P}_{sr} = 1$ and have the properties $\hat{P}_{rs}\hat{P}_{st} \leq \hat{P}_{rt}$, $\check{P}_{rs}\check{P}_{st} \leq \check{P}_{rt}$. Then it is possible to solve the system of simultaneous inequalities $\check{P}_{rs} \geq P_s/P_r$ for the P_r. The system $\hat{P}_{rs} \leq P_s/P_r$ is identical with this, so solutions automatically satisfy

$$\check{P}_{rs} \leq P_s/P_r \leq \hat{P}_{rs}$$

Now it is possible to describe all the price-indices P_{rs} between periods that are compatible with the data and form a consistent set: they are exactly those *having the form $P_{rs} = P_s/P_r$ where P_r is any solution of the above system of inequalities*. The condition for their existence is just the homogeneous consistency of the data. For any solution P_r there exists a homogeneous utility compatible with the data on the basis of which $P_{rs} = P_s/P_r$ is the price-index from period r to periods s. This will be shown by actual construction of such a utility.

Now to be remarked is the *extension property* of any given price-indices for a subset of the periods that are compatible with the data and together are consistent: *it is always possible to determine further price-indices involving all the other periods so that the collection price-indices so obtained between all periods are both compatible with the data and together are consistent*. There is an ambiguity here about a set of price indices being compatible with the data: they could be that with each taken separately, or in another stricter sense where they are taken simultaneously together. But in the conjunction with consistency the ambiguity loses effect. *For price-indices P_{rs} that are all independently compatible with the data*, the compatibility of each one with the data being established by means of a possibly different utility, *if they are all consistent there also they are jointly compatible* in that also there exists a single utility, homogeneous and compatible with the data, that establishes their compatibility with the data simultaneously.

This completes a description of the main concepts and results dealt with in this paper. Further remarks concern computation of the $m \times m$—matrix of generalized Laspeyres indices $\hat{P}_{rs}$, and hence also the generalized Paasche indices $\check{P}_{rs} = \hat{P}_{sr}^{-1}$, from the matrix of ordinary Laspeyres indices $L_{rs} = p_s x_r / p_r x_r$. An algorithm proposed goes as follows. The matrix L with elements L_{rs} is raised to powers in a sense that is a variation of the usual, in which $a + b$ means $\min[a, b]$. With the modification of matrix addition and multiplication that results associativity and distributivity laws are preserved, and matrix 'powers' can be defined in the usual way by repeated 'multiplication'. The condition for the powers $L, L^2, L^3, \ldots$ to converge is simply the homogeneous consistency of the data. Then for some $k \leq m$, $L^{k-1} = L^k$, and in that case also $L^k = L^{k+1} = \cdots$ so the calculation of powers can be broken-off as soon as one is found that is identical with its predecessor. Finding such a $k \leq m$ by this procedure is a test for homogeneous consistency; finding a diagonal element less than unity denies this condition and terminates the procedure. With such a k let $\hat{P} = L^k$. The elements $\hat{P}_{rs}$ of $\hat{P}$ are the generalized Laspeyres indices. A programme for this algorithm is available for the TI-59 programmable calculator applicable to $m \leq 6$, and another in Standard BASIC for a microcomputer.

1 Demand

With n commodities, Ω^n is the *commodity space* and Ω_n is the *price* or *budget space*. These are described by non-negative column and row vectors with n elements, Ω being the non-negative numbers. Then $x \in \Omega^n$, $p \in \Omega_n$ have a product $px \in \Omega$, giving the value of the commodity bundle x at the prices p. Any $(x, p) \in \Omega^n \times \Omega_n$ with $px > 0$ defines a *demand*, of quantities x at prices p, with expenditure given by $M = px$. Associated with it is the *budget vector* given by $u = M^{-1} p$ and such that $ux = 1$. Then (x, u) is the *normal demand* associated with $(x, p)(px > 0)$.

Some m periods of consumption are considered, and it is supposed that demands $(x_t, p_t)(t = 1, \ldots, m)$ are given for these. With expenditures $M_t = p_t x_t$ and budgets $u_t = M_t^{-1} p_t$, so that $u_t x_t = 1$, the associated normal demands are the (x_t, u_t). Then $L_{rs} = u_r x_s = p_r x_s / p_r x_r$ is the Laspeyres quantity index from r to s, or with r, s as base and current periods. It is such that $L_{rr} = 1$. Then the coefficients $D_{rs} = L_{rs} - 1$ are such that $D_{rr} = 0$. To be used also are the Laspeyres *chain-coefficients* $L_{rij \cdots ks} = L_{ri} L_{ij} \cdots L_{ks}$.

Any collection $D \subseteq \Omega^n \times \Omega_n$ of demands is a *demand relation*. Here we have a finite demand relation D with elements (x_t, p_t). For any demand (x, p), the collection of demands of the form (xt, p), where $t > 0$ is its *homogeneous extension*, and the homogeneous extension of a demand relation is the union of the homogeneous extension of its elements. A *homogeneous demand relation* has the property

$$xDp, t > 0 \rightarrow xtDp$$

making it identical with its homogeneous extension.

For a normal demand relation E, or one such that $xEu \rightarrow ux = 1$, homogeneity is expressed by the condition

$$xEu, t > 0 \rightarrow xtEt^{-1}u$$

If E is the normal demand relation associated with D, or the *normalization* of D, then this is the condition for D to be homogeneous.

2   Utility

A *utility relation* is any binary relation $R \subseteq \Omega^n \times \Omega^n$ that is reflexive, xRx, and transitive, $xRyRz \rightarrow xRz$, by which properties it is an order. Then the symmetric part $E = R \cap R'$, for which

$$xEy \leftrightarrow xRy \wedge xR'y \leftrightarrow xRy \wedge yRx$$

is a symmetric order, or an equivalence, and the antisymmetric part $P = R \cap \bar{R}'$, for which

$$xPy \leftrightarrow xRy \wedge x\bar{R}'Y \leftrightarrow xRy \wedge y\bar{R}x \leftrightarrow xRy \wedge \sim yRx$$

is irreflexive and transitive, or a strict order.

A *homogeneous, or conical*, utility relation is one that is a cone in $\Omega^n \times \Omega^n$, that is $xRy, t > 0 \rightarrow xtRyt$. Any $\phi : \Omega^n \rightarrow \Omega$ is a utility function, and it is homogeneous or conical if its graph is a cone, the condition for this being $\phi(xt) = \phi(x)t \ (t > 0)$. A utility function ϕ represents a utility relation R if $xRy \leftrightarrow \phi(x) \geq \phi(y)$. If ϕ is conical so is R.

3   Demand and utility

A demand (x, p) and a utility R are *compatible* if

(i) $py \leq px \rightarrow xRy$

(ii) $yRx \rightarrow py \geq px$ (3.1)

They are *homogeneously compatible* if (xt, p) and R are compatible for all $t > 0$, in other words if the homogeneous extension of (x, p) is compatible with R. If R is homogeneous, compatibility is equivalent to homogeneous compatibility. Demand and utility relations D and R are compatible if the elements of D are all compatible with R, and homogeneously compatible if the homogeneous extension of D is compatible with R.

A demand relation D is *consistent* if it is compatible with some utility relation, and *homogeneously consistent* if moreover that utility relation can be chosen to be homogeneous. Homogeneous consistency of any demand relation is equivalent to consistency of its homogeneous extension. That the former implies the latter is seen immediately, and the converse will be shown later.

It should be noted that (3.1 (ii)) in contrapositive is $py < px \rightarrow y\bar{R}x$, and, with the definition of P in section 2, this with (3.1 (i)) gives

$$py < px \rightarrow xPy \qquad (3.2)$$

so this is a consequence of (3.1).

4   Revealed preference

A relation $W \subset \Omega^n \times \Omega_n$ is defined by $xWu \equiv ux \leq 1$. Then xWu, that is $ux \leq 1$, means the commodity bundle x is *within* the budget u, and

$$Wu = [x : xWu] = [x : ux \leq 1]$$

is the *budget set* for u, whose elements are the commodity bundles within u.

The *revealed preference relation* of a demand (x, p) is $[(x, y) : py \leq px]$. For a normal demand $(x, u)(ux = 1)$ it is $(x, Wu) = [(x, y) : y \in Wu] = [(x, y) : uy \leq 1]$. The revealed homogeneous preference relation is the conical closure of the revealed preference relation, so it is $[(xt, y) : py \leq pxt, t > 0]$ for a demand and $\cup_{t>0}(xt, Wt^{-1}u)$ for the normal demand. The condition (3.1), which is a part of the requirement for compatibility between a demand and utility (x, p) and R, asserts simply that the utility relation contains the revealed preference relation. If the utility relation is homogeneous, this is equivalent to its containing the revealed homogeneous, this is equivalent to its containing the revealed homogeneous preference relation.

Let R_t be the revealed preference relation of the demand (x_t, p_t), and $\dot{R}_t$ the revealed homogeneous preference relation. Then, as remarked, compatibility of that demand with a utility R requires that

$$R_t \subseteq R \qquad (4.1)$$

and if R is homogeneous this is equivalent to

$$\dot{R}_t \subseteq R \qquad (4.2)$$

Now let R_D, the revealed preference relation of the given demand relation D, be defined as the transitive closure of the union of the revealed preference relations R_t of its elements, $R_D = \vec{\cup}_t R_t$. The compatibility of R with D requires (4.1) for all t, and because R is transitive this is equivalent to $R_D \subset R$. Also let $\dot{R}_D = \vec{\cup}_t \dot{R}_t$, the transitive closure of the union of the revealed homogeneous preference relation $\dot{R}_t$ of the elements of D, define the *revealed homogeneous preference relation* of D. Then, by similar argument, with (4.2), compatibility of D with a homogeneous R implies $\dot{R}_D \subseteq R$. While R_D is transitive from its construction, and reflexive at the points x_t, because R_t is reflexive at x_t, $\dot{R}_D$ is both transitive and conical, and reflexive on the cone through the x_t.

5   Revealed contradictions

A demand relation D with elements (x_r, p_r) is *compatible* with a utility relation R if

(i) $p_t x \leq p_t x_t \rightarrow x_t R x$

(ii) $x R x_t \rightarrow p_t x \geq p_t x_t$

$$(5.1)$$

and D is *consistent* if some compatible order R exists. It has been seen that (5.1) is equivalent to

$$R_D \subseteq R \tag{5.2}$$

Therefore, if D is compatible with R, $x R_D x_t \rightarrow x R x_t$ for any t and x, and also $p_t x < p_t x_t \rightarrow x \bar{R} x_t$. Therefore, on the hypothesis that D is compatible with some, R, the condition

$$x R_D x_t, p_t x < p_t x_t \tag{5.3}$$

implies $x R x_t, x \bar{R} x_t$ making a contradiction, so the hypothesis is impossible and D is inconsistent.

The condition (5.3) for any t and x is a *revealed contradiction*, denying the consistency of D. Thus:

> *The existence of a revealed contradiction is sufficient*
> *for D to be inconsistent.* (5.4)

Now it will be seen to be also necessary.

The condition for there to be no revealed contradictions is the denial of (5.3), for all t and x; equivalently

$$x R_D x_t \rightarrow p_t x \geq p_t x_t \tag{5.5}$$

But this is just the condition (5.1 (ii)) with $R = R_D$. Because (5.1 (i)) is equivalent to (5.2), and because in any case $R_D \subseteq R_D$ so (5.2) is satisfied with $R = R_D$, it is seen that (5.4) is necessary and sufficient for (5.1 (i) and (ii)) to be satisfied with $R = R_D$, in other words for D to be compatible with R_D. Thus:

> *The absence of revealed contradictions is necessary and*
> *sufficient for D to be compatible with R_D.* (5.6)

As a corollary:

> *The absence of revealed contradictions implies the consistency of D.* (5.7)

For consistency means the existence of some compatible order, and by (5.5) under this hypothesis R_D is one such order. Now with (5.5):

> *The absence of revealed contradictions is necessary and sufficient*
> *for the consistency of D and implies compatibility with R_D.* (5.8)

By exactly similar argument, $x\dot{R}_D x_t \theta$ and $p_r x < p_r x_r \theta$, for any r, x and $\theta > 0$, make a *homogeneously revealed contradiction* denying the homogeneous consistency of D, or the existence of a compatible homogeneous utility. Then $x\dot{R}_D x_t \theta \rightarrow p_r x \geq p_r x_r \theta$ for all r, x and $\theta > 0$ asserts the absence of homogeneously revealed contradictions. Then there is the following:

Theorem *For a demand relation to be compatible with some homogeneous utility relation, and so homogeneously consistent, it is necessary and sufficient that its revealed homogenous preference relation be one such relation, and for this the absence of homogeneously revealed contradictions is necessary and sufficient.*

This theorem holds unconditionally, regardless of whether or not D is finite. However, when D is finite the homogeneous consistency condition has a finite test, developed in the next two sections.

Because the revealed preference relation of the homogeneous extension of a demand relation is identical with its revealed homogeneous preference relation, it appears now, as remarked in section 3, that *homogeneous consistency of a demand relation is equivalent to consistency of its homogeneous extension.* For, as just seen, the first stated condition on D is equivalent to compatibility with $\dot{R}_D$ and the second with $R_{\dot{D}}$, so this conclusion follows from $\dot{R}_D = R_{\dot{D}}$.

6 Consistency

Though R_D, $\dot{R}_D$ and the L_{rs} which give the base for the following work are derived from D, they are also derivable from the normal demand relation E derived from D. Therefore there would be no loss in generality if only normal demand relations were considered.

As a preliminary, the definition of the revealed homogeneous preference relation $\dot{R}_D$ will be put in a more explicit from. This requires identification of the transitive closure of any relation R with its chain-extension $\vec{R}$. An R-chain is any sequence of elements $x, y, \ldots, z$ in which each has the relation $\vec{R}$ to its successor, that is $xRyR \ldots Rz$. Then the chain-extension R is the relation that holds between extremities of R-chains, so $x\vec{R}z \equiv (\vee y, \ldots)xRyR \ldots Rz$. The relation $\vec{R}$ so defined can be identified with the transitive closure of R, that is as the smallest transitive relation containing R, it being such that it is transitive, contains R and is contained in every transitive relation that contains R. Therefore $x\dot{R}_D y$ means x, y are extremities of a chain in the relation $\cup_t \dot{R}_t$. This means there exist $r, i, \ldots, k$ and $z_i, \ldots, z_k$ such that $xR_r z_i R_i \ldots z_k R_k y$. But, considering the form of the elements of the R_t, now we must have $x_r = x_r \theta_r$, $z_i = x_i \theta_i, \ldots, z_k = x_k \theta_k$ for some $\theta_r, \theta_i, \ldots, \theta_k > 0$, and $u_k y \leq \theta_k$. Accordingly, the condition $x\dot{R}_D x_s \theta_s \rightarrow u_s x \geq \theta_s$ *for all x, s and $\theta_s > 0$*, for the absence of homogeneously revealed contradictions, can be restated as the condition

$$x_r \theta_r \dot{R}_r x_i \theta_i \dot{R}_i \cdots x_k \theta_k \dot{R}_k x_s \theta_s \rightarrow U_s x_r \theta_r \geq \theta_s \qquad (6.1)$$

for all $r, i, \ldots, k, s$ and $\theta_r, \theta_i, \ldots, \theta_k, \theta_s > 0$. From the form of the elements of the $\dot{R}_t$, that is

$$u_r x_i \theta_i \leq \theta_r, \ldots, u_k x_s \theta_s \leq \theta_k \rightarrow u_s x_r \theta_r \geq \theta_s$$

or, in terms of the Laspeyres coefficients,

$$L_{ri} \leq \theta_r/\theta_i, \ldots, L_{ks} \leq \theta_k/\theta_s \rightarrow L_{sr} \geq \theta_s/\theta_r \tag{6.2}$$

Another way of stating this condition is that

$$(L_{ri}, \ldots, L_{ks}, L_{sr}) \leq (\theta_r/\theta_i, \ldots, \theta_k/\theta_s, \theta_s/\theta_r) \tag{6.3}$$

is impossible for all $r, i, \ldots, k, s$ *and* $\theta_r, \theta_i, \ldots, \theta_k, \theta_s > 0$. This condition will be denoted $\dot{K}$.

While theory based on homogeneity is here the main object, in the background is the further theory without that restriction. Some account of that is given here, but it is mainly given elsewhere as already indicated. The dots used in the notation are to distinguish features in this homogeneous theory from their counterparts without homogeneity. The homogeneous theory is required in dealing with price indices, but still it has its source in the more general theory. It is useful in this section and later to bring counterparts of the two theories together for recognition of the connections and the differences.

Condition (6.1) has been identified with the condition for the absence of homogeneously revealed contradictions that in the last section was shown necessary and sufficient for the consistency of the given demands, that is, for the existence of a homogeneous utility compatible with them all simultaneously. The weaker condition that is the counterpart without homogeneity, put in a form that assists comparison, is the condition K given by

$$(L_{ri}, \ldots, L_{ks}, L_{sr}) \leq (1, \ldots, 1, 1) \tag{6.4}$$

is impossible for all $r, i, \ldots, k, s$. By taking the θs all unity in (6.3), (6.4) is obtained, so (6.3) implies (6.4) as should be expected.

If compatibility between demand and utility is replaced by *strict compatibility*, by replacing cost-efficacy or cost-efficiency by their strict counterparts, which conditions in fact are equivalent to each other, and *strict consistency* of any demands means the existence of a strictly compatible utility, then the test for this condition which is a counterpart of (6.4) is the condition K^* given by

$$(L_{ri}, \ldots, L_{ks}, L_{sr}) \leq (1, \ldots, 1, 1) \tag{6.5}$$

is impossible for all $r, i, \ldots, k, s$ *unless* $x_r = x_i = \cdots = x_k = x_s$, *in which case the equality holds*. This is just a way of stating the condition of Houthakker (1950), know as the Strong Axiom of Revealed Preference, for when that condition is applied to a finite set of demand instead of to the infinite set associated with a demand function. Here the *finiteness is not essential* and is just a matter of notation, though in later results it does have an essential part. Corresponding to the results obtained for the less strict consistency, and for homogeneous consistency, as in the Theorem or section 5, *Houthakker's condition is necessary and sufficient for the existence of strictly compatible utility, and for the revealed preference relation to be one such utility.*

While (6.5) is the 'strict' counterpart of (6.4), the corresponding counterpart for (6.3) is the condition K given by

$$(L_{ri}, \ldots, L_{ks}, L_{sr}) \leq (\theta_r/\theta_i, \ldots, \theta_k/\theta_s, \theta_s/\theta_r) \tag{6.6}$$

is impossible for all $r, i, \ldots, k, s$ *and* $\theta_r, \theta_i, \ldots, \theta_k, \theta_s > 0$ *unless* $x_r\theta_r = x_i\theta_i = \cdots = x_s\theta_s$ *in which case the equality holds.*

Just as a dot signifies a condition associated which homogeneity, a star signifies belonging to the 'strict' theory. The various conditions that have been stated have the relations

$$\dot{K} \rightarrow K$$

$$\uparrow \qquad \uparrow$$

$$\dot{K}^* \rightarrow K^*$$

The main result of this section, which is about $\dot{K}$ in (6.3) being a consistency condition, will be part of a theorem in the next section where it is developed into another form.

It can be noted that (6.3) is equivalent to the same condition which $r, i, \ldots, k, s$ restricted to be all distinct. For the second condition is part of the first. Also, the inequalities stated in the first, involving a cycle of elements, can be partitioned into groups of inequalities involving simple cycles, each without repeated elements, showing that also the first follows from the second.

A finite consistency test is wanted, one that can be decided in a known finite number of steps. The last conclusion goes a step towards finding such a test, though it does not give one. That will be left to the next section. However, (6.4) and (6.5) taken with the indices all distinct already represent finite tests. But still this is not the case for Houthakker's condition (6.5), or for (6.4), when these are regarded as applying to a demand function (6.5), or for (6.4), when these are regarded as applying to a demand function, for which the number of cycles of distinct demands is unlimited.

7 Finite test

Theorem *For any finite demand relation D the following conditions are equivalent*

($\dot{H}$) *D is homogeneously consistent, that is, there exists a compatible homogeneous utility relation;*

($\dot{R}$) *D is compatible with its own revealed homogeneous utility relation $\dot{R}_D$;*

($\dot{K}$) $(L_{rs}, L_{st}, \ldots, L_{qr}) \leq (\theta_r/\theta_s, \theta_s/\theta_t, \ldots, \theta_q/\theta_r)$ *is impossible for all distinct* $r, s, \ldots, q$ *and* $\theta_r, \theta_s, \ldots, \theta_q > 0$;

($\dot{L}$) $L_{rst\cdots qr} \geq 1$ *for all distinct* $r, s, \ldots, q$.

Arguments for the equivalences between $\dot{H}$, $\dot{R}$ and $\dot{K}$ have already been given in the last two sections. It is enough now to show $\dot{K}$ and $\dot{L}$ are equivalent. By multiplying the inequalities stated for any case where $\dot{K}$ is denied, it follows that

$$L_{rst\cdots qr} < (\theta_r/\theta_s)(\theta_s/\theta_t)\cdots(\theta_q/\theta_r) = 1$$

contrary to $\dot{L}$. Thus $\dot{L} \to \dot{K}$. Now, contrary to $\dot{L}$, suppose $L_{rst\cdots qr} < 1$, and let

$$\theta_r = L_{rst\cdots qr}, \quad \theta_s = L_{st\cdots qr}, \ldots, \quad \theta_q = L_{qr}$$

Then

$$L_{rs} = \theta_r/\theta_s, \quad L_{st} = \theta_s/\theta_t, \ldots$$

and finally, $\theta_r < 1$ and $\theta_q = L_{qr}$ so that $L_{qr} < \theta_q/\theta_r$, showing a denial of K. Thus $\dot{K} \to \dot{L}$, and the two conditions are now equivalent.

Because the number of simple cycles that can be formed from m elements is finite and given by

$$\sum_{r=1}^{m}(r-1)!\binom{m}{r} = \sum_{r=1}^{m}(r-1)!m!/r!(m-r)!$$

$$= \sum_{r=1}^{m}(m-r+1)\cdots m/r$$

$\dot{L}$ is a finite test.

The counterpart of $\dot{K}$ for the general non-homogeneous theory has already been stated, and that for $\dot{L}$ is

(L) *There exist positive λs such that for all distinct $r, s, t, \ldots, q$*

$$(\lambda_r L_{rs} + \lambda_s L_{st} + \cdots + \lambda_q L_{qr})/(\lambda_r + \lambda_s + \cdots + \lambda_q) \geq 1$$

It can be noted that while $\dot{L}$ shows a finite test and $\dot{K}$ does not, L does not and K does.

There are several routes for proving the equivalence of K and L, all of some length. From that equivalence it is known that $\dot{L} \to L$. But this can be seen also directly. From the theorem that the geometric mean does not exceed the arithmetic,

$$(L_{rs} + L_{st} + \cdots + L_{qr})/k \geq L_{rst\cdots qr}^{1/k}$$

k being the number of elements in the cycle. Therefore $\dot{L}$ implies

$$(L_{rs} + L_{st} + \cdots + L_{qr})/k \geq 1$$

But this validates L with all the λs equal to unity.

The counterpart of L for the 'strict' theory, equivalent to Houthakker's revealed preference axiom, is

(L*) *There exist positive λs such that, for all distinct $r, s, t, \ldots, q$*

$$(\lambda_r L_{rs} + \lambda_s L_{st} + \cdots + \lambda_q L_{qr})/(\lambda_r + \lambda_s + \cdots + \lambda_q) \geq 1$$

the equality holding just when $x_r = x_s = x_t = \cdots = x_q$.

8 A system of inequalities

The test $L_{rs\cdots qr} \geq 1$ *for all distinct* $r, s, \ldots, q$, that was found for the homogeneous consistency of a demand relation is also the test for solubility of the system of inequalities

$$L_{rs} \geq \phi_s/\phi_r \quad \text{for all } r, s \tag{8.1}$$

for numbers ϕ_r $(r = 1, \ldots, m)$. Such numbers obtained by solving the inequalities will be identified as utility-levels for the demand periods, because for any demand period there exists a homogeneous utility compatible with the demands that identify them all as such, in that the numbers $X_{rs} = \phi_s/\phi_r$ are identified as quantity-indices, compatible with the data, and price indices correspond to these. By taking logarithms the system (7.1) comes into the form

$$a_{rs} \geq x_s - x_r \tag{8.2}$$

where $x_r = \log \phi_r$ and $a_{rs} = \log L_{rs}$. An account of the system in this from has been given in Afriat (1960), and in the last section here it is developed to suit needs of the present application.

The same system, in the additive from, arises also in the version of this theory unrestricted by homogeneity. It is required to find a positive solution of the system of homogeneous linear inequalities

$$\lambda_r (L_{rs} - 1) \geq \phi_s - \phi_r \tag{8.3}$$

That the ϕs be positive is inessential because they enter through their differences, and so a constant can always be added to make them so, but the restriction is essential. The λs occurring in solutions of (7.3) are identical with the λs that are solutions of (6.4), so they can be determined separately. With any λs so determined, and $a_{rs} = \lambda_r (L_{rs} - 1)$, (7.3) is in the from (7.2) for determining the ϕs. The ϕs and λs in any solution become utilities and marginal utilities at the demanded xs with a compatible utility that is constructed by means of the solution. In the case of homogeneous utility, $\lambda_r = \phi_r$, and with this substitution (7.3) reduces to (7.1).

An entirely different connection for the system (7.2) is with minimum paths in networks. With the coefficient a_{rs} as direct path-distances, a solution of (7.2) corresponds to the concept of a *subpotential* for the network, as described by Fiedler and Ptak (1967). Whereas there it is an auxiliary that came in later, here it is a principal objective and a starting point. Then there is the linear programming formula $A_{ij} = \min[x_j - x_i : a_{rs} \geq x_r - x_s]$ expressing the minimum path-distance A_{ij} as the minimum subpotential difference, as learnt from Edmunds (1973). It is familiar under the assumption $a_{rs} \geq 0$, and in the integer programming context. Close to hand in the 1960 account is this formula without the non-negativity restriction on the coefficients and a quite different method of proof.

9 Utility construction

Now to be considered is how, for any number $\phi_t > 0$ such that

$$u_s x_t \geq \phi_t/\phi_s \tag{9.1}$$

it is possible to construct a linearly homogeneous, or conical, utility that is compatible with the given demands D_t and such that

$$\phi(x_t) = \phi_t \tag{9.2}$$

The utility constructed will moreover be semi-increasing, $x < y \rightarrow \phi(x) < \phi(y)$, and, being both conical and superadditive, $\phi(x + y) \geq \phi(x) + (y)$; also it is concave.

The existence of numbers ϕ_t satisfying (9.1) is necessary and sufficient that there should exist any compatible homogeneous utility R at all, without further qualification. But here it is seen that if there exists one then also there exists one with these additional classical properties. A conclusion is that these classical properties are unobservable in the observational framework of choice under linear budgets, or are without empirical test or meaning and are just a property of the framework.

The consistency condition generally becomes more restrictive as additional restrictions are put on utility. Thus homogeneous consistency is more restrictive that the more general consistency that is free of the homogeneity. Then *classical consistency*, where utility is required to be representable by a utility function with the classical properties, might seem to be more restricted than general consistency, and also the same might be supposed for when homogeneity is added to both these conditions. But the contrary is a theorem: *the imposition of the classical properties make no difference whatsoever.*

Let

$$\phi(x) = \min_t \phi_t u_t x \tag{9.3}$$

so, for all x,

$$\phi(x) \leq \phi_t u_t x \quad \text{for all } t, \qquad \phi(x) = \phi_t u_t x \quad \text{for some } t \tag{9.4}$$

Then, with $x = x_t$, so $u_t x = 1$, we have $\phi(x_t) < \phi_t$. But from (9.1), $\phi_s u_s x_t \geq \phi_t$ for all s. Hence, with (9.3), $\phi(x_t) = \min_s \phi_s u_s x_t \geq \phi_t$. Thus (9.2) is shown.

Now further, from (9.4) with $\phi_t > 0$,

$$u_t x < 1 \rightarrow \phi_t u_t x < \phi_t \rightarrow \phi(x) < \phi_t$$

Hence, with (9.2), $u_t x < 1 \rightarrow \phi(x) < \phi(x_t)$, and similarly, or from here by continuity, $u_t x \leq 1 \rightarrow \phi(x) \leq \phi(x_t)$, showing that the utility $\phi(x)$ and the normal demand (x_t, u_t) are compatible.

10   Utility cost

Because

$$u_t = M_t^{-1} p_t \tag{10.1}$$

where

$$M_t = p_t x_t \tag{10.2}$$

and because $X_t = \phi_t(x_t)$, another statement of (9.1), in view of (9.2), is that.

$$p_s x_t / p_s x_s \geq X_t / X_s \qquad (10.3)$$

Then introducing

$$P_t = M_t / X_t \qquad (10.4)$$

so that, as a parallel to (10.2) $M_t = P_t X_t$, (10.3) and (10.4) give

$$p_s x_t / p_s x_s \geq (p_t x_t / P_t)/(p_s x_s / P_s) = (p_t x_t / p_s x_s)(P_s / P_t)$$

and consequently

$$p_s x_t / p_t x_t \geq P_s / P_t \qquad (10.5)$$

Or again, introducing

$$U_t = M_t^{-1} P_t \qquad (10.6)$$

in analogy with (10.1), so that $U_t X_t = 1$, this being, in analogy with the normalized budget identity $u_t x_t = 1$, an equivalent of (10.3), and also of (10.5), is that $u_s x_t \geq U_s / U_t$. Let $\theta(p)$ be the cost function associated with the classical homogeneous utility function $\phi(x)$, so that

$$\theta(p) = \min[px : \phi(x) \geq 1] \qquad (10.7)$$

this again being classical homogeneous, that is semi-increasing, concave and conical. Then by taking x in the form xt^{-1}, where $t > 0$,

$$\theta(p) = \min[pxt^{-1} : \phi(xt^{-1}) \geq 1] = \min[pxt^{-1} : \phi(x) \geq t]$$

because ϕ is conical. Then by taking $t = \phi(x)$, $\theta(p) = \min_x px(\phi(x))^{-1}$ is obtained as an alternative formula for θ. From this formula the functions θ and ϕ are such that

$$\theta(p)\phi(x) \leq px \qquad (10.8)$$

for all p, x with equality just in the case of compatibility between the demand (x, p) and the utility ϕ. For the equality signifies cost efficiency, and because ϕ is continuous this implies also cost effectiveness, and hence also the compatibility. Because ϕ is concave it is recovered from θ by the same formula by which θ is derived from it, with an exchange of roles between θ and ϕ; that is

$$\phi(x) = \min[px : \theta(p) \geq 1] = \min_p (\theta(p))^{-1} px \qquad (10.9)$$

In the case of a normal demand (x, u), that is one for which $ux = 1$, (10.8) becomes

$$\theta(u)\phi(x) \leq 1 \qquad (10.10)$$

with equality just in the case of a demand that is compatible with ϕ.

In section 9 it was shown that the function $\phi(x)$ constructed there is compatible with the given normal demands (x_t, u_t). Therefore $\theta(u_t)\phi(x_t) = 1$ for all t, while, by (10.10), $\theta(u_s)\phi(x_t) \leq 1$ for all s, t. Also it was shown that

$$\phi(x_t) = \phi_t \tag{10.11}$$

Hence, introducing

$$\theta_t = \phi_t^{-1} \tag{10.12}$$

it is shown that $\theta(u_t) = \theta_t$. It is possible to verify that also directly by inspection of the cost function. Thus, with $\phi(x) = \min_t \phi_t u_t x$, so that $\phi(x) \geq 1$ is equivalent to $\phi_t u_t x \geq 1$ for all t, which, with (10.12), is equivalent to $u_t x \geq \theta_t$ for all t, the cost function in (10.7) is also

$$\theta(u) = \min[ux : u_t x \geq \theta_t] \tag{10.13}$$

so that $\theta(u_t) \geq \theta_t$. Therefore, by (10.11) and (10.12), $\theta(u_t)\phi(x_t) \geq 1$. Then $u_t x_t = 1$ with (10.10) shows that $\theta(u_t)\phi(x_t) = 1$ and hence, again with (10.11) and (10.12), that $\theta(u_t) = \theta_t$.

By the linear programming duality theorem (Dantzig 1963) applied to (10.13), another formula for the cost function is

$$\theta(u) = \max\left[\sum s_t\theta_t : \sum s_t u_t \leq u\right] \tag{10.14}$$

Then, as known from the theory of linear programming, for any x, $\theta(u) \leq ux$ for all u if and only if x solves (10.13). Similarly, with the θ_t now variable while u is fixed, for any s_t, $\theta(u) \geq \sum s_t\theta_t$ for all θ_t if and only if the s_t solve (10.14).

If the θ_t are a strict solution of (9.1), that is $u_s x_t > \phi_t/\phi_s$ ($s \neq t$), then $x = x_t\theta_t$ is the unique solution of (10.13) when $u = u_t$. In just that case $\theta(u)$ is differentiable at the point $u = u_t$. In that case θ is locally linear, and has a unique support gradient, and the differential gradient which now exists coincides with it. Thus in this case $\theta(u) \leq ux$ for all u, and $\theta(u_t) = u_t x$ if and only if $x = x_t\theta_t$, so $\theta(u)$ has gradient $x_t\theta_t$ at $u = u_t$.

It can be added that this entire argument could have gone just as well with an interchange of roles between u and x. By solving $u_s x_t \geq \theta_s/\theta_t$ for the θ_t, a cost function θ could be constructed first, with the form originally given to ϕ, and then ϕ could have been derived. Also, ϕ need not have been given the polyhedral form (9.5). It could have been given the polytope form (10.13) or (10.14). Then θ would have had the polyhedral form (9.5).

11   Price and quantity

The method established for the determination of index numbers can be stated in a way that treats price and quantity both simultaneously and in a symmetrical fashion. With the given demands (x_t, p_t), numbers (X_t, P_t) should satisfy

$$p_s x_t \geq P_s X_t \quad \text{for all } s, t \tag{11.1}$$

Then, in particular,

$$p_t x_t = P_t X_t \tag{11.2}$$

Then division of (11.1) by (11.2) gives

$$p_s x_t / p_t x_t \geq P_s / Pt \tag{11.3}$$

as a condition for the 'price levels', and also

$$p_s x_t / p_s x_s \geq X_t / X_s \tag{11.4}$$

for 'quantity levels'. Reversely, starting with a solution P_t of (11.3), let X_t be determined from (11.2). Then X_t is a solution of (11.4) and the P_t and X_t together make a solution of (11.1). Just as well, the procedure could start with a solution X_t of (11.4) and go on similarly.

It has been established that the existence of solutions to these inequalities is necessary and sufficient for homogeneous consistency of the demand data. The investigation now concerns the identification of the numbers $P_{rs} = P_s / P_r$ obtained from solutions with *all possible* price indices that are compatible with the data, that is, derivable on the basis of compatible homogeneous utilities. Then it will be possible to go further with a description of all possible price indices in terms of closed intervals specified by formulae for their end-points, or limits.

For any utility order R, the derived utility–cost function $\rho(p, x) = \min[py :$ $yRx]$ is defined for all p, x if the sets Rx are closed. If R is a complete order and the sets Rx, xR are closed then, for any p, $\rho(p, x)$ is a utility function representing R (see Afriat, 1979). It follows that, for any p and q, there exists an increasing function $w(t)$, independent of x and carrying p, q as parameters, such that $\rho(p, x) = w(\rho(q, x))$ for all x.

If R is conical then so is $\rho(p, x)$ as a function of x, for any p. In that case so is $w(t)$ as a function of t. But a conical function of one variable must be homogeneous linear, so $w(t)$ has the form wt where w is a function of p, q independent of x. That is, $\rho(p, x) / \rho(q, x) = w$ is independent of x. Then w must have the form $w = \theta(p) / \theta(q)$ where $\theta(p)$ is a function of p alone, so it follows that $\rho(p, x) / (\theta(p)$ must be a function of x alone, and so $\rho(p, x) = \theta(p)\phi(x)$, where θ, ϕ are functions p, x alone. Now ϕ must be a utility that represents R, and be conical because ρ is conical in x. Then the condition for ϕ to be quasi-concave is that the sets Rx be convex. But because ϕ is conical this is also the condition that ϕ be concave (Berge, 1963). Moreover, because in any case $\rho(p, x)$ is concave conical in p, so also is $\theta(p)$.

The reflexivity of R gives in any case $\rho(p, x) \leq px$, so now $\theta(p)\phi(x) \leq px$ for all x. Hence, for all p, $\theta(p) \leq \min_x px(\phi(x))^{-1}$, while $\rho(p, x) = px$ for some x gives $\theta(p)\phi(x) = px$ some x, so that now $\theta(p) = \min px(\phi(x))^{-1}$. Similarly $\phi(x) \leq \min_p (\theta(p))^{-1} px$. Then let $\bar{\phi}(x) = \min_p (\theta(p))^{-1} px$, so $\phi(x) \leq \bar{\phi}(x)$ for all x and $\bar{\phi}$ is concave conical. Then, for any x, $\phi(x) = \bar{\phi}(x)$ is equivalent to $\theta(p)\phi(x) = px$ for some p. The condition for this to be so for any x is that $\phi(x)$ be quasi-concave, having a quasi-support p at x, for which

$$py < px \rightarrow \phi(y) < \phi(x), \quad py \leq px \rightarrow \phi(y) \leq \phi(x)$$

in other words the demand (x, p) is compatible with x for some p. This condition, which means that, with choice governed by ϕ, x could be demanded at some prices, can define compatibility between ϕ and x. The condition that ϕ be compatible with all x is just that it be quasi-concave, and that now is equivalent to $\phi(x) = \bar{\phi}(x)$ for all x. In any case, any x compatible with ϕ is also compatible with $\bar{\phi}$. Hence, if utility R is constrained by compatibility with given demands, if ϕ is acceptable then so is $\bar{\phi}$, and moreover ϕ and $\bar{\phi}$ have the same conjugate price function θ. This suggests that, instead of constructing a utility ϕ compatible with the data having a concave form that is a generally unwarranted restriction on utility and, for all we know now, might make some added restriction on price-index values, it is both possible and advantageous to construct the price function θ first instead, and so be free of such a suspicion. It has already been remarked that this might have been done instead, following an identical procedure as that for the ϕ, so in fact that issue is already disposed of. Form any compatible homogeneous utility a price function θ is derived, giving the $P_r = \theta(p_r)$ as a system of 'price-levels' compatible with the data, and determining the $P_{rs} = P_s/P_r$ as compatible prices. But the possible such P_r are already identified with the possible solutions of (11.3). Also, for any solution P_r and the θ that must exist, the X_r determined from (11.2) have the identification $X_r = \phi(X_r)$ where $\phi(x) = \min_p (\theta(p))^{-1} px$. This ϕ is concave conical. But also any other ϕ^*, not necessary concave but having the same conjugate θ, would do, so there is no inherent restriction to concave utilities here. For such a ϕ^*, generally $\phi^*(x) \leq \phi(x)$, while $\phi^*(x_r) = \phi(x_r)$ for all r, and all that is required of ϕ^* is that $\theta(x) = \min_p px(\phi^*(x))^{-1}$, and there are many ϕ^* for which this is so, that given being just one.

The argument in this section permits by-passing complications of the argument involving 'critical cost functions' that was used formerly, such as in the exposition of Afriat (1977b) for the special case of just two demand-periods. An interesting point is that the care taken in both arguments to avoid imposing on a compatible utility the requirement that also it be concave makes no difference at all to the range of possible values for a price-index.

12   Extension and exhaustion properties

For any coefficients a_{rs} $(r, s = 1, \ldots, k)$, consider the system $S(a)$ of simultaneous linear inequalities

$$a_{rs} \geq x_s - x_r \tag{12.1}$$

to be solved for numbers x_r. This is an alternative form for the system (7.1), and the form that applies directly to the system (7.3). Introduce *chain-coefficients*

$$a_{rij\cdots ks} = a_{ri} + a_{ij} + \cdots + a_{ks} \tag{12.2}$$

so that

$$a_{r\cdots s\cdots t} = a_{r\cdots s} + a_{s\cdots t} \tag{12.3}$$

If the system $S(a)$ has a solution x then

$$a_{ri} \geq x_i - x_r, \quad x_{ij} \geq x_j - x_i, \ldots, \quad a_{ks} \geq x_s - x_k$$

so by addition,

$$a_{r\ldots s} \geq x_s - x_r \tag{12.4}$$

In particular $a_{r\ldots r} \geq x_r - x_r = 0$, so that $a_{r\ldots r} \geq 0$, that is,

$$a_{ri} + a_{ij} + \cdots + a_{kr} \geq 0 \tag{12.5}$$

for every cyclic sequence of elements $r, i, j, \ldots, k, r$. This can be called the *cyclical non-negativity* condition C on the system $S(a)$, and it has been seen *necessary for the existence of a solution*. Because

$$a_{r\ldots s\ldots s\ldots r} = a_{r\ldots s\ldots r} + a_{s\ldots s}$$

the coefficient on a cycle with a repeated element s can be expressed as a sum of terms that are coefficients on cycles where the repetition multiplicity is reduced, and this decomposition can be performed on those terms and so forth until an expression is obtained with only simple cycles, without repeated elements. From this it follows that the condition C is equivalent to the same condition on cycles that are restricted to be simple, or have elements all distinct.

Under the condition C,

$$a_{r\ldots s\ldots s\ldots t} = a_{r\ldots s\ldots t} + a_{s\ldots s} \geq a_{r\ldots s\ldots t}$$

so the cancellation of a loop in a chain does not increase the coefficient along it. It follows that the *derived coefficient*

$$A_{rs} = \min_{ij\cdots} a_{rij\ldots s} \tag{12.6}$$

exists for any r, s and moreover

$$A_{rs} = a_{rij\ldots s} \tag{12.7}$$

for some simple chain $rij \cdots s$ *from r to s*. Thus C *is sufficient for the existence of the derived coefficients*. Also it is necessary. For if $a_{s\ldots s} < 0$ then for any r, t by taking the chain that goes from r to t, following the loop $s \cdots s$ any number K of times and then going from s to t, we have

$$A_{rt} \leq a_{rs} + K a_{s\ldots s} + a_{st} \to -\infty \quad (K \to \infty) \tag{12.8}$$

so A_{rt} cannot exists. Therefore also C *is sufficient for the existence of the derived coefficients*. Evidently then either the derived coefficients all exist or none do. Given that they exist, from (12.3) it follows that $A_{rs} + A_{st} \geq A_{rt}$, *so they satisfy the triangle inequality*.

The system $S(a)$ and the derived system $S(A)$, of inequalities

$$A_{rs} \geq x_s - x_r \tag{12.9}$$

have the same solutions. For from (12.4), any solution of (12.1) is a solution of (12.9). Also from $A_{rs} \leq a_{rs}$, that follows from the definition (12.6) of the A_{rs}, it is seen that any solution of (12.9) is a solution of (12.1).

The triangle inequality is necessary and sufficient for a system to be identical with its derived system, that is for $A_{rs} = a_{rs}$ for all r, s. It is necessary because any derived system has that property. Also it is sufficient. For the triangle inequality on $S(a)$ is equivalent to $a_{rij\cdots ks} \geq a_{rs}$, but (12.9) implies both that the derived coefficients A_{rs} exist and that $A_{rs} \geq a_{rs}$ which because of (12.8) is equivalent to (12.9).

Now the *extension property* for the solutions of a system that satisfies the triangle inequality will be proved. Let $S(A)$ be any such system, so if this is the derived system of some other system then this hypothesis must be valid.

A subsystem of $S(A)$ is obtained when the indices are restricted to any subset of $1, \ldots, n$. Without loss in generality consider the subsystem $S_{m-1}(A)$ on the subset of $1, \ldots, m - 1$. Let x_r $(r < m)$ be any solution for this subsystem, so that

$$A_{rs} \geq x_s - x_r \quad \text{for } r, s < m \tag{12.10}$$

Now consider any larger system obtained by adjoining a further element to the set of indices. Without loss in generality, let m be that element and $S_m(A)$ the system obtained. It will be shown that there exists x_m so that the x_r $(r \leq m)$ that extend the solution x_r $(r < m)$ of $S_{m-1}(A)$ are a solution of $S_m(A)$, that is

$$A_{rs} \geq x_s - x_r \quad \text{for } r, s \leq m \tag{12.11}$$

With the x_r $(r < m)$ satisfying (12.10), x_m has to satisfy

$$A_{rm} \geq x_m - xr \quad \text{for } r < m, \qquad A_{ms} \geq x_s - x_m \quad \text{for } s < m \tag{12.12}$$

Equivalent, $x_s - A_{ms} \leq x_m \leq x_r + A_{rm}$ for $r, s < m$. But a necessary and sufficient condition for the existence of such x_m is that $x_s - A_{ms} \leq x_r + A_{rm}$ for $r, s < m$, equivalently $A_{rm} + A_{ms} \geq x_s - x_r$ for $r, s < m$. By the triangle inequality, (12.11) implies this, so the existence of such x_m is now proved. Thus *any solution of $S_{m-1}(A)$ can be extended to a solution of $S_m(A)$.* Then by an inductive argument it follows that, for any $m \leq n$, any solution x_r $(r \leq m)$ of $S_m(A)$ can be extended to a solution of $S_n(A) = S(A)$, by adjunction of further elements x_r $(r > m)$. It can be concluded that *any system with the triangle inequality has a solution,* because the triangle inequality requires in particular that $A_{11} + A_{11} \geq A_{11}$, or equivalently $A_{11} \geq 0$. This assures that $S_1(A)$ has a solution x_1 and then any such solution x_1 can be extended to a solution x_r $(r \leq n)$ of $S(A)$.

From the foregoing, each of the conditions in the following sequence implies its successor: (i) The existence of a solution. (ii) The cyclical non-negativity test. (iii) The existence of the derived system. (iv) The existence of a solution for the derived system. (v) The existence of a solution.

It was shown first that (i) $\rightarrow$ (ii) $\rightarrow$ (iii). Then because any derived system satisfies the triangle inequality and any system with that property has a solution,

(iii) $\leftrightarrow$ (iv) is shown. Now the identity between the solutions of a system and its derived system shows (iv) $\leftrightarrow$ (i) and establishes equivalence between all the conditions, in particular between (i) and (ii).

The derived system $S(A)$ can be stated in the form

$$-A_{sr} \leq x_s - x_r \leq A_{rs} \quad (r \leq s)$$

requiring the differences $x_s - x_r$ $(r \leq s)$ to belong to the intervals $(-A_{sr}, A_{rs})$. The extension property of solutions assures also the *interval exhaustion property*, that *every point in these intervals is taken by some solution*. Whenever the derived system exists these intervals automatically are all non-empty.

An order U of the indices determined from the coefficients A_{rs} is given by the transitive closure $U = \vec{A}$ of the relation A given by $rAs \equiv A_{rs} \leq 0$. Also, any solution x determines an order $V(x)$ of the indices, where $rV(x)s \equiv x_s \leq x_r$. Whatever the solution, *this is always a refinements of the order U*, that is $V(x) \subset U$ for every solution x. Moreover, *for any order V that is a refinement of U, there always exists a solution x such that $V(x) = V$*. This *order exhaustion property* can be seen from the interval exhaustion property and also by means of the proof of the extension property of solutions by taking the extensions in the required order.

These results can all be translated to apply to a system in the form $a_{rs} \geq x_s/x_r$, now with *multiplicative chain coefficients*, $a_{rij\cdots ks} = a_{ri}a_{ij}\cdots a_{ks}$ and derived coefficients A_{rs} defined from these as before and satisfying *multiplicative triangle inequality* $A_{rs}A_{st} \geq A_{rt}$. The cyclical non-negativity test becomes $a_{rs}a_{st}\cdots a_{qr} \geq 1$. For any solution x, the ratios x_s/x_r are required to lie in the intervals $I_{rs} = (1/A_{sr}, A_{rs})$. From their form these intervals remind of the Paasche–Laspeyres (PL) interval $(1/L_{sr}, L_{rs})$. Also, the multiplicative chain coefficients correspond to the familiar procedure of multiplying chains of price indices, except that there are many chains with given extremities and here one is taken on which the coefficient is minimum. While the non-emptiness of the PL-intervals, whether or not the one index exceeds the other, is a well-known issue, there is no such issue at all with the intervals I_{rs} because *whenever they are defined they are non-empty*, this following from the multiplicative triangle inequality that gives

$$A_{rs}A_{sr} \geq A_{rr} \geq 1.$$

13 The power algorithm

For a system with coefficients a_{rs}, and any $k \leq m \leq n$, let

$$a_{rs}^{[k]} = \min_{i_2 i_k}(a_{ri_2} + a_{i_2 i_3} + \cdots + a_{i_k s}), \quad a_{rs}^{(m)} = \min_{k \leq m} a_{rs}^{[k]} \tag{13.1}$$

According to (12.6), if the derived coefficients exist any one has the form

$$A_{rs} = a_{ri} + a_{ij} + \cdots + a_{ks} \tag{13.2}$$

for some $i, j, \ldots, k$ making $r, i, j, \ldots, s$ all distinct except possibly for the coincidence of r and s. Because there are just n possible values $1, \ldots, n$ for the indices, it follows from (13.1) and (13.2) that $A_{rs} \geq a_{rs}^{(n)}$. But from the definition of the A_{rs} in (12.6) and from (13.1) again, also $A_{rs} \leq a_{rs}^{(n)}$, so now $A_{rs} = a_{rs}^{(n)}$, that is $A = a^{(n)}$. Now writing $+$ as $\cdot$ and min as $+$, (13.1) becomes

$$
\begin{aligned}
a_{rs}^{[k]} &= \sum_{i,\ldots i_{m-1}} a_{ri_1} \cdot a_{i_1 i_2} \cdots a_{i_{k-1}s} \\
&= (a \cdot a \cdots a)_{rs} \quad (k \text{ factors}) \\
&= (a^k)_{rs}
\end{aligned}
$$

that is $a^{[k]} = a^k$, where the 'power' a^k so defined is unambiguous because of associativity of 'multiplication' and 'addition' and the distributivity of 'multiplication' over 'addition' and is determined recurrently from

$$
a^1 = a \quad \text{and} \quad a^k = a \cdot a^{k-1} \tag{13.3}
$$

Then (13.2) becomes $a^{(m)} = \sum_1^m a^k$, and is determined from

$$
a^{(1)} = a \quad \text{and} \quad a^{(m)} = aa^{(m-1)} + a \tag{13.4}
$$

This algorithm with powers in the context of minimum paths in networks is from Bainbridge (1978). Observed now is a simplification that is applicable to the special case of importance here where $a_{rr} = 0$, or where $a_{rr} = 1$ in the multiplicative formulation. If $a_{rr} = 0$, in which case chains of any length include all those of lesser length, we have

$$
a \geq a^2 \geq \cdots \geq a^k \geq \cdots \geq a^m
$$

where the matrix relation $\geq$ means that relation simultaneously for all elements. Therefore in this case $a^{(m)} = a^m$. This with $A = a^{(n)}$, together with (13.3), shows that the matrix A of derived coefficients can be calculated by raising the matrix a of the original coefficients to successive powers, the nth power being A. Should $a^m = a^{m-1}$ for any $m \leq n$ then also $a^m = a^{m+1} = \cdots = a^n = \cdots$ so that $A = a^m$. But in any case the formula $A = a^n$ is valid. Then evidently $A = A^2 = \cdots$, so *the derived matrix is idempotent.* This property is characteristic of any matrix having the triangle inequality.

By taking exponentials, these procedures can be translated to apply to the system in the multiplicative form (7.1), $L_{rs} \geq \phi_s/\phi_r$ with $L_{rr} = 1$. Matrix powers have been defined in a sense where $+$ means min and $\cdot$ means $+$. Taking exponentials turns $+$ into $\cdot$ and leaves min as min, so we are back with $\cdot$ meaning $\cdot$. This makes $\hat{L} = L^n$ a formula for the derived coefficient matrix, where powers now are defined in the ordinary sense except that $+$ now means min. As before, n here can be replaced by any $m \leq n$ for which $L^m = L^{m+1}$, in particular by the first such m found.

References

Afriat, S.N. 1956. 'Theory of Economic Index Numbers'. Mimeographed. Department of Applied Economics, Cambridge.

1960. 'The system of inequalities $a_{rs} > X_s - X_r$'. *Research Memorandum No.* 18, Econometric Research Program, Princeton University, Princeton, NJ. *Proc. Cambridge Phil. Soc.*, **59** (1963), 125–33.

1964. 'The construction of utility functions from expenditure data'. *Cowles Foundation Discussion Paper No.* 144, Yale University. Paper presented at the First World Congress of the Econometric Society, Rome, September 1965. *International Economic Review*, **8** (1967), 67–77.

1967a. 'The Cost of Living Index'. In *Studies in Mathematical Economics: In Honor of Oskar Morgenstern*. Edited by M. Shubik. Princeton, NJ: Princeton University Press.

1970a. 'The Concept of a Price Index and Its Extension'. Paper presented at the Second World Congress of the Econometric Society, Cambridge, August 1970.

1970b. 'The Cost and Utility of Consumption'. Mimeographed. Department of Economics, University of North Carolina at Chapel Hill, North Carolina.

1970c. 'Direct and Indirect Utility'. Mimeographed. Department of Economics, University of North Carolina at Chapel Hill, North Carolina.

1972a. 'Revealed Preference Revealed'. Waterloo Economic Series No. 60, University of Waterloo, Ontario.

1972b. 'The Theory of International Comparisons of Real Income and Prices'. In *International Comparisons of Prices and Output*, Proceedings of the Conference at York University, Toronto, 1970. Edited by D. J. Daly, 13–84. Studies in Income and Wealth, vol. 37. New York: National Bureau of Economic Research.

1973. 'On a System of Inequalities in Demand Analysis: an Extension of the Classical Method'. *International Economic Review*, **14**, 460–72.

1974. 'Sum-symmetric matrices'. *Linear Algebra and its Applications*, **8**, 129–140.

1976. *Combinatorial Theory of Demand*. London: Input–Output Publishing Co.

1977a. 'Minimum paths and subpotentials in a valuated network'. Research Paper 7704, Department of Economics, University of Ottawa.

1977b. *The Price Index*. Cambridge and New York: Cambridge University Press.

1978a. '*Index Numbers in Theory and Practice* by R. G. D. Allen'. *Canadian Journal of Economics*, **11**, 367–9.

1978b. '*Theory of the Price Index* by Wolfgang Eichhorn and Joachim Voeller'. *Journal of Economic Literature*, **16**, 129–30.

1979. *Demand Functions and the Slutsky Matrix*. Princeton, NJ: Princeton University Press.

1980. 'Matrix Powers: Classical and Variations'. Paper presented at the Matrix Theory Conference, Auburn University, Auburn, Alabama, 19–22 March 1980.

Allen, R. G. D. 1975. *Index Numbers in Theory and Practice*. London: Macmillan.

Bainbridge, S. 1978. 'Power algorithm for minimum paths', private communication. Department of Mathematics, University of Ottawa, Ontario.

Berge, C. 1963. *Topological Space*. New York: Macmillan.

Berge, C. and Ghouila-Houri, A. 1965. *Programming, Games and Transportation Networks*. London: Methuen & Co. New York: John Wiley and Sons.

Dantzing, G. 1963. 'Linear Programming and Its Extensions'. Princeton, NJ: Princeton University Press.

Edmunds, J. 1973. 'Linear programming formula for minimum paths', private communication. Department of Combinatorics and Optimization, Faculty of Mathematics, University of Waterloo, Ontario.

Eichhorn, W. and Voeller, J. 1976. *Theory of the Price Index: Fisher's Test Approach and Generalizations*. Berlin, Heidelburg and New York: Springer Verlag.

Fiedler, M. and Ptak, V. 1967. 'Diagonally dominant matrices'. *Czech. Math J.*, **17**, 420–33.

Fisher, I. 1927. *The Making of Index Numbers*. Third edition. Boston and New York: Houghton Mifflin Company.

Geary, R. C. 1958. 'A note on the comparison of exchange rates and purchasing power between countries'. *J. Roy Stat. Soc.* A, **121**, 97–9.

Hicks, J. R. 1956. *A Revision of Demand Theory*. Oxford: Clarendon Press.

Houthakker, H. S. 1950. 'Revealed Preference and the Utility Function', *Economica*, New Series, **17**, 159–74.

Samuelson, P. A. 1947. *The Foundations of Economic Analysis*. Cambridge, Mass.: Harvard University Press.

Samuelson, P. A. and Swamy, S. 1974. 'Invariant Economic Index Numbers and Canonical Duality: Survey and Synthesis'. *American Economic Review*, **64**, 566–93.

Shephard, R. W. 1953. *Cost and Production Functions*. Princeton, NJ: Princeton University Press.

Theil, H. 1960. 'Best linear index numbers of prices and quantities'. *Econometrica*, **28**, 464–80.

1975–1976. *Theory and Measurement of Consumer Demand*. Two volumes. Amsterdam: North-Holland Publishing Company.

1979. *The System-wide Approach to Microeconomics*. The University of Chicago Press.

Yen, J. Y. 1975. *Shortest Path Network Problems*. Meisenheim am Glan: Verlag Anton Hain.

7
Index-number practice
under conditions of hyperinflation
—with particular reference to Peru

International Development Research Centre (IDRC), Ottawa, 1991.

Index-number practice
under conditions of hyperinflation
—with particular reference to Peru

PREFACE

The Consumer Price Index (CPI) is a summary, by means of a single number, of a changing relationship between commodities and consumers. Under normal conditions there are stabilities that maintain usual practice with the CPI as a social institution which is adequate for the needs it is designed to meet. Under extreme conditions, important changes take place that cannot be accounted by means of the CPI, or any single number. It may be necessary to monitor such changes on a regular basis. A review of essentials about the CPI will put the concept in a framework for a response to this need.

The 'Fleetwood map' is exploited in chapter 1, for a graphic representation of bias associated with a price index, particularly the bias in regard to different income classes.

Also taken up, in chapter 2, is the issue of replacing the arithmetic mean formula for the CPI by the corresponding geometric mean. Such a replacement provides an offset for the exaggeration of the inflation rate by the conventional CPI, and allows for the otherwise ignored 'change in the basket'. It also resolves outstanding questions to do with consistency. These issues are present whenever price indices are used, but they take on a greater importance with hyperinflation.

The marginal price index (MPI) method, as laid in chapter 1, is limited to providing a linear income relationship just for the period of the survey. It serves for making a comparison with the homogeneous linear relationship obtained from the average price index or API (=CPI) for that period, and so provides a means for investigating the high/low income bias that accompanies use of the CPI.

In chapter 3 we approach a method that enables an MPI relation to be constructed in any period, on the basis of data from two surveys. This would be comparable with the API relation obtained for any period, and so the matter of bias can be studied further.

There are arithmetic and geometric formula versions of this method[1], and results obtained with them could be compared. Here we provide an exposition of the method in a form where it is integrated with the geometric mean price index. Then it will be possible to study high/low income bias for that index, and compare it with that found for the arithmetic mean index, or conventional CPI, especially for the view that, as also with the matter of inflation exaggeration, the bias with the geometric index should be less.

To be well-conditioned, the method depends on prices changing at different rates from one survey period to the other, a typical circumstance with hyperinflation.

For an early familiarity with the 'linear expenditure system' related to this method, I am again indebted to Sir Richard Stone from the time of the project on "Consumers' Expenditures and Behaviour in the UK" which employed the model.[2] R. Frisch derived the system from a more general one, by imposition of the Slutsky conditions, required for consistency with utility maximization, which brought about a reduction in the parameters. L. R. Klein and H. Rubin brought forward its significance for the cost-of-living index problem.[3] I added considerations which included a point about indeterminacy related to location of the 'centre', otherwise hidden in a constant of integration.[4] Further developments are in chapter 3, especially about the way parameters are found from survey data, giving the approach a workable basis.

I have pleasure to thank very much Mario Berrios, International Development Research Centre, Ottawa, who initiated this project, and my participation in it. I am indebted also to John Kuiper for his collaboration, as in the investigation we carried out some years ago for the Economic Council of Canada, where ideas pursued now with a renewed relevance had a beginning. Since that time and especially recently he has had a wide experience of Peru, and this has been additionally valuable. My thanks are due similarly to Farid Matuk, Univeridad Catolica, Lima.

1 The Laspeyres and Paasche API formulae have precise MPI counterparts, with a corresponding role as limits, obtained simply by replacing consumption bundles by marginal bundles. For the counterpart of Fisher's 'ideal index', we have the MPI that comes out of Wald's "New Formula". In chapter 3 we deal instead with the geometric fixed-exponent MPI.

2 Richard Stone, *The Measurement of Consumers' Expenditure and Behaviour in the United Kingdom, 1920–1938*. Cambridge University Press, 1966.

3 Lawrence R. Klein and H. Rubin (1947), "A constant utility index of the cost of living". *Review of Economic Studies* 15, 38 (1947), 84–7.

4 "On Bernoullian Utility for Goods and Money", *Research Memorandum* No. 35 (December 1961), Econometric Research Program, Princeton University. *Metroeconomica* 15, 1 (1963), 38–46.

1
Fleetwood Maps

1. The CPI and Fleetwood

William Fleetwood, in 1707, took a bundle of goods a, which he supposed represented the life-style of a student, and calculated its cost A_1 in his day, and the coat A_0 in "H. IV days", 400 years earlier. If p_0, p_1 were the prices in those periods, we have[5]

$$A_0 = p_0 a, \quad A_1 = p_1 a.$$

One can understand these to be the incomes needed in the two periods that have the desired purchasing power, or maintain the standard of living or life-style precisely represented by the commodity bundle a. With the considerations to follow, it should be appreciated that Fleetwood had no significance to give to the ratio A_1/A_0.

The CPI can be understood as a concept by reference to Fleetwood's procedure. By sampling consumers' expenditures in some period, an estimate is made of the average consumption bundle $\bar{x}$ for the considered population, usually a specific more or less limited *target group*. Then[6]

$$P_{10} = p_1 \bar{x} / p_0 \bar{x} \qquad\qquad 1.1$$

is the CPI for the group, with 0, 1 as base and current periods, the prices in those periods being given by p_0, p_1. The outstanding use of it is to provide the relation

$$M_1 = P_{10} M_0 \qquad\qquad 1.2$$

between incomes M_0, M_1 which are judged to have the same purchasing power in those periods, with the prices that prevail. A certain condition is involved in any presumption of truth of this relation, for reflecting actual living costs in individual cases.

---

5 With prices given by a row vector p and quantities by a column vector x, px is the cost of the quantities x at the prices p.

6 We omit the date of the survey as immaterial. Here there is the position, to be explained further, that dating the quantities in the base period, and with that identifying the CPI with a Laspeyres index, as in textbooks, is not relevant to the practical matter. In any case, we are dealing not with the usual single theoretical individual but a diverse population.

One could say

$$\bar{M}_0 = p_0\bar{x}, \quad \bar{M}_1 = p_1\bar{x} \qquad\qquad 1.3$$

are the averages of individual incomes for the reference periods that maintain desired purchasing powers, and that the relation

$$\bar{M}_1 = P_{10}\bar{M}_0 \qquad\qquad 1.4$$

is exact, by the definition, stated in 1.1, of P_{10}.

2. Discrepancies with the CPI

With Fleetwood, the population consisted of a single individual, the student he was addressing, and there was the single bundle of goods x. But now we have a sample S of bundles, with $\bar{x}$ as the average of the $x \in S$. There is of course no actual consumer of this average bundle. Rather, the individual costs

$$M_0 = p_0x, \quad M_1 = p_1x \quad (x \in S) \qquad\qquad 2.1$$

with ratios which may be far from P_{10}, are associated with real consumers who have a diversity of life-styles. The cost averages are given by 1.3, and it is true that 1.4 shows the correct adjustment for the current average in relation to the base, obtained by means of the price index. Also, the use of 1.2 to adjust individual incomes currently would produce this correct current average. However, it cannot be said that the individual costs determined from 2.1 will satisfy 1.2, as would be required if practice with the price index is to be correct in regard to the real consumers.

Special circumstances would support this correctness:

(a) Prices all move in proportion, or have fixed ratios, so their vectors in different periods all lie on the same ray.
(b) Quantities in the various bundles have fixed ratios, or the bundles all lie on the same ray in the commodity space.

While (b) must be rejected (for reasons to be remarked later, even though this is the ideal condition for the use of price indices, as also will be elaborated), the tolerability of usual practice depends on an absence of systematic departure from (a). However, as likely with hyperinflation, departures from (a) could be extreme, with important consequences.

3. Fleetwood maps[7]

Our considerations will be assisted by a method of graphical representation, which can be introduced with an elaboration of Fleetwood's procedure, and use of the diagram shown below. This will lead to one proposal towards laying out data for

---

7 Afriat and Kuiper (1973), Afriat (1977), pp. 7 and 162ff, and Cameron (1987).

Fleetwood Map

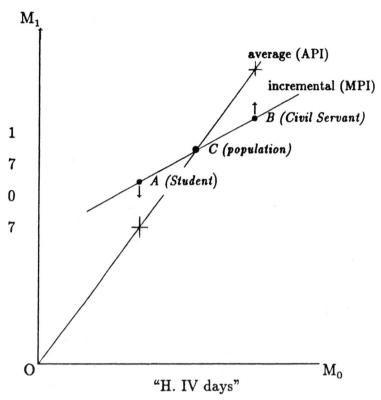

average (API)

incremental (MPI)

B *(Civil Servant)*

C *(population)*

A *(Student)*

M_1

1
7
0
7

O

M_0

"H. IV days"

monitoring the movement of prices, in a consistent scheme that contains the normal CPI as an element, and shows its place among others that are more informative. Then another proposal will be made, more basic and rudimentary, which could be auxiliary to this scheme, or an alternative.

The costs Fleetwood obtained for the requirements of his Student, represented by the bundle *a*, provide the coordinates for a point $A = (A_0, A_1)$, in the *Fleetwood or income space* $\mathcal{F}$ associated with the prices in the base and current periods 0, 1. If, as usual with 'price index' thinking, these costs are used just to provide the ratio A_1/A_0, which is the CPI for the population made by the single individual, and the slope of the ray from O to A, in effect we would be given knowledge of just the ray, without information of this important specific point on it.

Beside the Student, Fleetwood might just as well have considered another representative type in the population, with a different level of means, and life-style; say, the Civil Servant, whose typical consumption *b* provides a second point B in the income space. With these two types given equal weight, the average consumption bundle is the point.

$$c = \tfrac{1}{2}(a + b),$$ 3.1

in the commodity space, and the corresponding Fleetwood point, in the income space, is

$$C = \tfrac{1}{2}(A + B),$$ 3.2

which, in this case of equal weights, is the mid-point of the segment joining A, B. The ratio

$$P_{10} = C_1/C_0$$ 3.3

is the CPI for the population consisting of these two individuals. It is the slope of the ray from O to C, which is the graph of the relation

$$M_1 = P_{10}M_0$$ 3.4

in the income space. A purpose in the construction of the CPI is use of this relation for deciding the adjustment of incomes, from base to current period, in order that they keep pace with the change in prices and maintain their purchasing power.

4. Income class bias

In the way the diagram is drawn, a particular tendency is evident in the fortunes of those concerned, were they to receive this adjustment. The sense of it is indicated by the arrows attached to the points A, B. The Student has a shortage, and the Civil Servant an excess by exactly the same amount. The average adjustment is correct, but masked in this is the transfer of purchasing power that has taken place, from one individual to the other.

   With this illustrative case, it is not to be suggested that there is an absolute reason for the sense of the transfer. However, it has a likelihood in some circumstances. An obvious case is when prices for basic essentials, which absorb a large part of lower incomes, rise faster than those of luxury items, which are more for the rich. It is possible to have the cost of living rising much faster than the CPI for certain groups, defined by whatever characteristics, and at the same time significantly slower for others.[8]

5. API and MPI

During the 1970s in Canada, we had the case of food prices rising more rapidly than others. This was surmised to be to the disadvantage of the poor, who spent a

---

8 A case has been noted, I believe in Italy in the 1970s, where the CPI showed the 'level of prices' to be constant, while the cost of living was rising significantly for the poor, and falling for the rich.

greater part of income on food than the rich[9]. To investigate the matter[10], we in effect divided the population sample S into two equal parts S', S'' corresponding to incomes above and below the median. Dealing with the associated points in the income space, we have the overall average point C represented as the average of the average points A, B for the two classes. Joining A, B by a line, necessarily going through C, we compared its slope R_{10}, termed the *incremental* or *marginal price index* (MPI), with the slope P_{10} of the ray from O to C, this last being the *average price index* (API), with which we identify the CPI. We then had

$$B_{10} = R_{10}/P_{10} \qquad\qquad 5.1$$

as a coefficient reflecting the *bias* as between high and low incomes, resulting from indiscriminate use of the population CPI. This being found with a value <1 provided a confirmation of the original surmise which prompted the investigation. We also had a quantitative statement and graphical representation that contained further information.

The equation for the line joining A, B is

$$M_1 - C_1 = R_{10}(M_0 - C_0), \qquad\qquad 5.2$$

where

$$C_1 = P_{10}C_0, \qquad\qquad 5.3$$

which shows income average adjusted by the API, and deviations from the average adjusted by the MPI.

Replacement of the homogeneous linear relation 3.4 by this general linear relation eliminates the misallocation between the two income groups (however, there can still be faults with allocation within a group).

A commonly proposed response to the possible bias from reliance on a single overall price index is to construct a separate price index for each of the distinguished population groups. This is an impossible remedy, just as it is impossible to know the line joining A, B from being given the pair of rays from O going through A, B.[11]

6. Price index concept

What has been done instead is quite different. It was arrived at by going back to Fleetwood, and then returning some way towards 'price index' thinking which is thoroughly a part of ordinary economic discussion. In exploring for what may stand out as appropriate in conditions of acute hyperinflation, later we will have to approach Fleetwood again, and remain closer.

---

9 The point was made in a report "Prices and the Poor" issued by Health and Welfare Canada.
10 Intergovernmental Project on Consumers' Expenditures and Inflation, Economic Council of Canada, carried out with Professor J. Kuiper, University of Ottawa.
11 The price index and 'price level' being thoroughly ingrained in economic thinking and language obstructs appreciation of this point.

The 'homogeneity' that is inseparable from the 'price index', in both theory and practice, should have emphasis, since it is the first basis for that restrictive concept.[12] Also, it is of importance to us now.

In practice, the homogeneity is manifested, first and most simply, just in *the way a price index is used*. This is where it provides the slope to a homogeneous linear relation, in the income space, between incomes in two periods that have the same purchasing power, as in 3.4.

Another manifestation, now having reference to the commodity space, comes directly from formulae for price indices, and the way quantity data enter homogeneously, so the index depends on quantities in a data bundle only to the extent of their ratios, or the ray they determine. For instance, the Laspeyres index

$$P_{10} = p_1 x_0 / p_0 x_0 \qquad\qquad 6.1$$

is unchanged when x_0 is replaced by any point $x_0 t$ $(t > 0)$ on the same ray.

In consistency with this, in reference to a demand function, the expansion paths, or loci of consumption for different levels of income while prices are fixed, should be rays in the commodity space, or lines through the origin.

The basis that the price index can be given in utility theory brings out again the limitation of the concept, and the characteristic homogeneity, which then has further expressions.

7. Cost of living problem

When a utility is given, the relation between incomes that have the same purchasing power at different prices is determined, say

$$M_1 = F_{10}(M_0), \qquad\qquad 7.1$$

where the function F_{10} carries prices p_0, p_1 as parameters. The cost of living index problem arises from a utility not being given explicitly. Any utility that may be considered has to be inferred on the basis of fragmentary demand data, and a consistency is required of the data for such a utility to exist.

All that can be said about F_{10} as a consequence of its utility derivation is that it is a monotonic increasing function. However, with the use of a price index there is the offer that F_{10} has the special form

$$F_{10}(M_0) = P_{10} M_0, \qquad\qquad 7.2$$

where P_{10} is independent of M_0.

This special form has an implication about the utility, that it be representable by a function ϕ with the 'constant returns' property

$$\phi(xt) = \phi(x)t \quad (t > 0). \qquad\qquad 7.3$$

---

12 However, this escapes mention in most works.

An equivalent implication as concerns demand is that the expansions paths in the commodity space all be rays, or lines through the origin. *These restrictions therefore have to be in view whenever price indices are dealt with.*

8. Expansion paths

As a consequence, the quantity data used in price index formulae must be seen as specifying not single points in the commodity space, but expansion paths in the form of rays. By the same principle, any quantities demanded at the same prices must lie on the same ray, their difference being related to income level. Since expenditure surveys produce diverse sets of quantities with a single set of prices, here is a severe restriction on the data if the model is going to fit.

In ordinary circumstances, the CPI is a social institution that gives the service wanted of it. But as concerns changes one may need to know about under conditions of hyperinflation, it is not informative enough. At this point, with recognition of the nature of the price index as a concept, there can be doubt that all help that might be wanted can be found while staying with it.

Three procedures are illustrated together in the figure shown in §3. There is the isolated point of Fleetwood, the ray through an average point for the CPI, and then the modification of the ray into a general line by disaggregating to overall average point C into partial averages A and B. This diagram will be useful for further discussion.

9. Wald's "New Formula"

A. Wald (1939) made an approach to the cost of living problem directly, and perhaps unprecedently from being without the usual homogeneous 'price index' form of confinement being imposed at the start. His data had the form of a pair of expansion paths, for the base and current periods, in the form of general lines in the commodity space. His "New Formula", which he produced as a result, is a general linear relation between incomes with the same purchasing power. The MPI method described above, as a modification of the API method used for the CPI, also produces such a general linear relation, shown in 5.2.

Most price index formulae[13] involve data in the form of a pair of demand observations (p_0, x_0), (p_1, x_1). Here it has been argued that the consumption bundles really enter as determinants of expansion paths in the form of rays. Hence, Wald's data can be regarded as a modification where the rays are replaced by general lines.

10. Objections to linearity

The estimation of expansion paths in the form of general lines has had a following in econometrics. Also this form goes some way to overcome objections that can

---

13 Irving Fisher (1922) deals with approaching two hundred formulae.

be made to having rays as a model. But objections can still be made to this form. This is because expansion paths have a basic non-linearity, where with increasing income there is a turning away from inferior goods in favour of superior ones, making the paths definitely curved. In any case, there are obvious criticisms about expansion paths on either model, rays or lines, and we will consider these now. Our later proposal will avoid both, and also allow other factors to distinguish consumers, beside income.

There is a clear absurdity in taking expansion paths to be rays. It would say that consumers with twice the income just buy twice as much of everything. However, we know that the poor buy things the rich would rather not have, while the rich buy things the poor have never even seen.

When rays are replaced by general lines, that may be better, but still an absurdity remains. It would be to say that, give an extra $100 of income to a consumer on the threshold of subsistence, and to another glutted with affluence, and the extra goods they will buy, the incremental bundles, where we allow also negative quantities, will be identical. However, we expect these bundles to be completely different, and likely to contain elements with opposite sign.

From this evidence, though we may give some favour to the MPI method, as auxiliary to the API (=CPI) and working in a framework where they can be viewed together (as in the figure of §3), it is not going to be an adequate response to questions arising under conditions of hyperinflation. We will consider such questions, and arrive at procedures that take us again rather close to Fleetwood.

11. Information shortage

With hyperinflation, in reliance on macro-statistics from which details escape, there is the chance of critical thresholds being passed quickly without notice. There could be multiple unexpected failures, some without repair. For avoidance, or some warning about what might be taking place, statistics about critical areas are required. Beside groups in the population, these include facilities, institutions and so forth. What is wanted broadly in any case is a model of behaviour depending on price conditions. A most simple example, possibly appropriate for some such targets, would be a bundle of goods, representing factors for maintenance, or a particular performance, even just survival.

It may also be envisaged that certain payments be settled with reference to the cost of a specific bundle of goods, agreed in each case. A worker's pay or salary, for instance, or a part of it, might be determined from the current cost of some agreed bundle.

12. Group separation

The CPI has its target group, but provides for no other group distinction. With the MPI method, incomes are distinguished. But other factors could be significant as concerns exposure to extreme inflationary conditions, such as region, occupation, urban/rural, and other divisions that may be judged to enter.

An emphasis here, taken with all that has been said earlier, is on specific costs, as against cost ratios—in other words, putting aside 'price index' thinking, and returning to Fleetwood.

Apart from such dealings with specific income or other consumer groups, this is not to suggest displacement of the CPI as a social institution, bearing on the broad generality of money and transactions.

That being so, it should be of interest to lay out the structure in which the CPI is a particular element, the otherwise abandoned information contained in its data, and be able view relationships revealed in that way.

A step in that direction is shown already in the Fleetwood Map diagram in §3, from retention of the actual costs C_0, C_1 lost in the CPI ratio $P_{10} = C_1/C_0$, in other words, keeping the point C, otherwise lost in information of the ray through it.

13. Disaggregation

The sample S in the commodity space determines a collection of points in the income space, which have C as their average. When the population is split into subgroups, so correspondingly is S, and then T. With the MPI method, the population is divided into subgroups with income above and below the median, of the same size, each equal to half the population. The total weight on C is thus distributed equally on the points A, B of which it is the average (representing this, the dots marking A, B have been made half the size of the one marking C).

From this procedure, the broader principle of disaggregation of C in respect to any partition of the population can be gathered. Apart from income, as in the illustration, the partition may be made in respect to any factors, such as region, occupation, urban/regional, blue/white collar, or whatever. In that way a *Fleetwood* or *inflation map* is obtained, a scatter of points with weights proportional to group size attached to them, their average with those weights being C. From such a map it is possible to read the average income and average inflation factor, or CPI, for any group represented, and have a graphic view of the assemblage, revealing relations of groups to each other, and to the population average C.

2
Critique of the Conventional CPI

1. Substitution effect

When prices increase at different rates, there is a shift of demand away from goods with higher rates towards those with lower, or *substitution* takes places. This is a well known principle for the theory. It is also well known from practical consumer experience, and with hyperinflation it becomes a major factor. Then it is felt that this significant part of experience should be reflected in the construction of index numbers. From the sides of both methodological principal and of data practicality, how this should be managed has made a dilemma.

The conventional CPI practice, from its basic principle, gives no such needed accommodation. Its faithfulness to consumer realities depends on the opposite, that no substitution at all takes place. Any questioning about this usually rest with an admission about 'change in the basket of goods'. There has always been obscurity about how to proceed beyond that. For everyday practice under normal conditions, even if not so well with hyperinflation, the matter is put aside as a tolerable and even inevitable flaw in practical statistics.

If this 'change' matter should be taken further, there is the issue, which may at first seem most outstanding:

(i)   How should the change is to be known from the usually available data?

Then there is the further issue, just as important even though it may appear to be made more distant by the first:

(ii)   What use should be made of the knowledge?

These two issues will eventually be brought fully together in our considerations.

2. Review of CPI practice

A usual situation to consider is when a single bundle of goods a (the 'basket'—an average for the community, or the 'target group') is provided from a survey during a period, together with the prices p.[14] The expenditure associates with this bundle is therefore pa. The expenditure shares for the goods, or 'weights', are then

$$\omega_i = p_i a_i / pa. \qquad 2.1$$

In a subsequent period when the prices are p^r, the CPI is

$$P_r = p^r a / pa = \sum_i p_i^r a_i / pa$$

$$= \sum_i (p_i a_i / pa)(p_i^r / p_i) = \sum_i \omega_i (p_i^r / p_i), \qquad 2.2$$

with the survey period as 'base'. In going to any other subsequent period, say when the prices are instead p^s, we have the value

$$P_s = p^s a / pa = \sum_i \omega_i (p_i^s / p_i). \qquad 2.3$$

understood to reflect change in the 'level of prices', from one subsequent period to the other. It is as if

$$P_{r/s} = P_r / P_s \qquad 2.4$$

should serve as the CPI for period r with the period s base.[15]

Were a survey conducted in period s, to obtain a bundle a^s, and weights ω_i^s,

$$P_{rs} = p^r a^s / p^s a^s = \sum_i \omega_i^s (p_i^r / p_i^s) \qquad 2.5$$

would have claim to being another candidate for this comparison–CPI. Unless a^s happened to be on the same ray as a, in other words, there is no 'substitution', the two values obtained are generally different. But another fair candidate for the comparison index is

$$P_{rs} = \sum_i \omega_i (p_i^r / p_i^s), \qquad 2.6$$

where we use the old weights.[16] We now have three different indices, which could in principle all serve the same purpose. With either P_{rs}, another candidate for P_s is

$$\vec{P}_s = P_r P_{rs}, \qquad 2.7$$

obtained by 'chaining' the first index with the second, and it is not going to be the same as the direct P_s.

A variance between the practices found in USA and UK should be noted. In the USA the survey, with a large sample, is infrequent. In the UK, there are

14 We omit it for simplicity, but things dated in the period of the survey might have been tagged with a 0.
15 While P_r and P_s may be considered to have the Laspeyres index form, this certainly cannot, there being not just two dates involved, but three.
16 This index, determined from an arithmetic mean, does not have the property of chaining-consistency. However, when it is replaced by the corresponding geometric mean, we have an index, to be discussed later, which does have that property.

more frequent surveys, with a relatively small sample, and the index numbers are *chained*, so that, instead of the direct P_{rs}, we would have

$$\vec{P}_{rs} = P_{ri} P_{ij} \cdots P_{ks}, \hspace{3cm} 2.8$$

with chains of some length, using different weights. It is supposed the UK method, with the frequent update, has merit in making an allowance for 'change in the basket', or 'substitution'. However, over longer periods the US indices are also chained, and over short intervals the UK practice is the same as the US.

There is an ambivalence about UK practice, first forgetting about the past by starting a new index, and then remembering it by chaining with the old index. In making a comparison between different times, there must be something that is transported unchanged through time, to provide the yardstick.

In theoretical principle, as concerns price indices, utility is that yardstick. It is not any utility, but one with the special conical or homogeneity property, which makes equivalent incomes at different prices have a homogeneous linear relation, and demand to be such that the expansion paths are rays.

With survey data, a demand observation (p, a) is obtained for the community, in order to determine weights ω_i. Such data, with a sample of demands for a single set of prices, is no basis for elaborate utility construction. However, whatever should be the utility, it is outstanding that the ray through a should provide the expansion path for prices p. If there is going to be a yardstick, we will certainly have to keep a hold on this.[17] Yet with UK practice, and the US less frequently, it is let go. There can be some wondering about what should come out of doing that.

3. Geometric v. Arithmetic

Ideally, for consistency in either practice, one would like to have[18]

$$P_s = P_r P_{rs}. \hspace{3cm} 3.1$$

We have this in the singular case of the commodity bundles a and a^r, of the two surveys, being on the same ray. That is, the case no substitution—just the case outside present concern, which is with the possibility of substitution.

But in any case, there is an aspect here, in the hybrid of additive and multiplicative, where an arithmetic mean has to be a product of arithmetic means, that could strike some minds as unnatural.[19]

Where a survey used simply to determine weights ω_i, once and for all, there would still be this consistency difficulty with chaining, were we to continue using the arithmetic mean. From the usual formula, but with the modification of fixed

---

17 At least, while following usual practice with the arithmetic mean formula (see secs. 16–18).
18 This is the 'Chain Test' of Irving Fisher, otherwise stated $P_{rt} = P_{rs} P_{st}$.
19 Another bad case is Fisher's "Ideal Index", a geometric mean of arithmetic means.

weights, we have

$$P^a_{rs} = \sum_i \omega_i (p^r_i / p^s_i),$$ 3.2

p^r, p^s being price vectors for any two periods, r, s where s is current, and r is the base or comparison period. With this formula the price index, in principle a ratio of 'price levels', is estimated as an arithmetic mean of individual price ratios, with these weights. Except when the prices in the two periods are proportional, that is, the vectors are on the same ray, or have the relation $p^r \parallel p^s$, meaning $p^r = p^s \alpha$ for some $\alpha > 0$, we would not even have

$$P^a_{sr} = (P^a_{rs})^{-1},$$ 3.3

which is the Reversal Test of Irving Fisher, let alone the Chain Test. Here again is the syndrome of unfittingness of the arithmetic mean.

But why use the arithmetic mean? With the textbook view of the CPI as a Laspeyres properly put aside, one could just as well consider the geometric mean

$$P^g_{rs} = \prod_i (p^r_i / p^s_i)^{\omega_i},$$ 3.4

with the same fixed weights as exponents. This inevitably satisfies the Chain Test, so the chaining indices with this formula always has the desired consistency. One would only need calculate these indices relative to any one period, say 0, taken as base, and then we would have

$$P^g_{rs} = P^g_{r0} / P^g_{r0}.$$ 3.5

The inconsistency that accompanies chaining of usual indices may perhaps be ignored as a minor matter under normal conditions. With hyperinflation it can begin to be pronounced, and here is a compelling case for use of the fixed exponent geometric formula. There is yet another argument for using it, for the way it provides a response to 'change in the basket', or for dealing with the substitution problem, as becomes especially important with hyperinflation. This is elaborated in the next section.

The geometric mean is a reminder of a formula that used to be known as Palgrave's index. However, with that the weights or exponents are not fixed, but always dated in the base period, just as they are with the Laspeyres index.

By the general Theorem of the Mean, a geometric mean with, whatever exponents, does not exceed the corresponding arithmetic mean, the equality holding if and only if the numbers are all equal. Accordingly,

$$\prod_i (p^r_i / p^s_i)^{\omega_i} \le \sum_i \omega_i (p^r_i / p^s_i),$$ 3.6

the equality holding if and only if $p^r \parallel p^s$. This shows Palgrave's index does not exceed that of Laspeyres, and is equal to it only in the case of prices in the two periods being proportional.[20]

---

20 All price indices should agree under this condition.

4. Denial of substitution

When I offered to John Kuiper, shortly after he had returned from Peru, the geometric *v.* arithmetic argument, together with the enhancements concerning substitution about to be accounted, he promptly told me of someone he saw in Lima who had continually and emphatically submitted a very strong conviction in favour of the geometric. This is Dr Roberto Abousarda, former Deputy Minister of Finance.

As we have gathered, paths to that conviction can be various. And that notwithstanding, it may still take a shock of hyperinflation to give credible conviction to any departure from established custom with the CPI. In any case, from what I have understood, Señor Abousarda must have sympathy with arguments made above, as also I expect with those to follow.

With the data (p, a) obtained from a survey, points on the expansion ray specified by the bundle a are associated with different levels of income.[21] With the prices p, and any income M, the demand is given by

$$x = a(M/pa). \tag{4.1}$$

Then the *expenditure shares* for individual commodities are

$$\omega_i = p_i x_i / px = p_i a_i / pa. \tag{4.2}$$

By taking the *basic bundle*

$$b = a(1/pa) \tag{4.3}$$

which is associate with a unit of income, just as a is with the average income pa, we have

$$x = bM \tag{4.4}$$

as the demand for prices p with any income M. Also, the

$$\omega_i = p_i b_i \tag{4.5}$$

are the expenditure shares, serving as weights in the arithmetic formula, and exponents in the geometric. For demand at prices p, we then have

$$x_i = \omega_i M / p_i, \tag{4.6}$$

for any income M.

With price indices constructed from the arithmetic mean formula, consistency requires demand to be located on a single ray. With this ray specified by the basic bundle b, such a demand behaviour is obtained from the utility function

$$\phi(x) = \max \ [t : bt \leq x]. \tag{4.7}$$

Since $\phi(b) = 1$, this assigns a utility level 1 to the basic bundle b, and similarly a level $\phi(bM) = M$ to the bundle bM obtained with income M. The demand function which derives from this utility function is shown in equation 4.1.

---

21 Dealing with a price index involves all expansion paths being lines through the origin in the commodity space, or rays.

This model of behaviour, where demand is located always on a single fixed ray, whatever the prices, is so restrictive as to exclude exactly the phenomenon we are concerned to represent. This is the phenomenon of substitution, where when prices undergo changes with different rates, there is a movement of the location of demand from one ray to another.

5. Allowance for substitution

We have already found reason for using the geometric mean formula with fixed exponents, from considerations of consistency when indices are chained. The conventional CPI uses an arithmetic mean with fixed weights, given by expenditure shares obtained from a survey, and for consistency requires the fixed expansion ray.

Now by adopting the geometric formula with fixed exponents, again given by the surveyed expenditure shares, we will have the desirable consistency associated with that formula, and at the same time be able to abandon the rigidity of the fixed ray, for a model which gives a proper allowance for substitution.

This will come from a reference to equation 17.6, which, with the ω_i fixed, and p now regarded as variable[22], can be taken to determines

$$b_i = \omega_i / p_i \qquad\qquad 5.1$$

as elements of the basic bundle on the expansion ray associated with any prices p. As one would wish in an account of 'change in the basket', the quantity of a good in the basic bundle, or 'basket of goods' which is bought with each unit of expenditure, decreases with increase of its prices.[23]

Since bM is the commodity bundle on this ray obtained with income M, we have equation 17.7 as a statement of the demand function representing this behaviour. This is the demand function which derives from the utility function

$$\phi(x) = A \prod_i x_i^{\omega_i}, \qquad\qquad 5.2$$

with

$$\theta(p) = B \prod_i p_i^{\omega_i}, \qquad\qquad 5.3$$

where A, B are related by

$$AB = 1 / \prod_i \omega_i^{\omega_i}, \qquad\qquad 5.4$$

---

22 Originally it has the value provided by the survey data, and with the b, so provided also, enters into determination of the w_i, these then taken as fixed.

23 This 'change in the basket' has been a matter of concern for Mario Berrios and Bruno Seminario, regarding the *Indice de Precios al Consumidor (IPC)* constructed at the *Instituto Nacional de Estadistica (INE)*.

the utility level attained with an income M when the prices are p is given by

$$X = M/P, \qquad\qquad 5.5$$

where

$$P = \theta(p). \qquad\qquad 5.6$$

In consequence, for incomes M_r, M_s to attain the same level of utility when the prices are p^r, p^s it is required that

$$M_r/P_r = M_s/P_s, \qquad\qquad 5.7$$

where

$$P_r = \theta(p^r), \quad P_s = \theta(p^s). \qquad\qquad 5.8$$

That is,

$$M_r = P_{rs}M_s, \qquad\qquad 5.9$$

where P_{rs}, which from independence of M_r, M_s appears here in the role of a price index, is given by

$$P_{rs} = P_r/P_s = \prod_i (p_i^r/p_i^s)^{\omega_i}. \qquad\qquad 5.10$$

With this price index, there can also be inspection of the basic bundles associated with the prices, given by

$$b_i^r = \omega_i/p_i^r, \quad b_i^s = \omega_i/p_i^s. \qquad\qquad 5.11$$

These provide evidence of a 'change in the basket' underlying its use.

I hope this discourse on method with the geometric formula will give some satisfaction to Mario Berrios and Bruno Seminario, and others in Lima, who had concern about price index construction that did not allow for 'change in the basket', and of course to Roberto Abousarda, who I understand believed in the geometric formula anyway.

6. Stabilisation

Inflation is sustained by expectation, among other things. For there is the question why sell today if you can sell for more tomorrow, and why buy tomorrow if it is going to cost more than today. Hence with inflation expectation there are shortages of supply or excesses of demand, contributing to the rise of prices. Statements of the inflation rate influence expectation, making overstatement an addition to the inflationary forces.

By commodity substitution, when prices have changed at different rates, there is a reduction in the cost for attaining a given level of utility. The conventional CPI which employs the arithmetic mean formula, and rests on exclusion of substitution, is recognised to overstate the inflation rate. When prices change at very different rates, as usual with hyperinflation, the overstatement would be correspondingly great.

Out of respect for the stabilisation policy, here is yet another recommendation for the geometric formula over the usual arithmetic. Against that, and the other positive recommendations which alone are decisive enough, is the ordinary resistance to departure from custom regardless of its shortcomings. But also the linkage of wages to the CPI creates a support for the inflation exaggeration.

The MPI method, as laid out so far, is limited to providing a linear income relationship just for the period of the survey. It serves for making a comparison with the homogeneous linear relationship obtained from the API (=CPI) for that period, and so provides a means for investigating the high/low income bias that accompanies use of the CPI.

In the following, we will approach a method that enables an MPI relation to be constructed in any period, on the basis of data from two surveys. This would be comparable with the API relation obtained for any period, and so the matter of bias can be studied further.

Again, there are arithmetic and geometric formula versions of this method, and results obtained with them can have a comparison.

3
Geometric Mean Index and Income Bias

1. Expenditures

The utility function

$$\phi(x) = A \prod_i (x_i - c_i)^{\omega_i}, \qquad\qquad 1.1$$

where

$$A > 0, \quad \omega_i \geq 0, \quad \sum_i \omega_i = 1, \qquad\qquad 1.2$$

is associated with the demand function

$$x_i = c_i + (M - pc)\omega_i/p_i. \qquad\qquad 1.3$$

This system is specified by the *marginal expenditure shares* ω_i, the fractions in which extra income is distributed over the goods, which serve as exponents in the utility, and *central point c*.[24]

The expansion path associated with any prices p, or locus of demand while the prices remain fixed, is a line through the central point c, in the direction of the vector b with elements

$$b_i = \omega_i/p_i. \qquad\qquad 1.4$$

This vector b, which is such that $pb = 1$, specifies the extra bundle of goods bought with an extra unit of income, or the *marginal bundle*.

2. Purchasing power

Let

$$\theta(p) = B \prod_i p_i^{\omega_i}, \qquad\qquad 2.1$$

---

24 With prices given by a row vector p and quantities by a column vector x, px is the cost of the quantities x at the prices p.

where A, B are related by

$$AB = 1 \Big/ \prod_i \omega_i^{\omega_i}.$$

2.2

Then the utility attained with an income M, when the prices are p, is given by

$$X = (M - pc)/P,$$

2.3

where

$$P = \theta(p).$$

2.4

For incomes M_r, M_s to attain the same level of utility when the prices are p^r, p^s it is required that

$$(M_r - \mu_r)/P_r = (M_s - \mu_s)/P_s,$$

2.5

for *marginal price levels* given by

$$P_r = \theta(p^r), \quad P_s = \theta(p^s),$$

2.6

and *original incomes* by

$$\mu_r = p^r c, \quad \mu_s = p^s c.$$

2.7

That is,

$$M_r - \mu_r = P_{rs}(M_s - \mu_s),$$

2.8

where P_{rs}, which appears in this *linear puchasing power relation* as the *marginal price index*, is given by

$$P_{rs} = P_r/P_s - \prod_i (p_i^r/p_i^s)^{\omega_i}.$$

2.9

The marginal bundles associated with the prices are given by

$$b_i^r = \omega_i/p_i^r, \quad b_i^s = \omega_i/p_i^s.$$

2.10

3. Survey data

This system, which requires estimation of the marginal expenditure shares and the central point, can be based on survey data from two periods 0, 1.

The data provided from each survey have the form (p, a, b), with price p, an average bundle a, and a marginal bundle b.

It can be supposed that the average bundle a is diaggregated into average a', a'' for incomes above and below the median, so that $a = (a' + a'')\frac{1}{2}$, and with $d = a' - a''$, we have $b = d(1/pd)$.

The marginal expenditure shares are now

$$\omega_i = p_i b_i,$$

3.1

the average expenditure is

$$M = pa,$$ 3.2

and the average expenditure shares are

$$\sigma_i = p_i a_i / M.$$ 3.3

The central point is some point

$$c = a + b\theta,$$ 3.4

indeterminate on the line through a in the direction b, this line being identified with the linear expansion path L for the prices p. We require two such schemes of data to make an inference about the location of c on this line.

4. Shares

The required data now have the form

$$(p^r, a^r, b^r) \quad (r = 0, 1),$$ 4.1

and determine marginal expenditures shares

$$\omega_i^r = p_i^r b_i^r.$$ 4.2

The average expenditures are

$$M_r = P^r a^r,$$ 4.3

and the average expenditure shares are

$$\sigma_i^r = p_i^r a_i^r / M_r.$$ 4.4

For exact consistency of the data with the model, it is required that

$$\omega_i^0 = \omega_i^1, \quad \text{for all } i.$$ 4.5

Allowing for the normal violation of this condition, we take

$$\omega_i = \tfrac{1}{2}(\omega_i^0 + \omega_i^1)$$ 4.6

as an estimate of the marginal expenditure shares.

A correction can now be applied to the marginal bundles b^r that are included in the date, by replacing them with

$$b_i^r = \omega_i / p_i^r.$$ 4.7

For purposes of comparison, we can also deal with the homogeneous index, on the model with the arithmetic or geometric mean, with fixed weights or exponents, in either case given by the expenditure shares σ_i. Then consistency requires

$$\sigma_i^0 = \sigma_i^1, \quad \text{for all } i,$$ 4.8

and we can take

$$\sigma_i = \tfrac{1}{2}(\sigma_i^0 + \sigma_i^1).$$ 4.9

5. Central point

The expansion paths should be the lines L_r described by

$$x = a^r + b^r t, \qquad 5.1$$

with t as parameter. For exact consistency, these lines should intersect, their common point being the central point c of the system, so we would have

$$a^0 + b^0 \theta_0 = a^1 + b^1 \theta_1, \quad \text{for some } \theta_0, \theta_1. \qquad 5.2$$

Normally these will be skew lines. In any case, provided they are not parallel, there is a unique pair of points

$$c^0 = a^0 + b^0 \theta_0, \qquad c^1 = a^1 + b^1 \theta_1 \qquad 5.3$$

on the lines which have minimum distance. These are determined from the conditions

$$b^{0\prime} b^0 \theta_0 - b^{0\prime} b^1 \theta_1 = b^{0\prime} a^1 - b^{0\prime} a^0, \qquad 5.4$$

$$b^{1\prime} b^0 \theta_0 - b^{1\prime} b^1 \theta_1 = b^{1\prime} a^1 - b^{1\prime} a^0, \qquad 5.5$$

on the parameters. In the case where the lines do intersect, these would coincide in their common point c, to be the central point of the system. Otherwise take

$$c = \tfrac{1}{2}(c_0 + c_1). \qquad 5.6$$

With

$$M_r = p^r a^r \quad (r = 0, 1), \qquad 5.7$$

for goodness of fit we should have

$$a_i^r = c_i + (M_r - p^r c)\omega_i / p_i^r, \qquad 5.8$$

or suitably small discrepancies. In any case, to remove any discrepancy, we can now apply a correction to the average bundles a^r included in the data, replacing them by the bundles so determined.

6. Bias

For any periods when the prices are p^r, p^s we now have the income purchasing power relation

$$M_r - \mu_r = P_{rs}(M_s - \mu_s), \qquad 6.1$$

for original incomes given by

$$\mu_r = p^r c, \qquad \mu_s = p^s c, \qquad 6.2$$

and

$$P_{rs} = \prod_i (p_i^r / p_i^s)^{\omega_i} \tag{6.3}$$

is the marginal price index.

We also have the homogeneous linear relation

$$M_r = P_{rs}^* M_s, \tag{6.4}$$

where P_{rs}^* is a price index given by the arithmetic formula

$$P_{rs}^a = \sum_i \sigma_i (p_i^r / p_i^s), \tag{6.5}$$

or the geometric formula

$$P_{rs}^g = \prod_i (p_i^r / p_i^s)^{\sigma_i}. \tag{6.6}$$

In either case we have a bias index

$$B_{rs}^* = P_{rs} / P_{rs}^*, \tag{6.7}$$

reflecting a bias, as between high and low incomes, involved in using the homogeneous relation, this with value <1 signifying a bias in favour of high incomes.

Bibliography

Afriat, S. N. (1956). Theory of Economic Index Numbers (mimeo). Department of Applied Economics, Cambridge.

—— (1960). The Conceptual Problem of a Cost of Living Index. Stanford Meeting of the Econometric Society, August. Abstract in *Econometrica* 29, 3 (1961), 440.

—— (1961). On Bernoullian Utility for Goods and Money. *Research Memorandum* No. 35 (December), Econometric Research Program, Princeton University. *Metroeconomica* 15, 1 (1963), 38–46.

—— (1967). The Cost of Living Index. In Shubik (1997), Ch. 23, 335–65.

—— (1972). The Theory of International Comparisons of Real Income and Prices. In Daly (1972), Ch. I, 13–84.

—— (1976). On Wald's "New Formula" for the Cost of Living. In Eichhorn *et al.* (1978).

—— (1977). *The Price Index.* Cambridge University Press.

—— (1981). On the Constructibility of Consistent Price Indices Between Several Periods Simultaneously. In Deaton (1981), pp. 133–61.

—— (1989). *Logic of Choice and Economic Theory.* Oxford: Clarendon Press.

—— and Nuri T. Jazairi (1988). Fisher's Test Approach to Index Numbers. In Kotz and Johnson (1978).

—— and J. Kuiper (1975). Inflation Maps and the Total and Incremental Inflation Rates. Third World Congress of the Econometric Society, Toronto, August 20–6.

Allen, R. G. D. (1975). *Index Numbers in Theory and Practice.* London: Macmillan.

Cameron, Grant J. (1987). The Marginal Price Index Method: Construction from the Statistics Canada Survey of Family Expenditures—a Robust Approach. M.A. Thesis, Economics Department, University of Ottawa, March 16.

Daly, D. J. (ed). (1972). *International Comparisons of Prices and Output.* Proceedings of the Conference at York University, Toronto, 1970. National Bureau of Economic Research, Studies in Income and Wealth Volume 37. New York: Columbia University Press.

Deaton, Angus (ed). (1981). *Essays in Theory and Measurement of Demand: in honour of Sir Richard Stone.* Cambridge University Press.

Eichhorn, W., R. Henn, O. Opitz and R. W. Shephard (eds.) (1978). *Theory and Applications of Economic Indices.* Proceedings of an International Seminar at the University of Karlsruhe, 23 June–1 July, 1976. Würzburg: Physica-Verlag.

Fisher, Irving (1922). *The Making of Index Numbers.* Boston & New York: Houghton-Mifflin (3rd edition 1927).

Fleetwood, William (1707). *Chronicon Preciosum: Or, An Account of English Money, the Price of Corn, and Other Commodities, for the Last 600 Years—in a Letter to a Student in the University of Oxford.* London: T. Osborne in Gray's-Inn (anonymous 1st edition; 2nd edition 1745, in Codrington Library).

Instituto Nacional de Estadistica (INE) (1991). *Indice de Precios al Consumidor (IPC),* 1985–90 (spreadsheet data).

Jazairi, Nuri T. (1971). An Empirical Study of the Conventional and Statistical Theories of Index Numbers. *Oxford Institute of Economies and Statistics Bulletin* 33, 181–95.

——(1988). Afriat and Jazairi (1988).

Kendall, M. G. and A. Stuart (1967). *The Advanced Theory of Statistics* (2nd edition). Hafner Publishing Co. Volume 2, p. 349.

Keynes, J. M. (1930). *A Treatise on Money*. Volume I, *The Pure Theory of Money*. New York: Harcourt, Brace.

Klein, L. R. and H. Rubin (1947). A constant utility index of the cost of living. *Review of Economic Studies* 15 (38), 84–7.

Kotz, Samuel and Norman L. Johnson (1988). *Encyclopedia of Statistical Sciences.* New York: John Wiley & Sons.

Kuiper, J. (1975). Afriat and Kuiper (1975).

Liesner, Thelma and Mervyn King (eds.) (1975). *Indexing for Inflation.* Institute for Fiscal Studies monograph. London: Heinemann.

Morgenstern, Oskar (1963). *On the Accuracy of Economic Observations* (2nd edition) Princeton University Press.

Mudgett, Bruce D. (1951). *Index Numbers.* New York: John Wiley & Sons Inc.

OECD, Paris (1975). *Indexation of Financial Assets.*

Ruggles, Richard (1967). *Price Indexes and International Price Comparisons.* In *Ten Economic Studies in the Tradition of Irving Fisher.* New York: John Wiley & Sons.

Seminario, Bruno (1990). The Consumer Price Index: Methodology and Problems. Universidad Pacifico, Lima, August.

Shubik, Martin (ed.) (1967). *Studies in Mathematical Economics in Honor of Oskar Morgenstern.* Princeton University Press, 1967.

Stone, Richard (1951). *The Role of Measurement in Economics.* Cambridge University Press.

——(1966). The *Measurement of Consumers' Expenditure and Behaviour in the United Kingdom, 1920–1938.* Cambridge University Press.

Wald, A (1939). A New Formula for the Index of the Cost of Living. *Econometrica* 7 (4), 319–35.

Notation

Ω	the non-negative numbers
Ω^n	non-negative column vectors
$C = \Omega^n$	the commodity space
$x, y, \ldots \in C$	commodity bundles
Ω_n	non-negative row vectors
$B = \Omega_n$	the budget space
$u, v, \ldots \in B$	budget vectors
$p, q, \ldots \in B$	price vectors
	$p \in B, \ x \in C \Rightarrow px \in \Omega$
px	cost of commodity bundle x at prices p
$ux \leq 1$	budget constraint associated with budget vector u
$(p, x) \in B \times C$	demand element showing commodity bundle x demanded at prices p
$R \subset C \times C$	binary relation in C
xRy	x has relation R to y, means $(x, y) \in R$
xR	the set $\{y : xRy\}$ of elements to which x has the relation R
Rx	the set $\{y : yRx\}$ of elements which have the relation R to x
$\bar{R}$	the complement, $x\bar{R}y$ denies xRy
R'	the converse, $xR'y$ asserts yRx
$\vec{R}$	the transitive closure, $x\vec{R}y$ asserts $xRzRz'Rz'' \ldots Ry$ for some $z, z', z'', \ldots$
order R	reflexive xRx, transitive $xRyRz \Rightarrow xRz$ utility order, order in commodity space $xRy \Rightarrow xtRyt \ (t > 0)$ R homogeneous, or conical

$\varphi : C \rightarrow \Omega$ utility function

$\varphi(xt) = \varphi(x)t \ (t \geq 0)$

linearly homogeneous or conical,

graph $\{(x, y) : y = \varphi(x)\}$ is a cone

R represented by φ if $xRy \Leftrightarrow \varphi(x) \geq \varphi(y)$

Bibliography

I   Author's bibliography

Materials from my main published work in the economic index-number area, together with additional items.

Included are my two out of print books:

(1) *The Price Index*. Cambridge University Press, 1977.

(2) *Logic of Choice and Economic Theory*. Clarendon Press, Oxford, 1987 Part III on "The Cost of Living", 185–256.

Additional resources:

The calculation of index numbers of the standard and cost of living. Department of Applied Economics, Cambridge, 1956 (mimeo).

On index numbers in the theory of value and demand. Department of Applied Economics, Cambridge, 1956 (mimeo).

Theory of economic index numbers. Department of Applied Economics, Cambridge, 1956 (mimeo).

On value and demand and theory of index numbers of the standard and cost of living. Department of Applied Economics, Cambridge, 1956 (mimeo). *Bulletin of the Research Council of Israel,* 7 (Section F: Mathematics and Physics), 1 (December 1957).

Value and Expenditure. *Research Memorandum no.* 7 (February 1959), Economic Research Program, Princeton University.

Preferences and the theory of consumers' expenditures. Washington meeting of the Econometric Society, December 1959; abstract in *Econometrica*, 28, 3 (1960), 693–95.

The analysis of preferences. *Research Memorandum* No. 11 (January 1960), Econometric Research Program, Princeton University.

The system of inequalities $a_{rs} > x_s - x_r$. *Research Memorandum* No. 18 (October 1960), Econometric Research Program, Princeton University. *Proc. Cambridge Phil. Soc.* 59 (1963), 125–33.

The conceptual problem of a cost of living index. Stanford Meeting of the Econometric Society, August 1960; abstract in *Econometrica* 28, 3 (1961), 693–5.

Expenditure configurations. *Research Memoranda*, No. 21 (February 1961), Econometric Research Program, Princeton University.

The Cost of Living Index I. *Research Memoranda*, No. 24 (March 1961, Econometric Research Program, Princeton University. In *Studies in Mathematical Economics in Honor of Oskar Morgenstern*, edited by Martin Shubik, Chapter 23: 335–65. Princeton University Press, 1967.

The Cost of Living Index II. *Research Memoranda*, No. 27 (April 1961), Econometric Research Program, Princeton University.

The Cost of Living Index III. *Research Memoranda*, No. 29 (August 1961), Econometric Research Program, Princeton University.

On Bernoullian Utility for Goods and Money. *Research Memoranda*, No. 35 (December 1961), Econometric Research Program, Princeton University. *Metroeconomica* 15, 1 (1963), 38–46.

The algebra of revealed preference. Pittsburgh meeting of the Econometric Society, December 1962; abstract in *Econometrica* 31, 4 (1963), 755.

A Formula for Ranging the Cost of Living. In *Recent Advances in Mathematical Programming, Proceedings of the Chicago Symposium*, 1962, edited by R.L. Graves and P. Wolfe. New York: McGraw Hill, 1962.

An Identity Concerning the Relation between the Paasche and Laspeyres Indices. *Metroeconomica* 15, 2–3 (1963), 136–40.

The Method of Limits in the Theory of Index Numbers. Joint European Conference of the Institute of Mathematical Statistics and the Econometric Society, Copenhagen, July 1963. *Metroeconomica* 21, 2 (1969), 141–65.

The Construction of Utility Functions from Expenditure Data. *Cowles Foundation Discussion Paper* No. 144 (October 1964), Yale University. First World Congress of the Econometric Society, Rome, September 1965. *International Economic Review* 8, 1 (1967), 67–77.

Principles of choice and preference. *Research Report* No. 160 (February 1967), Economics Department, Purdue University.

The Cost and Utility of Consumption. Department of Economics, University of North Carolina, Chapel Hill, 1969 (mimeo).

The concept of a price index and its extension. Second World Congress of the Econometric Society, Cambridge, August 1970.

The Theory of International Comparisons of Real Income and Prices. In *International Comparisons of Prices and Output, Proceedings of the Conference at York University, Toronto, 1970*, edited by D. J. Daly. National Bureau of Economic Reasearch, Studies in Income and Wealth Volume 37, New York, 1972. (Ch. I, 13–84).

On a system of inequalities in demand analysis: an extension of the classical method. *International Economic Review* 14, 1973 (2), 460–72.

Measurement of the Purchasing Power of Incomes with Linear Expansion Data. *Journal of Econometrics* 2, 3 (1974), 343–64.

The Purchasing Power of Incomes. *Annals of Economic and Social Measurement* 4, 1 (Winter 1975), 199–200. Special Issue on Consumer Demand, Proceedings of the National Bureau of Economic Research Conference, NBER West Coast Center, Palo Alto, California, 2–3 May, 1974.

Inflation maps and the total and incremental inflation rates (with John Kuiper). Third World Congress of the Econometric Society, Toronto, 20–26 August 1975.

Inflation and purchasing power. Quantitative Methods and Forecasting Seminar, Department of Manpower and Immigration, Ottawa, 14 October 1975.

Consumers' Expenditures and Inflation. Government of Canada Interdepartmental Project 1975–77, Economic Council of Canada (ECC).

On Wald's "New Formula" for the Cost of Living. In *Theory and Application of Economic Indices*, edited by W. Eichhorn, R. Henn, O. Opitz, R. W. Shephard. Proceedings of an International Seminar at the University of Karlsruhe, 23 June–1 July, 1976. Würzburg: Physica-Verlag, 1978.

The marginal price index in theory and practice. Helsinki meeting of the Econometric Society, August 1976.

The Price Index. Cambridge University Press, 1977.

Index Numbers in Theory and Practice by R. G. D. Allen. *Canadian Journal of Economics* 11, 2 (May 1978), 367–9.

Theory of the Price Index: Fisher's Test Approach and Generalizations by Wolfgang Eichhorn and Joachim Voeller. *Journal of Economic Literature* 16 (March 1978), 129–30.

The power algorithm for generalized Laspeyres and Paasche indices. Athens meeting of the Econometric Society, September 1979.

Matrix powers: classical and variations. Matrix Theory Conference, Auburn, Alabama, 19–22 March 1980.

On the Constructibility of Consistent Price Indices Between Several Periods Simultaneously. In *Essays in Theory and Measurement of Demand: in honour of Sir Richard Stone*, edited by Angus Deaton. Cambridge University Press, 1981. pp 133–61.

The power algorithm for minimum paths, and price indices. Eleventh International Symposium on Mathematical Programming, University of Bonn, 23–27 August 1982.

The True Index. In *Demand, Equilibrium and Trade: Essays in Honour of Ivor F. Pearce*, edited by A. Ingham and A. M. Ulph. London: Macmillan, 1984. 37–56.

Logic of Choice and Economic Theory. Oxford: Clarendon Press, 1987. p. 592.

The price index, the concept in theory and practice, and its extensions. Institute of Socio-Economic Planning, Tsukuba University, 26 April 1988; also Economics Department, Osaka University, and Tohoku University, Sendei.

Fisher's Test Approach to Index Numbers (with Nuri Jazairi). *Encyclopedia of Statistical Sciences*, edited by S. Kotz and Norman L. Johnson. John Wiley & Sons, 1988.

The price index under conditions of hyperinflation—with particular reference to Peru. International Development Research Centre (IDRC), Ottawa, 2 April 1991.

High Inflation Measurement Problems. Bilkent University, Ankara, June 1993; National Statistics Day, Prime Ministry of Turkey, State Institute of Statistics, Ankara, 9 May 1994.

Intergroup structure of inflation in Turkey. International Statistical Institute 51st Session, İstanbul, 18–27 August 1997. With Cengis Erdoğan, State Institute of Statistics, Prime Ministry of Turkey.

II General bibliography

Aczel, J. and W. Eichhorn: Systems of functional equations determining price and productivity indices. *Utilitas Mathematica* 5 (1974), 213–26.

Allen, R. G. D.: The Economic Theory of Index Numbers. *Economica*, New Series 16, 63 (August 1949), 197–203.

—— Index Numbers of Volume and Price, in *International Trade Statistics*, ed. R.G.D. Allen and J. Edward Ely. New York, 1953.

—— Price Index Numbers. *International Statistical Review* 31 (1963), 281–301.

—— *Index Numbers in Theory and Practice*. London: Macmillan, 1975.

—— *The Price Index* by S. N. Afriat. *J. Roy Stat. Soc.* Series A (General) 141 (1978), 3, 418.

Allen, R. G. D., and A. L. Bowley: *Family Expenditure*. London, 1935.

Anderson, O.: Mehr Vorsicht mit Indexzahlen. *Allg. Statist. Arch.* 33 (1949), 472–9.

Antonelli, G. B.: *Sulla Teoria Matematica della Economia Pura* (1886). Reprinted in *Giornale degli Economisti* 10 (1951), 233–263.

Arrow, K. J.: The Measurement of Real Value Added. *Technical Report* 60. IMSSS, Stanford University, California, 1972.

Balk, B. M.: Second thoughts on Wald's cost of living index and Frisch's double expenditure method. *Econometrica* 49, 1981 (6), 1533–8.

—— Household-specific Price Index Numbers 1980–1982 (in Dutch). *Statistische Magazine* 4 (1984), 2, 5–17; Netherlands Central Bureau of Statistics, Voorburg.

—— The Behaviour of the Cost-of-living at Different Levels of Real Income: A Correction. *Economic Letters* 20 (1986), 301–2. See Finke and Lu (1984).

—— On calculating cost of living index numbers for arbitrary income levels. *Econometrica* 58 (1990), 1 (January), 75–92.

Ballegeer, N.: *The Price Index* by S. N. Afriat. *Reflets et Perspectives* Tomme XVIII no. 2, 1989.

Banerjee, Kali S.: *Cost of Living Index Numbers*. New York: Marcel Dekker, 1975.

Beath, John: *The Price Index* by S. N. Afriat. *The Economic Journal* Vol. 88, No. 351 (September 1978), 574.

Benedetti, Carlo: Teorie e tecniche dei numeri indici. *Metron* 22, 1–2 (December 1962), 3–97.

—— Ricerche su un tipo generalizzato di indice del costo della vita. *Metron* 27, 3–4 (December 1969), 3–40.

—— Vecchi e tradizionali indici dei prezzi ricondotti a moderni indici funzionali a costante utilita. *Metron* 30, 1–4 (December 1972), 1–20.

Bergson, A.: *National Income of the Soviet Union Since 1928*. Cambridge, Massachusetts: Harvard University Press, 1961.

Bernholz, Peter and Hans Jürgen Jaksch (1989). An Implausible Theory of Inflation. *Weltwirtschaftliches Archiv* 125 (2), 359–65.

Bowley, A. L.: Review of *The Making of Index Numbers* by Irving Fisher. *Economic Journal* 33 (1923), 90–94.

—— Notes on Index Numbers. *Economic Journal* 38 (June 1928), 216–237.

Braithwait, S. D.: The substitution bias of the Laspeyres Price Index: an analysis using estimated cost-of-living indexes. *American Economic Review* 70 (1980), 64–77.

Bruno, M., S. Fisher, E. Helpman, N. Liviatan and L. Meridor, eds.: *Lessons of Economic Stabilization and its Aftermath*. Cambridge, MA: MIT Press, 1991.

Brown, J. A. C., and A. Deaton: Models of Consumer Behaviour: A Survey. *Economic Journal* 82 (1972), 1145–1236.

Buscheguennce, S. S.: Sur une classe des hypersurfaces: ápropos de 'l'index idéal' de M. Irving Fischer. *Recueil Mathematique* (Moscow) 32 (1925), 625–631. (Russian title: Byushgens, S. S. Ob odnom klasse giperpoverkhnostey: po povodu 'idealnovo indeksa' Irving Fischer' a pokupatelnoi sili deneg. *Mathematischeskii Sbornik* 32 (1925), 625–631.)

Cameron, Grant J.: The Marginal Price Index Method: Construction from the Statistics Canada Survey of Family Expenditures—a Robust Approach. M.A. Thesis, Economics Department, University of Ottawa, March 16, 1987.

Canada, Government of : *Prices and The Poor—A Report of the National Council of Welfare on the Low-Income Consumer in the Canadian Market Place*. Ottawa: Health and Welfare Canada, 1974.

—— *Price Level Measurement: Proceedings of a Conference Sponsored by Statistics Canada*. Ministry of Supply and Services Canada, 1983.

Carli, G. R.: Del valore etc. *Opere Scelte*, 1764, Vol. 1, p. 299.

Carter, C. F., W. B. Reddaway, and Richard Stone: *The Measurement of Production Movements*. Cambridge University Press, 1948.

Central Statistical Office: *Method of Construction and Calculation of the Index of Retail Prices*, Studies in Official Statistics, No.6, 4th ed. H.M. Statistical Office, 1967.

—— *National Accounts Statistics, Sources and Methods*, 2nd ed. H.M. Statistical Office. 1970.

Chase, Arnold E.: Concepts and Uses of Price Indices. Division of Prices and Cost of Living, Bureau of Labor Statistics, US Department of Labor, Washington, DC. Paper presented at the American Statistical Association meeting, August 1960.

Christensen, L.R. and D.W. Jorgensen: U.S. Real Product and Real Factor Output, 1929–1967. *Review of Income and Wealth* 16 (1970), 19–50.

Cournot, A.: *Recherches sur les Principes Mathématiques de la Théorie des Richesses*. Paris: L. Hachette, 1838. (Researches into the Mathematical Principles of the Theory of Wealth. Trans. by N.T. Bacon, with an Essay on Cournot and a Bibliography on mathematical economics by I. Fisher, 1924. New York: Kelley Reprints of Economic Classics, 1960.)

Craig, J.: On the Elementary Treatment of Index Numbers, *Journal of the Royal Statistical Society* C 18 (1969), 141–152.

Crowe, W.R.: *Index Numbers—Theory and Applications*. London 1965.

Dahrendorf, Ralf: The 1974 Reith Lectures "The New Liberty: survival and justice in a changing world", 4th Lecture "On Difference" reproduced in *The Listener*, 5 December 1974, 724–6.

Dalén, Jörgen (1992). Computing Elementary Aggregates in the Swedish Consumer Price Index. *Journal of Official Statistics* 5 (2), 129–47.

Dalton, Kenneth (1993). Letter, *The Economist* November 27th, concerning inflation rate exaggeration; response to leader October 30th. Bureau of Labor Statistics, Washington, DC.

Daly, D. J. (ed.) (1972). *International Comparisons of Prices and Output. Proceedings of the Conference at York University, Toronto, 1970*. National Bureau of Economic Research, Studies in Income and Wealth Volume 37. New York: Columbia University Press.

Davidson, A.: *Money in the Real World*. London: Macmillan, 1974.

Deaton, Angus (1974). A reconsideration of the implications of additive preferences. *The Economic Journal* 84, 338–48.

—— (1979). *The Price Index* by S. N. Afriat. *J. Amer. Stat. Assoc.* 74, 365 (March), 251.

—— (ed.) *Essays in the Theory and Measurement of Demand: In Honour of Sir Richard Stone*. Cambridge University Press, 1981.

—— and J. Muellbauer (1980). *Economics and Consumer Behaviour*. Cambridge University Press.

Diewert, W.E.: Afriat and Revealed Preference Theory. *Review of Economic Studies* 40 (1973), 419–425.

—— Exact and Superlative Index Numbers. *Journal of Econometrics* 4 (1976), 115–45.

—— *The Price Index* by S. N. Afriat. *Canadian Journal of Economics* 12 (1979), 1 (February), 113–4.

—— The Theory of the Cost of Living Index and the Measurement of Welfare Change. In Canada (1983).

Divisia, F.: L'Indice Monétaire et la Théorie de la Monnaie. *Revue d'Economie Politique* 39 (1925), 980–1008.

—— L'Indice Monétaire et la Théorie de la Monnaie. *Societe anonyme du Recueil Sirley*, Paris, 1926.

—— *Economique Rationelle*. Paris, 1928.

Dobb, Maurice: *Welfare Economics and the Economics of Socialism*. Cambridge University Press, 1969.

Economist, The (1993). Leader, October 30th, concerning inflation rate exaggeration.

Edgeworth, F. Y.: A Defence of Index Numbers. *Economic Journal* 6 (1986), 132–42.

—— Third report of the British Association Committee for the purpose of investigating the best methods of ascertaining and measuring variation in the value of the monetary standard. 1889.

—— *Papers Relating to Political Economy*, Vol. 1. London, 1925.

—— The Plurality of Index Numbers. *Economic Journal* 35 (1925), 379–88.

Eichhorn, Wolfgang: *Functional Equations in Economics*. Applied Mathematics and Computation Series No. 11. Reading, Mass.: Addison-Wesley, 1972.

—— Zor axiomatischen Theorie des Preisindex. *Demonstratio Mathematica* 6 (1973), 561–73.

—— Fischer's Tests Revisited. *Econometrica* 44, 2 (March 1976), 247–56.

—— and Joachim Voeller: *Theory of the Price Index*. Berlin: Springer-Verlag, 1976.

—— Henn, O. Opitz and R. W. Shephard (eds.) (1978). *Theory and Applications of Economic Indices. Proceedings of an International Seminar at the University of Karlsruhe, 23 June–1 July, 1976*. Würzburg: Physica-Verlag.

Engel, E.: Die Productions und Consumptionsverhaltnisse des Konigreichs Sachsen, reprinted in *Bulletin de l'Institut International de Statistique* 9 Appendix (1857, 1895).

Finke, R. and W. Lu (1984). The Behavior of the Cost of Living at Different Levels of Real Income. *Economic Letters* 15, 223–8. See Balk (1986).

Fisher, Irving: Mathematical investigations in the theory of values and prices. *Transactions of the Connecticut Academy of Arts and Sciences* 9, 1892, 1–124.

—— *The Purchasing Power of Money*. New York: Macmillan, 1911.

—— Is 'utility' the most suitable term for the concept it is used to denote? *American Economic Review* 8, 1918, 335–7.

—— *The Making of Index Numbers*. Boston and New York: Houghton Mifflin, 1922 (3rd edition 1927).

—— Professor Bowley on Index Numbers. *Economic Journal* 33 (1923), 246–251.

—— A Statistical Method for Measuring Marginal Utility and Testing the Justice of a Progressive Income Tax. In *Economic Essays in Honor of John Bates Clark*. New York, 1927.

Fisher, F.M. and K. Shell: Taste and Quality Change in the Pure Theory of the True Cost of Living Index. In *Value, Capital and Growth, Papers in Honor of Sir John Hicks*, ed. By J.N. Wolfe. Edinburgh University Press, 1968.

—— *The Economic Theory of Price Indices*. New York: Academic Press, 1972.

Fisher, W.C.: The Tabular Standard in Massachusetts. *Quarterly Journal of Economics*, May 1913.

Fleetwood, William (1707). *Chronicon Preciosum: Or, An Account of English Money, the Price of Corn, and Other Commodities, for the Last 600 Years— in a Letter to a Student in the University of Oxford*. London: T. Osborne in Gray's-Inn (anonymous 1st edition; 2nd edition 1745, in Codrington Library, All Souls College, Oxford).

Forsyth, F. G. (1978). The Practical Construction of a Chain Price Index Number. *Journal of the Royal Statistical Society*, Series A, 141, 348–58.

Foster, William T.: Prefatory Note to *The Making of Index Numbers* by Irving Fisher (see above).

Fowler, R.F.: *Some Problems of Index Number Construction*. Studies in Official Statistics, Research Series, No.3. H.M. Statistical Office, 1970.

—— *Further Problems of Index Number Construction*. Studies in Official Statistics, Research Series, No.5. H.M. Statistical Office, 1973.

—— An Ambiguity in the Terminology of Index Number Construction. *Journal of the Royal Statistical Society* A 137 (1974), 75–88.

Frisch, Ragnar: Necessary and Sufficient Conditions Regarding the Form on an Index Number Which Shall Meet Certain of Fisher's Tests. *Journal of the American Statistical Association* 25 (1930), 397–406.

—— Annual Survey of General Economic Theory: The Problem of Index Numbers. *Econometrica* 4, 1 (1936), 1–39.

—— Some Basic Principles of Price of Living Measurements: A Survey Article. *Econometrica* 22 (1954),

Galbraith, J.K.: *Money*. Cambridge, Mass.: Houghton Mifflin, 1975.

Gamaletsos, T.: Further Analysis of Cross-Country Comparison of Consumer Expenditure Patterns. *European Economic Review* 4 (1973), 1–20.

Geary, R.C.: A Note on a Constant-utility Index of the Cost of Living. *Review of Economic Studies* 18 (1950), 64–66.

—— A note on the comparison of exchange rates and purchasing power between countries. *Journal of the Royal Statistical Society* A, 121 (1958), 97–9.

Georgescu-Roegen, N.: Choice and Revealed Preference. *Southern Economic Journal* 21 (1954), 119–130.

—— *Analytical Economics: Issues and Problems*. Cambridge, Massachusetts: Harvard University Press, 1966.

Gillingham, R. F. (1974). A Conceptual Framework for the Revised Consumer Price Index. Proceedings of the Business and Economics Section, American Statistical Association, 46–52.

Gorman, W.M.: Community Preference Fields. *Econometrica* 21 (1953), 63–80.

—— Some comments on Professor Hicks' revision of demand theory. *Metroeconomica* 9 (1957), 167–80.

—— On a Class of Preference Fields. *Metroeconomica* 13 (1961), 53–56.

——The structure of utility functions. *Review of Economic Studies* 35, 1968 (4), 367–90.

——Tricks with utility functions. In *Essays in Economic Analysis*, edited by M. J. Artis and A. R. Nobay. Cambridge University Press, 1976.

Gossling, W.F.: *Some Productive Consequences of Engel's Law*. London: Input-Output Publishing Co., 1974. (Occasional Paper No.2).

Green, H.A.J.: *Aggregation in Economic Analysis*. Princeton University Press, 1964.

Griliches. Z.: (ed.) *Price Indices and Quality Change—Studies in New Methods of Measurement*. Cambridge, Massachusetts: Harvard University Press, 1971.

Haberler, B. von: *Der Sinn der Indexzahlen*. Tubingen, 1927.

Hagemann, R. P. (1982). The Variability of Inflation Rates Across Household Types. *Journal of Money, Credit, and Banking* 14, 494–510.

Haley, James and Ghiath Shabsigh (1994). Monitoring Financial Stabilization in Moldova: The Role of Monetary Policy, Institutional Factors and Statistical Anomalies. Paper on Policy Analysis and Assessment of the International Monetary Fund No. 25 (December). IMF World Economic Studies Division, European II Department.

Harcourt, G., ed. (1977). *The Microeconomic Foundations of Macroeconomics*. London: Macmillan.

Hardy, G. H., J. E. Littlewood and G. Polya (1934). *Inequalities*. Cambridge University Press.

Hasenkamp, Georg: A Note on the Cost-of-Living Index. University of Bonn, January 1976. Presented at the European Meeting of the Econometric Society, Helsinki. August 1976.

Heyman, Daniel (1986). *Tres Ensayos sobre Inflacion y Politicas de Estabilizacion*. Santiago de Chile: CEPAL.

—— (1991). From sharp disinflation to hyperinflation, twice: the Argentinian experience. In Bruno et al (1991).

—— and Pablo Sanguinetti (1993). Fiscal Inconsistencies and High Inflation. *Journal of Development Economics*, forthcoming.

—— and Axel Leijonhufvud (1994). *High Inflation*. Oxford: Clarendon Press.

Hicks, J. R.: Consumers' surplus and index-numbers. *Review of Economic Studies* 9, 2 (1942), 126–37.

—— *Value and Capital*, 2nd ed. Oxford: The Clarendon Press, 1948.

—— *A Revision of Demand Theory*. Oxford: The Clarendon Press, 1956.

Hicks, J. R., and R. G. D. Allen: A reconsideration of the theory of value. *Economica*, New Series 1 (1934), 52–75, 196–219.

Hofsten, E. von: Witchcraft and Index Numbers. *Malayan Economic Review* 1 (1956), 6–14.

Hotelling, H.: Demand functions with limited budgets. *Econometrica* 3 (1935), 66–78.

Houthakker, H. S.: Revealed Preference and the Utility Function. *Economica*, New Series 17 (1950), 159–74.

—— La forme des courbes d'Engel. *Cahiers du Seminarie d'Econometrie* 2 (1953), 59–66.

—— An International Comparison of Household Expenditure Patterns, Commemorating the Centenary of Engel's Law. *Econometrica* 25 (1957), 532–551.

Ichimura, S.: A Critical Note on the Definition of Related Goods. *Review of Economic Studies* 18 (1951), 179–183.

ILO (1987). Resolution concerning consumer price indices, 5 November, 1987. The Fourteenth International Conference of Labour Staticians convened by the Governing Body of the ILO, Geneva, 28 October–6 November. In Turvey et al (1989), Appendix 1, 123–9.

Instituto Nacional de Estadistica (INE) (1991). Indice de Precios al Consumidor (IPC), 1985–90 (spreadsheet data).

Jaksch, Hans Jürgen (1989). Bernholz and Jaksch (1989).

Jazairi, Nuri T. (1971). An Empirical Study of the Conventional and Statistical Theories of Index Numbers. *Oxford Institute of Economics and Statistics Bulletin* 33, 181–95.

—— (1983). The present state of the theory and practice of index numbers. *Bulletin of the International Statistical Institute* 50, 122–47.

—— (1985). Log-Change Index Numbers. In Kotz and Johnson (1985–8), Volume 5.

—— (1988). Afriat and Jazairi (1988).

—— and Mirka Ondrack (1988). Logarithmic Index Numbers. In Kotz and Johnson (1988), Volume 9.

Jorgensen, D. and Slesnick (1983). Individual and Social Cost of Living Indexes. In Canada (1983).

Jevons, W.S.: *A serious fall in the value of gold ascertained and its social effects set forth*. London, 1863.

Kendall, M.G.: The Early History of Index Numbers. *International Statistical Review* 37 (1969), 1–12.

Kendall, M. G. and A. Stuart (1967). *The Advanced Theory of Statistics* (2nd edition). Hafner Publishing Co. Volume 2, p. 349.

Keynes, J.M.: *Treatise on Money, Vol. 1, The Pure Theory of Money*. New York: Harcourt Brace, 1930.

—— *The General Theory of Employment, Interest, and Money*, London: Macmillan, 1936.

Kirman, Alan (1994). Price Formation and Price Indices: Theoretical Problems and Empirical Studies of Particular Emerging Markets in Eastern Europe. European University Institute, San Domenico di Fiesole/Firenze. In collaboration with Fuad Aleskerov, Institute of Control Sciences, Moscow.

Klein, L.R. and H. Rubin: A Constant Utility Index of the Cost of Living. *Review of Economic Studies* 15 (1947), 84–7.

Kloek, T.: *Indexcijfers: Enige methodologische aspecten*. The Hague: Pasmans, 1966.

—— On quadratic approximations of cost of living and real income index numbers. *Report* 6710, Econometric Institute, Netherlands School of Economics, Rotterdam, 1967.

Konyus, A.A.: Problema istinovo indeksa stoimosti zhizni. *Ekonomicheskii Byulleten Konyunkturnovo Instituta* 3 (1924), 64–71. English trans.: The Problem of the True Index of the Cost of Living. *Econometrica* 7 (Jan. 1939), 10–29.

Konyus, A.A., and S.S. Byushgens: K probleme popupatelnoi cili deneg. Voprosi Konyunkturi 2 (1926), 151–171. English title: Conus, A.A. and S.S. Buscheguennce, On the problem of the purchasing power of money. The Problems of Economic Conditions, supplement to the *Economic Bulletin of the Conjuncture Institute* 2 (1926), 151–71.

Kotz, Samuel and Norman L. Johnson (1985–8). *Encyclopedia of Statistical Sciences*. New York: John Wiley & Sons.

Kuiper, John: MATOP: a generalized computer program for mathematical operations. Department of Economics. University of Ottawa. June 1974.

—— (1975). Afriat and Kuiper (1975).

Lange, O.: The Determinateness of the Utility Function. *Review of Economic Studies* 1 (1934). 218–224.

Laspeyres, E.: Hamburger Warenpreise 1850–1863. *Jahrbucher fur National-okonomie una Statistik* 3 (1864), 81 and 209.

—— Die Berechnung eiDer mittleren Waarenpreissteigerung. *Jahrbucher fur Nationalokonomie und Statistik* (Jena) 16 (1871).

Leacock, Stephen: Boarding-House Geometry. In *Literary Lapses*. Toronto: McClelland and Stewart, 1910.

Leijonhufvud, Axel.: *On Keynesian Economics and the Econonomics of Keynes*. Oxford University Press, 1968.

—— (1977). Cost and Consequences of Inflation. In Harcourt, ed. (1977). Repr. in Leijonhufvud (1981).

—— (1981). *Information and Coordination*. Oxford University Press.

—— (1984). Inflation and Economic Performance. In Siegel, ed. (1984).

—— (1992). High Inflations and Contemporary Monetary Theory. *Economic Notes*.

—— (1994). Heyman and Leijonhufvud (1994).

Leontief, W.: Composite Commodities and the Problem of Index Numbers. *Econometrica* 4 (1936), 39–59.

Lerner, A.P.: A Note on the Theory of Price Index Numbers. *Review of Economic Studies* (1935), 50–56.

Leser, C.E.V.: Forms of Engel Functions. *Econometrica* 31 (1963), 694–703.

Liesner, Thelma and Mervyn King (eds.) (1975). *Indexing for Inflation*. Institute for Fiscal Studies monograph. London: Heinemann.

Little, I.M.D.: *A Critique of Welfare Economics*. Oxford University Press, 1957.

Liviatan, Nissan, and Don Patinkin: On the Economic Theory of Price Indices. *Economic Development and Cultural Change* 9 (1961), 501–536.

Lloyd, P.J.: Substitution effects and biases in non-true price indices. *American Economic Review*, June 1975.

Lynch, John (1993). Private communication, IASC Conference, Siena (September). Central Statistical Service, Pretoria, Republic of South Africa.

Machlup, Fritz: Professor Hicks' revision of demand theory. *American Economic Review* 47 (1957), 119–35.

—— *Essays in Economic Semantics*. New York: W.W. Norton, 1967.

Malmquist, S.: Index Numbers and Indifference Surfaces. *Trabajos de Estadistica* 4 (1953), 209–242.

Malthus, Rev. T.R.: *The Measure of Value Stated and Illustrated with an Application of it to the Alteration in the Value of English Currency since 1790*. 1823.

—— *Definitions in Political Economy, preceded by An Inquiry into the Rules Which Ought to Guide Political Economists in the Definition and Use of their*

Terms; with Remarks on the Deviations from these Rules in their Writings. London, 1827.

—— *On the Meaning which is Most Usually and Most Correctly Attached to the Term Value of Commodities.* 1827.

Manser, Marilyn E. and Richard J. McDonald (1988). An analysis of substitution bias in measuring inflation, 1959–85. *Econometrica* 56 (4), 909–30.

Marris, Robin: *Economic Arithmetic.* London: Macmillan, 1958.

Marshall, A.: *Principles of Economics.* London: 1st ed. 1890, 8th ed. 1946.

Mathur, P.N.: Approximate Determination of Indifference Surfaces from Family Budget Data. *International Economic Review* 5 (1964), 294–303.

Maunder, W.F.: (ed.) *Bibliography of Index Numbers.* London: Athlone Press, 1970.

Merilees, W.J.: The case against Divisia index numbers as a basis in a social accounting system. *Review of Income and Wealth* 17 (1971), 81–85.

Michael, Robert T.: Variation across households in the rate of inflation. *NBER Working Paper* No. 74 (March 1975). Center for Economic Analysis of Human Behaviour and Social Institutions, Stanford, California. Journal of Money, Credit, and Banking 11, 32–46.

Mishan, E.J.: Theories of Consumers Behaviour: A Cynical View. *Economica* 28 (February 1961), 1–11.

Mitchell, W.C.: The Making and Using of Index Numbers. Bureau of Labour Statistics, Washington 1921, *Bulletin* 284.

Mitzutani, K.: New Formulae for Making Price and Quantity Index Numbers. Chapter 27 in *Essays in Mathematical Economics in Honor of Oskar Morgenstern*, ed. by Martin Shubik. Princeton University Press, 1967.

Morgan, D. D. V. (1981). Estimation of Retail Price Changes. *The Statistician* 30, 89–96.

Morgenstern, Oskar: *On the Accuracy of Economic Observations.* Princeton University Press, 1963.

—— Demand Theory Reconsidered. *Quarterly Journal of Economics* 62 (February 1948), 165–201. Reproduced in *The Evolution of Modern Demand Theory*, ed. by R.B. Ekelund et al. Lexington, Massachusetts: D.C. Heath and Co., 1972.

—— Thirteen Critical Points in Contemporary Economic Theory. *Working Paper* No.3 (April 1972), Department of Economics, New York University. *J. Econ. Literature* 10, (December 1972), 1163–1189.

Mudgett, Bruce D.: *Index Numbers.* New York: John Wiley and Sons, 1951.

Muellbauer, J.: Prices and Inequality: the United Kingdom Experience. *Economic Journal* 84 (1974).

—— The Political Economy of Price Indices. *Birkbeck Discussion Paper* No. 22 (March 1974).

—— Household Composition, Engel Curves and Welfare Comparisons between Households. *European Economdc Review* 5 (August 1974).

—— Aggregation, Income Distribution and Consumer Demand. *Review of Economic Studies* 17, 4 (October 1975), 525–543.

Nataf, André, and René Roy: Remarques et suggestions relatives aux nombres-indices. *Econometrica* 16 (1948), 330–346.

National Council of Welfare: *Prices and the Poor: A Report by the National Council of Welfare on the Low-Income Consumer in the Canadian Market-place.* Ottawa, April 1974.

Netherlands Central Bureau of Statistics (1982). *Private Consumption Expenditure and Price Index Numbers for the Netherlands 1951–1977.* Statistical Studies No. 33. The Hague: Staatsuitgeverij.

Nicholson, J. L.: The Measurement of Quality Changes. *Economic Journal* 77 (1967), 512–530.

Noe, N. N. and G. von Furstenberg (1972). The upward bias in the consumer price index due to substitution. *Journal of Political Economy* 80, 1280–94.

Ög-üt, Nurgül (1994). Private communication, SIS, 3 June.

Ondrack, Mirka (1988). Jazairi and Ondrack (1988).

OECD, Paris (1975). *Indexation of Financial Assets.*

Paasche, H.: Uber die Preisentwickelung der letzten Jahre, nach den Hamburger Borsennotierungen. *Jahrbucher fur Nationaloxonomie una Statistik (Jena)* 23 (1874), 168–178.

Paige, Deborah and Gottfried Bombach: *A Comparison of National Output and Productivity of the United Kingdom and the United States.* Joint Study by the Organisation for European Economic Co-operation and the Department of Applied Economics, University of Cambridge. OEEC, Paris, 1959.

Palerm, Angel (1990). Price Formation and Relative Price Variability in an Inflationary Environment: Mexico. PhD Thesis, University of California, Los Angeles.

Palgrave, R. H. I.: Currency and standard of value in England, France and India etc. *Memorandum* to the Royal Commission on Depression of Trade and Industry, Third Report, Appendix B, 1886.

Patinkin, Don: *Money, Interest, and Prices,* 2nd ed. New York: Harper and Row, 1965.

—— (1993). Israel's Stabilization Program of 1985, Or Some Simple Truths of Monetary Theory. *Journal of Economic Perspectives* 7, 2 (Spring), 103–28.

Pearce, I. F.: *A Contribution to Demand Analysis.* Oxford: The Clarendon Press, 1964.

Perroux, Francois: *Pouvoir et Economie*. Paris: Bordas, 1973.

Pfanzagl, J.: Zur Geschichte der Theorie des Lebenshaltungskostenindex. *Statistische Vierteljahresschrift* Bd. 8 (1955), 1–52.

Pfouts, R.W.: An Axiomatic Approach to Index Numbers. *Review of the International Statistical Institute*, Vol. 34, 2 (1966), 174–185.

Philips, L.: *Applied Consumption Analysis*. Amsterdam: North-Holland, 1974.

Pigou, A.C.: *The Economics of Welfare*. London: Macmillan, 1920.

Pollak, Robert: The Theory of the Cost of Living Index. *Discussion Paper* No. 11, Office of Prices and Living Conditions, U.S. Bureau of Labor Statistics, Washington. D.C., 1971.

—— (1980). Group Cost-of-Living Indexes. *Am. Econ. Rev.*, May.

—— (1981). The Social Cost of Living Index. *J. Public Econ.*

Prais, S. J.: Non-linear estimates of the Engel curves. *Review of Economic Studies* 20 (1952–53), 80–104.

Prais, S. J. and H. S. Houthakker: *The Analysis of Family Budgets*. Cambridge University Press. 1955.

Raj, B. (1987). Did the Cost-of-living in Canada Increase Faster for the Rich During the Period 1950–1980? *Empirical Economics* 12, 19–28.

Rajaoja, Vieno: A Study in the Theory of Demand Indexes. *Commentationes physico-mathematicae*, Fennica (Helsinki) 21 (1958), 1–96.

Ricardo, David: Proposals for an Economical and Secure Currency (1816). In *The Works of David Ricardo*, ed. by J. R. McCulloch, 1852, p. 400.

Rickard, J. A.: *The Price Index* by S. N. Afriat. *Mathematical Reviews* 58 (1979).

Robinson, J.: *Economic Heresies*. London: Macmillan, 1971.

Roy, René: Les index conomiques. *Revue d'Economie Politique* 41 (1927), 1251–1291.

—— *De l'utilité*. Actualités Scientific et Industrielles No. 930. Paris, 1942.

—— De la théorie de choix aux budgets de familles. *Econometrica* 17 (1949), 179–85.

Ruggles, Richard (1967). Price Indexes and International Price Comparisons. In *Ten Economic Studies in the Tradition of Irving Fisher*. New York: John Wiley & Sons.

Samuelson, P.A.: Some implications pf 'linearity'. *Review of Economic Studies* 15 (1949), 88–90.

—— Evaluation of Real National Income. *Oxford Economic Papers*, New Series 2, 1 (1950), 1–29.

—— *Foundations of Economic Analysis*. Harvard University Press, 1947.

—— Remembrances of Frisch. *European Economic Review*, 1974.

—— Analytical Notes on International Real-Income Measures. *Economic Journal* (September 1974), 595–608.

Samuelson, P.A., and S. Swamy: Invariant Economic Index Numbers and Canonical Duality: Survey and Synthesis. *American Economic Review*, Vol. 64, 4 (1974), 566–593.

Sato, K.: Ideal index numbers that almost satisfy factor reversal test. *Review of Economics and Statistics* 56 (1974), 549–552.

Schultz, H.: A misunderstanding in index number theory: the true Konus condition on cost of living index numbers and its limitations. *Econometrica* (January 1939), p. 109.

Schumpeter, Joseph A.: *History of Economic Analysis.* Oxford University Press, 1954.

Scrope, G. Poulett: An Examination of the Bank Charter Question, with an inquiry into the nature of a just standard of value etc. London, 1833.

Seminario, Bruno (1990). The Consumer Price Index: Methodology and Problems. Universidad Pacifico, Lima (August).

Shephard, R.W.: *Cost and Production Functions.* Princeton University Press, 1953.

—— *Theory of Cost and Production Functions.* Princeton University Press, 1970.

Sheshinski, E. and Y. Weiss (eds.) (1993). *Optimal Pricing, Inflation and the Cost of Price Adjustment.* Cambridge, Mass.: MIT Press.

Shubik, M.: A Curmudgeon's Guide to Microeconomics. *Journal of Economic Literature*, June 1970.

—— (ed.) *Studies in Mathematical Economics in Honor of Oskar Morgenstern.* Princeton University Press, 1967.

Siegel, B., ed. (1984). *Money in Crisis.* San Francisco: Pacific Institute.

Slutsky, E.E.: Sulla teoria del bilancio del consumatore. *Giornale degli Economisti* 51 (1915), 1–26. (Trans. by O. Ragusa: On the theory of the budget of the consumer. In *Readings in Price Theory*, ed. by G.J. Stigler and K.E. Boulding. Ch. 2, 27–65. Chicago: Irwin, Inc., 1952.)

Staehle, Hans: A Development of the Economic Theory of Price Index Numbers. *Review of Economic Studies* (1935), 163–188.

—— Annual Survey of Statistical Information: Family Budgets. *Econometrica* 2 (October 1934), 349–362.

State Institute of Statistics (SIS), Prime Ministry, Republic of Turkey, publications.

—— (1987a). Consumption Expenditures. Household Income and Consumption Expenditures Survey Results.

—— (1987b). Income Distribution. Household Income and Consumption Expenditures Survey Results.

—— (1990a). Wholesale and Consumer Price Indexes Monthly Bulletin, January – February – March. (SIS wholesale price index, 1981=100; consumer

10000000

price index, 1987=100. Contains detailed information of how the 1987=100 based urban consumer price index was prepared.)

—— (1990b). Social and Economic Characteristics of Population. Census of Population.

—— (1994a). Wholesale and Consumer Price Indexes Monthly Bulletin, March.

—— (1994b). Wholesale and Consumer Price Indexes Monthly Bulletin, June.

—— (1994c). Haber Bülteni, Nisan (April).

Stigler, G.J.: (chairman) *Report on the Price Statistics of the Federal Government*, National Bureau of Economic Research, General Series, No. 73. New York, 1961.

Stone, Richard: *The Role of Measurement in Economics*. Cambridge University Press. 1951.

—— Linear Expenditure Systems and Demand Analysis; an Application to the Pattern of British Demand. *Economic Journal* 64 (1954). 511–24.

—— *Quantity and Price Indexes in National Accounts*. Published by OEEC, Paris, 1956.

—— assisted by D.A. Rowe, W.J. Corlett, R. Hurstfield, and M. Potter. *The Measurement of Consumer's Expenditure and Behaviour in the United Kingdom, 1920–1938*, Vol. 1. Cambridge University Press, 1966.

Stuvel, G.: A New Index Number Formula. *Econometrica* 25 (1957), 123–31.

Subramanian, S.: On a Certain Conclusion of Frisch's. *Journal of the American Statistical Association* 29 (1934), 316–317.

Swamy, S.: Consistency of Fisher's Tests. *Econometrica* 33 (1965), 619–23.

Szulc, B. J. (1989). Price Indices Below the Basic Aggregation Level. In Turvey et al (1989), 167–78.

Theil, H.: *Economics and Information Theory*. Amsterdam: North Holland, 1967.

—— On the geometry and the numerical approximation of cost of living and real income indices. *De Economist* 116 (1968), 677–689.

—— A New Index Number Formula. *Review of Economics and Statistics* (1973), 498–502.

Tintner, Gerhard: Homogeneous Systems in Mathematical Economics. *Econometrica* 16, 4 (October 1948), 273–294.

Tommasi, Mariano (1993). Inflation and Relative Prices: Evidence from Argentina. In Sheshinski et al (1993).

Tornquist, L.: The Bank of Finland consumption price index. *Bank of Finland Monthly Bulletin* 10 (1936), 1–8.

Turvey, Ralph et al (1989). Consumer Price Indices: An ILO manual. Geneva: International Labour Office.

U.S. Congress: Joint Economic Committee, Government Price Statistics. Hearings before the subcommittee on Economic Statistics. 87th Congress, 1st Session.

Report of the Price Statistics Review Committee, Washington, D.C., Part 1, 5–99. Government Printing Office, 1961.

Ulmer, M.J.: *The Economic Theory of Cost of Living Index Numbers*. Columbia University Press, 1949.

Van Drill, J. and A. J. Hundepool (1984). *Private Consumption Expenditure and Price Index Numbers for the Netherlands 1977–1981*. Netherlands Central Bureau of Statistics, Voorburg.

Vartia, Yrjo O.: *Relative changes and economic indices* (in Finnish). A Licentiate Thesis, Department of Statistics, University of Helsinki, 1974.

—— Ideal log-change index numbers. *Discussion Paper* No. 2 (June 1976). The Research Institute of the Finnish Economy (ETLA). *Scandinavian Journal of Statistics* 3, 121–126.

—— Fisher's Five-Tuned Fork and Other Quantum Theories of Index Numbers. *Discussion Paper* No. 3 (June 1976). The Research Institute of the Finnish Economy (ETLA).

—— *Relative Changes and Index Numbers*. Helsinki: The Research Institute of the Finnish Economy, 1976.

Ville, J.: Sur les conditions d'existence d'une orphelimite totale et d'un indice du niveau des prix. *Annales de l'Université de Lyon*, 1946.

—— The Existence Conditions of a Total Utility Function. *Review of Economic Studies* 19 (1951–52), 128–32.

Viner, J.: The Utility Concept in Value Theory and its Critics. *Journal of Political Economy* 33 (1925), 369–87, 638–59.

Voeller, J.: *Theorie des Preis- und Lebenshaltungskostenindex*. Dissertation, Karlsruhe, 1974.

von Wright, Georg Henrik: *The Logic of Preference*. Edinburgh University Press, 1963.

Wald, A.: Zur Theorie der Preisindexziffern. *Zeitschrift fur Nationalokonomie* 8 (1937), 179–219.

—— A New Formula for the Index of the Cost of Living. *Econometrica* 7 (4) (1939), 319–35.

Walras, L.: *Eléments d'économie pure*. Paris: 1st ed. 1874, 5th ed. 1926.

Walsh, C.H.: *The Measurement of General Exchange-Value*. New York: Macmillan, 1901.

Walters, David (1993). Letter, *The Economist*, November 27th, concerning inflation rate exaggeration; response to leader, October 30th.

Wicksell, Knut: *Lectures on Political Economy. Volume II: Money*. London: Routledge, 1935.

Wold, H. O. A.: A synthesis of pure demand analysis. *Skandinavisk Aktuarietid-skrift* 26 (1943), 85–118, 221–263; ibid. 27 (1944), 69–120.

Index